Crises and Sequences in Political Development

Studies in Political Development, 7

Working within the theoretical framework established in the six previous volumes of the series, the authors identify and analyze key problems or crises that have arisen historically in the process of political development: identity, legitimacy, participation, distribution, and penetration. The Belgians and Canadians are, for example, discovering anew their crises of national identity; Americans now realize that they face a crisis of admitting new groups and a new generation to full political participation; the government of France, invulnerable for almost a decade under De Gaulle, discovered in the events of May 1968 a profound crisis of access and political participation.

Analysis of the five types of crisis led the authors to ask whether the ordering of crises might be decisive in the historical evolution of political systems. Would it be possible to identify significant sequences of crises and, therefore, construct typologies of political systems that would be based on dynamic patterns of development rather than on static characteristics? The concluding chapter discusses some of the problems inherent in the analysis of sequences.

Precisely because of the questions raised in this book, *Studies in Political Development* will continue with three additional volumes: a historical review, country by country, of European patterns of development; a volume on methodology, discussing empirical social science in the era after logical positivism; and an analysis of govern-

ment activities which have been important in the process of European statemaking—such activities as the organization of the armed forces, taxation, and control of the food supply. This last volume will consider, in addition, the implications of Western statemaking for theories of political development.

Crises and Sequences in Political Development is the seventh volume in the series "Studies in Political Development," sponsored by the Committee on Comparative Politics of the Social Science Research Council; its authors, each of whom has contributed one or more chapters in the volume, are Leonard Binder, James S. Coleman, Joseph LaPalombara, Lucian W. Pye, Sidney Verba, and Myron Weiner.

ences in

lopment

Studies in Political Development

"What is the meaning of 'political development,' and what characterizes 'modernization' in the realm of politics? What is the significance of the contention between old and new, between traditional values and modern practices for the stability and maintenance of political order? Above all, to what extent is it possible to accelerate and direct political change, and how can traditional societies be best transformed into democratic polities? These are the kinds of questions that plague the leaders of the new states. . . . These are the questions that must be answered by all who would help the new states in realizing their aspirations."—Lucian W. Pye

(Published titles listed
on backboard)

STUDIES IN
POLITICAL DEVELOPMENT

1. *Communications and Political Development*
Edited by Lucian W. Pye

2. *Bureaucracy and Political Development*
Edited by Joseph LaPalombara

3. *Political Modernization in Japan and Turkey*
Edited by Robert E. Ward and Dankwart A. Rustow

4. *Education and Political Development*
Edited by James S. Coleman

5. *Political Culture and Political Development*
Edited by Lucian W. Pye and Sidney Verba

6. *Political Parties and Political Development*
Edited by Joseph LaPalombara and Myron Weiner

7. *Crises and Sequences in Political Development*
by Leonard Binder, James S. Coleman, Joseph LaPalombara,
Lucian W. Pye, Sidney Verba, Myron Weiner

◈

Sponsored by the Committee on
Comparative Politics of the Social
Science Research Council

Crises and Sequences in Political Development

CONTRIBUTORS

Leonard Binder
James S. Coleman
Joseph LaPalombara
Lucian W. Pye
Sidney Verba
Myron Weiner

PRINCETON, NEW JERSEY
PRINCETON UNIVERSITY PRESS

1971

To
Pendleton Herring
and
Bryce Wood

FOREWORD

THIS SEVENTH volume in the series of Studies in Political Development constitutes a phase in a continuing research endeavor by members of the Committee on Comparative Politics of the Social Science Research Council. The effort began in the summer of 1963 at a workshop sponsored by the Committee at the Center for Advanced Study in the Behavioral Sciences at Palo Alto. Our focus at that time was on conceptualizing political systems, identifying their universal functions, and describing the processes of political modernization and development.

By the end of the workshop we had systematically reviewed contemporary usages of the notions of political modernization and development and found that they could be usefully reduced to the three key concepts of *equality*, *capacity*, and *differentiation*, which collectively we called the "development syndrome," that are defined by James S. Coleman in Chapter 2 of this volume. What began as a pragmatic exercise in collecting statements characterizing political modernization and development led in time to the analytical observation that the strains of development involve more than just the tensions of change, for inherent within modern societies are certain fundamental and dynamic contradictions unknown to traditional societies. Basic to the development syndrome are the contradictions among the rising demands for *equality*, which involves popular participation, adherence to universalistic laws, and respect for achievement performance; a greater need for *capacity* and for a more efficient and far-ranging governmental system; and an inexorable tendency toward greater *differentiation* as the divisions of labor and specialization of tasks become more widespread.

Much of recent literature on political development reflects to some degree or other the view that societies can be historically classified according to some variation of the three basic categories of "traditional," "transitional," and "modern," and that of these categories the initial and the terminated ones describe equilibrium states; hence they are relatively more stable, while the transitional category that encompasses much of the Third World is more tentative, unstable, and essentially inchoate. Through our investigations of the relationships of *equality*, *capacity*, and *differentiation*, we were led to the conclusion that while traditional social orders might not be spared internal tensions and contradictions the very essence of modernization is a dynamic state based on the need to manage and ameliorate the inescapable tensions inherent in the development syndrome. From the perspective given us by this approach, we have tended to see the problems of the currently developing countries of Africa and Asia as being closer to the persisting problems of the advanced industrial societies than to the state of affairs associated with traditional orders. Our approach has also led us to a greater appreciation of the presence of tension, conflict, and even violence in all societies that must cope with the development syndrome. To the extent that a more developed society is less plagued with instability and conflict than a developing country, it is only because more effort and resources can be mobilized for coping with the inherent tensions in the development syndrome.

From this concern with the tensions in the developmental process, the members of the project moved on to the identification and analysis of those key problems or crises that appear to have arisen historically in the process of political development. In tracing the contradictions and pressures basic to the development syndrome, and their interactions with the fundamental requirements for building both state and nation, we arrived at the five crises of *identity, legitimacy, participation, penetration,* and *distribution,* the discussion of which constitutes the bulk of this book.

Initially our concern was with the problems of development in the contemporary Afro-Asian world, an emphasis that is reflected in the chapters that were written earlier. Yet, increasingly in our search for greater historical perspective on the crises, we were led back to examinations of the earlier European experiences. Throughout this effort we have not been entirely comfortable with the term "crisis," for it could easily suggest an overly dramatic form of attracting attention. Frequently we found it useful to think of the five "crises" as being essentially "problem areas" that either plague a society or regime or demand the attention of its leaders and aware citizens. Yet on closer examination, we became increasingly convinced that the requirement of societies to cope with these five problems and the consequences of how they have been dealt with are so enduring and decisive in determining the subsequent character of the system that it was not inappropriate to refer to them as crises.

In arriving at a greater sense of historical perspective, we also became interested in the lasting consequences of the different sequences in which the crises were experienced. Countries that have clearly established their sense of national *identity* and achieve a broad recognition of the *legitimacy* of their system of government before they are confronted with the demand for universal *participation* in public affairs are, for example, significantly different from countries in which popular *participation* precedes either the *legitimization* of public institutions or the *penetration* of the governmental system into the mass of society.

Thus, in our effort to understand the separate crises we found that we had to place them in context with each other and to recognize that the ordering of the crises might be decisive in the historical evolution of all political systems. This led to the question of whether it might not be possible to identify different significant sequences of crises and, therefore, eventually construct typologies of political systems that would be based on different dynamic patterns of development rather than on static characteristics. The last chapter in this volume discusses some of the problems inherent in the analysis of sequences; it was originally drafted by Sidney Verba as an internal memorandum to alert the other authors to some of these problems.

Precisely because of both the difficulties and the promise of sequential analysis for comparative historical analysis, the next phase of the Committee's work will include two parallel projects. The first is a pragmatic testing of the utility of the concepts of crises and sequences in which a group of distinguished historians will seek to apply them in analyzing the different European patterns of development. The result of this effort will be a volume edited by Raymond Grew that will appear in this series. In addition, we are planning a volume on methodology and questions in the philosophy of science, to be edited by Leonard Binder, Sidney Verba, and Philip E. Converse, that will examine further some of the conceptual problems raised by our questions about crises and sequences in development.

This volume is, therefore, both a report on work accomplished and an introduction to a new departure in comparative analysis. This book is also noteworthy as an effort at collective theory building in the social sciences. If this were not a collective enterprise, the individual authors of this volume would probably have treated the subject of the entire volume, and even the subject of their particular chapters, in a different manner. The authors, while responsible for the chapters under their names, jointly developed all the basic concepts and the overall structure and therefore their names appear alphabetically on the title page.

The authors of this volume have many debts of appreciation which cannot be easily discharged, but we must acknowledge our thanks for the patient support and understanding of the other members of the Committee, who from time to time became participants and not mere observers of this novel effort at collective theory building. We benefited greatly from a conference held at Wentworth-by-the-Sea in June 1969, at which a distinguished company of historians discussed with us the problems of treating European history in terms of the crises and their sequences. We must single out Raymond Grew and Harry Eckstein for particular thanks because of their extended criticisms and guidance. Richard Hatch, formerly of M.I.T. and now retired on Cape Cod, helped prepare the manuscript for publication.

LUCIAN W. PYE

CONTENTS

FOREWORD   vii

1. Crises of Political Development by Leonard Binder   3

2. The Development Syndrome: Differentation-Equality-
   Capacity by James S. Coleman   73

3. Identity and the Political Culture by Lucian W. Pye   101

4. The Legitimacy Crisis by Lucian W. Pye   135

5. Political Participation: Crisis of the Political Process
   by Myron Weiner   159

6. Penetration: A Crisis of Governmental Capacity
   by Joseph LaPalombara   205

7. Distribution: A Crisis of Resource Management
   by Joseph LaPalombara   233

8. Sequences and Development by Sidney Verba   283

CONTRIBUTORS   317

INDEX   319

*Crises and Sequences in
Political Development*

CHAPTER 1

The Crises of Political Development[1]

LEONARD BINDER

And to think there may be more Worlds than one, is neither against Reason or Scripture. If God glorify'd himself in making one World, the more Worlds he made, the greater must be his Glory.—M. Fontenell, *Conversations with a Lady on the Plurality of Worlds*, trans. Glanvill, London, 1719

What is perceivable by one Ego must in principle be conceivable by every Ego. And though as a matter of fact it is not true that everyone stands or can stand in a relation of empathy or inward understanding with every other, as we ourselves, for instance, are unable to stand with the spirits that may frequent the remotest starry worlds, yet in point of principle, there exist essential possibilities therefore, that worlds of experience sundered in point of fact may still be united together through actual empirical connections into a single intersubjective world, the correlate of the unitary world of minds.—E. Husserl, *Ideas*, New York, 1962, p. 136

Part I. The Threshold of Modernity

FOR NEARLY ten generations Western man has been concerned with understanding and controlling the changing of his condition and circumstances. That the occurrence of change should require any special understanding is not immediately self-evident. The simple awareness of change does not appear to be a matter of significant rarity. Continuity and stability are ancient desiderata whose worth must depend upon the comprehension if not the experience of change. Surely the law of opposites applies here. Stability would not be valued if change were not known. What does appear to be significant, even if in no measurable sense, are two characteristics of modern Western man's intuition of the expansion and acceleration of history. The first of these is awareness of the length of the epoch of change, and the second is the prevalent, but by no means universal, favor with which change is anticipated if not experienced. The notion of the continuity of change is all but a logical contradiction, while the preference for

---

[1] I would like to acknowledge the helpful criticism and suggestions of my colleagues on the Comparative Politics Committee, fellow members of the New Nations Committee at Chicago, and faculty and students at the Center for Comparative Study of Political Development, also at Chicago.

change in itself is composed of a paradoxical combination of alienation and optimism—alienation from the present and optimism about
the future. Hegel taught that man's alienation was due to his ignorance, which was in turn due to his historicity. But why man should be
optimistic about a future he does not know is a mystery.

In Book Six of the *Ethics* Aristotle wrote, "scientific knowledge
is of things that are never other than they are. . . . So anything that
science knows scientifically must exist by an unalterable necessity. It
must therefore be eternal."[2] According to this definition, which precludes scientific knowledge of things that change, there can be no
scientific theory of political development insofar as it is concerned
with political change. There might be a scientific theory of politics
that is everywhere and at all times the same, but not insofar as politics
is manifested in particular ways in specific places, and not insofar as it
changes. Hence, if political development refers to particulars rather
than universals, it is not given to scientific understanding. Furthermore, when political development involves change, it is also not given
to scientific understanding. We are, therefore, faced with a dilemma
constructed on the one hand of the pretensions of scholars who are
trying to do the theoretically impossible, and on the other by the apparent agreement of many to give a general name to something which
is both particular and changing.

In Book Epsilon of the *Metaphysics* Aristotle wrote:

> We must first consider the accidental and point out that there
> can be no theory of it. . . . Some things are always and of neces-
> sity as they are . . . others are so, not of necessity, or not always,
> but usually . . . what is as it is neither always nor usually we say
> is accidental.

> Let us consider a particular event. Will it happen or not? It
> will if this other happens; if not, not. . . . Similarly if one jumps
> over to past events . . . for something that has happened now
> exists as present in something. Everything that follows will ac-
> cordingly be of necessity . . . this then will be the starting point
> for whatever happens by chance; and nothing else will explain its
> coming to be.[3]

[2] Aristotle, *The Ethics*, trans. J.A.K. Thomson (New York: Penguin Books,
1955), p. 174.
[3] Aristotle, *Metaphysics*, trans. Richard Hope (Ann Arbor: University of Michigan
Press, 1952), pp. 125-26.

There are two elements in these quotations that tend to bring theory and practice together: the category of the usual which is interposed between the accidental and the necessary, and the notion of necessity in a particular historical sequence. If the two elements might be brought together, one could speak of the possibility of a theory of the usual pattern of sequence in political development. It may well be that this is not the form of the theory that is expected. Certainly, many scholars are seeking a theory which describes the essence of political development in terms of integration, differentiation, or rationalization. If such a theory is sought, then a theory of sequence or even of frequent recurrence is of little importance in comparison with a theory able to determine the commendability of certain policies because they enhance the values of integration, differentiation, or rationalization. But if we are more concerned with how political development comes about than with what it is (although the two cannot be completely separated), then we shall have to construct our theory of accidents from empirical observations of the usual and of historical sequences.

It is patent, however, that the usual recurrence of an event is no warrant for the certainty of its future recurrence, and only in special circumstances can past events be used to determine statistical probabilities for the future. When Aristotle uses the term "usual" he does not, of course, necessarily refer to knowledge gained from observation of past events. The usual may refer to the condition of a class of phenomena at a given point in time without regard to how they got that way and what may become of them. It need not imply causality or historical sequence. The problems of political development may also have to be answered in terms of multiple causality and a plurality of development paths.

The idea of necessary sequences suggests that we will find the material for a theory of political development in history. We must be careful, however; even as the very idea of political development suggests that something in history changed, we cannot be certain under what conditions the future will continue to reflect the past. In another sense, everything that ever happened and ever will is already in history, but that history is not recorded—or not adequately recorded. Since we cannot recapture events which have not been recorded, and since the criteria for choosing events to be recorded cannot be events which have not yet occurred, then it follows that the history upon which we must rely is recorded history and not some ideal record of all events "as they really happened." As a consequence, the social scientist must correct history by means of his knowledge of the usual and of the probable sequences of necessity and not the other way around. The big question that remains now is whether political development does not itself imply the transcending of what had been usual or what had been thought of as necessary sequences in the past.

These issues may be illustrated by reference to the writings of Ibn Khaldun who proposed a science of history that could be used to correct or criticize inaccurate historical reports. Obviously, this science must rest on the assumption that we can know at least the limits of the possible in human affairs. In other words, Ibn Khaldun felt that he could distinguish between possible accidents and impossible ones.

Ibn Khaldun went beyond this theory of the possible. Since for him even possible events did not occur randomly but with a certain order, we can say that Ibn Khaldun elaborated a theory of the usual. There was an important cyclical aspect to his theory, but it was not of a metaphysical sort; he merely argued that there were only a few forms which societies could take, hence the same sort of things, including change sequences, would keep on happening. To be valid, his theory requires the assumption that certain elements, such as technology, warfare, social structure, science, economic structure, the scope of government, and so on, are static. Ibn Khaldun did not argue that nothing about these elements ever changed at all, but rather that all such changes occurred within what were, to him, well-known limits of growth and decline. Within such limits it is reasonable to talk of political development and decay. But do these terms have the same meaning when the limits are transcended? (Or are we deluding ourselves in the view that political development entails a real break with the past?)

Muhsin Mahdi summarizes Ibn Khaldun's theory as follows:

> Within this overall direction toward an end, culture undergoes change in certain respects, and these can be divided into two types: (a) when a culture is generated and corrupted; and (b) when a culture persists but its properties or common attributes change. . . . This generation and corruption of culture does not refer to the species "culture," but to individual cultures . . . and the cyclical life span of individual cultures is not the eternal and necessary being or cycle of *a* culture. . . . Examples of qualitative changes in culture are: Changes from primitive to civilized culture, the

change of solidarity from familial relations to tribal solidarity, to the greater solidarity of a whole people, to religious solidarity and to solidarity among urban groups; and the change of the primitive subsistence economy to the civilized economy of abundance. Examples of quantitative changes in culture are: the growth or diminution of the dominions, population and income of the state; the growth of the cities; and the increase or decrease of the number of men dedicated to learning. And examples of changes in place are: conquests and the movement of population from the desert or the countryside to the cities.[4]

For Ibn Khaldun, then, the basic dimensions of culture as a world phenomenon do not change even though particular cultures may change within the range of possible cultural configurations. Some cultures may even cease to exist. Despite his reference to economic factors, to mobility, to types of solidarity, and to the growth of learning (but not knowledge), Ibn Khaldun does not suggest that the known limits of culture can be transcended in the manner usually thought of when we talk of political development or of modernization. Since culture in its most general sense is not given to generation and corruption, at least to this extent it cannot be considered accidental. If particular cultures are unquestionably accidental, it is difficult to explain the starting point of a process of change, but not so difficult to explain the pattern of change so long as that change remains within the limits already known. Only if the limits of change are known can Ibn Khaldun's theory be taken as a valid extension of Aristotle's theory of accidents.

If, as Mahdi asserts, Ibn Khaldun remains essentially within the Aristotelian tradition, Hobbes is an important example of how Western philosophers transformed the classic use of history. Strauss writes:

> Hobbes is in touch with the systematic turning of political philosophy, and of philosophy altogether, to history, which took place in the sixteenth century. This turning is shown by the fact that now for the first time the methodic study of history is demanded. . . . What is felt as a lack is not so much the scientific writing of history . . . not even directions for the writing of history, but above all, methodical reading, methodical utilization of the histories already in existence. . . .

[4] Muhsin Mahdi, *Ibn Khaldun's Philosophy of History* (Chicago: University of Chicago Press, 1964), pp. 254-57.

. . . one does well to compare Hobbes's "composite" method with Aristotle's "genetic" method. Both philosophers are interested in the typical element of history, but each in a different way. When Aristotle depicts the genesis of the city as the perfect community out of primitive communities, the understanding of perfect organism is the main thread. . . . The understanding of the standard, which is set up from the outset and which does not change at all during the analysis of the genesis, dominates the testing of the individual stages of the development. Hobbes proceeds quite differently. For him, the imperfection of the primitive condition, or the state of nature, is perceived not by looking to the already, even if only cursorily clarified, idea of the state as the perfect community, but by fully understanding the state of nature. The standard for the test is not set up beforehand, but is to produce itself and to prove itself. Hobbes, therefore, does not follow Aristotle, but opens up the way to Hegel.

Thus real history has as its function to vouch for the possibility of further progress by perceptions of progress already made. . . . as a result of historical criticism man's limitations show themselves as limits set by himself, and therefore to be overpassed.[5]

Strauss's strong if unsympathetic presentation indicates that the project of an inquiry into political development is not new. Philosophically, at any rate, it has its roots in ancient times. There is, however, a profoundly important difference of approach between the ancients and the moderns.

Before the French Revolution it was not uncommon to speak of a single great cleavage in political thought between the ancients and the moderns. The proponents of the ancients believed that no more recent contribution could exceed the wisdom of Plato and Aristotle— unless, of course, it was concerned with adapting this ancient wisdom to the Christian revelation. The moderns, departing from the learned tradition, believed that new wisdom was possible and that it was even more likely that the wisdom of those who came later would be greater than that of those who came earlier. It is characteristic of revealed systems that the more ancient is revered above the more modern because it is closer to the source of knowledge. Reverence for the ancient philosophers could not be based on any such singular event, but only on the belief that no important new work of discovery was required

[5] Leo Strauss, *The Political Philosophy of Hobbes* (Chicago: University of Chicago Press, 1952), pp. 83-84, 104-05, 107.

once an outstanding philosopher had arrived at the truth. One of the more recondite, but relevant, points debated by the ancients and the moderns was the possibility of the plurality of worlds. If more than one world could exist, then more than one explanation of nature would be possible. This is what Whitehead meant when he wrote of "creative epochs."[6] But the same issue of the plurality of worlds is present in a somewhat lesser form in discussions of the nature of modernity or of development. Do the conditions of modernity or of development require a new philosophy, a new rhetoric of values, and a new social science, or can we rest contentedly in the conviction that as human nature does not change so does the human condition and so do human possibilities remain the same?

Those who believe that understanding modernizing change requires a new philosophy, that the modern world is in a social scientific sense a new "creative epoch," must also believe in the possibility, if not the probability, of a fundamental improvement of the human condition. The moderns tend to be more optimistic than the ancients in this sense, because the moderns deny that we have a knowledge of the eternal essence of man and of political society.

The world is, indeed, predictable when it is ruled by a knowable, living God. Since God is perfect and man but an image, God is perfectly knowable, but man remains an enigma. What appears to be man's free will is rooted in his imperfection both as knower and as thing to be known. (Surely, such a view is preferable to the blasphemous one which would divide the sciences according to whether they are divine or human, or according to whether they are natural or unnatural, as Harry Stack Sullivan might have put it.) Still, pious religionists believe that man's ignorance is defined by the fact that God revealed only so much of Himself as He deemed desirable. It is the philosophers who believe that some men can attain a complete knowledge of God.

The pious religionists, in their concern to justify the limitation of revelation and of our knowledge, assert that what we now know is adequate for policy. Man need not know why and ought not speculate. It is enough that he has been told what to do. The pious religionist is certain that our practical wisdom, to use the classical terminology, has been completed by revelation. But the philosophers insist that our practical wisdom must always fall short of our theoretical wisdom;

---

[6] A. N. Whitehead, *Process and Reality* (Cambridge, Eng.: Cambridge University Press, 1929), p. 116 passim.

we can arrive by speculation at an understanding of perfect beings, but never of imperfect beings. The statesman is compared to the doctor deciding whether to hazard a heart transplant—maybe the doctors of the fifth century were different. The religionists' view of the statesman would emphasize his ritual duties above issues of judgment, however. Every philosopher of political development will eagerly burden you with his wisdom regarding what political development looks like, that is, with his theory of the ideal and best regime. And every practitioner of development will tell you what activities development requires and which industrial, bureaucratic, and service rituals must be pursued.

But neither the theorists nor the practitioners have been lifted up high upon a distant peak. They are not the prophets of development, but only its priests and scribes. Its prophets were those great single-minded men of the nineteenth century who explained modernity as the progress of reason in human history, but each had his own definition of reason. Perhaps even more significant than their disagreements over the nature of reason were their disagreements regarding the consciousness of change. For some, consciousness was the great emancipator from delusion and unreason, but for others, consciousness rendered the essence of modernity neurosis. What is it that we are offering the struggling peoples of the developing areas: the optimistic future promised by our natural scientists and positivistic sociologists, or the neurosis of disenchantment and morbid nostalgia which gripped those who were lifted onto another mountain?

Modernization and the related notion of political development may be thought of as a necessary, usual, or accidental change in history. Dialectical theories of history are the most notable but not the only ones which postulate the speculative necessity of modernization. Such theories or philosophies of history hold that there is a single destiny for the world, though a people, a country, or even a continent may lead the rest or lag behind. The fate of all has been decided in an original creation. Individual men may dispose of their own souls in the enjoyment of personal moral responsibility, but the fate of nations, from the political, economic, and social points of view, has been laid down once and for all. The myopic observer may theorize about convergence and the consequences of culture-contact, but if history moves along a necessary path, the motive process is less significant than it would be were the outcome uncertain.

If, however, political development is thought of as usual and not necessary, a consideration of the processes of political development becomes relevant to determining where such development will occur and where it won't. If we knew and could identify the components of the process, we could conclude where development would necessarily occur. But the methodological implications of the "usual" are such that this category may be used even where our theory falls short of perfect predictability. If we knew *a priori* or *a posteriori* that a given political unit would not experience development, then our theory would not be concerned with a universal teleology but with the necessary order of causality in the world. If our knowledge is less complete, if our concepts are not so precise that they may not be applied to some of the wrong cases in the real world, then the applicability of our theory will be valid only some of the time for some of the countries studied. The usual can be expressed in a probabilistic or a statistical manner, or simply as a crude approximation of the empirical circumstances applying in many countries. An "ideal type" is closely related to the principle of speculative necessity, but an empirical approximation is closely related to the principles of a statistical generalization—except that it does not easily distinguish between accounting for some of the cases in all cases of change and accounting for some of the change in all or only some of the cases of change. These two applications of the notion of the "usual" share its essential feature, and that is the absence of a theory which explains everything in all cases.

If development is the consequence of accidental change in history, then presumably we could trace the causes of that unique event and we could guess at the likelihood of anything similar occurring. Recurrence is not of prime significance, though, because the theory of accidents tells us that the change from tradition to modernity was necessary given certain antecedent events, and any recurrence in somewhat different circumstances is a veritable historical redundancy from the point of view of the universal historian. Nevertheless, assuming that modernity will become thoroughly diffused, recurrence might have changed the pattern of diffusion. I think it is fairly well agreed that development or modernization did not occur in two unrelated circumstances at two different times but that the whole thing started once and was diffused by means of diverse processes. This circumstance may mean that the Western European development simply preempted the history of other areas and did not cause but only influenced their modernization. It is this uncertainty which leads us back to the theory of the usual, for if Western Europe did not cause the development of the rest of the world, in the sense of being both efficient and sufficient cause, then each case of development has to be traced back, as an accident, to European influences *and* to indigenous influences. A theory of development based on such case studies will be an empirical generalization based on the usual.

Whether Europe preempted the history of the world or even caused it, modernity appears to most of us as a great singular event, as an historical threshold. Even if all countries did not become modern at once, the world moved on to a situation in which history took a direction that it did not have before. If the idea of direction is too easily confused with the idea of a pre-modern progress toward modernity, then the new pattern of history might be described as one where the nature of historical causes changed. The economic parameters of political events changed. The cultural parameter of economic events changed. The political parameters of social events changed—or at least so it seems. The central point is that things are different after some point in history than they were before. This point can be called a threshold, and it may be thought of as a singular event or a broad band of history through which different countries pass at different times, some more rapidly, some more slowly, some even slipping back, and some seemingly hopelessly bogged down. If the threshold is thought of as a point in time then it merely divides the traditional from the modern and allows two principles for understanding the world. If the threshold is itself an historical period, then it affords us three principles of understanding: the traditional, the modernizing, and the modern. If the last point of view is accepted, it may further be questioned whether any country has reached the stage of the modern. Are we not all still modernizing?

A related question is whether the same principle of analysis ought to prevail both before and after the threshold has been experienced. If the traditional world was characterized by limited possibilities of change, corruption, and generation, and if these limitations were transcended in crossing the threshold to modernity, is the modern period characterized by a similar systemic limitation or does modernity entail breaking the cyclical limits of social process so that it spirals out into infinite possibilities?

It is this sense of new possibilities that is at the root of the amazing and often confusing efflorescence of the social sciences in recent times. On top of the ancient and ineradicable dualism of the real and the apparent there were erected dozens of systems presuming to be based upon a decisive empirical or speculative insight into the true nature of reality. Up to the threshold of modernity such flights of fancy were left to the religious mystics and the spiritual dialecticians, but with the break in history itself scholars permitted themselves the dismaying thought that if their ideas of the past were inadequate for an understanding of the present, then maybe we had never understood anything of reality at all. Wholly new ways of talking about social process were invented and somehow justified in an effort at least to explain the great events of modernization in Western Europe, if not to relate the fast-changing present to the remote and unchanging past.

It is impossible to prove that we have traversed an historical threshold or that we have, some time in the recent past, crossed over an historical watershed between tradition and modernity, or between a relatively unchanging society and culture and a relatively rapidly changing society and culture. If there was an historical watershed, it is almost impossible to locate it chronologically. Not all of the relevant changes, even if they have a common direction, can be said to have occurred at the same time; nor did particular sorts of change occur at the same time in all countries.

But if we are uncertain about the idea of an historical threshold, there seems to be less doubt about the occurrence of an intellectual threshold. Regardless of whether the change to modernity has been continuous or intermittent, the perception of this kind of change has been episodic. It was the more or less sudden realization of change which gave rise to contemporary forms and categories of social theory as part of the attempt to understand what European society was passing through. Theories of historical change dominated the thought of the nineteenth century. The early part of the century was more influenced by mechanistic, dialectical, and logical notions while the later part of the century saw greater emphasis upon organic, evolutionary, and romantic theories. History itself as a social science discipline was seriously offered as the master social science rather than the bastard of moral philosophy and story-telling.

The sense of change that led to this new emphasis on history and on innovation was brought about by particular changes, the explanations of which tended to be couched in universal terms. Thus, the breakdown of the feudal system and the rise of the bourgeoisie did not occur everywhere at the same time nor in the same way nor in the same degree, but the closely related rise of classical economic theory, which was inspired largely by events in Britain and France, was held to be universal in its applicability. If the historical changes which were partly explained by the new science of political economy did not occur everywhere at once, the spread of the theory itself, with appropriate modifications, helped to universalize historical change, as can be seen in the spread of classical economics in Germany.

A similar conclusion can be reached for the decline of benevolent despotism and the rise of new theories of the state as an abstract juridical, cultural, or spiritual entity. This development may have had its strongest manifestation in Germany, but the German theory of the state was paralleled by the work of the British Hegelians and the French legists.

The consequences of more efficient agricultural methods, of urbanization, and of the industrial revolution for social mobility and the restructuring of society led to the application of Newtonian physics to social analysis. The growth of the urban proletariat contributed directly to the Marxist theory of social classes as variable in history. The social dislocations and political tensions arising from these changes were at the root of utilitarianism and physiocratic thought. In short, contemporary sociological theory, itself of world significance, is the result of the attempt to explain historical changes which were originally quite restricted in their scope.

The diffusion of literacy and education in a few countries is directly related to the politicization of identity and the rise of nationalist thought. Nationalist ideas could then spread to intellectuals everywhere, even to those countries where popular political participation was far more limited. Where the improvement of communications and transport permitted, and where political conditions were properly conducive, the same spread of literacy and education permitted the growth and transformation of traditional bureaucracies into the distinctively modern institution that inspired so much of Weber's sociology. The idea of a modern bureaucracy was not limited to the countries in which it first came into being, but that idea could inspire the realization of administrative modernization even in the colonial territories of Asia and Africa.

Imperialism was not invented in the nineteenth century, but was intensified in a particular way because of European rivalries. Furthermore, the power differential between European and non-European countries, transformed an earlier and more benign curiosity about cultural diversity into the more loaded issues of social Darwinism and then cultural relativism, the forerunners of contemporary anthropology. The geographical displacement of people, the transformation of family and other kinship institutions, and the breakdown of traditional local communities and occupational patterns are at the back of theories of alienation and anomie. The full development of these ideas had to await the Freudian revolution in psychology, but both have remained key concepts in relating modernization to dynamic psychology and in explaining the different types of individual impacts of modernization.

It would be difficult to argue that all of these new ways of understanding social phenomena have a common intellectual ground any more than that they are based on universal and ubiquitous events. Nevertheless, it is not farfetched to suggest that there is a common epistemological thread which runs through them all and that is an epistemological dualism which is not new but which is at least intensified in modern thought. This epistemological dualism does not consist of the usual distinction between reality and appearance, but more particularly of the difference between purpose and function or between purposeful action and unintended consequences. Classical economics was the unseen hand, the metaphysical theory of the state postulated transcendental purposes. Marxist theory adapted the historical dialectic while other sociologies, especially those of Comte and Spencer, laid the groundwork for modern functionalism, romantic nationalism was thought to supersede individual wills just as did the general will, social Darwinism referred to laws of nature and not to individual moral responsibility, and certain undesirable psychological patterns were held to be the unintended consequences of social and historical changes which were similarly, at least originally, unintended.

When Europe tries to understand its own development, it has recourse to functional theory and to unintended consequences. Adam Smith and the doctrine of the "unseen hand" described a benign order of creation, not purposed by man but allowing the achievement of his individual purposes. The liberals argued that man-made order interfered with the progressive realization of a more beneficent order. The positivists and utilitarians thought that the happiness of individuals could best be attained by wise policies which accommodated the order of creation. The overwhelmingly accepted view was that politics was essentially a response to the historical forces of modernization.

Outside of Europe, the prevailing view has been the opposite. Politics is not a response to modernity, it must rather be the cause of modernity if modernity is to be achieved. A crude and simple way of putting this matter is to ask whether political development is thought to be the dependent variable and modernization the independent variable (European model), or whether modernization is considered the dependent variable and political development the independent variable (the extra-European model).

If it may be granted that we have passed over an intellectual threshold, we are still left with uncertainties regarding the significance of the historical threshold which is postulated by this intellectual revolution. History itself is seen in a new way as the story of change and by some even as the antithesis of social science. If the most important thing about history is its description of change, then, history describes what social science cannot investigate—unless, of course, change always or usually occurs in the same way. Contrariwise, there are social scientists who reject history in the sense that they argue that explanations of social events are essentially the same in all periods. There is still room to establish the middle ground, however, which would hold that despite observable regularities in human affairs there may also be important historical discontinuities. These discontinuities mark the difference or separation between one pattern of regularities and another. The idea of modernity appears to require this kind of thinking. By modernity we generally mean the historical conditions or patterns of observable social behavior and characteristic ideas which prevail in our era and did not prevail at some determinable period in the past.

Our understanding of the difference between the terms "political change" and "political development" is related to this concept of modernity. The easiest way to distinguish the use of these two terms is to limit the term political development to the political consequences of crossing an historical threshold. Political change would then be used only to describe change within an era during which the nature of social process was essentially unchanged. From this point of view, it might be said that both Aristotle and Ibn Khaldun have presented us with theories of political change which were brilliant explanations of the usual patterns of political events during the period in which each lived. However, Aristotle's theory, while not contradicting Ibn Khaldun, had not the categories to describe empirically the processes which most concerned Ibn Khaldun. Similarly, the theory of political change elaborated by Ibn Khaldun is not sufficient to explain the patterns of political change in the Middle East today.

The difference of temporal frames of reference has been emphasized in the preceding discussion, but we must be no less willing to consider the possibility that any given theory of political change may be restricted by a particular cultural frame. Even if our preferred explanation of historical development and modernity emphasized technology and science rather than those cultural elements which might be more difficult to diffuse throughout the world during any given era, it would be necessary to concede the possibility that, at any given moment, the new technology and science would not be evenly distributed throughout the world. The problem of diverse cultural frames which may have an equally limiting influence on explanatory generalizations is not essentially different. It may not be assumed that a theory of political change will be equally applicable everywhere during the same era.

The study of political development requires a theory of how the patterns of political life change from one set of regularities to another set of regularities. In the course of this transition, it is not clear whether we usually find an accompanying fundamental change of the whole system or whether there will only be changes in the political processes while the political system does not lose its identity. Even under such varying circumstances, each political system would probably undergo this transition but once. The limiting effects of both the temporal and cultural frames would have to be accounted for in any generalization about the process of transition itself. Actually, the historical and cultural limitations do not reinforce one another. Cultural differences cut across historical differences in such a way that the transition to modernity, which is still being accomplished by some states, is never precisely reproduced. The existence of underdevelopment in our own era gives us the opportunity of studying related patterns of transition, although it must be admitted that the process of political development differs greatly when there are many developed political systems as opposed to a situation in which there are no developed political systems—that is, when the world itself rather than a given country is on the threshold of modernity.

Part II. Equality, Capacity, and Differentiation

The idea of modernity is closely associated with important changes of orientation in a number of intellectual areas, and even with the creation of new disciplines such as economics and sociology. These intellectual efforts to understand contemporary events have not only provided us with a language for discussing modernity, they have at the same time tended to compartmentalize our ideas of modernity. Thus we have concepts for modernity derived from each of the disciplines; we have a few essentialist theories which appear to try harder to unify the disciplines themselves than to explain modernity; and we have theories which argue that the process of modernization starts within, or is caused by activity within, a single disciplinary area. The value of such theories must rest on the extent to which they can be used to elucidate historical modernity in such a manner as to unite the perspectives of the disciplines in a single empirical complex.

There is no way to prove that there is a generic modernity in the face of the situational differences which must always obscure the similarities among so-called modern states. It may seem to be a simple enough procedure to argue that modernization refers to whatever is common to the historical changing of European conditions, but the diversity of those events compels us to abstract certain salient elements that seem to be related to one another and to exclude those historical events which appear in recent times to comprise reactions to the progress of modernization. Obviously such a selection is not an empirical exercise but is rather an intellectual and possibly an ideological one. More particularly is this the case when the arguments made against some phases of modernity claim to represent yet newer and more contemporary manifestations of modernity.

The methodological problem we face in attempting to define modernity is, not surprisingly, the product of the intellectual modernization described in the preceding section. If we are certain that we have passed an intellectual threshold but uncertain about whether the world has passed an historical threshold, it is because we are uncertain of our intellectual tools. Two dominant themes of the modern social science disciplines are consciousness and functionalism. True consciousness, false consciousness, self-consciousness, group-consciousness—and the related notions of identity, intentionality, psychological phenomenology, transcendental phenomenology, the philosophy of mind, and the issues of solipsism—all derive from the Cartesian heritage of the modern world and reflect the realization that man does not or has not purposively shaped the social world in which he lives. Modernization is best understood as change which was not intended but which was possibly the consequence of too rational and too purposive a view of man.

"Functionalism" in our present use refers to the phenomenon of unintended consequences, what Merton referred to as latent function-

ality (positive or negative) and what Sartre has called countertotali-
ties.[7] The problem is a simple one, even if abstract: if consciousness is
determined by circumstances, and if circumstances are determined not
by what man proposes but by the unforeseen consequences of diver-
gently purposive human encounters, then how can consciousness ever
be an accurate guide to understanding the social world? In other
words, there is some doubt that the rationality of rational man is of the
kind that can grasp the rationality (or pattern, or structure) of the
social order. Ordinary commonsense understands social appearances,
but social reality is accessible, if at all, only to disciplined understanding.

The project of the modern social sciences, like that of contemporary
philosophy, is to link consciousness with the world by means of knowledge of how the world works—i.e., by knowledge of what causes
"functional" consequences when they are unintended. The age of
the Enlightenment gave us, as an alternative project for social science,
the goal of understanding the world by means of rational observation
and experiment. Consciousness was not thought to complicate observation, except insofar as irrational religious or supersititious beliefs
persisted. For Adam Smith the rationality of the individual and the
rationality of the "system" were linked by the order of creation (if not
by the genius of capitalism). An uncertain and often contradictory
route leads from Comte to Dilthey to Durkheim and on to Parsons,
for whom, finally, the rational and intelligible order is the same
for both individual and collectivity. A parallel route with a less self-
satisfying conclusion leads from Rousseau through Kant, Hegel, and
Marx to Weber. This route starts with the old idea that the moral
order depends upon the prevalence of moral individuals, denying the
ontological heterogeneity of individuals and collectivities. Kant coun-
terposed the self and other, and, retaining the good will, all but declared the subject to be master over object. Hegel, in turn, all but
declared that it is the world or object which determines the ego, or the
subject, or consciousness. Rational self-consciousness would permit the
ego "in-itself" to become "for-itself," that is, to transcend its own circumstances in its understanding of the world. Marx and Weber transformed the idea of the history of the world as the history of the
growth of rational consciousness into a periodization of historical con-
sciousnesses, one more material and the other more cultural, but both

[7] Jean-Paul Sartre, *Search for a Method* (New York: Vintage Books, Knopf,
1968), p. 164.

discovering, in their respective forms of economic and bureaucratic rationality, a final stage or at least a point beyond which further change would mean a decline. The project of the modern social sciences, then, is not to achieve a rational understanding of *any* set of regularities in the world, for that is merely rationality "in-itself." The goal is to attain rationality "for-itself," in the sense of a rationality which knows that it is about the empirical social world and about the main things which shape the history of that world: "For Necessity, Fate or the like, is just that about which we are unable to say what it is doing, what its definite laws and its positive content actually are, because it is the absolute pure notion itself, viewed as *being*, relation bare and simple, but irresistible, and immovable, whose work is merely the nothingness of individual existence."[8] Hegel condemned the search for an intellectual apparatus capable of understanding all possible worlds, an apparatus which would of necessity have been composed of abstract Kantian categories. He demanded, instead, a method for synthesizing the *experience* of the unique and the *intellection* of the universal. But for Hegel, unlike Marx and Weber, such synthetic knowledge was valid only for the present or the past; it was not applicable to events which had not yet occurred. It could not be valid for the future because the method required an effort to attain a consciousness of the immediate present, through acting in or on the world. It is true that Hegel insisted on the importance of transcending the stage of consciousness which came of action in the world while Marx did not; nevertheless, it was Marx and Weber who more readily believed in the intellectual accessibility of the political and social absolute than did Hegel. For most of us today modernity does not appear as a final stage which cannot be transcended, as a final opaque destiny. History has not ceased, even if it rumbles ominously close to a nuclear denouement.

We know that history has not ceased, and yet most of us cling stubbornly to an idea of modernity which hypostatizes reason. The past is tradition; the future—in which the world will go on despite the end of history—is modernity; and the present is transition. This schema has a wide acceptance even where both tradition and modernity are thought to be various. The three stages are often taken as ideal types, or alternatively, individuals are characterized in terms of whether they are traditionals, transitionals, or moderns. But hypostasis

8 G.W.F. Hegel, *The Phenomenology of Mind* (New York: Torchbooks, Harper and Row, 1967), p. 387.

is not history. The idea of modernity may be one of the attractions that lead away from tradition, but it functions as the *dialectical* rather than the *historical* opposite of tradition. What we hopefully call transitional is, of course, the synthesis of modernity as an idea and tradition as an empirical, historical configuration. This synthesis is transitional only in the sense that it is not a fixed arrangement, but an arrangement in which history continues to have meaning. This synthesis is modernity, but we do not recognize it because it is not a final stage. The idea of stages, which is not unrelated to the question about the occurrence of an historical threshold, is potentially misleading; but even more misleading is the substitution of the idea of modernity for the idea of the Hegelian absolute. This substitution accounts for the arbitrary tendency to think of modernity as univocal, when it is more reasonable to think of modernity as a complex of divergent and occasionally conflicting elements. The idea of the heterogeneity of modernity is certainly sustained by an examination of the way in which scholars in the social sciences have tried to explain modernity. At least we may say that the heterogeneity of modernity is sustained when we look at each of the disciplines by itself. There are, of course, those who believe that a higher level of knowledge is to be attained by means of a speculative unification of the disciplines, but they are confusing the false need for the logical unity of a set of analytical categories with the need to understand the contingent unity of a piece of empirical reality. When the divergences of the disciplines are reconciled, the definitional order which results is often at the expense of whatever explanatory value the separate disciplines have.

For present expository purposes it is impractical to attempt to employ all of the theoretical insights of the various disciplines. Instead we will use summary concepts derived from an examination of the specialized literature of the disciplines of economics, sociology, and anthropology. These summary concepts, which we have agreed to call equality, capacity, and differentiation (ECD), will serve as a shorthand description of the syndrome of modernity and they are meant to provide a statement of the heterogeneous context within which political development is to be understood.

If there are central notions of the way in which modernity has influenced development in each of the three areas of economy, society, and culture they are: for economics, *capacity*; for society, *differentiation*; and for culture, *equality*. These three ideas are central to the meaning of modernity. They are not exclusively limited, each to a single discipline, but for economics, differentiation and equality are subordinated to capacity; for society, equality and capacity are subordinated to differentiation; and for culture, capacity and differentiation are subordinated to equality.

Let us turn now to the disciplines themselves for a closer examination of these ideas—with apologies in advance for a treatment which is lengthy enough in the present context but still too brief to do justice to much important scholarship.

The most frequently used and the simplest definition of development in economic terms is higher income. This term is used with reference to the economic system, and it has no limitation with regard to historical period. Fluctuations in the level of income for a total society might occur under any conditions of technological achievement, and even as a consequence of changes in the weather. Indeed, for agricultural economies, the most significant changes will be the result of changes in the weather. But the strongest objection to the utility of this term is precisely in that it refers to the economic system and not the society, hence it does not account for changes in population size. An increase in population, simply by providing more labor, might produce an increase in total income but possibly one that is not commensurate with the increase in the number of mouths to be fed.

As a consequence of these objections some writers have insisted that higher per capita income be used as the definition of economic development, even though higher income, without regard to population size or growth, may be less value committed or less committed to certain types of economic theory. Presumably, the most rational economic approach would avoid attaching any noneconomic value to any one factor of production above any other. The idea of higher per capita income does refer to the difficulties that must eventually overtake those countries whose population growth exceeds the consequent increase in production, but this more humane concept leaves out of account the noneconomic consequences of increased income. It is fairly well agreed that the larger the total income of a society, the larger will be the portion available for government disposition. This proposition holds true under conditions of similar technological development and economic structure, and probably holds true even where per capita income may be falling. It is not a foregone conclusion that political development will result from governmental disposition of increased resources, but neither should such a possibility be precluded from any consideration of the political consequences of economic development.

Once it has been agreed that we must take population growth and welfare into account, our notion of economic development begins to spread all over the place. How much must income increase before we can say that a given economy is developed? Since the term may be used in relation to any previous state of the economic system, it does not seem to have much explanatory value for anything else. Granted that we discover an increase in per capita income, how great an increase is necessary in order to achieve an acceptable level of welfare? Even more difficult, how much of an increase is necessary to achieve political stability? Since there are some theorists who correlate economic development with democracy, it is also in order to ask how much economic development is necessary in order to achieve democracy?

While it is possible to discern some threshold of economic development by examining the distribution of per capita incomes for all countries, such static notions appear to have less and less relevance for the more advanced countries even as they continue to represent utopian and often unattainable goals for the poorer countries. A concept that has come into increasing use for the "developed" economies of the world is, therefore, the idea of the continuously expanding economy. This is a dynamic idea, it is process oriented, and it is open-ended with regard to political, technological, and welfare values. Or so it seems. But the main point is that this new concept of the state of economic development points to no threshold and designates no absolute quantities in terms of which the attainability of other desiderata might be considered. Political stability, the satisfaction of popular demands, the fulfillment of the ambitions of newly emerging generations—all these can be anticipated only within a perpetually optimistic setting.

There must obviously be some basic changes in economic structure if a constantly expanding economy is to be maintained. Searching for the nature of these changes, some observers have emphasized a particular change as decisive. Others have tried to suggest that a certain combination of changes will bring about development. We shall discuss some of the more interesting of these suggestions, even though it will be clear that some are so general and comprehensive in scope that they may entail other more specific ideas about the nature of economic development.

It is widely agreed that a developed economy is more complex than an underdeveloped one. Because this idea of complexity has many dimensions it is not clear whether it has any conceptual or theoretical unity. One way of viewing this complexity is to acknowledge that different kinds of products are being made and exchanged in a wide variety of indirect ways within a larger geographical context. Complexity would then refer to technology, transportation, banking and finance, style changes, consumer preferences, and many other elements that do not seem to fall within the scope of a single theory. Another way of referring to all of these things draws upon the more comprehensive but more abstract terminology of sociology. The complementary concepts of differentiation and specialization as they affect each of the factors of production, are the most relevant.

Another factor-oriented development concept is efficiency. While complexity is generally thought of as a pejorative in our culture, efficiency is a widely approved value, the approval stemming from the notion of economizing rather than from economic theory as such. In this limited practical sense of the term, efficiency may be found even in underdeveloped economies where the best use of available resources is made within the context of a given economic structure. In more abstract terms, however, efficiency refers to the operation of the markets for the various factors of production: an efficient market is one which approaches, as nearly as possible, the perfect market ideal of economic theory. This theoretical use of the term still has practical consequences for the price structure and the availability of the factors of production throughout the economy, while its more analytical aspect is evident in the use of the alternative term "integration."

In a manner of speaking, our single idea of efficiency has divided itself into two notions, both of which are relevant to the idea of development. Many of us have the sense that productive units in a modern economy tend to be more efficient than they are in a traditional economy—other things being equal. When we say that other things are equal, what can we mean except the changing of the traditional economy into a developed one? Presumably we must leave technology and the organization of production unchanged, and we must argue that development means greater efficiency as a consequence of more productive attitudes, fairer pricing (again factor markets), or different mixes of the factors of production (which may or may not entail a change in the organization of production).

Each of these three interpretations of efficiency appears in various theories of economic development. The argument for the importance of attitude change usually derives from psychological and cultural ideas of development, but there is a special variant—entrepreneurship—which has been of particular interest to economists. The theory of entrepreneurship has certain conservative biases. Although it may be possible that a sufficient number of persons with appropriate characteristics may be found in any society to permit that society to develop, whether under a capitalist or a socialist framework, the economic theory of entrepreneurship argues that it is the economic system itself which permits, encourages, or even produces entrepreneurial behavior. If all those individuals having entrepreneurial characteristics are from an ethnic, religious, or caste minority, then this form of economic development would seem to be precluded by the culture, modal personality, and economic structure of the majority community.

Fairer pricing, or the greater efficiency of factor markets throughout the whole system, might be thought of in terms of the "integration" of factor markets. The view does not require that factor prices be the same throughout the entire geographical area coinciding with the economic system; it merely insists that price differentials be justified in terms of costs such as transportation, storage, financing, and the like. One of the most intriguing aspects of the term integration is, of course, that it has terminological relevance for most other disciplines. It is not immediately clear that the use of a common terminology affords us a way of bridging the disciplinary gap, and it may simply put before us the temptation of believing that we have found the essence of the idea of development just because we have a single word for it. Nevertheless, economic integration has a significant economic meaning, and it also implies certain circumstantial interdependencies which, if they are not expressed in theoretical terms, are easily recognized as having substantial theoretical relevance for politics if not for culture and society. It is, in other words, difficult to conceive of an integrated economy under conditions of political, social, and cultural traditionality. At least two of the more significant political aspects of greater economic integration are increased availability of information and open access. It requires little elaboration to establish that perfect markets entail complete information regarding demand and supply and the free access of buyers and sellers to the market. We all know, however, that politics is not a market place even if it goes on in the market place.

The possibility of mixing or combining the factors of production in different proportions is also associated with the existence of a developed economy. Variability or flexibility or the possibility of choosing may be associated with development, but sometimes development is defined in terms of a particular way of combining the factors of production. Choice depends upon the availability of several technologies, but presumably one technology is the most efficient in any given situation. Furthermore, from a welfare point of view, the value of labor ought to be enhanced, generally by increasing the availability of land and capital. It is only as an interim solution that labor-intensive technologies are proposed for overpopulated countries. Since land is limited, it follows that a developed economy calls for an increasing use of capital relative to the other factors of production.

There are other indicators of economic development, but they seem to be less comprehensive, even though each has its impact on the social, the cultural, and the political subsystems. Not only may the value of labor increase, but it might also be argued that new kinds of value are added to products themselves. Varying the product to accommodate diverse tastes, packaging products to give aesthetic satisfaction, and even selling status along with the product are examples of new kinds of value. The service aspect of these values points to yet another way of describing economic development: the relative increase of tertiary production. Most of the developing countries are now concerned with increasing manufacturing or secondary production, yet the service sector has often developed more rapidly. This imbalance is the consequence of noneconomic development, particularly uncontrolled and unplanned urbanization. Urbanization, which creates new needs along with new jobs, is another characteristic feature of economic development. There are also circumstances in which the traditional needs, if not those unplanned needs that were acquired unintentionally, are maladaptive to the resources and technological possibilities of a particular economy. Under such circumstances economic development requires the capacity to alter established needs or to convince people that alternative foods and other products can supply those needs satisfactorily.

The last characteristic of our discussion of economic development has already been implied by several others. Economic development might be defined as the economic consequences of technological change, particularly the consequences of the substitution of mechanical or electronic energy for human energy. While a concern for human dignity may be associated with this view, there are also certain contradictory values linked with technological advance. Automation is but the latest term for dispensing with the need for certain kinds of manpower and subordinating other kinds of manpower to more efficient man-machine systems. The social and political implications of technological development have been as problematical as the related psychological implications.

Sociological theory appears to be particularly well adapted to the description of development because it is a new discipline whose creation is linked with modernization and development. As in the case of economics, however, we will find some concepts of a global type referring to the general characteristics of societies and some which are narrow in perspective.

One notion common to economics and sociology is complexity. Social development (in a disciplinary and not a value-oriented or ideological sense) means increased social complexity. This complexity may be described in terms of class, group, or structural-functional theory—and possibly many other ways besides. In Marxist terms development means the transformation of a structure of classes into a classless society or a simpler rather than a more complex society. A non-Marxist view might hold that development has actually entailed the emergence of a more complicated class structure through the addition of new classes without the elimination of the old. The two views may be held to converge in the sense that occupation is now more important than class. As occupational classes become more numerous, society is consequently more complex.

In terms of groups it can be argued that individuals now identify themselves in significant ways with many more groups, including some which did not even exist in the past. Extreme or distorted development is sometimes described as the elimination of all groups intervening between the individual and the state, including the family. There would also appear to be a stage of traditionality in which individuals seem to have belonged only to families and not to any other group. It is not certain that either of these limiting cases has ever been observed, but it is established that development has meant increasing the number of groups with which an individual is identified—even when these groups are not always independent of state control.

In terms of structural-functional theory, complexity is most frequently expressed as structural differentiation and functional specification. These two characteristics are not supposed to be separate tendencies. They are two ways of viewing the same phenomena. Structural differentiation, as a characteristic of modernity, need not be linked to any functional concept. Indeed linkage ought to be avoided in order to eschew the pitfalls of functional apriorism. Structural differentiation may entail class and group proliferation. Differentiation means that there are more structures in a modern society. It also means that it is easier, empirically, to distinguish among these structures. Structures may be distinguished in many ways, but principally in terms of role incumbents, role definition, and the goals associated with diverse roles.

Functional specificity is to be understood in terms of the particular variant of functional theory which is being employed. Thus, if one uses a scheme of four or seven functions, particular structures may be more readily associated with particular functions in a modern society than in a traditional society. If one is using a type of universal functionalism wherein every structure is said to have a function, modernization would presumably mean that many more structures would have unique functions and far fewer would have the same function. Where an undifferentiated notion of function is used as a synonym for system maintaining, as in the use of the terms "eufunctional" and "dysfunctional," the notion of functional specificity can have little meaning.

It stands to reason that the more structures there are, the easier is it to attribute specific functional consequences to particular structures. The discernment of particular structures is largely a matter of perspective and analytical orientation. Hence, it is possible to argue that conclusions regarding the degree of differentiation will depend upon culturally based perceptions of diverse purposes for which particular behaviors or strategies are specific.

Does this sort of complexity have a linear relationship with development? If it does, then the more developed a society, the more complex will it become. There will be more groups, more classes, more occupations, more structures, more roles—and more conflict. The more roles there are, the more likely is it that individuals playing more than one role will experience role conflict. It is not too difficult to foresee a point beyond which mere differentiation of structure would be dysfunctional in a political, psychological, or even an economic sense. But unless we have some way of designating the optimum level of differentiation, it is impossible to define social development in terms of a given level which will not be dysfunctional for other kinds of development. (This sort of analytical problem illustrates the tendency of our most abstract and theoretical definitions of development to outrun our naive understanding of the concept and to require some interdisciplinary definition. It also illustrates how the language of a particular discipline, insofar as it avoids ideological commitment, precludes us from dealing with matters which lie beyond disciplinary boundaries.)

Among other sociological ideas associated with development, only one seems as comprehensive as complexity, and that is the almost contrary idea of continuity, or the absence of social gaps. Actually, there is no well-elaborated theory of what a modern society or a developed society should look like, but the amount of writing on the pathologies of transitional or traditional societies is considerable. The "gap" idea as a way of characterizing underdeveloped societies received its most elaborate presentation by Shils in his *Political Development in the New States*.[9] In the first part of that study Shils described a model of underdevelopment that was characterized by gaps in the social, cultural, economic, psychological, and political spheres. A developed state is, therefore, characterized by an absence of gaps, or by continuity.

In sociological terms, continuity can mean either the existence of a complete array of classes, statuses, roles, etc., or a given configuration of these social structures. It is not at all clear what structures a complete social system would contain, but it is evident that a society lacking a bourgeoisie, an industrial labor class, an intelligentsia, or a bureaucracy would not satisfy our general idea of a developed society. How large should these groups be? Aside from very crude orders of magnitude, I doubt that anyone can say when a given class is so small that its smallness constitutes a gap or discontinuity.

Development as continuity cannot mean merely that all of a certain minimum of structures must exist. It also requires that these structures be found in a certain relationship. Once again, there are two ways in which we can understand this relationship or configuration. The first is a more or less quantitative understanding. A developed society must be characterized by the distribution of its individual members among classes, groups, occupations, and even among overlapping and interpenetrating structures. The second way of understanding a developed structural configuration is qualitative. It is composed of two main ideas. The first idea is that continuity refers to an optimum level of differentiation such that dysfunctional

---

[9] E. Shils, *Political Development in the New States* (New York: Humanities Press, 1962), p. 30.

consequences are minimized. The second idea is related and it would require that concrete structures be, in turn, so structurally linked as to eliminate gaps between structures and provide for an *integrated* society.

It is argued that a modern or developed society has a narrower, bell-shaped class pyramid. If the class pyramid is conceived of as a series of layers proportioned to the size of occupational and status groups in the society, then the widest stratum in a developed society will not be found at the bottom; it will be located between the bottom and the middle. The top part of the pyramid will not be sharply peaked. It will tend to be gently rounded and sloped toward the wider strata. The strata themselves will tend to be numerous and will appear thinner than those of a traditional society. There will be no discontinuity in the form of a gap or sudden nipping in of the sides of the bell-shaped pyramid.

Greater social mobility is another characteristic of a developed society. Movement between the various strata is more frequent, more rapid, and freer in both directions. Geographical mobility is also greater. Actually, the type of mobility generally associated with development is not exactly random, for there is some general expectation that the main direction of movement is upward socially and toward cities and industrial centers geographically.

Another social criterion of development thought to have special relevance to some kinds of political analysis is the growth of secondary interest associations. Secondary interest associations fall into the category of pressure groups, although they are not the only kind of group that exerts political pressure. The growth of these groups is explained with reference to the more general differentiation of the society and the increase in available information which permits persons that have similar interests to know one another and to join together and cooperate within the limits of those interests which are common and those which diverge. The political relevance of this trend is twofold. First, there is the relevance which emerges from group theory or the interpretation of all political life in terms of group pressures and competition. Second, there is a tendency for the government or the single party in both underdeveloped and totalitarian systems to organize secondary interest associations from the top.

In a developed society the salience and significance of the family declines. The size of the family appears to decline, but what really changes is the definition of the family and the binding character of traditional family obligations. While this change does not appear to have systemwide significance, and has perhaps little significance beyond the more restricted social system, it may in reality have the most profound importance for the pattern of development. It is patent that the character of elites will have much to do with role performance, whether social, political, or what have you. The character of elites is in part determined by origins in the traditional social structure as well as by the particular roles performed by the elites which happen to dominate in a given country. The transformation of the traditional family may be caused by the tension between traditional family obligations and the requirements of modern role performance, but the persistence of certain traditional family ties may also seriously affect role performance for modernizing elites. Where, in certain cases, the decline of the traditional family has little to do with role conflict, the transformation of the family may be determined by cultural and political factors that will thus indirectly determine the possibility of attaining satisfactory levels of modernizing performance on the part of elites. It should also be remembered that nonelite family structure will have significant political consequences consonant with prevailing levels and forms of popular political participation within the limits of the mobilization of the masses.

Since role conflict has already been discussed briefly, it need only be elaborated with respect to certain aspects frequently associated with modernization. The first of these aspects directs our attention to the separation of all roles from the personality of the individual. The psychological dimension of this separation is the need to integrate the personality, in the sense that pieces of the personality become attached to diverse roles. Presumably, the personality, insofar as it is a unity, would be expressed in the more diffuse roles which pass from tradition into modernity, such as those of kinship. But even in these areas there has been some pressure to perform in accordance with specified standards. Hence, while there may be some exaggeration in the statement that modernization requires the separation of *all* roles from the personality, it is only exaggeration and not prevarication.

One of the more problematical areas of confluence of role conflict, modernity, and personality is that of sex role differentiation. Traditionally and ideally, sex roles are not held to be related to personality except in pathological cases. In other words, from the social and cultural points of view, there are two and only two sex roles, which may be applied to typing many other roles—the occupational, socializational, consummatory, recreational, artistic, and so on. Some modern revisionists have argued for the separation of sex roles from all other roles, for the elimination of all outward symbolization of the dualistic sex role typing, and for the increased differentiation of sex roles by identifying rather than separating sex role and personality.

More generally, modernity is identified with a distinctive orientation toward and interpretation of human sexuality. Traditional repression of sexuality is said to have produced much human suffering, as well as social dislocation, political aberration, and cultural grotesquerie. But the contemporary attitude also appears to be paradoxical. In most other applications modernity is associated with self-consciousness, yet sexuality was the one thing about which traditional civilizations were self-conscious. Hence the modern attitude is supposed to be unself-conscious or "natural." It is assumed that this can be attained by an expressive permissiveness which may be artistic, educational, or, of course, practical. The central idea remains therapeutic, in keeping with the instrumental and anticonsummatory orientation of modernity.

By contrast, the treatment of sexual themes in the modern arts is often of the "can you take it" variety. Far from portraying human sexuality as a sort of biological quotidianality, modern films, plays, and novels (but not painting which lacks the subtlety, nor music which is too subtle) explore the rich and variegated associations and transmutations of sexuality revealed by means of the marvellously effective system of communication between the two entities of body and mind. For most of these artistic productions sexuality has the function of revelation; it substitutes for the significant turning point—or the climax—of the play. Truth is individualistic. Sexuality shatters the social framework and reveals the individuality which exists behind the facade of social role. The persistently individualistic bias of these artists emerges in their desire to demonstrate how a repressive sexual culture is injurious to society rather than how distortions of society are injurious to sexual culture. It is in this context that a modern counterideology has emerged that is more frankly hedonistic, prefers consummatory values to instrumental values, and emphasizes the importance of love without distinguishing eroticism and love. In general, this tendency attacks the formal institutionalization of sexuality in the West in its current arrangement of preadolescent sex-typing, ritual and class-based courtship, mildly hypocritical rules of chastity, and monogamous marriage.

The most contemporary of the modern orientations toward sexuality insists on the equality of the sexes and the de-differentiation of sex roles. There is also some inclination to de-differentiate sex-objects in terms of accepted cultural standards of desirability. This modern orientation would also enhance emotional and erotic capacity by the elimination of material, institutional, and cultural barriers to increased and more satisfactory sexual relationships. And, finally, this modern tendency insists on the acceptability of differentiated forms of sexuality, some of which are thought of as deviant, but many of which are simply treated by the culture as mysterious, sophisticated, subtle, or indulgent. It is in this last regard that "secondary" sex roles, rather than being de-differentiated in accordance with the current symbolism of "unisex" may be further differentiated in terms of personality variance.

A somewhat different slant on the problem of role conflict results from noting that it is characteristic of modern society that the home and the work-place are separated often by quite substantial distances. This separation of the locus of the performance of certain diverging if not conflicting roles has been noted and discussed by several writers. Such separation, while allowing divergent patterns to develop and be reinforced, also permits the traditional pattern to be preserved and reduces the potential of conflict between modern and traditional roles. Diffuse and specific roles may be maintained in diverse geographical locations, with the former allowing for the greater integration of the personality and the latter, presumably, fostering more of the alienation which is said to accompany modernization and industrialization.

A number of characterizations of sociological modernity focus on the increased importance of certain social segments. Perhaps the most widely accepted idea of this sort points to the increased importance of the middle sectors. (Some observers will speak of the middle class or classes, and others in vaguer terms like sectors.) It is usual, in traditional societies for the middle class to be small, however it may be defined. In modern societies, the middle class is larger, but is it the same middle class or a new and differentiated one? Even more important may be the question whether the middle class or the middle sectors are significant as a unit or rather in their diversity. The idea of the middle sectors has a vagueness which appeals to those who seek simple answers, and it suggests that social development is making the societies of the developing areas more like ours which is presumptively predominantly middle class. Middle class predominance is seen as a favorable characteristic, even if the process of the emergence of the middle sectors is somewhat disruptive for a time. When it is recognized that the middle strata in newly developing countries are quite different both occupationally and culturally from the early modern bourgeoisie of the West, some observers have had second thoughts.

Attempts to be more specific about the nature of this new middle class have led to narrower interpretations of the nature of social modernization based on the role played by various components of the middle strata. One of these groups is the intellectuals. A few writers have devoted much effort to describing the intellectuals, not only as exhibiting the most important single characteristic of the new middle class, but also as potentially playing the most important role in the process of modernization. Education, usually along Western lines, is the experience shared by most members of the middle classes in the emerging nations. There is also a widely observed difference in educational attainments between the elite and mass in these countries which favors the political elite, of course. Furthermore, even though the outstanding political leaders may be other things besides, they are frequently also intellectuals and recognize themselves as such. Very few countries are led by outspoken anti-intellectuals. The channels of Western influence are generally intellectual. The goals of development are usually expressed in the terms of Western intellectual thought. On the other hand, Western observers, particularly Americans, tend to be worried by the excessive prominence of intellectuals in politics.

Even more ambiguous is the assertion that increased bureaucratization is an extremely important aspect of modernization, a point of view almost standard in the literature influenced by Weber, although the interpretation of the consequences of bureaucratization varies considerably. Whereas most sociologists of the West have deplored the increasing bureaucratization of society as leading to alienation, atomization, and the like, the sociologists of the developing areas have generally approved of bureaucratization as leading to rationalization, hierarchicization, and effective mobilization. Two aspects of this theory require some caution. First, the process of bureaucratization is seen as essentially rational yet also cooperative in accordance with both the Weberian ideal type and some of the more recent social-psychologically oriented approaches to organization theory. The second is that bureaucratization is often confused with the increased importance and power of the bureaucracy. Insofar as the bureaucracy appears to play a more salient role, especially in politics, this approach is a specialized part of the middle sectors approach. The increased influence of the bureaucracy in political life contradicts the Weberian and other ideal models of administrative neutrality. This sort of a bureaucracy is not rational and in its empirical wholeness it is not wholly nor even always predominantly modern. In other words, the rise of the bureaucracy may counter the influence of the rise of bureaucratization. Bureaucratization, insofar as it is fostered by any group, may be the goal of others such as the intellectuals and the military who may seek rationalization and modernization, while the actual civil service functionaries pursue essentially traditional values, including those of cooperation and mutual aid.

The military are another group whose rise is associated with modernization, but the interpretation of the meaning of the rise of the military is in dispute. There are those who look upon the military as a special, particularly well-educated, well-disciplined, and mature segment of the middle strata. There are others who see the military as diluting the intellectual orientation of the middle sector and as political fumblers who rush into complex situations in the naive belief that military discipline will serve where ideological exhortation has failed. Perhaps the most frequent interpretation of military intervention depends upon the assumption that the traditional society has fallen apart, thus permitting force alone to prevail. As in the case of all the other theories about the middle sector and the special role of its components, a sounder approach would recognize that the military, like each of the other groups, can play diverse roles depending upon the social, political, and historical context and would avoid attributing sociologically universal functions to the middle sectors, bureaucracies, military organizations, technicians, or other experts like managers, and even religious hierarchies.

Finally, there are certain processes which bring about long-term change that are associated with modernization or social development. Urbanization is certainly one of the key aspects of development. The increased size of cities, the enhanced political importance of urban residents, the concentration of cultural, economic, and religious institutions in large cities, and the growth of a distinctively urban way of life are almost everywhere identified explicitly or implicitly with the process of development. Bureaucratization and industrialization, even alienation and atomization, all processes associated with development, may or may not occur to a significant extent, but urbanization is almost always found. The consequences of this process are also various, and while urbanization may entail many of the changes we have discussed in previous paragraphs, it is essentially a demographic process with open-ended implications. Industrialization does not necessarily accompany urbanization. The impact of urbanization on the traditional culture is indeterminate. But its impact on politics appears everywhere to have brought about populism, egalitarian, ideological politics, a preoccupation with distributive processes, and mass organization. Within the framework of urbanization itself, one of the greatest problems is the distorted development which results from the asymmetrical attractiveness of the often gigantically overgrown capital city as against the very low pulling power of provincial cities. The problems and the benefits of urbanization are unevenly distributed throughout the country and as a consequence, cities do not so much reflect particular hinterlands so much as they reflect a cross section of the entire country. The problems associated with urbanization will therefore vary with the social and ethnic structure of the particular country.

Industrialization is often said to be a prerequisite of development, if not the efficient cause of development. Some of the more extreme views would identify industrialization with development. From the sociological point of view, the importance of industrialization is expressed primarily in the creation of new classes, particularly in the creation of a new working class. The nature of entrepreneurship changes with industrialization, the role of the commercial classes changes, the influence of technicians and the educated increases, and the differentiation of occupations proceeds apace. Nevertheless, industrialization may not for the foreseeable future be separated from the consequences of increasing the size of the urban proletariat, which are probably not the same as the consequences of increasing the influence of the middle sectors.

Social atomization and alienation are processes that are also frequently associated with modernization, though they are more often discussed in the context of Western development than when the emerging countries of the non-West are under discussion. These two terms refer to obvious social pathologies and raise the question of whether they are necessary concomitants of development. In some sense, such social pathologies could be seen as the antithesis of development even if they were considered aspects of modernization. Both processes suggest the breakdown of society rather than its development. From this point of view, social modernization creates strains upon the political, economic, and cultural subsystems requiring their adaptation to socially pathological conditions or leading those subsystems to so influence the social subsystem as to bring it back toward health, integration, equilibrium, or development again. In the study of the developing areas we frequently come across descriptions of social pathology, but these descriptions are usually not explained as a necessary consequence of modernization (e.g., increased urbanization equals increased social deviance) but as the consequence of delayed or distorted development. Pathology is the characteristic feature of transition and not of arrival. Pathology represents the breakdown of tradition before modernity has taken hold. Furthermore, when viewed in the context of what are perceived to be the insistent and rigid collectivist structure of a traditional order, social atomization appears as a desirable attainment of individual freedom and equality, while alienation seems to be relevant only to the traditional order and not to society in general.

Unlike theories of economic development, not all ideas or theories of social development are optimistic. There are many writers who do not consider social development a benign process. Even more significant is the fact that most of the concepts connected with social development have implicit value orientations, while there are at least some economic notions that are relatively value free. One conceptualization of the process of social development comes closer to this economic ideal although it still has certain democratic, pluralistic biases. This idea associates social development with the capacity of a society to continually restructure itself in accordance with the demands of the environment. Since atomization and alienation are also forms of restructuring, it is important to emphasize that development entails adaptive restructuring, including a provision for the possibility of yet more restructuring in the future. Atomization (equality, individualism) is not necessarily excluded by this point of view, but alienation and the growth of social deviance are probably disallowed, since they reduce capacity for purposeful restructuring.

Let us turn now to a similar brief cataloguing of some of the concepts that are used to describe development from the cultural or anthropological point of view. Anthropologists have specialized for the most part in describing traditional and nonurban societies, while sociologists have described modern society and its problems. Nevertheless, in recent years more social anthropologists have entered into the colloquy with sociologists regarding cultural development in complex societies.

No single description can sum up the rich and varied interests of contemporary anthropology, yet one is tempted to say that much of anthropological theory is concerned more with form than substantive content. It is not a foregone conclusion that modernization or development represent substantive differences from the past, and one of the central problems of culture is that there may be diverse ways of doing the same thing as well as adaptive and imitative ways of trying to do new things. The functional interpretation of traditional cultures has tended to find them as rational in their way as are the so-called modern cultures. Of course, it is the culture that is rational and not individuals. Furthermore rationality is tied to goals such as stability or nonchange (hence nondevelopment) for the culture in question. Modernity may therefore be seen as another way of getting traditional things done rather than as more rational, more efficient, or more ethical.

The distinction between form and substance may suggest certain troublesome metaphysical implications which it is not our intention to introduce here. Our point is rather that a culture which is not self-conscious purports to present a system of values and valued practices which are sufficiently comprehensive for either a part or all of mankind. Contemporary social science casts doubt upon the validity of any such claim simply by juxtaposing many such systems even though some features of so-called primitive cultures may be preferred to some features of so-called civilized cultures. The primitive's preference for his own culture is not a matter of choice but of necessity in the Hegelian sense, whereas the sophisticated anthropologist's critique of modern society is only possible after the loss of innocence. The anthropologist may believe that there is no great difference in value between primitive and unself-conscious cultures and "advanced" self-conscious cultures, but the process of change from one to the other is not as simple as the "civilized" anthropologist's effort to reverse the process in order to understand a primitive culture.

Clifford Geertz has distinguished the conscious formation of political ideologies from the way in which undifferentiated political objects are imbedded in a total and integrated, unself-conscious culture.[10] For him, as for many others, the emergence of conscious, rational thought is the consequence of pathology—in this case, political breakdown or the loss of legitimacy. Leaving aside the large assumption regarding the integrated comprehensiveness of primitive or even premodern culture, we can recognize that this point of view is based on a functional orientation.

A rational and empirically relevant ideology is produced when it is needed, if it is produced at all. Theoretically, the need is society's and not the individual's, but the distinction between society and individuals may be criticized as formalistic. On the other hand, if some individuals have a "need" to produce new political ideologies when society has no similar need, then the distinction between society and individuals is again relevant. The same conclusion might be drawn for all those theorists whose efforts are unaccepted despite society's need. Obviously, not any rational and empirically relevant political ideology can be accepted, but only those suggestions which appear relevant to (whether for or against) the preexisting culture and which are indeed rational and empirical in relation to certain prevailing circumstances. Self-consciousness is not deemed to eliminate, transform, or even to greatly modify the functional requisites of society. The specific structures which serve society's needs may change, but the needs remain the same. The alternatives remain clear: either some new delusion or self-regarding interpretation of the political world is substituted, or else the "noble lie" becomes recognizable to all or nearly all. Under such circumstances functional theory offers societal reasons why individuals delude themselves, or itself provides the rational basis for upholding the noble lie. The consequence of the biologization of society is the psychologization of culture.

Paradoxically, the psychologization of culture works in at least two ways. Not only does it explain the acceptance of cultural phenomena and their effectiveness as a consequence of certain ubiquitous human needs regardless of the knowledge that these cultural phenomena are not absolutes, but it also attempts to evaluate cultures on the basis of whether they are conducive to the emergence of healthy modern personalities: the democratic personality, the mobile personality, the integrated personality, the achievement-oriented personality, the em-

---

[10] "Ideology as a Cultural System," in David E. Apter, *Ideology and Discontent* (New York: Free Press, 1964), p. 64.

pathetic personality, the ego-oriented personality, the entrepreneurial personality—above all, the pragmatic personality, capable of living with ambiguity, capable of accepting moderate hypocrisy, undisturbed by conventionalism, able to grasp the concept of the noble lie and to respond to it both rationally and emotionally, in the mode of the "as if." It need hardly be added that contemporary psychologism has immense significance for the association of modernity with equality and individualism.

Since a modern culture is self-conscious about the functional consequences of its patterns, one of the major issues in our own society is the extent to which we ought to preserve those cultural patterns which appeal to our emotions. The rejection of nonrational symbols has gone hand in hand with the rejection of various forms of group mystique. But rationality itself must rest on a ground of values which it can neither produce nor discover on its own. The more individualistic and the less group-oriented are those values, the more will such rationality be associated with private rather than public outcomes. The more that man is seen in psychological, or Freudian terms, the less will rationality be associated with social, political, and economic benefits to the society as a whole. The issue was stated by Freud in *Civilization and Its Discontents*, for though individual and group welfare are closely interdependent, they are not positively functional in each and every aspect. Emphasizing the areas of individual and group incompatibility instead of stressing areas of compatibility would appear to be a matter of choice—or of culture.

Cultural relativism, the equating of diverse cultures in terms of values, is possible only from a value-neutral standpoint, or, taking the preservation of system as the ultimate value, from the standpoint that all cultures are equally functional in preserving their sociopolitical systems. This view may have some validity insofar as we are concerned with established and isolated cultures which are not self-conscious in the sense that they understand the anthropologists' principles of functionalism as applied to their own culture. The absence of self-consciousness may be called lack of rationality, but the presence of self-consciousness need not lead to adaptiveness or responsiveness or to the better preservation of the culture. Just because cultural modernity implies a greater knowledge of human motivation, it need not also imply a more efficient preservation of social systems or even a more effective policy output on the part of the government. Recent cultural and (derivatively) ideological tendencies in the West suggest that cultural modernity may create grave social and political problems as easily as it provides new solutions to earlier problems. Indeed, there is a school that interprets modern society by emphasizing the negative consequences of modernization, particularly in cultural terms. This school has been nourished by the writings of romantic anthropologists among other romantic rejecters of the modern world.

The idea of cultural modernity takes account of how changes in society, technology, and economy affect culture, but it does not necessarily suggest that a modern culture responds and adapts to these changes in such a way as to preserve itself. It might be possible to distinguish between cultural modernity and cultural development according to how fully cultural change adapts to the other changes entailed in modernization, where adaptiveness is defined as contributing to the preservation of the system.

But culture is neither monolithic nor homogeneous except in the most primitive societies; nor are the processes of cultural preservation anywhere perfectly efficient. There are great traditions and little traditions. There are written traditions and oral traditions. There are intellectual, religious, and aesthetic traditions. There are social, moral, artistic, and professional values, rules, forms, styles and standards. And attached to each there are collections or systems of symbols, more and less elaborate, organized as ideologies, theories of legitimacy, *Weltanschauungen*, philosophies, sciences, histories, and identity resolutions. Some of these aspects of culture, some of the time, are more persistent than others. Some are more responsive to the changes of modernization and some less. Still, if we leave aside the question of eufunctional adaptiveness, it seems that there are a number of things that are entailed in cultural modernization which have been noticed by a variety of observers whose observations have been accepted to the extent that these characteristics have doubtlessly informed our own cultural understanding of the idea of development.

One of the most important contributions to our ideas of cultural modernization has come from Sir Henry Maine's contrast of the status basis of ancient law with the contractual basis of modern law. Contractualism provides the legal basis of Lockean individualism and equality. Maine's distinction was not the only dichotomous theory of modernization in which two principles were contrasted and in which tradition and modernity were both characterized by essential characteristics. The second most influential dichotomy is that of Tonnies between *Gemeinschaft* and *Gesellschaft* which was in part derived from

Maine's theory. Tonnies deplored the decline of the collectivity and the social atomization of modernity. The core idea might be pushed all the way back to the end of the Renaissance and the beginnings of modern empirical science from which the conscious comparison of the ancients and the moderns comes. As a consequence, most thinking about cultural modernization has been in the form of bimodal contrasts influenced by nineteenth-century social thought as interpreted by Weber in his contrast of traditional and rational legitimacy, by Durkheim and his contrast of the sacred and the secular, and by Parsons and his contrasting sets of pattern variables.

The sort of dichotomies we get contrasts traditional status and deference-oriented cultures with modern technologically and instrumentally oriented cultures. In traditional cultures individuals tend to be thought of in terms of their particularistic qualities rather than their common qualities. The abstraction of roles from personality is unknown, and in fact, the role is treated as if it were far less important than the individual personality. But both personality and role are subordinated to status which is in turn derived from the position which each person occupies in the total structure. The structure of the system may be influenced by technology and resources, but it is perceived and symbolized in words and behavior as a component of culture. Persons are born into positions in a traditional structure. The structure is comprised of statuses to which roles are attached. Deference behavior both reaffirms and symbolizes or expresses the structure of statuses. The structure is rigid. The cultural, as opposed to the sociological part of this traditionality appears in the values attached to status, stability, deference, and kinship, as well as to the ideas of structure and the symbolic systems of legitimation and expression. By contrast, the modern culture values skill, the pragmatic attainment of results, efficiency in the use of resources, the easy substitutability of similarly qualified persons, and the possibility of disregarding personality differences. Parsons describes these differences according to five pairs of dichotomous behavior patterns: universalism vs. particularism, achievement vs. ascription, affective neutrality vs. affectivity, specificity vs. diffuseness, and individual vs. collectivity orientation. Additional distinctions are made between instrumental (modern) and consummatory (traditional) value orientations and between egalitarian (modern) and elitist (traditional) orientations.

A second and important area of contrast focuses upon a general world view or ideological orientation in juxtaposing the traditional god-centered *Weltanschauung* with the man-centered rational *Weltan-schauung* which is said to characterize modern cultures. This dichotomy is patterned after the contrast between feudalism and capitalism in the sense that it represents only the most recent change in a series of stages of transformation, development, or dialectical evolution. The idea of the evolution of human thought is also derived from the controversy between the ancients and the moderns, since the adherents of the moderns believed that new knowledge could be discovered and advances made over the ancients, while the adherents of the ancients believed that knowledge itself was a limited sum and could not be aggrandized. Comte was explicit in his theory of the stages of the evolution of human thought from superstition to rationality, and he in turn influenced Dilthey who proposed a similar three-stage theory. The central idea can be summed up as a theory of the evolution of ontological ideas such that the more modern a culture, the more rational will those ideas become. The difficulty once again is in determining whether rationality is to be identified with social and political persistence or not. Since the overwhelming bias of most students of development is toward political and social stability, or toward the proliferation of idealized models of Western societies, the concept of rational ontological development is not often questioned. The whole idea could be boiled down to saying that it is the tendency for cultures to develop under the impact of modernization so as to become compatible with the persistence of a modern social and economic system. Exactly what configuration a culture needs in order to fulfill this purpose is not altogether clear, although the pattern variables already discussed are relevant at one level, and at the level of ontological ideas the metaphysical foundation of modern empirical science is similarly relevant.

Regardless of whether we tie these changes of world view and ideas of reality to the preservation of modern societies, or even to the creation of modern societies, one of the consequences of recent cultural change has been to reduce our concern with the hereafter, with considerations of the nature of God, and even with such questions as the degree of interest which God may have in our world. At least to a discernibly greater extent than ever before, man has become the measure of the importance of things.

Another related characteristic of cultural modernity is the favorable valuation of innovation as opposed to the maintenance of tradition. In modern societies change itself is viewed with favor and its occurrence is both more frequent and more sought after. It is a commonplace for merchants, actors, artists, teachers, and politicians to declare that they are offering something new to their clientele, and for their clientele to complain that they have been offered the same old thing. In traditional societies, so far are things the other way that innovations of some kinds are punishable in very severe ways.

In modern societies artistic failure is not the result of the failure to innovate alone. Innovation may lead to something of artistic value, or again it may not. Such new forms as the "happening" serve to break down all established criteria of aesthetic judgment and make nonrepetitiveness the ultimate basis of the art form. Comparison and judgment become difficult if not impossible, and the novelty and intensity of the experience become the only criteria. No doubt novelty has something to do with intensity, but this can only be discovered through repetition, a method precluded by pressing one modern cultural virtue to its extreme. When innovation itself becomes formalized and routinized, it thereby contradicts another principle of cultural modernity: the preference for achievement above form. Traditional cultures are said to emphasize and value form above substance. It is the form of legal documents or petitions which determines whether they are to be honored and not the validity of the applicant's case. It is the form of bureaucratic communication that is more important than what bureaucrats actually write to one another. It is the form of respecting one's parents that is more important than filial love. It is the form of bargaining in the market which is more important than the final sale price. It is the formal legitimacy of the government and not its performance which is important. In the arts, it is the repetition of received forms rather than creativity which constitutes art. Obviously, if modern culture rejects form alone as sufficient so must it also reject the mere rejection of received traditional forms.

Another contrast to which we have already referred is that between science and magic. Though the place of magic in primitive and prescientific societies can be interpreted in a functional manner, such an interpretation refers magic to certain social values and not to the purposive goal of magic as means of understanding and controlling both the human and nonhuman environment. The elimination of magic may weaken the society in certain ways, but the growth of science will certainly strengthen it in other ways. From the cultural point of view science involves much more than a mere ability to cope with the physical environment more effectively. It also means a new understanding of knowledge, the means of its discovery, a new relationship between theory and practice, the value of experiment and research, and the goal of education. Two other aspects of the modern valuation of science are worthy of mention. One of these is the recognition that access to the secrets of science is through intellectual ability as well as by means of any other institutional paths that may be established. Traditionally, access to magical knowledge was through initiation and often ascription. The modern view values access based on ability rather than initiation and ascription although there are increasingly occasions on which security or other considerations have mitigated against completely open access to scientific knowledge. Commercial rivalries also mitigate free access to scientific knowledge, which tends to be treated as is property in those societies where private property is strongly valued. (Is this a modern or a traditional value?) In a similar manner, and this is our second aspect, nations may deny access to scientific knowledge to the savants of other nations, or they may offer access selectively in accordance with policy. Hence, even though there may be a modern ideology of science which is identified with egalitarian social values and universalist principles, it is hard to derive these values from the observation of prevalent practice. Instead, it is in the denial of equal access that we can discover the typically modern realization of the equality of men. Access to scientific knowledge is denied not as in the case of magic because it will lose its effectiveness once revealed, but because scientific knowledge is effective and once revealed will lose its knower his advantage.

In a modern culture change itself tends to be seen as progress or development and hence beneficial. The traditional view is to see all change within a framework of cyclical recurrence so that all events can be understood with reference to some past event and some past historical context. The range or the limits of the possible are already known so that there can be nothing really new under the sun. This distinction between the traditional and modern view of change is itself a product of cultural differences, for the idea of what is change and what is not depends upon criteria of significance. Hence, if events are evaluated in terms of certain moral considerations, it might be argued that the future will give us little really significantly new knowledge of an ethical kind so all events will be familiar from an ethical point of view. If our valuation of events tends toward other sorts of things than the ethical we may more easily discern nonrecurrent changes, evolutions, and even progress.

Of particular importance for politics is the identification of modern cultural values with goal orientation as opposed to traditional ritualism. While this distinction borrows much from the one between substance and form, we are here more concerned with purposes. The reason why this distinction is important for political analysis is that some modern definitions of politics hold that politics is primarily concerned with goal attainment. Obviously, traditional politics could not have been similarly concerned if we can validly distinguish the traditional and the modern on these grounds. A dependent definition of politics will also be seen to be culture bound. Traditional politics might better be defined as maintaining all things in their proper and fixed relationship as designated by the culture itself. It is possible to derive from these considerations that culture in its broadest sense was more determinative of politics in traditional systems whereas politics is more determinative of culture in developed systems.

The notion of cultural modernity is not to be entirely separated from the idea of integration either. There are at least two ways in which cultural integration is related to modernity aside from the vague prescription of integrating the culture with the society and the more significant idea of integrating culture and personality. The most important idea is that of integrating the great and the many small traditions into a unified system. Very often the greatest task facing the new nation will be to build a nation out of a collection of tribes or of isolated communities. Even when all of these traditionally isolated groups share a common language, or a common religion, and other significant cultural features, there are often important local differences which are enhanced by the lack of literacy or the absence of close contact with the centers of the tradition, or the lack of suitable cultural mediators. Not only do the localities grow apart from one another, but it is apparent that without literacy, without formal institutions, and without frequent contact, the localities have probably never really grasped the nature of the great tradition and have never fully discarded more primitive local practices of a primeval type. Modernization involves an increasing ease and frequency of contacts between the great and small traditions, thus precipitating a kind of cultural sorting-out process. This process is often affected by political attempts to include or exclude either groups of people or particular cultures. But the idea of the integration of the great and small traditions does not necessarily mean a *gleichschaltung*. Presumably the two may fit together in such a way that many features of the small tradition can be incorporated into the great and even made applicable to the whole population which is now identified with the dominant cultural pattern.

The second idea of integration has to do with the integration of the traditional culture with alien great traditions or what is sometimes referred to as the world culture. The notion of a worldwide modern culture is a difficult one, although it is possible to point to certain common elements of modern culture such as those we have discussed, and to use those as indicators of modernity rather than as a statement of what a whole culture is like. The fact that the world culture is seen as a collection of certain traits makes it easier to contemplate integration of a particular tradition with world culture rather than with a specific manifestation of modern culture as lived in some modern Western state. It is, of course, particular modern cultures that have an impact on traditional cultures, and the adaptive response has usually been to choose aspects of the alien culture which appear to be least alien or most universal as the least damaging to the traditional culture in question. Viewed in a more dynamic way, cultural modernity is the ability to accept and integrate new cultural forms the value of which may be recognized even though they are developed in alien cultures.

The whole issue of contact with alien cultures brings up the matter of self-consciousness of one's own culture. It is primarily through comparison and the recognition that the same things may be done in different ways that one can raise questions about the arbitrariness of one's own tradition. Ultimately, self-consciousness may be referred to some sort of universal theory of culture and human society, but traditional values are more urgently called into question by alien challenges than by philosophical speculation which is a part of the traditional culture itself. It is therefore argued that a modern culture is capable of objectivizing its self-view through comparison with other cultures. Putting the matter the other way around some would say that only a culture which is capable of viewing another culture objectively is capable of viewing itself objectively. Only such a culture is capable of adaptation and borrowing, and only such a culture is truly developed.

Among the byproducts of measuring modernity and cultural excellence by successful borrowing has been the amazing willingness of so many developing countries to borrow so many of the developed art forms of the West. A fully developed culture, it is assumed, must demonstrate its development by expressing its cultural content through the entire range of extant art forms. In literature this has meant borrowing such forms as the novel and short story and play, not to mention borrowings of metrical rhythmic, and verse forms. In painting and the graphic arts all the media used in Paris and now New York will be found in Near Eastern and African capitals, and even styles such as abstraction, expressionism, primitivism, pop and op are quickly copied. In music and even in architecture the same sort of thing is true. A developed culture is, therefore, said to exhibit all the developed forms of the arts as means of self-expression. These art forms are all to be integrated into the existing tradition. How this is to be done is a more difficult question. The usual answer to this question is to express the most traditional themes within the framework of borrowed forms.

As had already been suggested, one of the most significant consequences of modernization for culture has been the politicization of culture. The main historical reason for politicization has been imperialism and the Western Christian attack on non-Western cultures. An ideological source of politicization has been the rise of nationalism, first in the West but also among the new nations (as that term implies) as the basis of deciding upon the legitimate limits of the political community. But the transformation of the politicization of culture into routine administrative policy is due to the new participatory politics which have been the result of modernization. The most relevant factors are, first, the movement of large numbers of people out of their traditional settings into large cities; second, these people remain predominantly traditional in their cultural orientations; third, the breakdown of traditional legitimacy makes the new rulers paradoxically more dependent upon traditional legitimizing symbols insofar as the uneducated masses are concerned; fourth, the need to rid the country of imperialism, to withstand external threats, or to industrialize makes the new leadership depend upon mass support. These factors have led to urgent but ambivalent cultural policies in the developing countries. Modern art forms are used in an effort to demonstrate the proud progress the country is making while popular and traditional themes are expressed in an effort to win over the masses. The results are not very satisfactory, so that these countries fall short of one of the more deplored aspects of cultural modernity: a highly elaborated arrangement for producing and disseminating mass culture. The television, movies, and popular press are all ill-adapted to the needs and desires of the masses, but the masses take what they can get anyway so long as it is economically attainable. In place of mass culture, or the effective adaptation of the traditional cultures of which the masses are aware, we find a substitute culture of populism. Populism is often no more than propaganda or an attempt at a more modern legitimation of the regime which has no traditional claim. On the other hand it may represent a genuine aspiration to find authentic cultural roots and may therefore be a way station on the road back toward the indigenous tradition. Above all, populism represents the desire to close the cultural gap between the elite and the masses. Populism as an element of the political culture, at least, is an indication of modernization and the adaptation of culture to the participant style of modern politics.

Reexamining briefly the ground we have covered, it is clear that in economics, not every characterization of development refers to capacity. Structural economic changes, increased complexity, and the growth of tertiary production all have reference to differentiation. Increasing per capita income, increasing the productivity of labor, and increasing the efficiency of factor markets all have egalitarian consequences. Nevertheless, the significance of all these factors is understandable only in terms of increased economic capacity. Policy will often decide which of the three aspects of modernity is to be most stressed in a given economic system.

A similar argument can be made for the various interpretations of social development except that more of these ideas, such as complexity, stratification, role conflict, urbanization, and industrialization, obviously refer to differentiation. The enhanced importance of certain groups such as the bureaucracy, the technocracy, the military, and entrepreneurs is related to capacity; while mobility, the decline of the family, and the atomization of society are related to the modern condition of equality.

The rational culture of modernity is the rational culture of individuals, and the antirational culture which is the contemporary antithesis is the culture of subjectivity. Mass culture is egalitarian to an extreme degree, but it is also the only way in which modern culture relates to a whole society. The preservation of the culture of the elite may indicate the emergence of a modern pattern of cultural differentiation, just as borrowing or innovation for the sake of innovation reveal the demand for if not the realization of an increased creative capacity.

The modernization syndrome is a collection of tendencies witnessed in the recent past and, in part, predicted by some insightful writers. There is nothing of the "crystal ball" in the modernization syndrome. What is questionable is whether these tendencies are likely to continue and become enhanced with the passage of time. Is there a point after which diminution commences? Does the curve flatten out? Is there a continuous and stable influence of the tendencies of the modernization syndrome on political things? Many of those concerned with modernization have envisioned a glorious conclusion to this inevitable progress along the lines of our "ECD" to a marvellously stable social and cultural equilibrium: the life of reason within the perfect state be it democratic, technocratic, or theocratic. Others have viewed with alarm the increasing entrenchment of baseless values and contractual relationships, and they have predicted a catastrophic breakdown which would result in the creation of a more organic, integrated community.

We have defined the components of the modernization syndrome as characteristic tendencies found in culture, society, and economy, at least, which vary in degree as well as diversity of empirical manifestation. In attempting to account for the path of modernization we may rely on those who believed that man's destiny was inevitable and undirectional progress, or those who saw it simply as a struggle with tradition, or those who saw the path as necessarily indirect and dialectical.

The first two views are relevant to our investigation in that the first emphasizes the nonpurposive character of modernity and the second treats modernity as an explicit goal of policy. Both orientations are valid, and possible even for the same country at the same time, although the first is more generally applicable to the developed countries of the West and the second is more relevant to the experience of the underdeveloped countries of the non-West. Both these views suggest the univocal character of generic modernity, and do not allow for their own mutual interactions, not to speak of situations in which some elements of modernity might not accord with other elements.

The key concept in the view of the dialecticians is that of contradiction, the contradiction of tradition and modernity, or the contradictions inherent in any historical system such as capitalism. The concept of contradiction has great popularity even outside of Marxist circles because it was fundamental to Weber's treatment of ideology. Just as bourgeois norms and Protestantism were compatible, so the ideological incompatibility of charisma and routinization will produce the breakdown of the charismatic polity. The "contradiction thinkers" use their key concept to account for either or both growth and breakdown.

Most thinkers of the past emphasized one or another feature of modernity, as S. Drescher points out in identifying the Positivists and Saint Simonians with science, Tocqueville with democracy, and Marx with capitalism. Others were concerned with the "contractualization" of society or with the loss of an absolute validation of ethical norms.[11] Because of this univocal emphasis, notions like contradiction were thought to govern the relations between traditional institutions and emerging modern institutions. The more pluralistic conception of modernity employed in this book adds yet a further dimension of complexity, for the difficulty of the path toward modernization may be due to the contradictions within modernity itself as much as to the conflict of tradition and modernity. Both types of conflict can explain why modernization is so frequently problematical, and it should be obvious that the pessimistic, traditional thinker would stress the inner contradictions of modernity while the optimistic, modern thinker would recognize the persistent pernicious rear-guard action of tradition.

From this brief discussion we can derive two types of contradiction and three related patterns of modernization. The two types of contradiction are internal contradiction and external contradiction. The three patterns of modernization are: (1) the pattern caused by the internal contradiction of tradition, (2) the pattern caused by the contradiction of tradition and modernity, and (3) the pattern caused by the internal contradictions of modernity.

In the present work we shall rather be more concerned with the second and especially with the third pattern of inner contradictions within modernization as defined by our modernization syndrome. This emphasis results from our concern to understand modernity, and it is in part motivated by the widely shared doubts about modernity that have emerged even in the so-called developed countries. But it is necessary to add that this general orientation should not mislead us to the wrong conclusion that the ideal components of the modernization syndrome must always lead to empirical contradiction and political conflict. All that can be asserted is that under certain circumstances, to be elaborated in subsequent chapters, the components

---

[11] Seymour Drescher, *Dilemmas of Democracy* (Pittsburgh: University of Pittsburgh Press, 1968), p. 1.

of the syndrome may be found in conflict, and the intensity of the conflict may grow to the point where the historian might discern the occurrence of a political crisis.

In other circumstances the source of political tensions may not be the inner contradictions of modernity so much as the external contradictions of modernity and tradition. This situation is more relevant to those countries where traditional structures are persistent and politically constitutive, where modernity is the goal of policy, and where the political process appears as the independent variable. The tradition which contradicts modernity in those countries is in each case a specific tradition, and its impact on political life will vary accordingly. But there are elements in the modernization syndrome itself which appear to encourage the reassertion of traditional ideas. Perhaps it is not the logical contradiction of the elements of modernity so much as the contradiction between the extreme intensification of the characteristics of modernity and the limits of human endurance. Frequently these traditional ideas have themselves been universalized, nationalized, and secularized, but they are opposed to the values of modernity. They have been developed into a powerful counterattack on the history of recent times and against the basis of modernity. As in the case of modernization itself this counterattack has not been limited to a single country or part of the world, but it has become diffused throughout the world.

Part III. The Crises of Political Development

The starting point of this chapter was the consciousness of change, but it was pointed out that change is not a new idea. What is new is the manner in which change is viewed, the mode of this consciousness, and the correlative concept of change. The ancients knew and attempted to conjure with the extremes of constant Heraclitean flux and the permanence of the Platonic essences. Modern man does not believe that change is random, and he does not believe that his present world is the best of all possible worlds. If he starts from a Kantian launching pad in his quest for the future, he will choose the target of a rationally contrived utopia with the assurance born of the Enlightenment's confidence in human reason. If he starts from an Hegelian beginning he will accept the hypothesis that we must back into the future, that the path of mankind is functionally determined by his attempt to resolve existing contradictions. The future is thus created out of the unintended consequences of the solution of earlier contradictions. Even though there will be new contradictions, the Hegelian believes that the future must, can, or eventually will be better than the present. Consequently, change is essentially, if not immediately and tangibly, beneficial. Consciousness is the psychosomatic condition resulting from the activity of ontological reasoning, whether of the more complacent, Kantian man-dominates-world sort or the more anguished, Hegelian world-dominates-man sort. We have called modern man an alienated optimist, alienated from the present and optimistic about his own reason—or at least his understanding. The conscious rationality which characterizes modern man's approach to his social world has raised questions and continues to raise questions regarding his own nature in the light of the order of his society, about the justification of the order of that society, about his freedom to alter that order, about the material resources available to him or the material limitations imposed on him, and about the resources and limitations of his society vis-à-vis the challenges and opportunities of its material and social environment.

Without a doubt these five questions are not the only questions that have been raised by modern man's consciousness of change, but they appear to be the most generally relevant questions insofar as modernization has affected politics. Since politics is not an innovation of the modern era, not all of these questions are new, but they have received some new answers.

The political path to modernity involves critical changes of identity from the religious to the ethnic and from the parochial to the societal. It involves critical changes in legitimacy from transcendental to immanent sources. It involves critical changes in political participation from elite to mass and from family to group. It involves critical changes of distribution from status and privilege to ability, achievement, and the control and management of capital. And it involves critical changes in the degree of administrative and legal penetration into social structure and out to the remote regions of the country. Let us examine each of these issues in the light of the three components of the modernization syndrome.

The identity crisis refers to the subjective, but not always emotional, basis of membership in a political community. More precisely, the problem of political identity might be stated as the tension between the culturally and psychologically determined sense of personal-group identity and the political definition of the community. In a traditional setting it would appear that these two elements were not often mutually determinative and that prevailing attitudes and values did not require that they should be. The modern identity crisis arises, in part, from the insistence that subjective identity and objective political identifications coincide. In addition, one can discern problems arising from shifts in the cultural basis of identity away from religion toward nationalism. There are other problems which are the product of a tension between the concept of the national interest and universally applicable values. Finally, there is a range of identity problems which have resulted from the rapidly increasing and disruptive social mobility which is a concomitant of development.

No one has better stated the problem of political alienation, and hence the essentially political nature of individual identity, than Rousseau in the opening sentence of the *Social Contract*. With the French Revolution the full implication of Aristotle's obscure dictum that man is a political animal began to impress itself upon a world where the ideological justification of the *ancien régime* was no longer compelling, where the argument that the individual ought to subordinate himself to the collectivity of which he was a part brought the dialectical response which asked what it meant to be a "part," and where a tremendous population explosion and a tremendous technological explosion were about to burst forth. The Saint Simonians, the Positivists, and the Utilitarians grew ever more enthusiastic about the possibilities of the future as they contemplated the application of an expanding science to an ever more complicated civilization. If there were to be no contradictions in the realization of the ideal social order then it must be empirically practical to disaggregate existing societies and recombine them in an infinite variety of ways. Individual identity is thus atomistic and self-contained, but yet, in the aggregate, determinative of the community and the polity. The emphasis on equality at once enhanced the significance of the individual while minimizing the significance of individual differences. Equality postulated identity of interests, and if not the equal value of each individual to the state, then, at least the equal value of the state to each individual. Yet, somewhat paradoxically, the modern doctrine of equality rendered the political element the most important to individual identity, since it interpreted human nature in terms of material needs and it saw the state as the source of requiting those needs.

Positivists and Marxists shared the view that the technological advances of modern times have permitted man to achieve that which no previous generation could hope for. Technological progress has now allowed all men to live in material plenty, to enjoy leisure, and to avoid the social evils attendant upon want. But in order to achieve these benefits it was argued that those individuals identified as members of the political community had to be organized in productive and administrative institutions according to a rational principle. Productive and administrative capacity depends upon the rational integration or organization of those human atoms which share a common identity. Comte and Engels shared this simple idea.

Others were less optimistic about the consequences of the application of this modern version of reason to human affairs. Hegel wrote of the problem of reconciling man as subject with man as object. Marx dealt with the same question in elaborating on the idea of the alienation of labor. Others were concerned with the opposition of reason and faith; and since life after death was based on faith, then reason led to a pessimistic preoccupation with death as the terminus—hence goal—hence meaningless end of life. Nietzsche, in particular, related rational consciousness with the existentialist understanding of the anguish associated with man's radical freedom and the opening of all moral options. The point is not that the very freedom to choose creates anxiety, but that any given choice must close a great multiplicity if not an infinite variety of alternative choices. Death determines the finitude of life, and since any given life pattern is grossly incommensurate with the totality of life and, hence, with the meaning of life, then any individual life is in grave danger of being meaningless. This tragic circumstance of the modern individual is manifested in the thematic instrumental notion of modernity: differentiation. Capacity requires differentiation but differentiation also reconciles the ends of equality with those of capacity. Any given reconciliation may or may not work for a particular community, but differentiation does not relate to all aspects of individual identity and so the potential for self-alienation remains. Similarly, particular patterns of differentiation may enhance the possibilities of individual adjustment. In this connection it is at least interesting to remember that Marx rejected the necessity of differentiation in his famous vision of Communist man hunting in the morning, manufacturing during the afternoon, and writing books at night.

The problem of identity has manifested itself in diverse countries in a variety of ways, and it will continue to constitute an important area of political concern. In any one country it may not have come to the surface as the primary political problem, but for modern civilization as a whole it is obviously possible to speak of the political significance of the identity crisis. The identity crisis is not the crisis of any country necessarily, but it is a crisis of our era. As a crisis of political development it does not tell us about particular countries, but it tells us which question to ask about particular countries and it gives us a way of understanding the meaning of great political events in particular countries.

The crisis of legitimacy refers to the change in the nature of the ultimate authority to which political obligation is owed. Political instability always involves some effect on legitimacy, and traditional politics have known significant changes in sources and types of legitimacy without becoming discernibly or significantly modern. The critical aspect of legitimacy change in modern times is the tendency for the source of political legitimacy to be shifted from the transcendental to the immanent. The commitment to an immanent source of political authority has spread into cultures still bereft of the ideational justifications for this new departure—another characteristic of modernity. The decline of the sacred character of political legitimacy is directly related to the newer understanding of the conventional basis of the state. What is the more remarkable is that the growth of the idea of the natural basis of the state did not bring a revival of transcendant theories. Instead a second variety of immanent legitimacy was produced. The first of the immanent theories of legitimacy related political obligation to an act of will, manifested as contracting, and representing some form of political rationality. The second theory abandoned the ideas of either human purposiveness or of the rational pursuit of self-interest and substituted for them the irrational and uncontrolled processes of history and the unfolding of the human mind.

These two theories of legitimacy, the contractual and the nationalist, are closely linked with the problem of political identity, and each expresses the problem of equality, and hence of democracy, in its own way. Regardless of whether political identity is thought to be determined objectively or subjectively, by an act of contracting or by an accident of birth, the legitimate order which prevails over such a community must relate itself to the principle of democracy. The democratic idea may be stretched, adjusted, distorted, but it must somehow be applied to reconcile the immanence of authority and the principle of equality. Under modern conditions a legitimate government is elected by the people, or is trustee for the people, or

works in the interest of the people, or is a reflection of certain qualities of the people, or reflects what the people will become in the
future.

The principle of equality does not necessarily require that the
regime accomplish anything. It may be sufficient that the government
symbolizes equality by means of doctrinal utterances or merely by
reaffirming the shared identity of individuals. The true nature of
democratic performance or the valid empirical test of democracy are
matters in dispute among democratic theorists of the liberal democracies, the peoples' democracies, and the third world. Furthermore, all
regimes seem to fall somewhat short of even their own ideal. These
unfortunate circumstances have combined to foster the popular reduc-
tionist theory of legitimacy as merely psychological—a matter of
belief. The psychological theory of legitimacy is characteristically
modern in its acceptance of the "alienation of reason" but it is also
characteristically individualistic and egalitarian in the sense employed
in our modernization syndrome.[12]

The concern with capacity leads to tension with the principle of
democracy because capacity requires efficiency and democracy is probably inefficient in all things except in the task of realizing the normative ends of democracy itself. Bearing this exception in mind we can
discover a contradiction within this aspect of capacity itself, for the
capacity of a regime will, in part, depend upon the degree to which
the announced goals of the regime are thought to be legitimate.

The modern requirement of capacity raises at least two questions
which are relevant to the legitimacy crisis. These are, first, the legitimacy of the goals for which the political capacity of either or both
government and nongovernmental structures are used, and second,
the impact on the legitimacy of governmental structures deriving
from the success or failure to implement effectively the policies announced or fixed in statutes. A regime which employs its political
capacity for nonlegitimate goals or that fails to implement policies
which symbolize the practical application of system legitimacy runs
great risks where political participation is open and where political
capacity is diffused among nongovernmental structures.

Legitimacy may be differentiated in a variety of ways, some of
which will enhance the possibility of a legitimacy crisis and others tend-
ing to reconcile equality and capacity. The most important aspect of

[12] L. Kolakowski, *The Alienation of Reason* (New York: Anchor Books, Doubleday, 1969).

legitimacy differentiation is that the ideas of the central principle of legitimacy may differ in accordance with class, region, ethnicity, religion, language, belief, education, age, intelligence, socialization, and/or in accordance with the experience of participation, distribution, and penetration. Similarly, the diversity of citizen and subject groups may be dealt with by differentiating both goals and methods of implementation of legitimate goals in accordance with the circumstances or preferences of each group. Legitimacy can be and often is differentiated in terms of particular criteria, such as the relevant political, administrative, and juridical spheres of validity of various political structures for the country as a whole or for certain regions of the country or for certain groups.

The third problem is that of the individual's freedom to alter the social order in which he finds himself. Now the rationality that is attributed to modern man and his isolation as a political component in the calculus of modern politics would appear to justify each individual acting in terms of his own reason and according to his own interest to change the system, or to influence its political decisions. Democracy presupposes the political participation of all citizens—at least from time to time.

The participation crisis represents the most apparent and ubiquitous form in which contemporary political change has occurred. Many observers have been inclined to point to the growth of populistic or democratic politics as the most characteristic feature of political development. The general sense of the term participation refers to involvement in the political process. The political process need not be conceived of as having any particular outcome; it may be examined as a purposeless activity or it may be defined as organized activity aimed at giving normative precision to the policy decisions made for a whole society. Whether consciously purposeful or not, participants in the political process have an effect on government policy and particularly on the performance of what Almond has called the process functions or what Easton has termed the input of demands and supports.

The major form in which the participation crisis appears is in the increase in the number of persons participating in the political process. Concomitantly with the increase in number, it may be expected that new groups previously excluded from legitimate (or nonlegitimate) political participation are also admitted. Ultimately, the direction of an uncontrolled and expanding participation crisis is the unregulated admission of all groups to nearly equal participation. Generally the participation crisis is manifested in the growth of parties and mass movements, but also in the politicization of caste and ethnic groups or in strikes and even demonstrations of political support. The point to remember, however, is that while the crisis of political participation in Western Europe took the form of the expansion of the suffrage and the growth of mass electoral parties, the same sort of critical change has taken place in other parts of the world but often without the growth of suffrage and certainly without the expansion of a truly effective franchise.

The ideal of universal adult suffrage and the principle of one man one vote (including equitable apportionment) are indications of the modern egalitarian perspective on participation. This attitude is even carried to the extreme of establishing legislative bodies at all levels of decision-making so as to eliminate, in theory if not in practice, any distinction between government and people, or between the rulers and the ruled, a goal more nearly attainable under conditions of decentralization characterized by a minimal hierarchy of deliberative and legislative bodies. The principle of autonomy or self-regulation expresses the ideal of democratic participation which is meaningful self-rule. Similarly, representation entails differentiating citizens and decision-makers, so that the principle of equality militates in favor of immediate deliberation and minimizes representation. The plebiscite and the referendum are also devices for achieving egalitarian results.

The implication of participation for capacity is readily understood. It is widely held that decentralization and diffusion of responsibility weaken efficiency and capacity. Hence, the achievement of near equality in participation would probably gravely limit capacity. Capacity must, in turn, be strengthened by limiting the access of participants to the decision-makers and often by limiting the availability of relevant information which might be indispensable to the rational planning of strategy by nongovernmental participants.

Many democratic theorists believe that limited mass participation leads to more salutary political results, and it has been noted that the least cultured, the least educated, and the poorest most often neglect to use the franchise. Today, such self-disenfranchisement is a source of embarrassment and the target of reformers. Capacity, therefore, must be seen from two points of view. It includes a concern with the capacity of citizens to participate as well as a concern with the capacity of a government to operate despite mass political participation. Citizen capacity is enhanced by organization through such groups as parties, pressure groups, or ad hoc movements, but individuals must in turn subordinate themselves to collectivities which articulate and aggregate. As is implied in the use of these terms, such organizations, limiting equality, may be thought of as "functional" to the system even while diminishing the individual's scope of activity.

Once again differentiation may be thought of as reconciling some of the divergences between egalitarian participation and the structures of access and information. The most effective means of achieving such a reconciliation is probably through representation, and a second method is through the legitimate activity of secondary interest associations. Through these devices the diffuse and energy-consuming methods of direct participation can be directed toward sustaining the representative or interest organization.

Participation may also be differentiated in terms of the diverse capacities which individuals have. Not all citizens are uniformly strategically situated with regard to the political process and not every participation crisis is a crisis of mass participation. Groups and parties, and particularly their leadership are more easily able to be effective participants. The same is also true of the educated, the wealthy, the aristocratic, and the skilled. The incumbents of certain institutional roles, such as the military, students, or members of parliaments, have greater participatory resources than do others. These strategically better situated participants can also create crises by pressing their advantage, as might be said of members of the provincial assemblies in India, or students in Turkey, or the military in Syria, or industrialists in the United States.

The crisis of distribution is associated with the rapid increase in the popular demand for material benefits from the government and with the contemporary belief that governments are responsible for the level of living in any given country. These phenomena have been described as the revolution of rising expectations, and the extreme optimism of these "attitudinal revolutionaries" has been increasingly demonstrated in recent years. It is clear that traditional governments did not see the problems of distribution as very great, nor did they conceive of them as centrally political. Only small numbers of people had to be taken into consideration and only small quantities of material goods or relatively small sums of money were involved. As Eisenstadt has put it, the political goals of traditional governments were culturally determined. Whenever the rulers sought what Eisenstadt termed "autonomous" political goals involving redistribution, or even additional distribution, some disturbance of the old system was inevitable. The crisis of distribution reflects the contemporary situation in which the narrow swing from culturally determined goals and limited "autonomous" goals has been changed to political goals that are predominantly of the sort that are not culturally predetermined but set by the need to emulate the most advanced countries. Wherever there is enough cultural strength to avoid simply aping the West, national pride requires a more equitable distribution of material benefits.

The principle of equality would require that all citizens be granted the same or a similar material standard regardless of how much more or less they might get under the rules of free competition. The pressure for equalization is frequently mitigated by insisting that only equality of opportunity is relevant but not equality of initial economic circumstances. Another limiting device frequently used in conjunction with other policies is to include in material distributions only those who have been admitted to full political participation.

Capacity is thought by many to be a function of the pattern of distribution of the transferable resources of each state. Capacity is clearly related to the resource base of each country, and capacity with regard to distribution entails both these resources and the bureaucratic and planning skills needed to ensure their wise use. In this sense capacity not only denies the ultimate validity of egalitarian distribution but also affirms the allocative responsibility of government and of its specialized structures of distribution.

Differentiation helps to limit conflict between equality and capacity insofar as it justifies all or any nonegalitarian distributions. Relevant differentia might be the development or possession of skills, including the more efficient exploitation of earlier opportunities to acquire skills. Contrarily, it is also well known that differentiation is all but a prerequisite of increased modern system-capacities. Differentiation encourages further the decline of egalitarian conformity while sustaining the centralization of authority through offering incentive payments or rewards to those who would serve the goals of the state or of a given organization. There are, however, principles upon which differentiation may be based that conflict with the achievement of greater efficiency. It will be the case that distribution policies will be justified in terms of the goal of greater productivity, but contrary arguments are frequently heard today in the United States. The diverse principles of differentiation prevalent in any society will determine whether the consequences of differentiation sustain the existing distributive pattern or encourage redistribution.

The fifth problem concerns the relations between the modern political community and its environment. Assuming that the citizen can identify with that community, that he believes its social order to be legitimate, that he reaches a reasonable adjustment between his level of participation and the benefits allocated to him, none of these resolutions is complete or satisfactory for modern man unless they are equally satisfying when viewed in a wider context. An identity is meaningful only in comparison with other possible even unattainable, but existent identities for all but the highly parochial. Similarly, it is the case that the other dimensions of modern political development are at least potentially comparable in significance.

It is highly characteristic of the modern era that the perspective by means of which such comparison is undertaken is broadly national. The terminal political community, or the sovereign state, is the basis of comparison and rightly so, because modern identity is so closely tied to political life. Our lives, our prospects, our perspectives, our cultural orientation, and to a considerable extent the possibility of achieving a reasonable identity resolution are determined by the political context in which we are born, brought up, and live. Very few are those who can migrate and successfully leave behind the limitations of original political attachments, and fewer still can transcend those limits and "live" in more than one culture, or live in a world culture created by themselves and perhaps a few others.

One of the reasons for this very significant modern phenomenon is the recent growth in the depth and extent of central political control. Government has penetrated into structures that were previously insulated from society or even thought of as independent components of society. Government has also extended its control to the more inaccessible parts of the national territory. The impact of the modern notion of equality on the idea of administrative penetration has been to equalize the political obligation of all citizens and, most importantly, to insist that the component parts of the community are individual citizens and not collectivities.

In the earliest stages of political development, the policies of defensive modernization engaged in by traditional regimes as a means of self-preservation led to increased penetration (which enhanced participation). Military defense against the imperialist West imposed all sorts of requirements for new fiscal resources, new sources for recruiting soldiers, new skills, and experts to teach these new skills. Imperialism led to guerrilla wars and clandestine resistance against the alien in the remote parts of the country, while nationalism and political independence have increased the desire to mobilize all of the resources of the newly emergent countries. As a consequence of these and more events, governments have desired, have tried and succeeded or failed to extend the power and authority of the administrative center. This extension was attempted into the more remote parts of the country and, perhaps more significantly, into the compartmentalized, primordial structures of traditional society. It is the latter tendency of political development that has led us to refer to this last area of critical change as the crisis of penetration.

The capacity of the modern citizen is not unaffected by the problem of penetration, for even though its consequence is that increasing demands are made upon him, a concomitant of the greater effectiveness of the government in dealing with its material and social environment may be some expansion of the scope of possibilities for the individual. The relationship between the problem of penetration and capacity is an obvious one, particularly where there are traditional resistances, divergences of identity, legitimacy doubts, participatory limitations, and distributive injustices or imbalances. To achieve a greater capacity to cope with both domestic and external challenges, mobilization and rationalization are often required. Though neither need necessarily be the explicit goal of policy, both can be. The range of application of government activities will be extended and the substantive scope of government activities will be increased, or at least attempts in this direction will be made.

Differentiation, as we have seen, cuts both ways, in being a prerequisite of efficient penetration, but possibly setting limits to the scope or range of government activity or the social groupings that are to be affected. Governmental efficiency cannot, short of war, alliance, or federation, greatly change the supply of material or social resources at its disposal, but it can use this supply more or less efficiently. Organizational or instrumental efficiency under modern conditions usually depends upon the skillful mix of talents, the subdivision of specializations and of tasks, and the rational coordination of all these in pursuit of a well-defined goal. In the real political world it is not always or even usually the case that all social groupings can be equally subject to government "output" activities. The importance of such equal subjection is ideological though and not necessarily instrumental, because the achievement of certain tasks may require the mobilization of some groups and not others.

It is not at all certain that the type of activity referred to under these terms will be manifested in a political crisis wherein the issue is made explicit. They need not become crises, and there need not be five of them, although historically they often do become crises and few of the five are avoided. Nevertheless, it may be preferable to see these as five processes of development proceeding simultaneously. Each is an area of possible conflict.

Another factor of importance is that these crises or processes are not mutually exclusive. Participation affects distribution. Legitimacy affects both penetration and distribution; penetration affects identity. And so on. The significance of this overlapping emerges more clearly when we consider the problems of sequence.

How, it may be asked, can we consider the sequences of processes which are empirically ambiguous? The answer is that sequence is not significant until consciousness of the problem renders one of these areas of political concern an explicit issue. It is the shift from functionally determined change with normative consequences to a normatively defined issue that may turn the process into a crisis. Should this shift occur, we all know that it has happened. The sequence of the occurrence of the crises is then empirically unambiguous and, of course, variable from case to case. But it does not seem, from an a priori examination of the theory, that the sequence of crises can be wholly arbitrary. Not only are there external factors operating to create awareness of events in other political systems, but because these processes overlap analytically as well as empirically, a crisis in one area will predictably affect other areas. In other words, these processes are dialectically related. Still, the effect that a given intensity of change in one area will have on other areas is a problem for empirical research, and it may be that no situationally transferable generalizations will be produced. Microanalytical changes, then, occur as elements of five ongoing processes, and macroanalytical sequences may be discovered when change reaches crisis proportions. Presumably, some sequences of crises will produce smoother paths to modernity and some more difficult transitions.

This theory cannot tell us what kind of regimes modern political systems will have, but the idea of political development is that in modern systems identity will be politicized, legitimacy will be based in part on performance, governments will be capable of mobilizing national resources, the majority of the adult population will be participant citizens, political access will be ubiquitous, and material allocations will be rational, principled, and public.

It may be helpful at this point to summarize our argument in the form of a paradigm illustrating the possible relationship of the modernization syndrome and the crises of political development.

PARADIGM OF THE MODERNIZATION SYNDROME AND
THE CRISES OF POLITICAL DEVELOPMENT

	SYNDROME COMPONENTS		
Crises	*Equality*	*Capacity*	*Differentiation*
Identity	politicization of identity	productive and administrative integration	individual adjustment, specificity of interests
Legitimacy	democracy, psychological legitimacy	definition of goals and implementation	spheres of political, administrative and judicial validity; divergent doctrines
Participation	voting, deliberating, self-regulation	information, access	decision-making structures, representation, interest groups
Distribution	equality of opportunity, achievement, standardization of welfare level	resource base, education, capital accumulation, allocation to general and particular goals	redistribution, equalization, incentives
Penetration	equalization of obligation and duties, individualization of citizenship	mobilization, rationalization, scope, range	technical, legal, intellectual specialization and coordination

If we reexamine these five areas of critical change, or these five crises of political development, the crisis of identity, the crisis of legitimacy, the crisis of participation, the crisis of distribution, and the crisis of penetration, we will find that all five types of change may occur without any concomitant strengthening of the political institutions of the country affected. The institutions might change, but they need not become stable nor effective. Popular legitimacy may be required ideologically, but, in fact, no government may acquire such legitimacy. A national identity may become established, but it may not reflect the identity resolutions of the masses. Mass popular political participation may be attained through plebiscites without building solid party organizations. Policies of egalitarian income distribution may be pursued, but effective development planning and sound investment organizations may not be created. The modern bureaucratic and security administrations may penetrate the most private or the most remote segments of society, but they may only succeed in breaking down the traditional social compartments without constructing any substitutes.

Political development, according to this definition, refers to changes in the type and style of politics. It refers to the informal political process that must always be a challenge to the formal processes, and to the new requirements that are demanded of institutions if they are to maintain stability and cope responsibly with social conflict. Perhaps the most frequent and dangerous manifestation of these processes as crises is within the more developed of the systems which have been affected by modernization, for in many of these countries it is, or has been, smugly assumed that the crises have been passed. But the Belgians and the Canadians are discovering anew their crisis of national identity; the Americans now realize that they face a crisis of admitting new groups and a new generation to full political participation; the government of France, invulnerable for almost a decade under De Gaulle, discovered in the events of May 1968 a profound crisis of access and political participation; the partition of Germany perpetuates the problems of identity and legitimacy; distribution remains the greatest problem in Italy; Czechoslovakia appears to be in the midst of a crisis of penetration; and the crisis of legitimacy in Belgium and the Netherlands is only barely decently covered.

In working with any given selection of broadly defined processes of political development or modernization, it is well to bear in mind the limited sort of theoretical claims that can be made for such a selection and the consequent methodological strictures which must accompany their use as guides and coordinators of research. We have started from the assumption that we are imbedded in history so that our perspectives can never hope to transcend our circumstances. On the other hand, there is no reason to transcend the very condition of understanding change. It is only because we are situated in history that we are able to differentiate historical events from both an empirical and evaluative perspective. While certain situational limitations cannot be overcome, accepting our circumstances need not eventuate in a narrow parochialism. It is important to retain the historical perspectives of past periods and to understand the views of our contemporaries who adhere to opposing ideologies or come from the developing countries. It is also important to apply the perspectives of intellectual history itself to this problem of modernization. Nevertheless, with all of these efforts to avoid the pitfalls of a purely private ideology, and even worse, of an individualistic terminology, it cannot be expected that Western scholars could wholly escape the influences of their own political cultures, nor should they desire to do so if they want to communicate matters of everyday political significance. Furthermore, political specialists will tend to emphasize the primacy of politics, itself an optimistic orientation since the primacy of politics usually points to the purposive and rational goal-seeking elements in political life.

The five crises of political development are orienting concepts, but they are not operationalized. They are not stated as empirical events nor as complex processes, the components of which may be known in every case. In the terminology of Marion J. Levy, Jr., they are the functional requisites of a modern or developed political system, but the structural requisites, i.e., the historical processes by which these ubiquitous modern political phenomena manifest themselves in particular countries are the phenomena to be described, operationalized, measured, tested for continuity and change, and predicted.[13] When these things have been accomplished in a sufficient number of cases, maybe then we can hazard a general theory of political development. In the meantime, the crucial test will be whether historians can recognize and agree on the characterization of these processes in the countries they know.

Part IV. Patterns of Crisis Resolution

Earlier we distinguished between the frequent optimism of the moderns and the pessimistic tendency of the ancients. In point of fact, though, the moderns have been divided between those who optimistically believe that man is infinitely adaptable, even in the face of the rapid urbanization and revolutionary technological advance of modern civilization, and those who believe that material modernization will outrun man's ability to adapt his inherited political wisdom

[13] Marion J. Levy, Jr., *The Structure of Society* (Princeton: Princeton University Press, 1952), pp. 71ff.

and his inherited political institutions. Similarly, we may divide our "pessimistic" ancients into two classes, those who believe, while holding that the political ideal is unattainable, that we can more consistently approximate the best possible arrangement and those who believe that the corruption and cyclical decline of all historical polities is inevitable. Combining these points of view we get a sum of four orientations toward, or theories of, political development:

	Ancients	*Moderns*
Optimistic	modernization permits realization of best possible system (less than ideal)	modernization permits transcending traditional limits on attaining political ideal
Pessimistic	modernization causes more rapid and more complete corruption of the political system	modernization leads to the nadir of mass politics

Whether they like it or not, the liberal democrats of the West must be cast in the role of the "optimistic ancients." They tend to identify the liberal democratic regime with the Aristotelian polity or as the best of all possible regimes. As the polity was based on class distinctions and upon "organic solidarities," so does the liberal democratic regime recognize and legitimize distinctions among its citizens, but modernization allows us the possibility of admitting all groups to full political participation. Political development may therefore be defined as the process of admitting all groups and all interests, including newly recognized interests and new generations, into full political participation without disrupting the efficient working of the political system and without limiting the ability of the system to choose and pursue policy goals.

The "pessimistic ancients" believe that the unlimited legitimation of pluralism, egalitarianism, and participation will cause the decline of all virtue, corrupting the rational political process and rendering the determination of policy a matter of requiting the lowest common consumer demand.

The "modern optimists" tend more and more to see the process of political development as an increasingly rational application of empirical or cybernetic method to the implementation of policy which is determined by the effective demands of participant citizens. Modernization permits more and more of these demands to be met with less and less significant difficulty of choice as we accumulate knowledge and technological capacity.

The "pessimistic moderns," of whom the number is rapidly increasing these days, believe that mass alienation and increasingly efficient tyranny are the inevitable consequences of the dehumanizing capacities of modern technology, against which the only remedy is cyclical, destructive, and anarchic revolution, which will temporarily reduce tyranny and exploitation.

Even at this early stage in our investigation it may be helpful to suggest that there are ways of coping with the crises of political development which are to some extent derivative from these four normative orientations toward modernization. The first of these has received the greatest attention in Western scholarship and that is institutionalization. As we have seen the crises do not necessarily manifest themselves as critical, episodic, political upheavals in all countries. The crises as general phenomena of development are, in certain countries, likely to be manifested as recurrent issues. They may be coped with by the gradual arrangement of certain standardized patterns of response. Where the crises have more of an intense episodic character, the institutionalization of a system response may be more difficult—but not impossible. Gradualism does not appear to be absolutely necessary, but it evidently helps just as it probably helps when all the crises do not occur at the same time.

There are three types of institutionalization which come to mind in considering crisis management. The first is the least useful but probably the most popular, and that is the belief that a particular political institution, a bureaucracy, a party, a parliament, or an electoral procedure is the solution to a crisis. If we emphasize the process side of our crises we will recognize that the crisis is dealt with through the institutionalization of a complex pattern of interaction among many groups and individuals. For the country in question there emerges a political structural requisite of modernity. Now this political structure or institutionalized process may be specific for each crisis, or, and this is the third type of institutionalization, it may be a generalized crisis management process. Examples of the last two may be helpful in clarifying the difference. In his work on the group process in India, Myron Weiner described how the resort to limited violence became an institutionalized part of the distribution crisis process.[14] In Egypt, by contrast, various political crises, of identity in 1957, distribution in 1961, and of penetration in 1967, led to repeated enactments of the reorganization of the mass national political movement.[15] In Uruguay, crises threatening the regime and often leading to violence have been resolved by the signature of "pactos" between the Colorados and the Blancos. A similar process of dealing with severe crises in Belgium has been described as "auctioning" by A. Zolberg.[16] It is important to bear in mind these differences in the institutionalization of crisis solutions (1) through regular procedures which stabilize innovation, (2) through informal but regular procedures which may make the solution of other crises more difficult, and (3) through procedures which are not specific to the crisis problems but which are relevant to the preservation of the existing system and possibly only postponing the full impact of the crisis. Are constitution-making in France and the extension of the suffrage in Great Britain crisis management processes, or do they represent successful institutionalization?

The second type of solution is that preferred by the "pessimistic ancients." Since they have little hope that the human condition can be improved by innovation and since they view the effect of modernization in the light of the ancient critique of democracy, they prefer to resist institutional change if possible and to propose ad hoc adjustments when necessary. There is some affinity of this approach for the last of the three institutional approaches since that sort of solution does not change existing institutions so much as it changes the groups benefiting from them. In any case, the pessimistic ancients prefer ad hoc management in order to preserve existing institutions as much as possible. Mosca's advocacy of cooptation and Pareto's doctrine of the circulation of elites illustrate the inclination of these people very well. The most salient aspect of a purely ad hoc approach is the absence of a cumulative quality to the experience of coping with the crises of political development. This pattern is particularly relevant to the traditional bureaucratic regimes which sought to cope with the West through defensive modernization.

The third type of solution is that preferred by the enthusiastic

---

[14] Myron Weiner, *The Politics of Scarcity* (Chicago: University of Chicago Press, 1962).

[15] Leonard Binder, "Political Recruitment and Participation in Egypt," in Joseph LaPalombara and M. Weiner, eds., *Political Parties and Political Development* (Princeton: Princeton University Press, 1969), p. 218.

[16] Aristide Zolberg, "Belgium," unpublished paper discussing political crises.

"optimistic moderns." Their faith in science and in the benevolent progress of history leads them to this preference for what we shall call evolutionary solutions. No elite has been able to sustain this pattern without some reversion to the others on occasion, but of those who are inclined in this direction the leaders of Russia and China are most noteworthy, followed by some liberal American leaders and then the more radical leaders and ex-leaders of the third world, including Nasser, Sukarno, Castro, and Ben Bella. They do not seek to establish institutionalized processes but to prepare for a more complete transformation of the political order. They generally prefer increased centralization of control, increased rationality, and increased automation of decision-making and implementation. Each manifestation of crisis must be countered by a further advance toward utopia. The dialectic of crisis and political response is an evolution toward the creation of the efficient administrative state in which there will be no politics.

The fourth kind of solution preferred by the "pessimistic moderns" might be likened to Schumpeter's notion of "creative destruction." Their normative evaluation of political development insofar as it means adapting to the exigencies of modernity is negative. They believe political development ought to mean resisting the institutional and administrative pressures of modernity and preserving or enhancing the consequences of equality and differentiation while limiting the influence of capacity. To strengthen this resistance to modernization the moral significance of small *gemeinschaftlich* communities has been praised and aesthetic values have been preferred to rational or instrumental values. Planning and providing for the future are similarly disregarded because the future is already upon us and its coercive rationality is precisely what must be escaped. In this sense destruction and the refusal to conform to institutionalized patterns is thought of as creative.

Doubtlessly this pessimistic view is a reaction to what Weber called the disenchantment of the modern world, and insofar as it advocates a politics that is at once aesthetic and therapeutic it has a certain appeal to all of us: If only we could use the differentiated individual identity as the measure of all things political. So would the romantic that is in all of us respond. But the scientist that is in some of us must also consider that the premise upon which "creative destruction" is based is largely false because it is clear that the political future is unknown, that modernity is an opportunity and not a destiny, and that political development is not an inevitability but a challenge. It is further clear that this challenge manifests itself with kaleidoscopic variety as it intrudes into each historical setting. So while we must beware of the platitudinous reconciliation of opposites we ought not lose sight of the scope for aesthetic creativity and for social healing in advancing our understanding of political development.

distribution adequately responsive to the demands generated by the imperatives of equality.[3] The acquisition of such a performance capacity is, in turn, a decisive factor in the resolution of the problems of *identity* and *legitimacy*.

DIFFERENTIATION

Before turning to an examination of the relationships among the three components of the development syndrome, it is in point to give each of them a working definition. The concept of differentiation, like the concepts of evolution and development with which it has frequently been made synonymous, is used loosely in a variety of ways.[4] For our purposes differentiation refers to the process of progressive separation and specialization of roles, institutional spheres, and associations in societies undergoing modernization. The assumption has been that the more highly developed a political system becomes, the greater will be its structural complexity and the larger the number of explicit and functionally specific administrative and political structures it will have.[5]

The historical pattern of differentiation in the major industrial societies has not been uniform. In some cases economic development preceded political development whereas in others political development seems to have come before at least many kinds of socio-eco-

[3] James S. Coleman, ed., *Education and Political Development* (Princeton: Princeton University Press, 1965), p. 26.

[4] It can refer both to a process and the result of such process. It has been used to describe any form of difference (sex, age, generation, race, religion, etc.) among individuals or human aggregates. The unit in which differentiation occurs has been variously the whole organic world; a particular species (phylogeny); an individual organism (ontogeny); and any human aggregation. Originally, in biology, differentiation as a process was viewed as synonymous with development; among developmental psychologists it is regarded as only one analytical aspect or phase in development. Among contemporary sociologists it is used variously as being synonymous with social stratification, ethnic diversity, associational proliferation, and so forth. Some of the common modifiers are "value," "status," "generation," "occupation," "role," "structure," and "system." Fred W. Riggs finds the concept differentiation so laden with multiple meanings that he has rejected it for the term "diffraction." *Administration in Developing Countries: The Theory of Prismatic Society* (Boston: Houghton, Mifflin, 1964), pp. 24-25.

[5] Like the terms "complexity" or "specialization," differentiation "describes the ways through which the main social functions or the major institutional spheres of society become disassociated from one another, attached to specialized collectivities and roles, and organized in relatively specific and autonomous symbolic and organizational frameworks within the confines of the same institutionalized system." S. N. Eisenstadt, "Social Change, Differentiation, and Evolution," *American Sociological Review*, 29 (June 1964), 376. See also Neil J. Smelser, "Mechanisms and Change peed Adjustment to Change," in Bert F. Hoselitz and Wilbert E. Moore, eds., *Industrialization and Society* (UNESCO: Mouton, 1963), pp. 32-56.

nomic development. However, in many of them political, economic, and social differentiation has occurred in a relatively synchronous manner. Noting Durkheim's insight concerning the role of integrative mechanisms under conditions of growing social heterogeneity, Neil Smelser has pointed out that:

> ... one of the concomitants of a growing division of labor is an *increase* in mechanisms to coordinate and solidify the interaction among individuals with increasingly diversified interests. . . . Differentiation alone . . . is not sufficient for modernization. Development proceeds as a contrapuntal interplay between differentiation (which is divisive of established society) and integration (which unites differentiated structures on a new basis). Paradoxically, however, the process of integration itself produces more differentiated structures—e.g., trade unions, associations, political parties, and a mushrooming state apparatus. . . . As social systems grow more complex, political systems are modified accordingly.[6]

There is considerable historical evidence that in the evolution of most major industrialized societies the contrapuntal interplay has been of the nature suggested by Smelser. This has not, however, been the pattern of differentiation in most of the developing countries with which we are primarily concerned. Indeed, in most of the new states of Asia and Africa the process has not been synchronous. "The story of the diffusion of the world culture," Pye reminds us, "has been one of countless efforts to establish modern organizational forms in traditional, status-oriented societies."[7]

EQUALITY

Equality is the second major element in our conceptualization of the political development syndrome. Whether viewed as a factual trend, a perceived technological possibility, or simply as the dominant aspiration underlying the drive for change, egalitarianism pervades all aspects of modern political life and culture and all forms of mod-

[6] N. J. Smelser, "Mechanisms and Change," *op.cit.*, pp. 41-42.
[7] Lucian W. Pye, *Politics, Personality, and Nation-Building: Burma's Search for Identity* (New Haven: Yale University Press, 1962), p. 38. He adds that "the whole range of modern political roles—from the civil servant on the planning board to the administrator in the district, from the cabinet minister and leader of political parties to the local party organizer—have appeared in transitional societies not through response to the internal needs of the society itself, but in response to supranational and foreign concepts of the appropriate standards of modern governmental and political behavior." (p. 43)

ern political ideology.[8] For our purposes three components of the concept of equality are indicative of and significant for political development: (1) national citizenship; (2) a universalistic legal order; and (3) achievement norms.

Citizenship connotes that basic human equality derived from one's full membership in a national political community and embodied in equal formal rights possessed by all citizens. In the historical development of the contemporary nation-state the struggle for equality has successively endowed the status of citizen with rights in virtually all spheres of life.[9] The distinctiveness of the egalitarian aspect of this evolved concept of citizenship is the fact that the nation-state and not just a privileged segment is the community of reference; citizens are legitimately concerned with both the input (participation) and the output (distribution) functions of government; and "whether liberal-democratic or totalitarian . . . one of the principal objects and justifications of [modern] politics is assumed to be a constant improvement in the social and material welfare of the common man . . . through technological and social innovation."[10]

The prevalence of universalistic over particularistic norms in a government's relations with the citizenry is crucial for the realization of the equal rights of citizenship as defined above. They dictate equality before the law (isonomy). This means not only equality of treatment in the application and adjudication of the law, but also the equal

[8] The most penetrating discussion of this proposition, in comparative and historical perspective, is Lloyd Fallers, "Equality, Modernity, and Democracy in the New States," in Clifford Geertz, ed., *Old Societies and New States* (London: Free Press, 1964), pp. 204-19. See also Rolf Dahrendorf, *Class and Class Conflict in Industrial Society* (Stanford: Stanford University Press, 1957), pp. 61-64, and T. H. Marshall, *Class, Citizenship, and Social Development* (Garden City: Doubleday, 1964), pp. 65-122.

[9] T. H. Marshall has categorized these citizenship rights into three types: *civil* (individual freedoms under law), *political* (universal suffrage), and *social* (welfare and education). Speaking of England, he observed that "civil rights came first, and were established in something like their modern form before the first Reform Act was passed in 1832. Political rights came next, and their extension was one of the main features of the nineteenth century, although the principle of universal political citizenship was not recognized until 1918. [But] it was not until the twentieth century that . . . [social rights] . . . attained to equal partnership with the other two elements of citizenship." *Op.cit.*, p. 83.

[10] Fallers, *op.cit.*, p. 205. "Under whatever regime, the hallmarks of a modern state are a vastly expanded set of functions and demands. Public services come to include education, social security, and public works while civic duties involve new forms of loyalty, tax payment and . . . military service. The tendency, moreover, is for services and obligations to become universal: schooling for all children, a road into every village, conscription for all men, and a tax out of every pay envelope. Hence political modernization clearly has egalitarian tendencies." R. E. Ward and D. A. Rustow, eds., *Political Modernization in Japan and Turkey* (Princeton: Princeton University Press, 1964), p. 5.

right to defend and to assert all other rights. Moreover, a differentiated universalistic legal order is essential for the development of central bureaucratic authority.[11]

The predominance of achievement over ascriptive norms in the allocation of political and bureaucratic roles is the third major component of the egalitarian dimension of the development syndrome. Achievement norms, coupled with the universal citizenship right to education, assure equality of initial opportunity. The right to education is of strategic importance in a modern society because allocation to the more highly valued roles in the stratification system increasingly depends upon educational achievement. Although the final outcome of the increasingly tight fit between education and social mobility may be what T. H. Marshall calls a "structure of unequal status fairly apportioned to unequal abilities," the imperative of equality and achievement norms is met if there has been an "equal right to display and develop differences, or inequalities . . . an equal right to be recognized as unequal."[12]

These three elements—universal adult citizenship (equality in distribution claims and participant rights and duties), the prevalence of universalistic norms in government relations with the citizenry (equality in legal privileges and deprivations), and the predominance of achievement criteria (the psychic equality of opportunity) in recruitment and allocation to political and bureaucratic roles—are the main components in the drive for equality, one of the three interacting elements in the development syndrome.

CAPACITY

Our concept of political development refers to a special capacity. It is an integrative, responsive, adaptive, and innovative capacity. It is a capacity not only to overcome the divisions and manage the tensions created by increased differentiation, but to respond to or contain the participatory and distributive demands generated by the

[11] Talcott Parsons regards the development of a general legal system of universalistic norms as a crucial aspect of social evolution, "a distinctive new step, which more than the industrial revolution itself, ushered in the *modern* era of social evolution." Such a system—which he makes one of his six evolutionary universals—is an "integrated system of universalistic norms, applicable to the society as a whole rather than to a few functional or segmental sectors, highly generalized in terms of principles and standards, and relatively independent of both the religious agencies that legitimize the normative order of the society and vested interest groups in the operative sector, particularly in government." "Evolutionary Universals in Society," *American Sociological Review*, 29 (June 1964), 350-53.

[12] T. H. Marshall, *op.cit.*, p. 109.

imperatives of equality. It is also a capacity to innovate and to manage continuous change. It includes the notion of adaptation which Talcott Parsons has made central to his definition of an "evolutionary universal."

> An evolutionary universal . . . is a complex of structures and associated processes the development of which so increases the long-run adaptive capacity of living systems in a given class that only systems that develop the complex can attain certain higher levels of general adaptive capacity. . . . Adaptation should mean not merely passive "adjustment" to environmental conditions, but rather the capacity of a living system to cope with its environment. This capacity includes an active concern with mastery, or the ability to change the environment to meet the needs of the system, as well as an ability to survive in the face of its unalterable features. Hence the capacity to cope with broad ranges of environmental factors, through adjustment or active control, or both, is crucial.[13]

Yet conceptually, developmental capacity goes beyond this broad notion of adaptation. It includes in addition the power constantly to create new and enhanced capacity to plan, implement, and manipulate new change as part of the process of achieving new goals. It is, in short, a "creative" and not just a "survival" or "adaptive" capacity that is the hallmark of a developing polity.[14]

The main attributes of a developing polity included in this concept of creative capacity are *scope, effectiveness, and rationality*. Scope

[13] Talcott Parsons, *op.cit.*, pp. 340-41. The notion of capacity is also central to Gabriel Almond's capability approach in his "Political Systems and Political Change," *The American Behavioral Scientist*, 6 (June 1963), in which he states (at p. 8): "The criterion of political change, then, is the acquisition of a new capability . . . [which gives] . . . a political system the possibility of responding efficiently, and more or less autonomously, to a new range of problems." It is also similar to Marshall Sahlins' concept of "thermodynamic accomplishment" as a criterion of development: "revolutionary all-round advance occurs when and where new sources of energy are tapped, or major technological achievement has its organizational counterpart, higher levels of integration." Marshall D. Sahlins and Elman R. Service, *Evolution and Culture* (Ann Arbor: University of Michigan Press, 1960), pp. 33-35.

[14] Clifford Geertz makes this point with characteristic brilliance: "The growth of a modern state within a traditional social context represents, therefore, not merely the shifting or transfer of a fixed quantity of power between groups in such a manner that aggregatively the gains of certain groups or individuals match the losses of others, but rather the creation of a new and more efficient machine for the production of power itself, and thus an increase in the general political capacity of the society. This is much more genuinely "revolutionary" phenomena than a mere redistribution, however radical, of power within a given system." "The Integrative Revolution," in Geertz, ed., *op.cit.* (above, n. 8), p. 121.

is reflected in the characteristically large volume and wide range of political and administrative decisions.[15] Effectiveness is revealed not only in the efficacy of those decisions, but also in the capacity for reasonably predictable and continuous goal attainment. Since scope and effectiveness are aspects of a developing polity's performance, they are directly dependent upon the third attribute, namely, the predominance of rationality in governmental decision-making. Rationalization of government is historically and logically associated with the secularization of government, that is, with the differentiation of government processes and procedures from religious organization, influence, and control.[16] This historic differentiation is marked by the emergence of a centralized civil bureaucracy staffed by personnel whose recruitment and status mobility are governed by achievement norms, and whose decisions reflect what Weber termed *formal* rationality (i.e., procedural formalization and the consistency of principle in decision-making). The peculiarly modern feature of this development is not the existence of centralized bureaucracy. Rather it is the predominance, pervasiveness, and institutionalization of a rational-secular orientation in political and administrative processes. This orientation is an absolutely indispensable ingredient in the creative capacity of a developing polity.

CONGRUENCES AND CONTRADICTIONS IN THE DEVELOPMENT SYNDROME

The foregoing is a specification of the basic dimensions of the development syndrome. The process of modernization, particularly among contemporary developing countries, underscores the wide empirical variations in initial institutional patterns, in traditional-modern mixes, in structural configurations, and in sequence and timing. Although the limits of structural and sequential variability in successful modernization remain unclear, the concepts of differentiation, equality, and capacity are heuristically useful in our search for a clearer working conception of the political modernization process.

Both congruences and contradictions are logically inherent in the contrapuntal interplay of the process of differentiation, the quest for equality, and the development of creative polity capacity. The differentiation of roles, institutional spheres, and functionally specific associations—and the specialization and interdependence this presumably involves—is obviously crucial to the development and maintenance of

---

[15] R. E. Ward and D. A. Rustow, *op.cit.*, p. 7.
[16] Talcott Parsons, *op.cit.*, pp. 351ff.

a creative polity capacity. It is also obvious, although it has not always been so recognized, that such differentiation thrusts an enormous and potentially unbearable integrative burden upon the polity.[17] A sustained integrative capacity is thus crucial for the successful institutionalization of capacity-producing differentiation. There is a similar reciprocal dependence between equality and capacity. Equality can release unbounded human energy and talent for the pursuit of polity goals, it furthers "penetration" of the society by the polity, and, through citizenship, it alone can assure the development of a sense of identity, civic obligation, and integration. Yet the realization of these capacity-producing potentialities of equality is directly dependent upon polity capacity as reflected in the effective enforcement of public policies guaranteeing and regulating political participation, resource mobilization and distribution, and access to education. Finally, there is a mutual dependence between differentiation and equality. Only full equality of opportunity via the education system will meet the specialized manpower and professional requirements of an increasingly differentiated and complex society and polity. The reverse is also true: only the expanding opportunities of such a society and polity can provide that status mobility and flexibility requisite for the maintenance of some sort of moving equilibrium between mobility aspirations and available careers "open to talent." The three elements in the syndrome are clearly both congruent and interdependent.

There is also an incongruent and conflictive potential inherent in their interplay. Polity capacity, particularly when the pressure is for an integrative "survival" capacity, may require the maintenance of structural fusion or an explicit policy of de-differentiation. It may also require the preservation or creation of hierarchy. Certainly the historical course of modernization in the Soviet Union, Japan, Turkey, and Mexico points this up, as do policies of deliberate fusion or de-differentiation and hierarchism at crisis points in the modernization of the West.[18] Because they can contain and exploit them both, established polities possessing creative capacity for sustained growth can allow—indeed, encourage—both differentiation and egalitarianism.

---

[17] ". . . [at] each more advanced level or stage of differentiation, the increased autonomy of each sphere creates more complex problems of integrating these specialized activities into one systemic framework. . . . Recognition of the integrative problems that are attendant on new levels of differentiation constitutes the main theoretical implication of the concept of differentiation." S. N. Eisenstadt, "Social Change, Differentiation, and Evolution," *op.cit.*, p. 377.

[18] S. N. Eisenstadt, "Breakdown of Modernization," *Economic Development and Cultural Change*, 12 (July 1964), 363-66.

Ironically, those lacking such an established capacity gravitate toward policies of containment and regulation of egalitarianism, policies that, if protracted, stunt their acquisition of the very creative capability they require and consciously seek to achieve. Finally, there is also an incongruity inherent in the functional need of a society for both status differentiation (hierarchy) and equality.[19] In any functioning society there are obvious structural limits to the full realization of equality.[20] As Moore has argued, "positions must be unequally rewarded because of differences in their functional importance and differences in talent within populations."[21] The type of creative capacity we are talking about is clearly impossible without the stimulus of individual and collective motivation and striving, and only status differentiation can produce that.[22] The equality-hierarchy contradiction is, as Dahrendorf has argued, the lasting determinant of social tension and conflict, and therefore of development.[23]

Because of these inherent contradictions among the elements of the development syndrome, the process of development and modernization must be regarded as interminable. We cannot logically envisage a state of affairs characterized at once by total equality, irreducible differentiation, and absolute capacity. Moreover, not only is development interminable, but the course it takes in concrete polities is extremely variable and unpredictable. As in the development among institutional spheres, the modernization process is one of interacting leads and lags in differentiation, in the realization of equality, and in the acquisition of enhanced capacity. Individual political systems begin their course of evolution possessing varying modernization

[19] Seymour Martin Lipset and Hans L. Zetterberg, "A Theory of Social Mobility," *Transactions of the Third World Congress of Sociology*, 2 (1956), 169.

[20] Talcott Parsons makes status differentiation one of his six evolutionary universals: "A 'prestige' position is a generalized prerequisite of responsible concentration of leadership." *Op.cit.*, p. 344.

[21] Wilbert E. Moore, *Social Change* (Englewood Cliffs: Prentice-Hall, 1963), p. 83.

[22] "Writers from the time of the Greek civilization on have pointed to the need for tenure positions and the inheritance of social position as a requirement for the stability of complex societies . . . the division of labor requires differential rewards in prestige and privilege as the means of motivating individuals to carry out the more difficult leadership or other positions requiring a great deal of intelligence and training." S. M. Lipset and H. L. Zetterberg, *op.cit.*, p. 169.

[23] Rolf Dahrendorf, *op.cit.*, p. 64 and passim. David E. Apter has argued that "Systems able to employ . . . [this tension between equality and hierarchy] . . . will be able to generate a continuous development process." *The Politics of Modernization* (Chicago: University of Chicago Press, 1965), p. 73. Cf. Arnold S. Feldman, "Violence and Volatility: The Likelihood of Revolution," in Harry Eckstein, ed., *Internal War* (Glencoe: Free Press, 1964), pp. 119-23.

potentials.[24] In the process of development a variety of both endogenous and exogenous factors, as well as the idiosyncratic interplay (lead and lag in sequence, timing, and rate of change) among elements in the syndrome, all combine to determine what Arnold Feldman has called the "forms of change,"[25] as well as the level of development (i.e., integrative and performance capacity) achieved. This is why there is such an extraordinary variety in the actual pattern of political modernization in the contemporary world.

Part II. The Development Syndrome in the Developing Areas

Undoubtedly the most compelling reason for our preoccupation with patterns of political development is our remarkable opportunity to conduct comparative studies of the political modernization process in the newly developing countries. In this quest for greater understanding the insightful analysis of S. N. Eisenstadt has been most illuminating. His synoptic characterization of the pattern of "breakdowns" in their political modernization warrants quotation at some length:

> In almost all these countries attempts were made to establish modern political and social frameworks and institutions . . . [there was a development] . . . of highly differentiated political structure in terms of specific political roles and institutions, of the centralization of the polity, and of . . . specific political goals and orientations . . . [there was] . . . a growing extension of the scope of the central legal, administrative, and political activities and their permeation into all spheres and regions of the society . . . [as well as] the weakening of traditional elites and traditional legitimation of rulers and . . . the establishment of some sort of ideological and often also institutional accountability of the rulers to the ruled . . . [there also developed] . . . the structural propensity to continuous change. . . . [But, despite all of this] . . . they did not develop within them a viable institutional structure which was able to deal with the problems generated by the socio-demographic and structural changes, and at least in the

---

[24] Cf. R. E. Ward and D. A. Rustow, op.cit., pp. 437-68.

[25] Arnold S. Feldman, "Violence and Volatility: The Likelihood of Revolution," op.cit., p. 124. He states: "By forms of change, I mean sequence, or the order in which different institutions change; rate, or the rapidity of change in one or several of the institutions experiencing industrialization; timing, or the intervals between component changes, especially the leads and lags that result from these intervals."

political field, they changed to less differentiated, less flexible, institutional frameworks which were able to cope with a smaller range of problems.[26]

Eisenstadt also observes that a complete reversion to a traditional, pre-modern political system has not occurred. Indeed, despite the "breakdown" in polity capacity, the egalitarian imperative and ethos remain vigorous and the process of social change continues.

> [The new elites] . . . had portrayed their own legitimation in secularized modern terms and symbols—in terms of symbols of social movements or of legal rationality and efficiency. . . . [Moreover] . . . they did not abandon the idea of the citizen as distinct from the older (traditional or colonial) idea of a subject . . . [and] . . . they rarely set themselves actively against the expansion of all of the social aspects or processes of modernization, such as education, economic development and industrialization, or rural development.[27]

The reasons for this general pattern of abortive developments are very complex, and far too few empirical studies have been made to permit firm generalization. Some likely explanations might be suggested, however, if we examined these societies in terms of the three elements in the development syndrome. We will be concerned, therefore, with the manner in which and degree to which differentiation has occurred, with the role of egalitarianism, and with the sources and nature of the capacity of their polities.

DIFFERENTIATION: THE PROBLEM OF BALANCE AND MIX

We have already noted the variations in patterns of "temporal sequence" of modernization among the different institutional spheres in the major industrial countries, and that by contrast in most of the new states a highly differentiated politico-administrative superstructure—with its full panoply of universalistic norms, achievement criteria, and functionally specific roles—was imposed upon a relatively unintegrated artificial cluster of culturally heterogeneous peoples with whom there was no meaningful historical, symbolic, affective, or representative link. There are at least three issues raised by the question of sequence: (1) the applicability of the so-called dif-

---

[26] "Breakdown of Modernization," op.cit., pp. 346-47.
[27] Ibid., pp. 347-48.

ferentiation model for understanding the processes of change in the developing countries; (2) the problems of mixing modern and traditional modes of differentiation; and (3) the problems resulting from unbalanced differentiation in the various institutional spheres.

A fashionable framework which has been used by some social scientists for studying change is the so-called differentiation model. This model assumes that the original unit that undergoes development "contains, in embryonic form, fused together, all the basic modes of social functions that later become structurally differentiated."[28] Development is seen as increased specialization and differentiation within an "evolving whole," with more efficient functional performance of the differentiated parts, and consequently greater interdependence and integration among those parts. Without serious qualification this model clearly has little relevance for the developing countries with which we are concerned. It reflects the uncritical acceptance of biological analogy or homology,[29] as well as the differentiation-cum-integration notions of Herbert Spencer and his many successors, all of whom took for granted the original and continuing solidarity of the "evolving whole." As we have already observed, Neil Smelser has recently reinterpreted his use of the differentiation model by stressing that differentiation is divisive of established society and that development requires integration of the differentiated structures on a new basis.[30]

The crucial fact is that with few exceptions none of the developing countries is or ever has been an integrated whole in the sense en-

[28] Amitai Etzioni, "The Epigenesis of Political Unification," in Eva and Amitai Etzioni, eds., *Social Change: Sources, Patterns, and Consequences* (New York, Basic Books, 1964), p. 482. Etzioni suggests that for the study of the development of political units that are not "evolving wholes" (e.g., contemporary Ghana or late medieval France), the "epigenesis" or "accumulation model" is heuristically more rewarding. Unlike anthropologists and most sociologists (who, for very good theoretical and methodological reasons, have concentrated in the main on small-scale relatively homogeneous cultural units—such as preliterate tribes—or "small groups"), political scientists and macro-sociologists have been and are primarily concerned with the development of large-scale entities such as the nation-state. In all but a few instances the historical political development of these latter units has not been a phenomenon of "evolving wholes," but the progressive integration of a medley of pre-existing smaller scale wholes into a larger, entirely new whole.

[29] ". . . development psychology postulates one regulative principle of development . . . which states that wherever development occurs, it proceeds from a state of relative globality and lack of differentiation to a state of increasing differentiation, articulation, and hierarchic integration." Heinz Werner, "The Concept of Development from a Comparative and Organismic Point of View," in Dale B. Harris, ed., *The Concept of Development* (Minneapolis: University of Minnesota Press, 1957), p. 126.

[30] N. J. Smelser, *op.cit.*, pp. 41-42.

visaged by the differentiation model.[31] Indeed, their integrative problems are four-dimensional, as reflected in the following:

(*1*) *primordial differentiation*, that is, the original and as yet unbridged—indeed, frequently intensified—lines of cleavage (ethnic, tribal, religious, linguistic, sectional, and so forth) with which they commenced their existence as a political entity;[32]

(*2*) *modernizing differentiation*, that is, the "fragmentation" into subsystems straining toward autonomy within the modern sector as a result of the pluralizing (i.e., differentiating) impact of economic and social modernization;

(*3*) *compounded differentiation*, as manifested in those explosive situations where the lines of cleavage of (1) and (2) coincide and are mutually reinforcing; and

(*4*) *uneven differentiation*, as reflected particularly in the wide gap between the highly differentiated politico-administrative superstructure imported from the West on the one hand, and the medley of fragmented elements in the society over which it has been placed, on the other.

This is the integrative load thrust on the new polities. Their already fragile capacity is simultaneously challenged to contain (or "domesticate," as Geertz would put it) the divisiveness of (1), hopefully by avoiding (3), as well as to develop new integrative mechanisms to bridge the discontinuities of (2) and (4).

The second issue raised by the variation in the temporal sequence of differentiation as between the older states and the newer states concerns the role of tradition in modernization. It is generally recognized that it can be both supportive and obstructive.[33] That is, modernization does not require the extinction of tradition. On the contrary, as Pye has put it, we must consider "what mixture, or rather fusion, of traditional and modern patterns will lead to national development . . . the effective operation of the society depends upon whether the traditional patterns of behavior tend to reinforce and give greater substance and clarity to the modern superstructure pattern of relationships or whether they tend to undermine and dis-

[31] Arnold S. Feldman, *op.cit.*, pp. 120-21.

[32] C. Geertz, *op.cit.*, pp. 105-57.

[33] David E. Apter, "The Role of Traditionalism in the Political Modernization of Ghana and Uganda," *World Politics*, 13 (October 1960), 45-68; and S. N. Eisenstadt, "Initial Institutional Patterns of Political Modernization," *Civilizations*, 19 (March 1962), 461-74.

rupt the superstructure."[34] Once this general proposition is made, that is, that we must think in terms not of replacement but of fusional (or isolative or conflictive) mixtures, there are two crucial distinctions to be noted. One is whether the country concerned has already achieved national integration and, therefore, has a national tradition that can be exploited for modernization purposes. This was true in the case of England and Japan; indeed, what Ward and Rustow call a "reinforcing dualism" (congruent exploitable traditions) was particularly striking in the modernization of Japan.[35] Most developing countries, however, are legatees of highly pluralistic traditions that reflect very different, frequently conflicting or incongruent, cultural patterns. They are countries that have no single national tradition, and any self-conscious effort to exploit one particular traditional pattern out of the melange available could heighten tension, provoke conflict, or have only local or sectional relevance.

The second distinction to be made regarding the role of tradition in modernization is semantical in character, but it is not trivial. The concept of tradition has come to be used so carelessly that, unless qualified, it has no analytical power. The issue turns on whether the term is viewed chronologically, that is, whether it refers to what existed in the old days before modernization occurred, or whether it connotes a set of distinctive attributes (e.g., ascription, particularism, diffuseness, etc.). In concrete "traditional" societies the two frequently coincide, but in many cases they do not.[36] To put the issue another way, a traditional trait, attitude, behavioral pattern, mode of differentiation, etc., can be typologically identical, and therefore by definition congruent with its modern counterpart, or it can be typologically different and fortuitously supportive of or instrumentally exploitable

---

[34] *Op.cit.*, p. 38. S. N. Eisenstadt notes that "the concrete patterns of structural differentiation, which have taken place even in most European countries, show a great variety of ways in which traditional elements and orientations have been incorporated within the more differentiated modern frameworks of ways in which ascriptive and particularistic criteria have spread and become crystallized within these frameworks. . . ." *Modernization: Growth and Diversity, op.cit.*, p. 10.

[35] R. E. Ward and D. A. Rustow, *op.cit.*, pp. 444ff. They point out how the traditional Japanese mode of status differentiation helped to maximize order, obedience, and discipline in the difficult early stages of the new society. See also Stanley Rothman, "Modernity and Tradition in Britain," *Social Research*, 26 (Autumn 1961), 297-320.

[36] See Lloyd Fallers, *op.cit.* (pp. 158-219), for several examples of "modern" attributes found in chronologically traditional polities. In David Apter's study of Ashanti and Buganda (*op.cit.*, pp. 45-68) both societies are subsumed under the rubric of chronological traditionalism, but typologically or attributively Buganda was considerably more "modern" than Ashanti.

for modernization, either for a particular phase or permanently. This latter point is important because what is typologically traditional (hierarchism or ascription) might be, at certain stages of modernization, more positively supportive of the process than what is typologically modern (e.g., achievement norms), yet at later stages it could become an obstacle to further development. In short, the modernizing potential of traditional-modern mixes is a function of several different circumstances: (a) typological trait congruence, (b) permanently compatible fusion, and (c) a transitional exploitable mix in which the modern and traditional elements are not permanently compatible. These distinctions are made with due regard to the fact that typological modernity and traditionality are only ideal-type constructs; concrete institutions, traits, and patterns are always mixed.

The reason for dwelling on the issue of tradition is that the limits of its exploitability as well as the high revolutionary potential of certain forms of fusion are not always fully recognized. Where primordial lines of cleavage (ethnic, tribal, religious, and status hierarchies) coincide with the fragmentation resulting from modernizing differentiation—what we called "composite differentiation"—the former are strengthened and perpetuated, and the resultant likelihood of disruptive political action, including political secession or civil war, is extraordinarily high. Under these conditions the dualism, the fusion of the traditional and the modern, is not reinforcing but dysfunctional for overall development.[37] In circumstances such as these, where "nonreinforcing dualisms" pervade the whole society, the governing elites directly and solely confront the full burden of tension-management and conflict-containment. They are denied the load-carrying, conflict-solving support of intermediate or primary structures characteristic of more integrated societies where modernizing differentiation crosscuts primordial lines of cleavage.

Once this general characterization has been stated, it should be noted that there are examples of successful reinforcing dualism in newly developing countries; that is, there are situations in which

[37] For examples of dysfunctional fusion see S. E. Harrison, *India: The Most Dangerous Decades* (Princeton: Princeton University Press, 1960), pp. 100ff; René Lemarchand, *The Politics of Fragmentation* (Berkeley and Los Angeles: University of California Press, 1964); James S. Coleman and Carl G. Rosberg, Jr., *Political Parties and National Integration in Tropical Africa* (Berkeley: University of California Press, 1964), pp. 689-91; and Myron Weiner, *The Politics of Scarcity: Public Pressure and Political Response in India* (Chicago: University of Chicago Press, 1962), pp. 36-72.

tradition has contributed positively to integration and development. The traditional pattern of role differentiation in Northern Nigeria has been reasonably congruent with the modern bureaucratic role structure developed under colonial rule and continued in the post-colonial period of accelerated modernization.[38] Here the discontinuity between the traditional and modern has been minimal; however, the congruence is more akin to the dualism that prevailed in Japan during the early stages of modernization, namely, a rigidly hierarchical, essentially authoritarian pattern of role differentiation congruent only with a statist mode and period of development. Another interesting example is the congruence between the traditional role pattern in India and the role structure of the Congress Party. In this case, Myron Weiner found that one factor accounting for the effectiveness of a modern highly differentiated association (the Congress Party) was the adaptiveness of certain traditional political roles.[39]

The third issue concerns the markedly uneven differentiation, particularly as manifest in the gross imbalance between the highly differentiated bureaucratic-administrative sphere and other institutional spheres characteristic of most developing countries. This has at least three significant aspects affecting polity capacity: (1) the statist orientation of governing elites, (2) the high vulnerability of elites in statist regimes that are also populistic, and (3) the inter-elite power struggle. On the first point, the governing elites in most new states are firm believers in the "primacy of the polity," and to them the polity is limited to the authoritative structures of government in which they are ensconced. Moreover, they are generally ill-disposed to encourage or even tolerate a pattern of development that would lead to greater differentiation and autonomy in nongovernmental institutional spheres or in nonbureaucratic parts of the political system. Their general outlook on economic growth has been summarized with characteristic directness by Edward Shils:

> They envisage a system in which the initiative, on the whole, will come from the politicians and the civil service, while the populace, if made sufficiently enthusiastic on behalf of the na-

---

[38] C. Sylvester Whitaker, *The Politics of Tradition: Continuity and Change in Northern Nigeria, 1946-1966* (Princeton: Princeton University Press, 1970). This case of dualism supports the integration of Northern Nigeria, but heightens the disintegrative potential of Nigeria as a whole.

[39] Myron Weiner, "Traditional Role Performance and the Development of Modern Political Parties: The Indian Case," *Journal of Politics*, 26 (November 1964), 830-49.

tional ideal, will carry out their schemes. They conduct a policy which aims to create socialistic, governmentally initiated, controlled, or operated enterprises, because they assume that the initiative for productive economic activity is lacking in the population.[40]

In postcolonial new states there tends to be a reassertion of bureaucratic (civil or military) predominance over nonbureaucratic sectors of the political system as evidenced by the seizure of power by the military establishment, the atrophying of mass nationalist movements after their raison d'être disappears through independence, and the general trend toward the emergence of a party-state governing apparatus.[41]

This statist orientation of elites in the developing countries is explained by a variety of factors, including, Edward Shils suggests, the charismatic legacy of traditional life. Their political socialization in what was essentially a bureaucratic-authoritarian colonial system is also a crucial consideration. They are statists because they inherited a statist system and knew no other. Another factor is the weakness or alien character of the private sector in their countries. The close ties with socialist and communist elements in European countries in the course of their higher education abroad are also of importance. Beyond these considerations there is the fact that differentiation creates conditions leading to tension and conflict that can place an unbearable load on the already fragile machinery of government, or, even more, undermine the legitimacy of the incumbent elites and even challenge their control over government.

Statist regimes catapulted into power through the manipulation of populistic slogans and high-output expectations are quite obviously peculiarly vulnerable to popular disaffection. The legitimacy of the government in a modern polity is dependent not only upon the continual resolution of the problem of integration but most uniquely and

[40] Edward Shils, "The Concentration and Dispersion of Charisma," *World Politics*, 10 (October 1958), 1-19.

[41] Fred W. Riggs, "Bureaucrats and Political Development: A Paradoxical View," in Joseph LaPalombara, ed., *Bureaucracy and Political Development* (Princeton: Princeton University Press, 1963), pp. 120-67. S. N. Eisenstadt in *Essays in Sociological Aspects of Political and Economic Development* (Hague: Mouton, 1961), who notes (p. 301) that "social and institutional differentiation which would facilitate the emergence of diversified centers of power and prestige in the society . . . (as well as) . . . the development of relatively autonomous groups and organizations in society," are the consequences of such statist systems. On the postcolonial emergence of party-state regimes in Africa, see James S. Coleman and Carl G. Rosberg, Jr., *op.cit.*, pp. 655-78.

emphatically upon performance, distributive output, and goal attainment. Governing elites in new states, which in the main lack traditional supports for their legitimacy, are particularly dependent upon fulfillment of goals promised during their climb to power. They are, Fallers observes, "held directly responsible for the welfare and progress of their people in a way that was less true in the West during comparable phases of modernization."[42] This is one of the explanations for the tendency of such elites to give in so readily to the demands of various groups that would be effectively resisted by governments more secure in the bases of their legitimacy. The logical corollary of the "primacy of the polity" in goal determination is exclusiveness of responsibility for goal fulfillment.

The imbalance in differentiation—and the consequent discontinuity —between the polity and other spheres also heightens the significance of inter-elite politics. Elite differentiation in developing countries is the source of continuous tension and conflict. Because the rewards and stakes are so high, politics tends to be almost an exclusive phenomena of competing elites in the authoritative structures. During the terminal stages of the colonial period in what are now the new states political elites monopolized the scene, partly because members of the bureaucratic elite were predominantly aliens and therefore on their way out, but mainly because the ideology of nationalism endowed the political elites with a transcendent and seemingly incontestable legitimacy. After independence the bureaucratic elites (both civil and military) were rapidly indigenized, and, in addition, a new indigenous technical elite concerned with economic and social development began to emerge in due course. This postcolonial differentiation of elites was accompanied by a characteristic strain toward autonomy on the part of the elites in the upper reaches of the status hierarchies in each of the differentiated spheres (the dominant political party, the civil bureaucracy, the military establishment, and the new technocratic cadres in planning and development ministries). The characteristic result of this confrontation of differentiated elites is a struggle for supremacy at the center.

> Conflicts . . . [among these elites] . . . are common after a
> modernizing country becomes independent. . . . Each tries to
> manipulate and control the others. Political leaders seek to ma-
> nipulate their civil servants, military officers, and leading profes-
> sionals in order to prevent them from exercising a potential veto

[42] Op.cit., p. 192.

over legitimacy. Ordinarily what occurs is friction and intense conflict between representatives of party bureaucracy, military bureaucracy, and civil service.[43]

In many new states the pattern of postcolonial development flowing from this conflict is not toward greater differentiation, but, as we have already seen, toward conscious de-differentiation within the politico-administrative superstructure, as well as in other institutional spheres of the modern sector, by whichever elite gains supremacy. The latter tends in most instances to be the leadership of the dominant party, but examples of successful intervention by the military elite are well known. This process of deliberate de-differentiation is particularly visible and most self-consciously pursued in those states known variously as "movement regimes," "revolutionary-centralizing one-party states," and "mobilization systems."[44]

The imbalance between the polity and other institutional spheres in society is, of course, only the most glaring example of uneven differentiation and malintegration affecting the political development process in modernizing countries. Uneven structural change among other institutional spheres and a persisting gap between the processes of differentiation and the development of new modes of integration, are also characteristic of the modernization process in most of these societies. The conditions they create are usually politically destabilizing.

> . . . [differentiation] . . . bites unevenly into the established social and economic structure. And throughout the society, the differentiation occasioned by agricultural, industrial and urban changes always proceeds in a seesaw relationship with integration: the two forces continuously breed lags and bottlenecks. The faster the tempo of modernization, the more severe are the discontinuities. This unevenness creates anomia in the classical sense,

---

[43] Apter, *op.cit.*, p. 221. S. N. Eisenstadt, in comparative and historical perspective, has generalized this proposition, arguing that "the growing differentiation and increasing interdependence among the various more autonomous and diversified institutional spheres increases the probability that one sphere will attempt to dominate the other coercively, by restricting and regimenting their tendencies toward autonomy. This probably is especially strong with respect to the . . . [political sphere], because it is "especially prone to 'totalistic' orientations that tend to negate the autonomy of other spheres." "Change, Differentiation, and Evolution," *op.cit.*, p. 381.

[44] See Robert C. Tucker, "Towards a Comparative Politics of Movement-Regimes," *American Political Science Review*, 15 (June 1961), 281-89; and James S. Coleman and Carl G. Rosberg, *op.cit.*, pp. 662-63. For historical examples of de-differentiation see S. N. Eisenstadt, *The Political Systems of Empires* (London: Free Press, 1963).

for it generates disharmony between life experiences and the normative framework by which these experiences are regulated . . . social movements appeal most to those who have been dislodged from old social ties by differentiation but who have not been integrated into the new social order.[45]

EQUALITY: THE PROBLEMS OF EXPECTATIONS AND DEMANDS

The explanation for the strength and pervasiveness of egalitarian pressures in the developing areas is more complex than such phrases as the "will to be modern" or the "revolt of the masses" would lead one to believe. Many of the traditional cultures of these areas had strikingly egalitarian features. "In the traditional civilization of Islam and China," Weiner observes, "the ideal if not always the practice of equality had an honorable and often commanding place in the culture."[46] Fallers has also observed that

. . . in traditional Africa, even in the larger kingdoms with their elaborate political hierarchies, [there was] a kind of egalitarianism that seems to have had two principal roots. One of these was the pattern of kinship and family structure, which over much of the continent rested upon exogamous unilineal descent groups . . . the other factor [was] the absence of literary religious traditions, which might have provided the basis for more clearly differentiated elite subcultures.[47]

How determinative such traditional egalitarian culture elements have been in shaping the perspectives and behavioral dispositions of the immediate past and current generation of peoples in the developing countries remains unclear.[48] Traditional African egalitarianism re-

[45] N. J. Smelser, *op.cit.*, p. 44. See also S. N. Eisenstadt, *Essays on Sociological Aspects of Political and Economic Development, op.cit.*, pp. 12-22, and Daniel Lerner, *The Passing of Traditional Society* (Glencoe: Free Press, 1958), pp. 84-85.

[46] Myron Weiner, "The Struggle for Equality in India," *Foreign Affairs* (July 1962), 1. Lloyd Fallers, *op.cit.*, p. 173, notes that although Islamic societies of the medieval period exhibited great inequalities of wealth and power, they remained "comparatively fluid and open to talent." In both China and the Ottoman Empire recruitment to bureaucratic office was governed predominantly by ascriptive rather than achievement criteria.

[47] *Ibid.*, p. 180.

[48] Cf. Robert A. LeVine, "The Role of the Family in Authority Systems: A Cross-Cultural Application of Stimulus-Generalization Theory," *Behavioral Science*, 5, (October 1960); Sidney Verba, "The Comparative Study of Political Socialization," (unpublished); Frederick W. Frey, "Political Socialization in Developing Nations," (unpublished); C. S. Whitaker, Jr., "Three Perspectives on Hierarchy," *Journal of Commonwealth Political Studies*, 3 (March 1965), 1-19.

ceives considerable emphasis in efforts to formulate modern African ideologies.[49] On the other hand, Weiner notes that despite the gross historic inequalities that characterized traditional India and the relative absence of the idea of social equality in Hinduism, the principle of equality has been central to the program of the Indian Congress Party both as a pre-independence nationalist movement and as a post-colonial governing party.[50]

The Western presence or model, whether transmitted through a colonial experience or not, has obviously been a major factor in the diffusion of modern ideas of equality in the developing countries. Both Christian evangelism and Western education were carriers of the egalitarian ideal, and the patent contradictions between the ideal and the realities of the colonial situation brought it into sharper focus and undoubtedly increased its emotive power. The socializing impact of modern secular political and bureaucratic ideas and institutions introduced in these areas also has been of no little significance. The imported model included at least the legal fiction of universal suffrage as well as the stress upon universalistic and achievement norms. Tocqueville long ago pointed out the peculiarly dynamic and contagious character of the idea of equality. Once men are equal in some respects, they are inexorably driven to become equal in all respects. It is the psychic component in equality that makes the quest for equality "totalistic."

The passion for equality is less the product of Western precept than of the humiliating and infuriating inequalities that historically have characterized the relationship between the former colonial countries and the West. Protest against what they feel to have been their debasement by the West is reinforced by their own tendency to lack self-confidence. This fusion of sentiments—rebelliousness and insecurity—is an extraordinarily powerful revolutionary element in their quest for equality. The agitation for self-determination and the extinction of the Western presence in these areas was not inspired by the desire to recover the lost freedom of an historic nation. Rather, its object was to remove what was regarded as the chief obstacle to progress toward a new era of equality in which so-called dependent peoples could, as Dr. Nnamdi Azikiwe of Nigeria once put it, "walk

---

[49] Charles F. Andrain, "Democracy and Socialism: Ideologies of African Leaders," in David E. Apter, ed., *Ideology and Discontent* (New York: Free Press, 1964), pp. 156ff.; and Thomas Hodgkin and Ruth Schacter Morgenthau, "Mali," in James S. Coleman and Carl G. Rosberg, eds., *op.cit.*, pp. 216-58.

[50] *Op.cit.*, pp. 2-9.

majestically with the other races of mankind."[51] Individual strivings for equality have been and are obviously present within each society; the crucial point is that individual self-realization is not regarded as psychically achieved unless one's race has likewise gained full acceptance and equality. This is among the reasons why, despite a pervasive de facto elitism and hierarchism, the rhetoric of self-assertion in the developing countries has been so markedly populistic and egalitarian.[52]

The pervasive spread of the egalitarian ethos in developing countries has been and remains a central driving force for change; it also, ironically, has created or aggravated some of their most vexing problems of modernization. Three of these problems are particularly significant: (1) by creating excessive demands it has either gravely weakened or it has destroyed the capacity of many new states to launch or to carry on sustained modernization; (2) the integrative task of the polity has been aggravated because the impact of egalitarianism in culturally fragmented societies tends to activate and reinforce divisive primordial ties; and (3) the revolutionary potential of disaffected groups is heightened as a result of severe imbalance between expanding educational output and limited career opportunities. Although these problems may be viewed as short-term pathologies—and in some cases may prove to be so—they may also lead to what Eisenstadt calls "breakdowns in modernization," possibly arresting political development for generations to come.

The dominant political characteristic of most of the developing countries is, as Eisenstadt puts it, the "marked discrepancy between the demands of different groups—parties, cliques, bureaucracy, army, regional groups—and the response and ability of the central rulers to deal with these demands."[53] Put more quaintly by John Dorsey, we are in "the presence of permeation of low-information-energy societies with the information and values of high-energy societies."[54] In

[51] James S. Coleman, *Nigeria: Background to Nationalism* (Los Angeles: University of California Press, 1958), p. 410.

[52] Clifford Geertz has critically analyzed the force generated by the fusion of the quest for personal identity, for a realization of the self, and the kind to be associated with a collectivity that participates equally in the main arena of world affairs: "The two motives are . . . most intimately related, because citizenship in a truly modern state has more and more become the most broadly negotiable claim to personal significance, and because what Mazzini called the demand to exist and have a name is to such a great extent fired by a humiliating sense of exclusion from the important centers of power in world society." *Op.cit.*, p. 108.

[53] S. N. Eisenstadt, "Breakdowns in Modernization," *op.cit.*, p. 350.

[54] Joseph LaPalombara, *op.cit.*, pp. 28, 318-59.

situations where the capacity-load ratio is already precarious, the enormous demands generated by the imperatives of equality are frequently more than the polity can bear. Not only have statist policies prevented the development of intervening aggregative structures, but demands tend to be thrust upon the polity in an unrestrained, intermittent, unpredictable, and totalistic manner. This state of affairs accounts in large measure for the coercion-capitulation syndrome described by Eisenstadt. ". . . the policies undertaken by the rulers in these societies have been characterized by continuous oscillation between the attempts at controlling all the major power positions and groups in the society and monopolizing the positions of effective control, on the one hand, and a continuous giving in to the demands of various groups, on the other hand."[55] Governing elites are vulnerable to egalitarian demands not only because they are statists whose continued legitimacy depends heavily upon distributive output and goal-achievement, a point already noted, but also because they are prisoners of the modern egalitarian ideologies that they articulated in their quest for control over central state power.

The introduction of universal suffrage and the concept of the participant citizen in unintegrated pluralistic societies has the perverse effect of politicizing—thereby freezing and strengthening—existing parochialisms. This is but another way of emphasizing once again the high incidence of politically dysfunctional dualisms in differentiation. Political organizations are formed and political appeals are made along pre-existing lines of traditional differentiation. The reasons are stark and simple: in most developing countries primordial loyalties are tenaciously persistent; and they continue, over the short run at least, to provide the strongest, most reliable base for political action or appeal.[56] Equally paradoxical is the fact that the introduction of achievement norms for recruitment to bureaucratic office can accentuate and intensify divisions among different ethnic, regional, or tribal groups. As Adam Curle has argued: "It is a sad fact that, once the

[55] S. N. Eisenstadt, *op.cit.*, p. 361.

[56] Myron Weiner, *op.cit.*, pp. 36-72, J. S. Coleman, *op.cit.*, pp. 329-31; 388-90; C. Geertz, *op.cit.*, who notes (p. 122) that in Ceylon, "The first definite move toward a resolute popularly based, social reform government led . . . not to heightened national unity, but to the reverse—increased linguistic, racial, regional, and religious parochialism. . . . The institution of universal suffrage made the temptation to court the masses by appealing to traditional loyalties virtually irresistible."

process of development starts in one sector of a society, the inequalities within that society tend to increase."[57] And in developing societies the most cohesive and identifiable sectors of the population among which inequalities exist, and are therefore increased, are ethnic, tribal, linguistic, religious, and so on in character. There is a law of unequal development advantage, and demographic groups whose members may be culturally more disposed to modernization, and who thereby already possess more relevant skills and education, have a differential advantage for further development once achievement criteria are made the determinants of status mobility. This tendency is made all the more pronounced because of the very tight fit between educational achievement and occupational mobility in most developing countries.[58] In any event, this process of uneven development and its corollary, the reinforcement of existing primordial divisions, continues according to its own logic and dynamic unless the state exerts countervailing influences, such as an enforced ethnic quota system or a deliberate program of leveling up less-developed or less-advantaged groups.[59] Over the short-run, however, such policies can have the ironic effect of intensifying the very problem they seek to surmount.

The high expectations and popular demands generated by egalitarianism, coupled with the vulnerability of governing elites previously noted, have frequently resulted in a vast expansion in education facilities completely unrelated to the availability of jobs and careers. Indeed, this imbalance in the development process is one of the most striking examples of the politically destabilizing consequences of incongruence between the extension of equality (universal educational opportunity) and increased differentiation (expansion of the modern occupational system), of the tension-producing lead and lag reflected in uneven development among different institutional spheres, and of the pendulum swing to the capitulation side of the oscillation syndrome described by Eisenstadt. The result is the creation in many new states of large numbers of educated unemployed who are "a

[57] Adam Curle, *The Role of Education in Developing Societies* (Accra: Ghana University Press, 1961), pp. 7-8.

[58] Philip J. Foster, "Secondary Schools and Social Mobility in a West African Nation," *Sociology of Education*, 37 (Winter 1963), 153. The tight fit results from the weakness of the private sector, the fact that most opportunities for salaried employment are in the government service, and the fact that recruitment into that service emphasizes educational qualifications.

[59] James S. Coleman, ed., *Education and Political Development*, pp. 26-27.

more serious source of alienation and political disaffection than are industrial workers."[60] A most significant aspect of this increase in the revolutionary potential in these states is that it is not solely the result of mass demonstrations and demands for educational expansion. Indeed, C. Arnold Anderson has emphasized that "premature dispersion of educational resources in actuality as often results from collectivist notions about equality held by the elite as from populist ideas."[61] Compulsive egalitarianism by modernizing elites can mean failure to achieve modernizing goals as well as loss of their own legitimacy.

MODERNIZING CAPACITY: THE PROBLEM OF INTEGRATION AND
PERFORMANCE

The three elements in the development syndrome (differentiation-equality-capacity) are interdependent and can be mutually supportive or conflictive; but they are not coordinate. Political development, or any kind of development for that matter, ultimately depends upon polity capacity and in a modernizing polity we should think in terms of modernizing capacity having two major dimensions: (1) an *integrative* dimension, as manifest in effective "domestication" of primordialism and the successive reintegration of society at each new level, phase, or extension of structural differentiation; and (2) a *performance* dimension, as reflected in effective public policies aimed at maximizing the realization of the civil, political, and social rights associated with the notion of equality and citizenship in a modern state, *insofar* as the overall capacity of the system for further development is not destroyed. Some of the special problems faced by developing countries attempting to achieve these two dimensions of capacity have been analyzed in the foregoing sections. It now remains for us to examine briefly the notion of modernizing capacity.

Scope and effectiveness are two aspects of the creative capacity of a developing polity that we discussed in the opening sections. Apart from the heavy load the polity of a modernizing country must bear as a consequence of the anomalies of differentiation and the excesses of egalitarianism, there are other incapacitating factors at work. There are mutually reinforcing weaknesses in the structure and the functioning of the machinery of government.[62] One such weakness may be incompetence and inefficiency—possibly due mainly to inexperience—of much of the personnel manning authoritative structures.

---

[60] Lloyd Fallers, *op.cit.*, p. 192.   [61] J. S. Coleman, ed., *op.cit.*, p. 521.
[62] These are examined exhaustively in LaPalombara, *op.cit.*, and Fred W. Riggs, *op.cit.*

A second major weakness is the discontinuous and fragmented character of the political communication network which limits both increase in scope and effectiveness of penetration. Finally, there is the excessive centralization and statism of most developing countries, which we have previously noted. This not only means greater vulnerability as a result of nonfulfillment of populist expectations it also means heightened inefficiency. Above all it means the absence of critically important supportive capacity in the society at large. Polity capacity is not solely a function of organizational technology or the efficiency of bureaucratic personnel and machinery; it is also a function of the extent to which the society itself—the economic, social, and political infrastructure—can absorb, deflect, or respond to the wide range of demands generated in a modernizing country and thereby minimize or obviate explicit government involvement. It is further a function of a type of political culture of participation that operates to restrain, moderate, or postpone demands or in other ways reduce the decisional load upon formal administrative structures. It is this very important buttressing, deflecting, absorbing, and containing dimension in the nonbureaucratic spheres of a polity's capacity that most developing countries lack and are not soon likely to realize.

Newly modernizing countries confront other aspects of the configuration of circumstances that militate against the primacy of rationality in political and governmental decisions, the third attribute of a modern polity so critical for the development of creative polity capacity. Foremost among these are the acute ambiguities in the normative and value systems of these countries. This has a profoundly negative affect upon both the integrative and performance capacities of a polity. Indeed, in contemplating this basic weakness many analysts have stressed the absolute essentiality of charismatic leadership and some form of utopian ideal—what David Apter calls "political religion."[63] The case has been made in these terms by Neil Smelser:

> . . . Political leaders will increase their effectiveness by open and vigorous commitment to utopian and xenophobic nationalism. This commitment serves as a powerful instrument for attaining three of their most important ends: (a) the enhancement of their own legitimacy by endowing themselves with the mission for creating the nation-state; (b) the procurement of otherwise im-

[63] David E. Apter, "Political Religion in the New Nations," in C. Geertz, ed., op.cit., pp. 57-104. See also Gideon Sjoberg, *Political Structure, Ideology, and Economic Development* (Bloomington: Indiana University Press, 1963).

possible sacrifices from a populace which may be committed to modernization in the abstract but which resists the concrete breaks with traditional ways; (c) the use of their claim to legitimacy to hold down protests and to prevent generalized symbols such as communism from spreading to all sorts of particular grievances.[64]

The atmosphere likely to be created by this formula is obviously not compatible with the predominance of rationality in political and administrative decision-making. However, ideology—including utopian and xenophobic nationalism—might well have the same function in development as tradition previously discussed, namely, at certain, usually early, stages of development it can enhance the capacity of the polity, but at later stages it may no longer be compatible with or functional to development.[65]

SUMMARY

Within the framework of an evolutionary perspective we have conceptualized development as a dialectical process reflecting a continuous interaction among differentiation, the drive for equality, and the integrative, responsive, and adaptive capacity of the polity. This contrapuntal interplay we termed the development syndrome, and we endeavored to specify both the conflicting and congruent aspects inherent in this interaction in all political systems. In concentrating our analysis upon the newly developing countries of this epoch the conflicting elements in the dialectic of their patterns and potentialities for development have been highlighted. The same would have been true had we concentrated on developing countries in any earlier historical epoch, or upon the various developing and stagnating countries in the more industrialized Northern Hemisphere. From the evolutionary perspective the process of political development is neither linear in pattern nor temporal in sequence; rather it is the consequence of the evolving dialectic among the three dimensions of the development syndrome. Some long-established contemporary polities may cease to develop and become arrested at a level of differentiation, equality, and capacity beyond which no significant further development can occur—at least in this epoch; some of the newer polities, on the other hand, possessed of a high evolutionary potential, may make quantum "leapfrogging" advances. What are certain are the main elements in the dialectic; what are not certain are the forms of the outcome.

[64] Smelser, op.cit., p. 47.
[65] Alexander Eckstein, "Economic Development and Political Change in Communist Systems," World Politics, 22 (July 1970), 483.

CHAPTER 3

IDENTITY AND THE POLITICAL CULTURE

LUCIAN W. PYE

IN THE PRECEDING chapter James Coleman has explored the complex dynamics of what we have chosen to call the development syndrome; and he had the occasion to observe that political development does not usually involve an orderly sequencing of events, but rather that there are constant stress and strain among the demands for equality, the processes of differentiation, and the need for greater capacity. Modernization also involves a ceaseless straining and tugging between the developmental processes and the requirement that the political system maintain itself as an effective integrated system capable of performing the universal functions basic to all political systems.

These conflicts and the ensuing tensions provide much of the drama, anxiety, and excitement in the politics of the developing areas. They are also the cause of the breakdown of some systems and of the drift toward ineffectualness and stagnation. The pulls between development and system maintenance set the stage for the conflicting counsels which say, at one and the same time, that "too much is being tried," and "not enough is being done." Similarly, in analyzing this conflict some observers may arrive at the conclusion that the only solution is revolution, while others hold that evolution is always possible if correct steps are taken. Indeed, there are few matters that tax the art of political judgment more than that of evaluating the probable outcome of any particular struggle between the demands for change and the need for order.

A moment's reflection will bring to mind a number of countries in which the almost unanimous forecast of foreigners for years on end has been that the pressures for change are inexorable, that older rulers will inevitably be toppled from power; and yet year after year old ways have lasted, with only minimal adaptations, proving that the tenacity of self-preservation of political systems is apparently one of the most enduring forces in human affairs. On the other hand, for other countries the forecast has been for rapid and even smooth acceptance of change, for the leaders seem bent on modernizing the lives of their people; but then suddenly the political system proves to have been of brittle substance and the effort to bend it has left it so shattered that the government is incapable of carrying out what were once merely routine operations.

A critical question of political development, both for the theorist and the policymaker, is that of foreseeing the probable consequences of strains among the different aspects of the development syndrome in different countries. There is probably no substitute for deep familiarity with existing conditions; but as a check for those with intimate knowledge and as a guide to more general theory building, it is useful to categorize the most significant problems that appear to dominate the modernization process and arise out of the inherent tensions in the development syndrome. As we have already indicated in the Introduction, these problems can then be readily grouped under the headings of five historically and analytically definable crises: identity, legitimacy, participation, penetration, and distribution.

In discussing now in greater detail the crises of identity and legitimacy in this chapter and the next, we shall be dealing primarily with the ways in which the development syndrome of equality, capacity, and differentiation tends to create problems in people's orientations toward political action, that is, in the political perceptions, cognitions, evaluations, and affective sentiments of those who make up any political system. In other words, identity and legitimacy are the crises of the political culture; for they determine how people come to understand politics, how they view authority, what they feel is the proper and right role of government, and what is to be the character and intensity of their loyalties to the particular system.

Since both the identity and legitimacy crises are fundamentally problems of attitude and sentiment (more particularly, the differences between rulers and the masses), it may be helpful at the outset before treating the crises separately to note some of the common problems of political cultures in the currently developing countries and some of the more general respects in which these late developing countries have different problems from those of earlier nation-states that evolved in Europe.

In a relatively stable political system in which all functions and processes tend to reinforce and support each other there is likely to be a coherent political culture in which the orientations of both the citizens and leaders are mutually compatible. However, even in the most stable systems and the most homogeneous populations there will still be significant differences in the outlooks of political leaders and common citizens. Those who on a workaday basis deal with power, and have been recruited to significant roles of responsibility and influence in a political system, must view politics from a significantly different perspective from those who remain primarily observers or only participating citizens. It is therefore important to note that in all political systems there are at least two political cultures, an elite political culture and a mass political culture.[1]

The elite political culture involves the attitudes, sentiments, and behavior patterns of those who through the operation of the political recruitment function have been brought to active roles within the political system and have a direct effect on the outputs of the system. The elite political culture thus involves primarily those in the authoritative structures but also the leadership elements of the nonauthoritative structures and processes. At the heart of the problem of elite political culture and development is the question of the qualities necessary for effective political leadership in the formulation and execution of national policies.

The mass political culture is formed by the attitudes and orientations toward politics of the population as a whole, including the participating citizens and the rank-and-file members of both the authoritative and the nonauthoritative structures who do not significantly control the outputs of the system. Central to the relationship of mass political culture to political development is the question of the sentiments and values that make it possible for people to work together effectively in seeking collective goals.[2] In many countries there may not be a well-defined commonly shared mass political culture, but rather there are several different mass political cultures differentiated according to class, region, ethnic community, or social grouping. Such a diversity of attitudes and opinions need not cause problems of either identity or legitimacy, for stable political development does not require a homogeneous political culture. Indeed, as we shall see, in some respects a society that is accustomed to pluralism may be better able to cope with continuing change.

It is readily apparent that any change in the equality, capacity, and

[1] See in particular the contributions of Robert E. Ward on Japan, Myron Weiner on India, and Robert Scott on Mexico in Lucian W. Pye and Sidney Verba, *Political Culture and Political Development* (Princeton: Princeton University Press, 1965).

[2] The classic study of the democratic citizen and political culture is Gabriel A. Almond and Sidney Verba, *The Civic Culture* (Princeton: Princeton University Press, 1963; Boston: Little, Brown, 1965).

differentiation dimensions of the development syndrome must affect both the elite and the mass political cultures. Such changes, to the extent that they are accommodated by the cultures, represent the normal dynamics of modernizing societies. A crisis begins to occur when the particular character of either the mass or the elite culture, or both, causes the inherent strains between, say, capacity and equality to become greatly magnified and perceived as a major threat to rulers or subjects or both. The result may then be that people question the basic unity of the society, causing an identity crisis, or they may question the proprieties of government, causing a legitimacy crisis.

Political cultures, and their propensities for crises, are governed not just by political events alone but also by the general parameters of the polity—the conditions of the economy and society, the level of technology, the extent of communications, and the degree of isolation or awareness of other cultures. It is, of course, gross differences in many of these parametric considerations which account for some of the most significant differences between the character of the political cultures and hence some of the characteristics of the crises experienced by the early developing European political systems and the currently developing nations. In the first instance the European systems evolved under conditions of low technological advancement and thus the communities had little difficulty in realizing the political capabilities necessary to utilize the highest potentials of existing technology. Indeed for a time it appeared that advances in technology could be readily translated into greater political capabilities and thus people could feel that their political systems were "advancing" at a rate more or less consistent with general advances in knowledge. In contrast, among the late developing countries a constant source of frustration contributing to identity and legitimacy crises is the awareness that one's own society lacks the ability to mobilize effectively existing technologies and to achieve the levels of well-being and national strengths that exist in other societies.

The difference between early and late developers is also a distinction between intransitive and transitive processes, between innovating out of internal dynamic forces and responding to existing models. In the late developing countries purposive and conscious development has been at the forefront of at least elite if not mass awareness.

The fact that the late developing nations have had to react more to the existence if not to the precise models represented by the more developed states has also had the consequence of giving greater saliency to the political sector in these societies. This in turn has probably had the dual effect of giving greater urgency to the crises and of suggesting that in these cases development is directly related to some notion of the "capacity" of the system to deal with problems.

The distinction between early and late developers should not, however, be carried too far. Although English institutions were later to become the model for many African and Asian leaders in search of national development, it would be wrong to believe that the English themselves were insensitive to the possibility that history offered them models. Indeed, it is doubtful that England was ever so isolated as to lack models, for even before the 17th century Englishmen thought that they could and should draw on the Greeks, the Romans, and even Venice, imperial China, and the Old Testament. And even though the late developers such as Japan and Turkey have sensed the need to modernize rapidly because of the threatening nature of the international environment, it is true that the earliest developing states also had to react to their neighbors and the wider setting of politics. For example, King John was in part led to Magna Carta by his defeat in France, and the Civil War of 1642 broke out in part because the Irish rebellion demanded an army be raised at a time when the country did not trust the king enough to raise an army.

Possibly the main differences between early and late developers is that before 1700 models exerted a different pressure in that they were less psychologically threatening and seemed to be more tentative. In the 18th century a whole series of quite explicit constitutional models were elaborated but gradually these have been narrowed down as the European societies moved toward less ambiguous views of the essential qualities of a modern policy. At the same time, the international environment has probably become less physically threatening to weak states as we have moved into the postcolonial era. However, the psychic threat of not being able to keep up with international standards is probably more severe today and in domestic politics elites do tend to feel a greater need to convey a sense of national accomplishment in development if they are to preserve their power than did the elites of earlier periods.

In the majority of contemporary developing countries there is a gap between desired performance and actual action, between aspirations and the power to act, between words and deeds. In some situations this gap appears only because the vision of development has produced naïve and unrealistic aspirations. Presumably time itself will take care of such quasi-magical views of politics that assume that merely a restatement of the ultimate goals of the system can produce changes throughout the system. Therefore we need not concern ourselves unduly with such problems of development. Rather we should focus on the more complex problem of why so often even apparently rational and realistic goals of political and economic development seem to lie beyond the reach of aspiring leaders. Among the new states the most common pattern has been that, after a phase of euphoria and illusion, the real problems of development gradually assert themselves so that even the most soberly formulated plans for economic development seem to overtax the system, and the most sincere efforts at democratic reform fail to ignite the hoped-for responses in the citizenry.[3] This general problem of realizing a higher level of performance of the political system is usually associated with a large number of other problems of the political culture that in turn are related to those difficulties we have termed the identity and the legitimacy crises. The limited capabilities of developing political systems stem in the first instance from the incoherent character of their political culture.[4]

An almost universal feature of the political cultures of developing societies is the absence of a widely shared understanding as to what should be the generally expected limits and potentialities of political action. The erratic and unpredictable course of modern history, which has suddenly brought isolated colonial territories into world prominence, would be enough to confuse and dazzle anyone's judgment about the nature of political events. Change, however, has left deeper divisions among the people of most of these countries because widely different political socialization processes have produced inordinately sharp cleavages between the generations and among social classes.

In these countries, for example, many political activists learned about the potentialities of politics through the excitement of participating in nationalist movements, and hence they continue to believe that politics should be an intensely emotional activity, spurred on by the most dramatic, extreme, and even violent language. Others

---

[3] For a general analysis of the problems and frustrations of national development see: Rupert Emerson, *From Empire to Nation* (Cambridge: Harvard University Press, 1960); Samuel P. Huntington, *Political Order in Changing Societies* (New Haven: Yale University Press, 1968).

[4] For a detailed analysis of the relevance of the degree of coherence and integration of the political culture for political development see Sidney Verba, "Comparative Political Culture" in Pye and Verba, eds., *op.cit.*

in the same society, and of nearly the same generation, may have come to politics out of ambitions to be admitted to the security of careers in a colonial civil service, and their language of politics has been legal formulas and bureaucratic regulations. Still others may have an older outlook on politics, and, seeing it in more traditional terms, they tend to relate government with status, authority, and the inherent rights of rulers and potentates. In the same society others may think of politics as providing the main chance for personal advancement in which the rewards are great and effort minimal. For others, politics is a chance for public service and a means of nation building.[5]

The fact that people have not been systematically inducted into a coherent political culture through a common political socialization process means that personal expectations can easily be disappointed, particularly as the more powerful rudely impose their views on all others. Ambitious young Ugandians, trained at missionary schools and dreaming of modernizing their land in the spirit of contemporary times, suddenly discovered that successful politics demanded that they conform to archaic and abject forms of deference in yielding always to the authority of a feudalistic court and ruler, the Kabaka. Dedicated Filipino students consumed with democratic ideals have had to dampen their enthusiasms as they discover that in their elders' politics every *quid* must have its *quo*, and all depend upon a calculated bargaining process. And so it occurs in country after country: people are constantly being jarred by discovering that the ways they were taught to view the working of politics are not in line with reality. In some countries, as in Uganda, the frustrations became too great and the pressures for change brought an end to old authorities; more often the result is as in the Philippines, where the individual gradually learns to accept and accommodate to dated practices, but with declining commitment.

A second major problem of political cultures that typically tends to affect the capabilities of developing systems is uncertainty and confusion over what should be the persisting role of traditional values and concepts in changing societies. In discussing the social and economic aspect of development it is proper for theorists to postulate a

[5] For a more extended discussion of these different general approaches to politics, based upon the communication socialization processes typical of developing societies see Lucian W. Pye, ed., *Communications and Political Development* (Princeton: Princeton University Press, 1963) Chaps. 7, 8, and 9.

relatively direct relationship between the decline in traditional modes of behavior, such as reliance upon particularisms and functionally diffuse relationships, and an increase in more "modern" forms, such as universalistic standards and more functionally specific relationships. In politics, however, the problem is more complex because all political systems are deeply wedded to a particular place and time. The vital importance of the individuality of every polity means that its history is of enduring significance. Political systems cannot seek to advance by merely denying their past. Somehow or other they must seek to come to terms with what they once represented even as they take on new forms and new content. In all the ten national case studies reported in *Political Culture and Political Development* the problem of the relationship of tradition to change was a central theme.[6]

Another characteristic common to the political cultures of systems undergoing the stresses of development is a general tendency to overemphasize the value of words and ideologies and to discount pragmatic considerations. Frequently both leaders and followers anxiously cling to the optimistic and heroic world of slogans and pronouncements about the glorious future to be built rather than face honestly the frustrating problems of the moment. A lack of realism is also to be seen in the violent shifts of mood in which compulsive optimism gives way to bitter cynicism. Aggressive, but only verbal, attacks on the government and the contemporary leaders are frequently only another form of a common refusal to confront honestly immediate realities.[7]

In large measure this tendency to emphasize the ideological and symbolic aspects of politics stems from the fact that the political socialization process in changing societies is not geared to an ongoing contemporary political process but rather is focused on an undefined and as yet vague future. Nationalist politics before there is a nation can only gain sustained strength by playing upon people's hopes and dreams about a future in which there will in fact be a nation.

The dilemma is that the very process of nation building requires

[6] This is as true of the older systems of Europe as of the contemporary developing areas of Africa and Asia. See especially Richard Rose, "England: The Traditionally Modern Political Culture"; Sidney Verba, "Germany: The Remaking of Political Culture"; Joseph LaPalombara, "Italy: Fragmented, Isolated, and Alienated" in Pye and Verba, eds., *op.cit.*

[7] Aristide R. Zolberg, "The Structure of Political Conflict in the New States of Tropical Africa," *American Political Science Review*, 62 (March 1968), 70-87.

that people be trained to look forward to the realization of the developed nation; but the more the individual ties his own sense of political identity to a visionary world of the future, the less comfortable he is with operating in terms of the realities of the moment. Students in colonial settings were often exposed to textbook versions of democracy that gave them completely unrealistic concepts about the actual model of democratic politics, and after independence youth may still be exposed to the appeals of democratic ideals. Once such people discover, however, that conditions in their country do not measure up to their ideals, they do not have a solid and realistic identity to fall back upon. Thus, they are at a disadvantage in directing their energies toward transforming current conditions to be more in line with their ideals. They tend either to cling to the vocabulary of idealistic politics that first brought them a sense of identity, or they are inclined to strike out bitterly against those who they feel have denied them their sense of political identities.[8]

Another common problem of political cultures in the new states is the prevailing widespread uncertainty about how existing roles in the political system can be effectively utilized. Leaders who appear to have all the necessary authority and power frequently do not use even the readily available resources to further objectives they have set for themselves. Subordinate officials hesitate to assume initiative, and all who do not have official positions sense little responsibility for political matters even though they may appear to be influential members of the community.[9]

In many such cases the difficulty is that the feelings toward authority that are essential to the individual's sense of identity are not appropriate to the kind of authority required for a developing political system. The individual leader may feel that his personal dignity and status require that he adopt an aloof and reserved attitude when the requirements of leadership call for aggressive involvement. In seeking to confirm his ideal of self-identity he may undermine confidence in the efficacy of public authority. Confusion about individual

[8] Seymour Martin Lipset is engaged in a comparative study of the politics of youth in various developing countries, a preliminary report of which is contained in his "University Students and Politics in Underdeveloped Countries," *Minerva*, 3 (Autumn 1964), 15-56.

[9] S. N. Eisenstadt, "Breakdown of Modernization," *Economic Development and Cultural Change*, 12 (July 1964), 345-67; Ann Ruth Willner, "The Neotraditional Accommodation to Political Independence: The Case of Indonesia," in Lucian W. Pye, ed., *Cases in Comparative Politics: Asia* (Boston: Little, Brown, 1970).

identity can thus contribute to uncertainties about legitimacy, and within the political culture the identity problem of leaders can add to the intensity of a general legitimacy crisis.[10]

The prospect of reducing the gap between wish and performance usually depends upon the resolution of tensions or the institutionalization of more vivid patterns of behavior, and especially of authority within the political culture. This means clarifying both individual and collective feelings of identity and the establishment of more effective authority that will have all the potency of acknowledged legitimacy. Thus we come again to the problems of identity and legitimacy that seemingly are related to most of the problems of the political cultures of the developing countries. It is time to examine each crisis in greater detail.

The Identity Crisis

There are numerous ways of describing and defining the identity crisis in the developmental process. In many respects the concept deals with the sentiments of nationalism and the feelings of a people that they are bound together in common association. This sense of identity with a particular political system and a territorially defined community tends to be a sovereign sentiment in modern, stable societies, riding supreme over other subordinate sentiments of association with class or profession, region or locality. It would be possible to treat systematically many aspects of the identity crisis according to the terms and concepts customarily employed in studying the sociological, economic, cultural, and communications bases of nationalism.[11] By employing the term identity crisis, which is borrowed from psychology, we intend to indicate a need to expand our study of nationalism to include quite specifically the psychological dimensions of the individual's feeling toward membership in the polity.[12]

In the process of political development an identity crisis occurs when a community finds that what it had once unquestionably accepted as the physical and psychological definitions of its collective

[10] For a discussion of the role of Gandhi's personality in creating a stronger sense of Indian identity and authority see Lloyd I. Rudolph and Susanne Rudolph, *The Modernity of Tradition* (Chicago: University of Chicago Press, 1967).

[11] Much of the problem of nationalism and of what we mean by the identity crisis has been masterfully explored with the pioneering techniques of communications research by Karl W. Deutsch in *Nationalism and Social Communication* (Cambridge: M.I.T. Press; New York: John Wiley and Sons, 1953).

[12] For an excellent general discussion of nationalism in such terms see Dankwart A. Rustow, *A World of Nations* (Washington: Brookings Institution, 1967) Chap. II.

self are no longer acceptable under new historic conditions. In order for the political system to achieve a new level of performance, in terms of change whether in scope, intensity, or structural and procedural forms, it is necessary for the participants in the system to redefine who they are and how they are different from all other political or social systems. Historically, nations and communities can have profound traumatic experiences, as for example in war and national disaster, but such shaking events need not necessarily produce an identity crisis. On the other hand, such gradual and undramatic forces as the diffusion of world communications can shake a formerly isolated community's foundation of identity by making its people aware of a whole new universe of political action.[18] The identity crisis is thus a phase of growth that the political system must inevitably experience whenever its basic forms are substantially changed. It is a sign of growth and change, not of weakness or abnormality.

Historically, the Western impact on Asia and Africa was often violent in its initial stages, but such conflict did not always bring on identity crises. Such crises began only when people in new challenged societies felt that they were confronted not with merely another classical conflict with foreigners but with a significant turn in history that called for a re-evaluation of existing values and practice. It is thus the interpretations a society gives to its experiences that govern the extent to which it enters into an identity crisis. The introduction of colonial rule in much of Asia did not, for example, usually precipitate such a crisis; indeed, in much of colonial Southeast Asia the news of the victory of Japan over Russia in 1905 was far more dramatic in creating a new sense of self-awareness. The test is not the objective stress and strain that society is exposed to, but rather the experience of having to adopt a new framework for viewing the self and its relations with others.

FOUR TYPES OF IDENTITY CRISES

There are four fundamental forms of the identity crisis. The first relates to feelings about territory and the relationship of geographical space to nationalist sentiments. The second occurs when the social structure and particularly the class divisions are so great as to preclude effective national unity. The third involves the conflict between ethnic or other subnational identifications and commitments to a common national identity. The fourth form of identity crisis arises out

---

[18] Daniel Lerner, *The Passing of Traditional Societies* (Glencoe: Free Press, 1958).

of the psychological consequences of rapid social change and ambivalent feelings toward outsiders. This type of identity crisis generally takes the form of deeply mixed feelings about the modern world and one's own historical traditions.

The four are possible because people can divide over the ways in which they identify themselves toward place, class, ethnicity, and time or history. We have somewhat arbitrarily excluded from the category of identity crises breakdowns that occur from deep ideological divisions. Where the divisions occur out of basic beliefs and confessional identifications, such as with religious divisions, we can treat them as identity crises along the lines of ethnic or subnational conflicts. Where the ideology is more in the nature of political programs and orientations we shall treat them as contributing to one of the other appropriate crises. Ideological crisis over the structure of government would thus be part of a legitimacy crisis; ideological confrontations over the end goals of public policy that challenge the entire system would be either a distribution or a penetration crisis; ideological conflicts over who should be involved in the management of power would be a participation crisis.

In now examining the four basic types of identity crises we can only outline their main dimensions and suggest some of their complications. The full analysis of an identity crisis calls for the details that can only be achieved by a case study.

National Identity and Territory. In its most elementary form the issue of national identity involves an appreciation of the geographic boundaries of the nation and the acceptance by all within those boundaries that they share with each other a distinctive and common bond of ultimate association. In many of the new countries the identity crisis immediately became a problem because of the artificial nature of their physical boundaries.[14] In other situations the boundaries the colonial empires left behind were imprecise, and there had been little emotional attachment to them.[15] In time, however, a greater sense of national awareness is likely to transform imprecise boundaries into intensely felt boundary conflicts. In Southeast Asia, for example, every

[14] For a discussion of the nature of boundaries for the new states of Africa see R. J. Harrison Church, *Environment and Politics in West Africa* (Princeton: Van Nostrand, 1963).

[15] In the Sino-Indian border dispute, for example, the strong Indian emotional reaction only came with the Chinese defeat of the Indian army and not when it was first discovered that the Chinese were building roads in what the government of India had long considered Indian territory.

country has a potential boundary problem with one or more of its neighbors, and during the last decade there has been a steady increase in the frequency and intensity of territorial conflicts between states in the region.

Once the polity has been clearly related to a specific geographical territory, the identity crisis assumes the more complex form of establishing among a people first the knowledge and then the conviction that they as individuals belong to a polity and that the government is in a fundamental sense theirs. In many of the former colonial countries, and also in some of the older underdeveloped nations, large segments of the population have been uninformed about their national government. Evidence suggests that even today nearly half the people in northeastern Thailand have never heard of their king and do not know that they are ruled by a government in far-off Bangkok, and in rural Laos over 75 percent of the people do not know of the existence of their king.

Although in popular literature there has been some discussion of such concepts as the "territorial imperative" and speculation about an animal's instinctive feelings of identification with a particular territory, there has been little work in the social sciences to explain the importance of territory for politics.[16] Yet in all versions of patriotism there are expressions of deep felt ties to one's homeland. Associations with childhood haunts and memories of natural surroundings are apparently universally important in contributing to the most elementary feelings of national identity.

The significance of territory in the question of national identity involves more than just sentiment for physical or natural glories. A basic part of human politics is that it appears to routinely take on a geographical or special form and its boundaries tend to become territorial. Although at times political systems have been organized along blood or tribal lines, the tendency is generally toward the recognition of territorial units. In the modern world the concepts of sovereignty and territory are inexorably linked, and it is generally assumed that any land is controlled by someone, and that if a polity does not exert sovereignty over some territory, then another political system will.

This territorial basis of politics, which is self-evident, is, however, significant because it means that there is always a parochial element

---

[16] An exceptional study of the psychology of nationalism that does deal with the nature of human sentiments toward land is Leonard W. Doob, *Patriotism and Nationalism: Their Psychological Foundations* (New Haven: Yale University Press, 1964).

in political development which does not appear when we speak about economic or social development. Loyalty to a location is fundamental to modern politics, and while certain forms of social and economic modernization may seem to lead to ever more universalistic commitments this is not the pattern for political development. Instead the commitment to a territory and the fact that political identity begins with particular geographic considerations means that in political development there is always a strain between the need to cling to the parochial memories that go with territorial identifications and the need to adopt more universalistic sentiments.

Thus in a very fundamental sense the first step in the building of a polity involves the establishment of its territorial boundaries. An identity crisis based on territorial considerations can occur whenever the accidents of history cause the arbitrary definition of a new polity or when an old polity is given new boundaries. The crisis continues as long as significant elements of the population within that territory fail to recognize any association with the governing system or when majority elements of the system fail to accept territorially marginal populations as having the same claim of identification with the system as they have. As long as there are any fundamental doubts as to what land belongs to what governing community and what are the boundary limits of the collective territory of a community, then there is an identity crisis.

The resolution of such a territorial form of identity crisis generally calls for changes in the basic social and economic parameters of the system and the establishment of a more sophisticated technological infrastructure for bringing together all the outlying geographic territories. The improvement of communications, the building of roads, the expansion of the national economy into all the back areas, the spread of a national educational system, the symbolic presence of representatives of the national authority can all contribute to the resolution of this form of national identity crisis. Indeed, the underlying trend of technological advancement is possibly the most fundamental historical fact in reducing the prevalence of this form of the identity question.

Identity and Class. Social structure and more particularly class differences are a second source of national identity problems. Where the chasm between classes is so great that there is no sense of common interests a country does indeed become, as Disraeli said of 19th-century England, "two nations." It is noteworthy that in European national development the leading architects of nationalism such as Bismarck and Frederick the Great were highly sensitive to the need to ensure that the lower classes received some visible benefits from the new state in order to counter the divisive effects of class differences.

In spite of the importance that class has played in providing a basis for primary political identifications and in spite of the intensity of class conflicts in European history, there have in fact been singularly few identity crises based on the divisions of class. Aside from the dramatic cases of the French and Russian revolutions and possibly the Irish rebellion, the pull of class has failed to obstruct the ultimate growth of nationalism.

In the contemporary world it is possibly only in Latin and more particularly Central America that social structure can be clearly identified as the critical factor preventing the growth of a sense of cohesive national identity. In Africa, the Middle East, and Asia class distinctions either hardly exist or are more than compensated for by the ties of religion and tradition.

Thus instead of class differences providing a widespread cause of national identity problems, the historic paradox of nationalism has been that the very frustrations of class distinctions have more often provided a rich source for extreme expression of national fervor. In this sense class and social structure are factors influencing patterns of participation in national politics and not so much the causes of conflicting national identities.

Therefore it would seem that social structure and class divisions are much more relevant for the crises of participation and penetration and less the cause of deep problems of national identity. The exception would be those cases in which a national polity does not exist because the ruling oligarchy based on class factors prevents the masses of the people from having any sense of national identification. But even among oligarchical systems such practices are rare, for most such rulers are prepared to allow, if not encourage, all subjects to have some sense of national identification as long as the masses are denied effective participation.

National Identity and Ethnic Divisions. The third basic type of identity crisis occurs when a state cannot perform as a fully effective national unit because significant elements of the population hold higher allegiance to subnational groupings. This is the identity crisis that arises when the "state" functions of the "nation-state" cannot be satisfactorily carried out because they are not supported by a full sense of "nationhood."

The literature on European nationalism is rich with discussions of the nature of a "national community" and of the assumed right that all "nations" should have their "self-determination" in the form of their own "state." Indeed, the basic logic of the nation-state system is premised on the assumption that statehood is somehow related to nationhood. The identity problem arises when there is not a ready "fit" between the reach of the state and the sense of a community. The common problem, of course, has been with the clash between majority and minority groups and the difficulty of having all elements feel that the state belongs equally to everyone.

In Europe, regional and linguistic differences had to be overcome in the building of even those countries such as France and Britain that now seem to have exceedingly high levels of national consciousness. The recent emergence of Scottish nationalism, the tensions between the two parts of Belgium, and the serious eruption of Quebec separatism dramatize the possibility that even the most apparently stable of the "older" states can be threatened by recurring identity problems.

Elsewhere in Europe the principal problem of ethnicity and national identity has tended historically to appear most sharply with the end of empires and the struggle to establish new states (as occurred at the end of World War I). For Asia and Africa the same phenomenon of the end of empire came with World War II, and suddenly many of these societies discovered that they had acute ethnic divisions.

Yet it is significant that in the European effort to redraw the map there was a conscious awareness of the problem of minority peoples and the fact that the minority peoples also represent historic communities, while in Asia and Africa the more common assumption at the time of independence was that reaction to the previous rule had produced a form of nationalism that had made irrelevant questions of older ethnic and linguistic differences. The language of nationalism thus often obscured the fact that nationalist leaders were not seen by all the people in their countries as championing their interests, but rather the leaders were seen as representing only the interests of whatever ethnic or communal group to which they belonged.

There is no need here to list the large number of identity crises arising out of ethnic and communal differences that are currently plaguing political development in Africa and Asia. The continuing need to grapple with linguistic and communal differences has in some countries, such as possibly India, helped to strengthen a more general sense of national identity. In other countries the divisions in tribe and ethnic groups seem only to become deeper as the shared experience of colonial rule recedes in memories and the political struggle becomes more intense.

There are two basic ways in which identity crises based upon ethnic or subnational groups can be resolved: either by assimilation or by accommodation based upon some degree of mutual respect and tolerance.

Karl W. Deutsch has suggested six dynamic factors that appear to determine the rate of assimilation: degree of similarity of communication habits; the level of learning capacity on the one side and the teaching capacity on the other; the frequency of contacts; the material rewards and penalties; the values and desires of both groups; and finally the existence of any social and political symbols and actual barriers to assimilation.[17] On the basis of these considerations it would seem that relatively few of the identity crises in the currently developing world are likely to be resolved by assimilation.

Resolution by accommodation requires not only a degree of tolerance but a belief that the common support of nationhood is more beneficial to each group involved than is their separate and competitive existences. The troublesome question, of course, is always whether one group or another is paying too high or too low a price for membership. This is why the resolution of such an identity crisis generally requires the growth of feelings of "blind" loyalty to the total system so that people will not feel that they must constantly calculate benefit and loss from their mutual associations. The question of identity thus merges into the larger problem of loyalty and national pride. Political development cannot advance far without the growth of this profound sense of identification of the ruled with their rulers and with a system of rule. The need for such a development points to the ultimate limitation of colonialism as an agent of nation building; for although the most enlightened colonial administrations could perform all the other functions of a political system, foreign adminis-

---

[17] Karl W. Deutsch, *op.cit.*, pp. 130-36.

trators could never meet the test of inspiring commitment evocation, the function directly related to the sense of basic identification.[18]

The spirit of loyalty and the need for national identification rest in the last analysis upon a people's feelings for the uniqueness of their polity and for the dignity of their nation. Yet the developmental process inevitably raises issues with respect to precisely the matters of uniqueness and dignity. The challenge of cultural change, the demand that the old be rejected in favor of new ways, the connection between a heritage of foreign administration and the first steps of modern political development, and the need to incorporate minority elements who are manifestly less culturally advanced are all haunting problems that tend to undermine the necessary sense of pride and self-respect. The identity crisis thus focuses on some of the most explosive and emotion-laden issues in political development.[19] This brings us to the fourth form of identity crisis.

Identity Crisis and Social Change. The fourth basic form of identity crisis is peculiar to the contemporary world in that it depends upon rapid social change and a sharp awareness of gross differences in national power and well-being. This is the sense of identity crisis that undermines the confidence of new states as the leaders and the articulate publics are perplexed over how much of their old traditions they should seek to maintain and how much they should change in order to become a part of the new and modern world. Self-consciously leaders and intellectuals speak of their "rootlessness" and their need to find a national identity. The problem of self-awareness is compounded because of the gross differences between the "they" of the modern world and the "we" of the local community.

[18] The fact that the converse pattern of emotions, that of the colonial administrators feeling that they had ties of affection for their subjugated peoples, was so often possible, frequently made colonial governments feel that they were more positively accepted by subject peoples than in fact was the case. Indeed, one of the ironies and profound paradoxes of colonial rule in Asia was that many colonial administrators who developed the strongest attachment to their subjects and their indigenous cultures were insensitive to the limitations of their role in the ultimate political development of the colony. There was thus an element of personal tragedy in the careers of some of these officials who found it difficult to appreciate that in spite of their affection for their former subjects they could have no useful role in post-independence developments.

[19] For analyses of such problems of self-respect and group humiliation see O. Mannoni, *Prospero and Caliban* (New York: Praeger, 1956); Leonard W. Doob, *Becoming More Civilized* (New Haven: Yale University Press, 1960); John Plamenatz, *On Alien Rule and Self-Government* (London: Longmans, 1960); and Lucian W. Pye, *Politics, Personality and Nation Building* (New Haven: Yale University Press, 1962).

In the development of the older states of Europe there was little chance for this form of identity crisis; first, because social change was less abrupt and psychically stressful when the older nations were being formed, and second, because there was a less sharp sense of the psychically threatening differences between the "they" and the "we" among the different European communities since all shared to some degree a common heritage. The emergence of national differences occurred against the background of shared histories of having once been a part of classical and Roman civilization and later of Christendom. Thus, the balance between sentiments of distinction and similarity was one thing for Europeans as they saw the emergence of not only their separate states but a nation-state system and quite a different matter for Africans and Asians who must reconcile being parts of different civilizations as they try to combine in their individual and national identities elements of both their historical traditions and the modern world. Within Europe it was possible to follow the lead of others without raising deep questions about whether one was being a traitor to one's own heritage. Today the intellectuals in changing societies complain that they are "rootless," that they no longer have any connection with the wellsprings of their old civilization, and that since they are not a part of Western civilization they are not authentically of the modern world.[20] It is generally recognized that these feelings of rootlessness toward the past and ambivalence toward the future can assume many complex forms and affect behavior in a variety of ways. With respect to our concern with the problem of political development and the identity crisis, it is useful to distinguish three rather common ways in which transitional people tend to relate a sense of history to feelings of individual identity.[21]

The first of these involves those people who react to their present state of confusion by strongly orienting their historical outlook toward the past. They include people who tend to glorify the history of the country, particularly before it was exposed to the Western impact. Most of them would claim that there is an organic and somewhat

[20] For the classic analysis of this problem among Indian intellectuals see Edward Shils, "The Intellectual between Tradition and Modernity: The Indian Situation," *Comparative Studies in Society and History* (The Hague: Mouton, 1961) Supp. I.

[21] These three patterns are modifications of the three-way classification which Robert J. Lifton employed in analyzing the imagery of Japanese youth, see his "Individual Patterns in Historical Change: Imagery of Japanese Youth," *Comparative Studies in Society and History*, 6 (July 1964), 369-83.

mystical connection between themselves and the collective spirit that inspired their history and their culture. People with this orientation tend to be quite explicitly and openly concerned with matters of race, culture, and religion. They may be anxious about the vitality of the folk spirit. Above all, however, as fundamentalists they are concerned with the search for the authenticity of their own culture and their own history.[22]

If we explore the content of the vision of the past-oriented people, we tend to find that beneath their exhortations about the virtues of the past there is in fact a latent admiration for the modern world and for the contemporary traditions of science and development. This can be seen in the way in which they generally use contemporary standards of excellence in extolling the past. The universal practice is that of finding the present in their own history. Indians will speak of ancient village-based democracy, Africans talk of the greatness and glories of forgotten black empires, Chinese talk of an earlier age of invention and science, and Indonesians will claim that they once had a method of decision-making that was rational and democratic as well as soul-satisfying and effortless.

It would seem that for many of these people there is a psychological need to cleanse the new and to make it fully acceptable by first wrapping it in the trappings of the old. We should not conclude, however, that these are people who desire or even admire the modern world and who are merely trying to fool themselves or who lack the courage to admit that they must accept new ways. On the contrary, such people are in fact often intensely unhappy with the present. They find something disturbing both in the ways in which the modern world has been corrupted within their society and in the ways in which what remains of their old culture has been distorted.

A second reaction to the uncertainties of the contemporary world involves people who adopt a strongly futuristic orientation. These people tend to glorify a future that they believe lies beyond both the remnants of the old culture and the contemporary forms of Western civilization. Such people feel that it is going to be possible to create in the Afro-Asian world a new civilization that will be pure

---

[22] For a very sensitive analysis of these attitudes see J. R. Levenson, "History and Value: Tensions of Intellectual Choice in Modern China" in Arthur Wright, ed., *Studies in Chinese Thought* (Chicago: University of Chicago Press, 1953); and also, Mary Matossian, "Ideologies of Delayed Industrialization: Some Tensions and Ambiguities," in *Economic Development and Cultural Change*, 6 (April 1958), 217-28.

and more deserving of respect and reverence than anything that has been known in the past.[23] In the main these people tend to join radical movements and often feel that in Communism they have found a more modern and advanced way of social order than anything known in the Western world.[24]

The future-oriented reaction, like the past-oriented, reflects a feeling of contempt for the contemporary world and a need to seek an identity in terms of models and forms that are not immediately available within the culture. At the same time even the most intensely future-oriented people have a latent concern with the past and with the historic roots of their culture and race, for their interest is always in glorifying an "African" or an "Asian" or some other highly particularistic identity. The future must have its parochial associations and its ties with the past. The truth seems to be that many people who feel the need to relate themselves to a distant future are doing so because they find it hard to face squarely the history of their own recent past because it contains within it too many remembrances that are disturbing and repugnant. Their hope seems to be to look so far into the future that they can in fact recover the past and thus gain a new identity.[25]

The third and possibly most common orientation is one of focusing on the present and avoiding as much as possible all questions about the meaning of the past or the prospect for the future. People so oriented accept the fact that their lives must be filled with anachronism, and that there is much of the old and the new in their environment, and that both must somehow be incorporated into their daily life pattern. Those who look to the immediate present are usually able to see many virtues in both the modern world and the remnants of their traditional culture, and, up to a point, these present-oriented people are able to accommodate themselves to the contradictions and anachronisms inherent in transitional societies. When placed under stress, however, they are likely to cast about for a perspective on both their past and their future prospects and to grope for a deeper sense of identity.

[23] See the discussion of utopianism in John H. Kautsky, *Political Change in Underdeveloped Countries* (New York: John Wiley, 1963), Chaps. II and III.

[24] For a detailed discussion of the dynamics of this appeal of Communism among Chinese Malayans see Lucian W. Pye, *Guerrilla Communism in Malaya* (Princeton: Princeton University Press, 1964).

[25] For the uses of the part played by Ataturk see Dankwart A. Rustow, *op.cit.*, Chaps. I and V. See also Robert E. Ward and Dankwart A. Rustow, eds., *Political Modernization in Japan and Turkey* (Princeton: Princeton University Press, 1964).

Most of those who focus their lives on the present do so merely because their lives are full enough coping with day-to-day problems. There is usually also a need to keep themselves oriented to the present because of the humiliations of recent history. Throughout much of history colonialism was not seen as a particularly disgraceful relationship, but once independence has been gained, retrospective reflections tend to disturb a people's sense of self-esteem.

The easy acceptance of the early periods of colonial rule of "protection" is understandable because it was frankly seen as being based on dependency, which is a relatively comfortable and psychologically secure form of relationship. All humans must experience complete and protracted dependency, for it is the very mark of human-ness; and many of the most positive and long-enduring sentiments of men stem from the time of their acceptance of dependency. With development people have ambivalent feelings toward their sentiments related to dependency, and the search for individual identity inevitably involves an assertion for independence in which any continuing cravings for dependency must be veiled. In asserting independence an individual may in fact be giving only a new form of expression to his needs for dependency, for he may be primarily anxious to hold the continued esteem of his former protector, even as he attacks him. Thus as a colonial people become more and more like their rulers and as the gaps in cultural differences begin to disappear, the relationship of dependency gives way to feelings of being discriminated against and of being treated as inferiors.[26]

Those who are present-oriented tend to find it equally difficult to look to the future because of uncertainty over what they should make of the future and anxiety about how much command they have over their future. To modernize can often seem too much like merely trying to copy the ways of the people who once humiliated one's nation.[27] Anxieties can also arise over the possibilities of failure in carrying out the tasks of modernization. These fears of failure can be particularly disturbing because of latent anxieties over whether one's people may indeed be inferior and whether one's rulers do in fact have the ability to rule. In the struggle for independence it was possible for people to declare that they would rather be free and misruled by their own people than remain subjugated; but as time goes by, ineffectual government and incompetence can become in-

[26] For a psychologically perceptive appreciation of the changing dynamics of the colonial relationship see O. Mannoni, *op.cit.*

[27] Everett Hagen, *On the Theory of Social Change* (Homewood, Ill.: Dorsey Press, 1962), Chaps. 9 and 10.

creasingly embarrassing and psychologically disturbing. Thus the very objective of modernizing can be seen as a threat that may provide evidence that one's own people are different from if not inferior to those who are now the international elite.

The present-oriented reaction that tends to be the dominant one in most transitional societies thus includes people who find it difficult to look either too far into the past or who have deeply ambivalent feelings about the future. Basic to the outlook of these people is an anxiety about being absorbed by the West. With respect to this last feeling there can be a need to resist even friendly and helpful overtures. The result is often a diffuse sense of suspicion and uneasiness toward all foreigners.

In all three of these reactions—or patterns of orientation—we can note a fundamental paradox in which the past and the future tend to become mixed, and behind any explicit concern for the one there tends to be a latent feeling about the other. In trying to put together a sense of individual identity people may try to ignore parts of their past collective experience or to overlook much that makes up the contemporary world. But inevitably all the matters that would be kept out of mind tend to creep in, and at times even become unconsciously the dominant motive force guiding the collective behavior of the people. The result is a sense of ambivalence about the proper direction of development and confusion over the legitimate aspirations of the individual.

As long as individuals have profound uncertainties about the meaning of history it is difficult for them to band together to give their society a common sense of national identity. On the other hand, as individual leaders struggle to clarify their own personal feelings of identity they are likely to give expression to some of the deepest sentiments of a people who share many of the same problems of personal identity. If the leaders are successful in articulating for themselves satisfying new identities, they are also likely in the process to succeed in giving expression to new collective feelings of identity. There is thus an interacting process between the level of individual identity and that of national identity.[28]

Patterns in Resolving Identity Crises

Although in our discussion of the four general types of identity crises that revolve around orientations toward territory, class, ethni-

[28] For a statement of the psychological relations between the "great man" and the ideology of a people in crises see Erik H. Erikson, *Young Man Luther* (New

city, and time or social change we have mentioned the conditions that might be conducive to the resolution of each type of crisis, it should be apparent that precisely because identity involves the search for a sense of uniqueness, it is peculiarly difficult to arrive at any generalizations about the essential character of a resolved identity crisis. Much depends upon the particular issues in the crisis and the substantive character of the specific cultures involved. This does create some difficulty in relating identity crises to the other basic crises of development. The particular manner in which, say, an ethnically based identity crisis has been resolved may place major constraints on the possible approach to such other crises as the participation, penetration, or distribution crises. The national sense of unity may require that special considerations be given to a particular minority.

Since the resolution of the identity crisis is so fundamental to the very establishment of the nation in the first instance, it is usually a crisis that occurs early in the sequence of development crises. Also since the identity crisis deals above all with the issue of unity or national coherence, it is generally a matter that tests the national leadership. There are in fact a wide range of strategies available to national leaders in seeking to counter identity problems, ranging from heavy investments in educational systems to insure the desired socialization of the next generation to a variety of cultural, linguistic, and communication policies.

Instead of seeking to discuss the various possible strategies or the general consequences of various particular ways in which identity crises might be resolved, it may be more useful to focus our analysis upon the more general matter of the relationship of identity crises with different forms of elite political cultures. Thus instead of treating specific strategies or particularistic features of identity problems, we can arrive at a level of generalization that will be more useful in relating our analysis to the other crises if we employ a somewhat more general typology of elite orientations toward problems of national unity and disunity.

IDENTITY CRISIS WITH AN EXPANDING ELITE CULTURE

We may begin our survey by noting the situation that exists when an elite political culture is prepared to share its standards and norms

York: W. W. Norton, 1958); and Lucian W. Pye, "Personal Identity and Political Ideology," in Dwaine Marvick, ed., *Political Decision Makers* (New York: Free Press, 1962).

with the mass culture and when the elite insists that all members of the polity can have a meaningful place within the system if they accept the essential spirit of the elite culture. Historically we can see that in many European countries and in the United States it was precisely the resolution of the national identity crisis on these terms that made it possible at a somewhat later date to resolve the problem of the participation crises in a relatively orderly fashion. If the elite can set a clear model of the essential spirit of politics for the entire society, then, as new groups are brought into politics, there can be a process of coherent induction that will strengthen rather than weaken the polity. The participation crises will thus become not a threat to the system but actually a stage of reinforcing the bases of the nation.

This is possibly the sequence that occurred in the Anglo-Saxon pattern of nation building. In England, well before the Reform Bills and the expansion of suffrage, the political class had established standards of governmental performance and of citizenship conduct that left no room for ambiguity over what constituted proper conduct for Englishmen in public affairs. The sequence of power moving from the aristocracy to the mercantile class to laboring groups and on to the technocratic and managerial classes has been relatively smooth in England precisely because the identity crises that might have been serious at each stage were resolved by the existing elite culture providing room for the new class if the latter in turn accommodated to the essential spirit of the dominant political culture.[29]

In the United States the pattern has been similar, with each new immigrant community being accepted into the total system once it had accepted in turn its obligation to become "Americanized." The important point was that each minority group could appeal to the standards inherent in the dominant culture in order to gain protection and a place in the system. A closer historical analysis of why this process worked more successfully in some American communities than in others might yield many insights of high relevance for the problem of newly emerging countries confronted with the need to resolve identity crises while also increasing participation. There has, for example, been a significant difference between New York City, where a multitude of separate ethnic communities have all sought in varying degrees to accommodate themselves to the dominant

[29] Richard Rose, *Politics in England* (Boston: Little, Brown, 1964), Chaps. II-IV and XI.

American culture, and Boston, where there was a much more bipolar confrontation between Yankee and Irish.[30]

Turning to the contemporary developing world, it appears that two of the most successful countries, Japan and Turkey, experienced identity crises under this particular condition. In Japan the alliance of lower samurai, outside daimyos, and chonen or merchants who supported the Meiji Restoration were not motivated by democratic or equalitarian sentiments; yet the leaders did seek early to establish a sense of national mystique that embraced all Japanese. For example, the code of the samurai, once the possession of a small elite class, was translated into the spirit of Bushido that was applicable to all Japanese. As the leadership set about devising new institutions of government, drawing up new laws, and promulgating a new constitution, it also asked the population as a whole to enter into a common effort to modernize Japanese society. Starting with a more ethnically homogeneous population than most transitional societies, but a society that had been sharply divided by feudal classes and categories, the Japanese leadership was able to create remarkably common bonds at a relatively early stage of the modernization process. Of course the Japanese were not spared the fundamental issue of how to relate their own traditions to modern and foreign ways that is a part of the identity crisis of all late modernizing societies; but the fact that they were able to work out early the problem of the relationship of elite and mass political cultures meant that their society could confront the issues of further changes in identity as a result of foreign influence on a relatively united basis. Thus all elements of Japanese society, both leaders and followers, could share the same anxieties of inferiority, the same feeling of having to catch up with the West while protecting essential old values. The expansionist character of the Japanese elite culture in finding a respectable place for the mass culture in the national identity ensured that Japan would not be faced with a crisis of internal relationships while also trying to cope with the crises caused by foreign pressures.[31]

The story of Ataturk's remarkable efforts to initiate and guide

---

[30] Cf. the analysis of the manner and degree of integration of various immigrant groups into American society in New York in Nathan Glazer and David P. Moynihan, *Beyond the Melting Pot* (Cambridge: M.I.T. and Harvard University Presses, 1963).

[31] See Robert E. Ward, "Political Modernization and Political Culture in Japan," *World Politics*, 15 (1963), 569-96; Marius B. Jansen, *Sakamoto Ryoma and Meiji Restoration* (Princeton: Princeton University Press, 1961).

rapid political development can also be seen as primarily directed toward establishing an elite culture that would share its standards with the mass culture if the latter developed certain characteristics. It was not just a case of rulers seeking to make the masses change their ways—a practice as old as politics—but rather with Ataturk the elite had first to change its ways before it could ask the population to follow practices consistent with the inherent standards of the new elite culture. For example, before asking the people to adopt a more secular outlook on social and political life the government itself had to accept the proposition that its authority was only secularly based, and thus elite and mass could seek together a new basis for national identity in terms of more secular orientation.[32]

Another example of a transitional society able to resolve fairly satisfactorily its identity crises because of the openness of its elite culture is the Philippines. Although there is much in Philippine culture and social stratification that supports hierarchical relationships and inequality, yet the basic elite political culture is highly democratic and responsible to the pragmatic spirit of competitive popular politics.[33] Many people might also classify India in this group, while others might feel, with Weiner, that the Indian elite culture does not as yet contain the standards that in the future will be basic to the Indian sense of identity, and that the Indian mass political culture may in time prove to hold the ingredients of what will be the dominant political culture.

IDENTITY CRISIS WITH AN EXCLUSIVE ELITE CULTURE

A second category of identity crises involves those societies in which the elite political culture seeks to provide a common basis of national identity, but specific features of this culture tend to exclude significant elements of the population, leaving them uncertain as to their proper place within the nation. The minority elements may not be formally or organizationally excluded from political involvement, but a sense of national identity is being created without regard to the sensitiveness of minority culture. The national leadership may be sincerely anxious to provide a solution to the nation's identity crisis, but in its efforts to form and maintain an elite political culture it can be seen as

[32] For more detailed comparisons of the similarities and differences in the Japanese and Turkish experiences see Robert E. Ward and Dankwart A. Rustow, eds., *Turkey and Japan: A Comparative Study of Modernization* (Princeton: Princeton University Press, 1964).

[33] See Thelma Jean Grossholtz, *The Philippine Political System* (Boston: Little, Brown, 1964).

threatening the security of particular subgroups. Thus these groups may feel that their identities are being challenged while at the same time they are not being given a reasonable alternative national identity.

This particular type of identity crisis is most commonly associated with countries with a significant number of minority ethnic groups, and where the dominant ethnic group in shaping the elite political culture feels it necessary for the sake of national unity to restrain, disable, and even threaten the continued existence of the minority communities. For example, in Burma the national leadership has sought to create a sense of Burmese nationhood, but the various minority groups consisting of the Shans, Karens, Chins, and Kachins have all felt that Burmese identity based on the elite political culture is in fact only the political expression of Burmese Buddhist culture. These minority groups tend to feel that they are being asked to give up more in terms of their separate traditional identities than they are likely to gain in return by accepting the new national Burmese identity. There is also, moreover, a feeling that the elite political culture has so defined the new national identity that it will permanently favor the dominant community and handicap all minority peoples.[34]

In some cases the differences between the dominant community shaping the elite political culture and the minority communities may be extremely subtle and not related to conspicuous ethnic characteristics. This type of identity crisis seems to exist in Indonesia to the extent that the elite culture is seen as favoring the Javanese in preference to all other communities. In Vietnam there has been danger that a similar form of crisis may develop between the Catholics in positions of influence and the Buddhist leaders seeking influence.

We should note that in some cases the elite's efforts to find a stronger common bond with parts of the mass of the population can create precisely this form of an identity crisis for other elements of the society. The effort in Pakistan, for example, to establish an "Islamic state," has unquestionably raised the problem for all non-Moslems in the country.

IDENTITY CRISES WITH A CLOSED ELITE

Our discussion now logically leads to a consideration of identity crises in countries in which the elite political culture explicitly sug-

[34] On the problem of the minorities in Burma see Hugh Tinker, *The Union of Burma* (Oxford: Oxford University Press, 1957); G. Fairbairn, "Some Minority

gests that there should be two basic identities in the nation; one that is related to the elite culture, and the other with a mass culture. This is similar to the pattern in many traditional societies in which the population was expected to follow their limiting customs and the leaders were born to their positions. In some of the transitional societies there may be many members of the elite culture who still retain such traditionalist views, but it seems that the only countries explicitly advancing such an outlook while also striving for greater modernization and development are the racially divided countries such as South Africa and Rhodesia.

Except for these extreme situations there is little relationship between this form of identity crisis and political development. In some countries in which there is a modernizing oligarchy dominating the elite culture, the initial efforts at stimulating development may be coupled with an attempt to prevent expanded participation in the society and hence an effort to create two separate senses of identity. This situation can occur in countries such as Ethiopia, in which there is a powerful and widespread respect for hierarchy and a belief in the divine and just bases of a ruling house and a nobility.[35] In most transitional societies, however, if the leadership has any success in advancing development, the elite culture will have to make some accommodations to the mass, and hence the identity crisis is likely to change at an early stage to conform to the pattern we have discussed above as occurring with a restrictive elite culture.

IDENTITY CRISES WITH A PAROCHIAL ELITE CULTURE

As an aftermath of nationalist revolution there can be a serious form of identity crisis in which the elite culture aggressively upholds many parochial and traditionalist values while minority elements in the society may feel that they are more modernized and more a part of the developed world. The elite may explicitly champion political and economic development goals but reject the leadership of those most appropriately trained and skilled for carrying out development on the grounds that they are too "Westernized" and no longer reflect

---

Problems in Burma," *Far Eastern Survey*, 28, 97-105; J. Silberstein, "Politics in the Shan State: The Question of Succession from the Union of Burma," *The Journal of Asian Studies*, 18, 43-48.

[35] Donald Levin has employed considerable anthropological data to demonstrate that the Ethiopian attitudes toward authority have helped to preserve the historic identity of the country but are at present impeding modernization. See "Ethiopian Political Culture, Source of Stability and Impediment to Development," in Pye and Verba, *op.cit.*

the values of the people. This is the form of identity crisis that occurs when the demands for equality are given complete precedence over the requirements for capacity.

There is no doubt that appeals to parochial sentiments can generate great force, and in many of the identity crises the problem is precisely that the elite can no longer effectively appeal to such basic sentiments. On the other hand, if stressing parochial values results in a conspicuous decline in capacity that will in turn affect the performance of critical functions, then almost certainly national self-confidence will decline. This is the form of crisis that nearly caused a serious breakdown in the political system of Ceylon. The problem was not just that the Sinhalese-Buddhist leaders arbitrarily pushed aside the talents of more Westernized communities and the potential loyalties of the Tamils, but that the continued frustration of economic development created deep and lasting feelings of aggressive inferiority on the part of the Sinhalese majority. To the extent that this elite culture lost its ability to represent itself as an acceptable model for the entire country, the responsibility for development was shifted to another leadership group.[36]

The example of Ceylon during the years before the change in leadership in 1964 stands out because it contrasts so sharply with those ex-colonial countries in which the dominant elite comes generally from the better-educated and more Westernized classes. The elite political culture of Nehru's India, for example, represented the most Westernized segment of the country, and the same situation is found in most of the ex-colonial countries of Africa. Indeed, in the main, identity crises based on an excessively parochial elite have been associated largely with countries that have not experienced colonialism. In Nationalist China, for example, the political class has been generally less exposed to cosmopolitan ways than most of the other elites in the society. Chiang Kai-shek and his most intimate associates do not speak any foreign languages, and their wives tend to be more parochially traditional than the leaders of nongovernmental segments of Chinese society. Although the politics of pre-Communist China has generally been discussed in terms of such categories as conservative and liberal, authoritarian and democratic, it is possibly more useful to recognize that the alienation of many critical sectors of Chinese society stemmed

[36] For an excellent analysis of these troubles in the Ceylonese political culture see Howard Wriggins, *Ceylon: Dilemma of a New Nation* (Princeton: Princeton University Press, 1961).

largely from the fact that they viewed their political leaders as excessively parochial.[37]

It should be observed that in many ex-colonial countries the emergence of a parochial elite culture has occurred without a transfer in power from one group of leaders to another. This has been the pattern when a nationalist leadership has become frustrated with its initial efforts at establishing Westernized institutions. Thus, for example, in the early years of his rule U Nu sought to champion strong modernizing and even secularizing programs of development, but as Burma experienced mounting difficulties he increasingly sought to identify his leadership with traditionalistic sentiments.[38] It was possible to observe much the same trend in Indonesian politics when Sukarno, before falling from power, gradually abandoned his earlier version of Westernized socialism in favor of more traditional practices and slogans. The fundamental contradictions inherent in the clash of old and new readily cause governments to vacillate between the extremes of aggressively seeking modernization and of articulating parochial sentiments. It is questionable whether the emergence of a parochial elite culture can provide enduring stability. Retreats into parochialism can only be temporary resting stages, for the pressures of the modern world cannot be that easily denied.

IDENTITY CRISIS WITH A SYNTHETIC ELITE CULTURE

An extreme form of identity crisis is found in ex-colonial countries without a dominant culture that is the normal way of life of a particular group or community. In these countries the ideal of the state is not reflected in the norms and practices of particular people but only lingers in the traditions of the past colonial rulers. Therefore the need is to create a synthetic elite culture that rests heavily upon the institutions introduced through foreign rule, but that must somehow be accepted as expressing a legitimate form of nationalism. This type of identity crisis occurs most frequently when the society is divided among a variety of ethnic or communal groups and, although one community may have dominant political influence, it cannot claim to be the expression of the national ideal without creating profound

[37] For an analysis of republican China which clearly demonstrates the dominant role of the more parochial and less cosmopolitan segments of Chinese society see Paul M. A. Linebarger, *The Government in Republican China* (New York: McGraw-Hill, 1939); and Ch'ien Tuan-sheng, *The Government and Politics of China* (Cambridge: Harvard University Press, 1950).

[38] Cf. Richard A. Butwell, *U Nu of Burma* (Stanford: Stanford University Press, 1963).

unrest and outright opposition of all the other groups, who together may constitute a majority of the total population.

Malaysia provides possibly the best example of this type of an identity crisis. The dominant political culture represents a continuation of the traditions of British Malaya in which the Malays had a special role. The national identity must ultimately depend upon an awareness of Malayan citizenship that is not Malay, Chinese, or Indian, but an amalgam of the ideals of British rule and Malayan tradition. Whether Malaysia will be able to resolve its identity problem is as much a matter of Malays realizing that the political culture of the country cannot be just an expression of their own particular ethnic culture as it is of the Chinese accepting the need to take on a new basic identity in their adopted country.

So far the Federation of Malaysia has been able to cope with development problems, in part, for the paradoxical reason that all communities have been sensitive to the problem of identity and of the dangers of communal divisiveness. Thus some leaders of all groups have been willing to avoid being excessively provocative in pressing their particular ethnic interests. The Malaysians, in short, cannot pretend that they do not have an identity problem, and they have generally been forced to be more realistic and less given to illusions than many other developing countries. This delicate situation of conspicuously divided communal groups has thus in an odd fashion helped to make Malaysia for at least the first decade of independence one of the more successfully developing countries in Southeast Asia. Yet this balance has been a most delicate one, as revealed first in the divorce between Singapore and the Federation and second in the outbreaks of social violence after the elections of 1969.

The synthetic nature of their elite cultures confronts countries in this category with the constant danger of fragmentation and severe internal tensions. In spite of such manifest liabilities they do, however, have the compensating advantages of being able to build upon the fundamental truth that political development must inevitably call for the creation of a new sense of identity that must in large measure be a synthetic product of contemporary history.

IDENTITY CRISES WITHOUT A MODEL ELITE CULTURE

The most extreme form of identity crisis arises when a new nation has no active elite culture and the people are unresolved as to who should set the standards for the country. This is the identity crisis common to former colonial countries that lacked a traditional culture for the whole country and in which the colonial experience failed to produce a satisfactory elite culture. Most often these are countries that were arbitrarily created by the decisions of Europeans, who drew boundaries with little regard to the locations of tribal and community grouping. At the moment the former Belgian Congo presents the most dramatic example of such an identity crisis.

The significance of this kind of identity crisis is that it helps to emphasize the degree to which national identity springs from a fundamental awareness that territory is the ultimate defining basis for the concept of community. Other forms of identity can be associated with biological lineage and cultural associations; but national identity must include a sense of boundary and geography. The importance of geographical boundaries for building a sense of national identity can be seen from the fact that, although many of the boundaries in Africa, the Middle East, and even in Southeast Asia were the arbitrary products of colonialism, there has been remarkably little readiness on the part of any of the new nationalist leaders to make adjustments in boundaries. What was once arbitrary and trivial quickly becomes fundamental and vital.[39]

Leadership and Competence

Our analysis has clearly illuminated the crucial role of leadership in resolving identity problems and creating the basis for national unity. Demonstrations of competency and effectiveness in any number of governmental functions can give the sense of pride and self-respect necessary for building an adequate feeling of national identity. Governments that just talk about the problem of identity, such as Sukarno's did in Indonesia, cannot solve their main problems; they must get on with the practical problems of raising the level of performance of their political systems.

In this respect the problem of identity for political systems is much the same as that for the individual, for, as Erikson has pointed out, the crisis of identity in the development of a personality is likely to be resolved only as the individual develops some skill, some dexterity in the command of a tool, some demonstration of regular competence in task-oriented enterprises.[40] In the case of the political system,

[39] For an interesting general discussion of the role of boundaries in nation building see Stephen B. Jones, "Boundary Concepts in the Setting of Place and Time," *Association of American Geographers Annals*, 49 (September 1959), 241-55.

[40] Erik H. Erikson, *Young Man Luther* (New York: Norton, 1958).

people can come to have a sense of strong identification with their particular national system only when it functions in a reasonably distinctive and gratifying manner. The people may come to develop a greater sense of national identity as they observe the responsiveness of their political system to the articulation of interests, and a sense of competency in their leaders' ability to aggregate these interests into just and acceptable public polities. Or they may find that merely out of the effective maintenance of order can come a sense of local pride, and the effective mobilization and allocation of resources for even modest and unambitious enterprises can set the stage for positive and enduring identification with the system.

In speaking of the vital importance of leadership in raising the level of performance we are alluding to the critical place of authority in politics and of the crises of legitimacy in national development. If leaders are to inspire a population and to direct a society to higher levels of performance, their words and actions must carry an aura of legitimacy. If a people are to gain satisfaction from the ways in which their polity performs, they must first accept as right and proper that the inherent functions of the political system can and must be performed in new ways. In short, if a polity is to resolve its identity crises through more effective governmental performance and a rise in political capabilities, it must also resolve any issues of legitimacy.

With this close relationship between these two crises of the political culture in mind, let us turn to an examination of the legitimacy crisis.

CHAPTER 4

The Legitimacy Crisis

LUCIAN W. PYE

WE HAVE NOTED that the problems of identity and legitimacy are closely related and in many respects overlap. In stable systems the basic political socialization process that gives a people a sense of identity also provides a recognition of the legitimate scope of all forms of acceptable authority in the system. Conversely a people may, through coming to accept the legitimacy of particular structures and authorities, develop a sense of their national identity.

There is, however, a clear distinction between the identity and legitimacy crises. A people may have an unambiguous sense of their unique identity as a national community but lack agreement over what should be the proper and accepted division of authority among various political structures capable of wielding power. There is, above all, the need in all political systems to specify what particular structures shall be considered to be the authoritative ones and what are to be the supporting political ones.

Thus the satisfactory resolution of the identity crisis may not involve the settling of the legitimacy crisis. Often in the developmental process we find that after a people have achieved a greater sense of common identity the resulting spirit of greater equality may leave them less prepared to accept the apparently arbitrary distinctions associated with those claiming authority. This possibility points to the fact that the legitimacy crisis is peculiarly linked to the stresses between equality and capacity in the developmental syndrome. Since legitimacy is an attribute of the political system, it is associated particularly with the performance of the governmental structure, and, hence, it is fundamental in determining the capacity of the system. On the other hand, the acknowledgment of legitimacy resides with the people, and it is only likely to be given when those in authority seem to appreciate the principles of equality and accept distinctions as being only the realities of appropriate forms of differentiation. Thus all advances in the developmental syndrome, with any concomitant changes in the relationships among equality, capacity, and differentiation, are likely to produce reactions that affect legitimacy and can bring on a major crisis.

The fact that legitimacy involves both the performance capacity of the system and the sentiments of the population toward governmental authority means that any one of the other crises whether of identity, participation, penetration, or distribution, can ultimately culminate in a problem of legitimacy, for in a sense all crises raise questions about legitimacy. Analytically, however, we can distinguish between other crises that inevitably raise some question of legitimacy and a situation in which there is a fundamental crisis about the bases of legitimacy of authority. In the former cases the issues are clearly defined by the nature of the particular crisis, and the matter of legitimacy comes into play only to the extent that all forms of institutionalized behavior involve some mystique of legitimacy. In a genuine legitimacy crisis the challenge is to the basic constitutional dimensions of the system and to the most generalized claims of leadership of those in authority.

In this analysis we shall therefore define a legitimacy crisis as a breakdown in the constitutional structure and performance of government that arises out of differences over the proper nature of authority for the system. A legitimacy crisis can thus take the form of a change in the fundamental structure or character of a government, a change in the source from which it claims to derive its ultimate authority, or a change in the ideals it professes to represent. Basic to a legitimacy crisis is a change in the way in which governmental authority is conceived or itself acts.

If, for example, a monarchy were replaced by a republic but there was no substantial change in class or popular participation, the event, if accompanied by tension and a sense of crisis, would be a legitimacy crisis. If, however, the change was primarily inspired by popular demands for broadening the basis of government, the event would more likely be a participation crisis. The Russian, Chinese, and French revolutions all changed the basis of legitimacy in their respective countries but none were legitimacy crises as defined here because all were more centrally crises of participation and distribution. Some interpretations of the American revolution would make it essentially a legitimacy crisis, while other interpretations would make it too a participation and distribution crisis.

In the contemporary world most coups d'etat are examples of legitimacy crises for they represent the replacement of civilian rule with military rule in order to achieve a new and greater sense of authority in the system with little or no change with respect to identity, participation, penetration, or distribution. The fall of such charismatic leaders as Sukarno, Nkrumah, and U Nu and their replacement by military governments represented primarily the collapse of one form of authority and a desperate effort to establish a new one. According to some analyses the overthrow of King Farouk and the final establishment of the Nasser regime involved an effort to create the impression that a participation and a distribution crisis had occurred while in fact the change was limited primarily to an alteration in the nature of governmental authority and hence it was a legitimacy crisis.

Precisely because all government and politics involve questions of legitimacy and authority, it is necessary to stress the limits to our definition of a legitimacy crisis. As we have noted, all the other crises do ultimately pose problems of legitimacy and therefore we must limit our concept of a legitimacy crisis to a breakdown in the constitutional basis of government. We should, however, also note that when a system has a peculiarly strong sense of legitimacy and authority it may be able to avoid the other crises. Thus a dramatic resolution of a legitimacy crisis can set the stage for a society to be spared, for a time at least, the other crises.

The fact that the basic question of legitimacy and the more limited concept of a legitimacy crisis stand in such close association with the other crises is important for our theory of both political systems and the sequence of crises. With respect to conceptualizing the political system in general, it is apparent that the question of legitimacy is closely linked to all the other crises because the resolution of each does in part contribute to the building of government. The question of identity is one of providing the basic sense of unity for the nation and of, in a sense, filling the physical space with a coherent society, and thus of creating the foundations for supporting the governmental structure which in turn becomes the basic mechanism for converting the consequences of "participation" into the output of "distribution" and which expands its own capacity through greater "penetration."

With respect to the sequence of crises, the questions of the creation and maintenance of the basic institutions of government are directly affected by the outcome or the onset of the other crises. On the other hand, well established and firmly institutionalized structures and processes of government can greatly reduce and even completely overcome the strains that might arise from situations of potential crisis in the other areas of nation building.

The Causes of Legitimacy Crises

The basic cause of the legitimacy crisis is the fact that the development syndrome always produces a widening of perception on the part of ever larger numbers of people and therefore an increase in sensitivities about the possibilities of alternative ways of doing things in all phases of life. Psychologically, the development process is thus a broadening one in which people steadily learn that there are fewer and fewer absolute limits of life. Awareness of alternatives suggests the need for choice, and choice calls for standards for measuring efficiency. The appreciation of alternatives is thus the starting point of rationality and the beginning point of the search for secular standards of authority. What we are suggesting is that Max Weber's distinction between traditional authority and rational-legal authority[1] involves far more than just a difference in style and spirit, and that it rests in the last analysis upon the degree to which the people perceive the possibility for alternative courses of actions.

More specifically we can identify four principal causes or sources of legitimacy crises in the development process. First, there is the breakdown of governmental institutions that occurs because of conflicting or inadequate bases for claiming authority in the society. Second, governmental structures may disintegrate because there is excessive and uninstitutionalized competition for power. Third, national leaders and the governmental divisions of authority may collapse because the justifications for their ideological or pragmatic claims to authority have been based on unacceptable readings of history or faulty predictions of future developments. Finally, and probably most basically, a legitimacy crisis may arise because people have been inappropriately socialized and their feelings about authority are not functional for the efforts of the current leaders.

CONFLICTING OR INADEQUATE BASIS FOR AUTHORITY

The historically most straightforward type of legitimacy crises occur when governmental leaders, often faced with a critical need for

[1] Max Weber, *The Theory of Social and Economic Organization*, trans. A. M. Henderson and Talcott Parsons (New York: Oxford University Press, 1947).

greater state power and capacity, are unable to find a popularly acceptable rationale for an expanded authority or they discover that the assertion of claims for the legitimacy of new state authorities conflict with other authorities in the society.

In the case of the development of European states the most common form of legitimacy crisis arose from the need to overcome other forms of authority. Thus, for example, the typical legitimacy crisis in Europe involved a clash of church-state relations. Secular state authority had to compete against religious, parochial, and other forms of institutionalized authority in societies in which the erosion of authority that is related to industrialization and social modernization had not as yet disrupted the more traditional bonds of society.

In contemporary developing countries legitimacy crises are more commonly related to the inadequacy of any form of authority in the society rather than a problem of entrenched nongovernmental authority. It is true in some Latin American countries the social positions of the oligarchy and less so that of the church has prevented the institutional development of the state. Also in a few areas religious and tribal authorities have clashed directly with the authority of the state. In the main, however, in Africa and Asia the old forms of authority have lost their basis for effectively structuring life, and the state finds that rather than having to compete explicitly with other authorities it cannot even find enough substance in the old myths of authority to help build its own sense of authority.

Indeed, the general historical trend seems to be in the direction of creating ever more wide-spread authority crises in all societies. This of course is because the spread of both differentiations, as the result of greater specialization and division of labor, and equality, as the result of communication and ideological development, has eroded the claims of all manner of authorities.

Where the legitimacy crisis arises from a conflicting basis of authority the most effective outcome calls for the drawing together of a new secular form of state authority based upon law. As Samuel P. Huntington has observed, "First, political modernization involves the rationalization of authority, the replacement of a large number of traditional, religious, familial, and ethnic political authority. This change implies that government is the product of man, not of nature or of God, and that a well-ordered society must have a determinate human source of final authority, obedience to whose positive law takes precedence over other obligations."[2] Huntington goes on to make the point that in traditional societies man felt "impotent before nature and assumed that their obligation was to discover and comply with fundamental law."[3] As Weber first observed, the very essence of traditional authority was the acceptance of an unchanging and unchangeable law that stood above all human institutions, and that the legal authority of a modern nation was based in a sense on the legitimacy of men applying intelligence to the changing and the improvement of laws. Huntington, in elaborating upon Weber's ideal types of authority, notes that in medieval Europe "Law was variously defined in terms of divine law, natural law, the law of reason, common law, and custom,"[4] but that, as modernization began in the 16th century on the continent and the 17th century in England, there arose the need for a new concept of authority that took the form of the "simple idea of sovereignty itself," which in turn was expressed in the doctrine of the divine right of kings and in the concept that there was a living authority which could change, even arbitrarily, the laws of the land. Thus, by opening men's perceptions to the possibility of change and the manipulation of the political environment, the age of absolutism did serve an elementary function in starting Europe on the road to modernization. The doctrines of divine right, sovereignty, and supremacy of the state "helped political modernization by legitimizing the concentration of authority and the breakdown of the medieval pluralistic political order. They were the seventeenth century counterparts of the theories of party supremacy and national sovereignty that are today employed to break down the authority of traditional, local, tribal, and religious bodies."[5]

Modernization, however, calls for more than just the building of state authority and the weakening of parochial bonds; it also requires that there be a substantial rise in the total level of power in the system.[6] It is noteworthy that in Western political thought little attention has been paid to the concept of absolute levels or amounts of power in a system. Instead the focus has been upon making power into a relative concept in terms of particular relationships, and upon the

[2] Samuel P. Huntington, *Political Order in Changing Societies* (New Haven: Yale University Press, 1968), p. 34.

[3] *Ibid.*, p. 99.　　　　[4] *Ibid.*　　　　[5] *Ibid.*, p. 102.

[6] For a discussion of the concept of levels of power in political development, see Frederick W. Frey, *The Turkish Political Elite* (Cambridge: M.I.T. Press, 1965), Chap. 13 and especially pp. 406-19; and "Political Development, Power and Communications in Turkey," in Lucian W. Pye, ed., *Communications and Political Development* (Princeton: Princeton University Press, 1963), pp. 298-305.

question of the distribution of power in a system. It is true that Carl J. Friedrich in beginning his classic analysis of authority observed that before there can be checks and balances on power in a state there must be power to be divided.[7] Before there can be a question of legitimacy and authority there must be the realities of power; and the sorrow of many developing countries is that they have no institutions capable of directing and managing all the tasks that must be accomplished if these countries are to achieve their goals of modernization.

Thus in a fundamental sense the legitimacy crisis in the contemporary developing areas has tended to be an authority crisis that reflects an underlying impotence. National leaders with great responsibilities do not have an easy command of power, and there is not an automatic and complete acceptance of the authority of governmental institutions. In the new states the individual leaders find that they do not occupy offices that give them clearly recognized ranges of authority; instead they must personally impose their wills and create for themselves the necessary acceptance of authority.

EXCESSIVE AND UNINSTITUTIONALIZED COMPETITION

This brings me to the second basic cause of legitimacy crises, the tendency for political competition to become raw power struggles when there are no stable institutions for channeling and ordering politics. The result is a somewhat more serious crisis since it involves not only the lack of bases for authority but also the breakdown of elite unity. In our first causes of legitimacy crises the national leadership was frustrated because it could not mobilize enough authority to run the country, in the second category the leadership is itself divided and cannot give form to even the governmental institutions.

Historically the European patterns of nation building contained few cases of this extreme form of legitimacy crisis. The closest examples probably occurred when the larger empires dissolved and the resulting national units lacked the necessary institutions to gain stability and the struggles for power became peculiarly harsh and brutal, as for example in some of the Balkan states. This pattern, however, is much clearer in the cases of the dissolution of the empires in the Middle East, Asia, and Africa. Indeed, with the end of the Ottoman Empire and the formation of the new states of the Middle East there was a constant series of legitimacy crises as intense and uninstitutionalized

[7] Carl J. Friedrich, *Man and His Government* (New York: McGraw-Hill, 1963).

struggles for power increasingly gravitated toward a situation of coups and countercoups.

The archetypical form of legitimacy crisis that arises from excessive uninstitutionalized power struggles is of course military rule based upon coup d'etat.[8] The inability of civilian rulers to contain the forces of the society and rule effectively encourages the ultimate arbitrators of force, the military, to intervene and to act out their other role as the ultimate defenders of the state ideal. When the military acts only to restore order the result can be an intense but limited legitimacy crisis. Yet the need to rely upon the military can become more enduring, and in time even the military may divide and fail to give the society order (as in the case of the warlord period in China).

This form of legitimacy crisis has been well characterized by Samuel P. Huntington's analysis of "praetorianism," a condition of society which encourages military intervention because much of society has been politicized but there are no adequate institutions to channel the competition.[9] "Countries which have political armies also have political clergies, political universities, political bureaucracies, political labor unions, and political corporations. Society as a whole is out-of-joint, not just the military."[10]

Thus in sum it can be said that whenever the old forms of authority have either been completely eliminated or greatly weakened by the dynamics of social change and new forms of authority are still to be accepted, there often seems to be an undue amount of naked, but relatively weak, power in the politics of new states. When power has not been institutionalized into legitimate authority, it does seem crude and even ruthless.[11] However, once power has been transformed into

[8] Of the thirty-five countries of black Africa, there have been fourteen successful coups and several failed military insurrections and mutinies; in the twenty countries of Asia there have been eight successful coups and insurgencies in most of them; in the twenty-two countries of Latin America only eight have not experienced a successful coup since 1946, and of these eight countries four have experienced military wrath and two insurgencies. See Edward Luttwak, *Coup d'Etat* (New York: Alfred Knopf, 1969), App. C.

[9] Huntington, *op.cit.*, Chap. 4.

[10] *Ibid.*, p. 194.

[11] Martin Kilson in an extremely subtle and sophisticated analysis of the authority problem in the modernization of Africa in general and Sierra Leone in particular has suggested that the effects of social and economic changes are not a simple and direct decline of traditional authorities and the emergence of new attitudes and new power centers. Instead he found that often social change provides new opportunities and new resources for power for traditional leaders, but as they expanded their involvements in their changing social and economic environment they could gain short-run advantages, but in time they were seen as leaders who had left their scope of authority and thus they weakened their claims to traditional authority. Their position thus

authority by the process of legitimization it requires less physical input to achieve the same effect. Thus it is that out of excessive power struggles leaders seek to transform their naked power into an acceptable form of legitimacy. One common approach is to claim a mixture of historical precedence and future promises which can either provide the basis for resolving the crisis or can become the cause of another form of legitimacy crisis.

UNACCEPTABLE HISTORICAL INTERPRETATIONS AND FAULTY PROMISES

The third principal source of legitimacy crises is the collapse of leadership which may occur when a people reject the leader's claim to historical precedence for their actions or their promises of future accomplishment. Leaders are given support on the grounds that they will revive old institutions or create a bright new world, and when accomplishment fails to match promise, the legitimacy of the governing institutions are brought into question.

In Europe this particular cause of legitimacy crises generally took the form of constitutional crises in which the leader's interpretations of history were seen by other power seekers as being invalid. Monarchs seeking to cling to their old prerogatives or parliamentarians stubbornly adhering to their own interpretations of republican "rules of the game" have in their different ways caused institutional and hence legitimacy crises.

In the newer states the tendency has more often been for leaders to champion ideologies that promise bright futures rather than appeal to memories of the old order. One of the most common uses of ideology in these societies is to evoke images and tap emotions that will provide the ruler with the mystique of authority.[12] The great danger of course is that when promises are not realized the authority of the leaders may quickly erode.

The delicate balance between the need to stimulate the aspirations of a society and the danger of disappointment points to the deeper questions of how social and political power is generated in changing societies, how power becomes transformed into authority, and what the moral and psychological bases are for recognizing different forms of authority. It is troublesome that at this stage in the history of the

had to depend more upon power. See Martin L. Kilson, Jr., *Political Change in a West African State* (Cambridge: Harvard University Press, 1966).

[12] For a discussion of the role of ideology in the new states see Charles W. Anderson, Fred R. van der Mehden, Crawford Young, *Issues of Political Development*, (Englewood Cliffs, N.J.: Prentice-Hall, 1967), Chaps. 9-11.

social sciences we should know so little about the dynamics of these historical processes. Our tendency has often been to "explain" such processes by merely employing new terms for describing them. Thus in analyzing the need for rationalizing authority in the developmental process we speak of the need for greater "institutionalization" and for the "internalization of new norms," yet we can specify very little as to what is actually involved in the behavior of individuals that justifies the use of such terms.[13]

Traditionally the analysis of authority and legitimacy lay at the very heart of political science. In early years of the behavioral revolution when attention was shifted away from such macro-concepts as the "state" and "sovereignty" to the actual actions of individuals, political scientists came to have less and less to say about the nature of such collective and abstract concepts as authority and legitimacy. More recently the behavioral approach has returned to a concern with macro-analysis, but as yet we have just begun to deal with authority and legitimacy on the basis of more contemporary concepts of political psychology and sociology. It is perhaps understandable that in seeking out new approaches there would have been a tendency to ignore old concepts and old problems. Yet this is most unfortunate, for unquestionably the behavioral approach with its emphasis upon both patterns of aggregate behavior and the subjective psychological realms have a great deal to offer in illuminating the psychological basis for the mystique of legitimacy and the dynamics of authority. In the past the concept of legitimacy was closely linked to the study of morality and normative theory, but as David Easton has observed legitimacy is a psychological, not a moral concept.[14]

DISFUNCTIONAL SOCIALIZATION PROCESSES

We can now turn to the last and possibly most fundamental cause of legitimacy crisis: the inappropriate ways in which people in a society have been taught about the nature of authority. This is a problem distinctive to rapidly changing societies in that people are instilled with views about politics and authority that are realistic at one time but which produce false expectations under new conditions. Furthermore with rapid but erratic change the various agents of

---

[13] I have discussed this problem in greater detail in "Bureaucratic Development and the Psychology of Institutionalization," in Ralph Braibanti, ed., *Political and Administrative Development* (Durham, N.C.: Duke University Press, 1969).

[14] David Easton, *The Political System: An Inquiry Into the State of Political Science* (New York: Alfred A. Knopf, 1953), p. 132.

political socialization may encourage quite different political orientations and consequently people may not develop strong commitments to the new standards of legitimacy.

It is not possible here for us to treat in any detail the basis in the socialization process for the establishment of attitudes and sentiments relating to authority and the emergence of legitimacy crises.[15] It is noteworthy, however, that in most traditional societies a prime stress in socialization is the instilling of respect and deference for authority. Children were expected to accept without question the authority of parents, and subjects were expected to defer completely to their political and social superiors. The comforts of dependency were the main rewards for being dutiful.

In transitional societies, in which social and political institutions have been weakened and their authority undermined, it is generally true that children in the first instance are still socialized to accept the complete and unquestioned authority of parents. Dependency is still a reality, and parents continue to teach their children as they themselves were taught. The result is that in many such societies people are still being taught to expect more of authority than any public authority is capable of being. Hence a basis is established for a sense of general dissatisfaction about any form of leadership in the society. By expecting more than is realistic a people will be constantly frustrated with the authorities, cynical about their particular leaders, and always looking for new leaders who will be able to live up to their ideals about what authority should be able to do.[16]

People in such societies thus grow up with a view of the world that is sharply divided between those who are powerless and those who are omnipotent. Those without authority are expected to keep their place and not criticize the conduct of those who have authority. Those in power feel it improper to be called upon to justify their authority; they believe that they should only have to display it in an appropriate manner. On the basis of such a socialization process sentiments about authority within the more explicitly political realm

[15] For an excellent selection of studies and a complete bibliography, see Jack Dennis and Frederick W. Frey, eds., *Exploration of Political Socialization: A Reader of Contemporary Research* (New York: John Wiley and Sons, 1970).

[16] The heavy emphasis upon filial piety in traditional Confucian culture and the unrelenting pressures to accept authority and order in the Chinese socialization process seem to lie at the heart of the extreme form of authority crisis which has plagued the Chinese modernization process. For a detailed analysis of this phenomenon see Lucian W. Pye, *The Spirit of Chinese Politics: A Psychocultural Study of the Authority Crisis in Political Development* (Cambridge: M.I.T. Press, 1968).

are likely to be complex and potentially explosive. Young people who find it impossible to express any form of revolt against paternal authority in their homes may express their aggressive feelings against other forms of authority that appear less threatening, and thus they may be strongly impelled to attack forms of political authority if any legitimacy is given to such attacks.[17]

Conversely, the leaders themselves may feel deeply unsure of their own authority and thus not be able to utilize the power available to them in an instrumental and pragmatic fashion. They may feel compelled to prove their powers by acting in arbitrary ways. Beneath these uncertain attitudes toward authority of both leaders and citizens there is frequently a more fundamental problem, that of a lack of self-esteem. Socialization processes within the family that leave people with an expectation of authoritarian ways generally will undermine the individual's sense of self-respect. The result is that subsequently those who do gain positions of power will feel driven to act in autocratic ways while those who remain common citizens are likely to have a sense of anomie.[18]

In addition to being able to incorporate psychological insights into any new theories about the processes of legitimization, we should also be able to enrich our theoretical understanding of this basic political process by utilizing recent research in anthropology. By systematically juxtaposing cultural sentiments, religious traditions, social practices, and leadership styles we can gain new dimensions of understanding what is represented by the concept of legitimacy in different settings.[19] Case studies of village life provide another important approach to understanding the gap in feelings about authority

[17] Leonard Binder, "Egypt's Integrative Revolution," in Lucian W. Pye and Sidney Verba, eds., *Political Culture and Political Development* (Princeton: Princeton University Press, 1965).

[18] Richard Rose, "Tradition and Modernization in England's Political Culture," in Pye and Verba, *op.cit.*

[19] There is, for example, a rich body of literature on Indian attitudes toward authority, power, morality, and leadership. See Myron Weiner, "Struggle Against Power in India," *World Politics*, 8 (April 1966); Joan V. Bondurant, "Satyagraha Versus Duragraha: The Limits of Symbolic Violence," in G. Ramachandran and T. K. Mahadevan, eds., *Gandhi: His Relevance for Our Times* (Bombay: Bharatiya Bhavan, 1969); Joan V. Bondurant and Margaret W. Fisher, "Ethics in Action: Contrasting Approaches to Social and Political Problems in Modern India," *Australian Journal of Politics and History*, 12 (August 1966); David H. Bayley, "The Pedagogy of Democracy: Coercive Public Protest in India," *American Political Science Review*, 61 (September 1962); and Richard L. Park and Irene Tinker, eds., *Leadership and Political Institutions in India* (Princeton: Princeton University Press, 1959).

between the most traditional and the more modern segments of transitional societies.[20]

A combination of both psychological and comparative sociological approaches suggests that the basic stability of governmental institutions is strongly influenced by the degree to which socializing agents reinforce or contradict each other in forming the community's sentiment about authority. Harry Eckstein's recent researches have shown, for example, that the patterns of authority in a society outside of the narrowly political realm can affect the stability of the regime; where there is congruence in style and value there is a higher likelihood for stable democracy than when there are discontinuities in authority patterns.[21]

Clearly the problem of legitimacy crises arising out of contradictory socialization practices is much greater with the contemporary developing countries than it was with the early developing states of Europe. The revolution in communications and the lack of coherence between family and public institutions in countries with both parochial orders and contemporary international influences creates a much more extreme situation than anything known in Europe.

The process of overcoming a legitimacy crisis produced by disfunctional socialization must be slow and undramatic. Eventually as the government establishes itself it can project an image of its authority which demands attention and thus compels the other socializing agents to reflect the new realities about governmental authority.

Dynamic Leadership and the Resolution of Legitimacy Crises

In part, the resolution of all legitimacy crises regardless of initial causes calls for dynamic leadership. Government institutions can only overcome their weaknesses and command public respect if those in responsible positions act to provide true leadership. In the last analysis government institutions are institutions of decision and of human inspiration.

It is necessary to stress the importance of dynamic human leadership in conquering legitimacy crises precisely because an inherent bias

[20] For an excellent recent study of changing patterns of legitimacy in rural India see Richard Fox, *From Zamindas to Ballot Box* (Ithaca: Cornell University Press, 1969).

[21] Harry Eckstein, *Division and Cohesion in Democracy* (Princeton: Princeton University Press, 1966); and "Authority Relations and Governmental Performance: A Theoretical Framework," Princeton Center for International Studies, Workshop on the Social Bases of Stable Rule (mimeo., 1968).

in political science has been a tendency to conceive of the myths of authority and legitimacy as being basically static and always threatened by change. Max Weber in vividly constructing his classic three ideal types of authority—the traditional, charismatic, and rational-legal—contributed greatly to the standard view that authority is strongest when conditions are the most stable. Yet for the purposes of trying to understand the legitimacy crisis in the new states the ideal type approach tends to obscure the problem, which should be that of asking what mixtures of lingering traditions, dynamic leadership, and national policies can best create a constructive sense of order. The problem in any developing country is not one of the existence or nonexistence of any particular form of authority, but rather that of the existence of degrees of authority and legitimacy with respect to the different problems and tasks that the new states confront. Richard Rose has recently developed a complex typology of the authority of regimes, based upon the mix in the degrees of support and compliance that each can command, that has the virtue of emphasizing the extent to which legitimacy is a relative concept.[22]

The analysis of the resolution of legitimacy crises calls for the discussion of charismatic leadership. Since the time of Weber, and more particularly after so many shrill and demagogic leaders have appeared in the postindependence era, a great deal has been written about the nature of charisma.[23] Recent studies that have sought to identify the personality qualities of great leaders, to relate cultural traits and crisis situations to the prevalence of charismatic leaders, and to distinguish the spontaneous or genuine from the manipulative or false political prophets have all contributed to a better understanding of how leaders and societies cope with the problems of establishing and strengthening legitimacy.[24]

[22] Richard Rose, "Dynamic Tendencies in the Authority of Regimes," *World Politics*, 21 (July 1969), 602-28.

[23] See in particular, Edward Shils, "The Concentration and Dispersion of Charisma," *World Politics*, 11 (October 1958); and "Charisma, Order, and Status" (mimeo.); Robert C. Tucker, "The Theory of Charismatic Leadership," *Daedalus* (Summer 1968).

[24] This literature on charisma can be roughly divided into two groups. The first consists of studies that concentrate on the qualities of the man, as for example Erik H. Erikson in his *Young Man Luther* (New York: Norton, 1958). The other body of writings has focused more on the relationship of leader to public and tends to associate charisma with the latter, holding that the vital element of charisma resides in the eyes of the beholder. See for example, Ann Ruth Willner, "Charismatic Political Leadership: A Theory" (Princeton Center of International Studies: Monograph 32, 1968), and "The Rise and Role of Charismatic Leaders," *Annals of the American Academy of Political and Social Science*, 358 (March 1965).

There has been a tendency to conceive of charismatic authority as being in sharp contrast to traditional authority on the one side and rational-legal authority on the other. This view as encouraged by Weber's discussion of the "routinization of charisma," by which he meant that the great leader might establish out of his authority new institutions that would be either a reestablishment of a form of traditional authority or the introduction of a national-legal system of authority. In spite of these tendencies to treat analytically the three types of authority as being distinctive and separate, Dankwart A. Rustow is right in reminding us that in political legitimacy there must be some balancing mix of all three, and that in historical situations we cannot find any one of them in pure form.[25] Thus a legitimacy crisis is not associated with the disappearance of one form of authority and the establishment of another, but rather with a change in the mixture of institutional legitimacy and the personal legitimacy of rulers.

The tendency to treat the building of authority through leadership as a matter of charismatic mystique has tended to obscure the critical role of choice and decision-making that can be critical in resolving legitimacy crises. Today the leaders of the new states in particular are faced with some very cruel dilemmas as they seek to establish effective governmental institutions that can blend parochial traditions and international standards. Modern communications through "shrinking" the world force people to recognize that they are different from others. As people learn about other systems and the norms which seem to govern them, they often become more critical of the assumptions that uphold their own systems of authority.[26] The awareness of foreign societies may not only create greater problems of managing extra-systemic relations but it may also affect people's attitudes toward the domestic performance of their own

---

[25] Rustow has two useful formulas for expressing these relationships:

$$\frac{\text{Political}}{\text{Stability}} = \frac{\text{Legitimacy of}}{\text{Institutions}} + \frac{\text{Personal Legitimacy}}{\text{of Rulers}}$$

and

$$\frac{\text{Political}}{\text{Legitimacy}} = \frac{\text{Traditional}}{\text{Legitimacy}} + \frac{\text{Rational-}}{\text{Legal}} + \frac{\text{Charismatic}}{\text{Legitimacy}}$$

Dankwart A. Rustow, *A World of Nations* (Brookings Institution, 1967), p. 157.

[26] Cf. Herbert Hyman, "Mass Media and Political Socialization: The Role of Patterns of Communication," in L. W. Pye, ed., *Communications and Political Development, op.cit.*

systems. Thus in developing countries the link between foreign and domestic affairs may be peculiarly intimate.

It is often said that the leaders of some of the newly emerging countries are excessively absorbed with world affairs and that in particular they find it difficult to get the West off their minds. The implication of such observations is usually that if such leaders would only concentrate more fully on domestic affairs they would be able to realize more substantial accomplishments. There is considerable truth in such criticism in particular cases, but in general it is important to note that this concern with the outside world is symptomatic of a fundamental feature of the legitimacy crisis. Leaders must, in a sense, constantly react to the standards that are assumed to underlie the foreign and particularly the Western world because the population in their countries is constantly inclined to criticize, explicitly or implicitly, the very authority of their national leaders on the basis of such foreign standards. Nationalist leaders are therefore often quick to find fault with Western performance, partly because they recognize that they must bring into question the propriety and efficacy of Western norms of authority if they are to strengthen the legitimacy of their own authority. If people have less to admire in foreign systems, they may have more to respect in their own. Unfortunately, however, the problem is considerably more complex for leaders seeking to develop their nations. For even as they are anxious to maintain their own mystique of authority they may also, with respect to many other areas of life, want to make their populations more aware of modern standards and the potentialities of alternative practices. As we analyze more closely the nature of legitimacy crises we find that in nearly all cases these profound problems tend to take the form of extremely awkward dilemmas for the current leadership of the country. Indeed, since the resolution of the legitimacy crisis depends so greatly upon leadership capabilities, it is useful to conclude our analysis of this particular crisis by reviewing some of the basic dilemmas of choice that leaders frequently must cope with in order to establish their authority.

The Dilemma of Firmness and Accommodation

The fundamental confrontation with the outside world, which so often initiates the developmental process, inevitably poses for national leaders the cruel choice of either remaining firm in their adherence to traditional norms or accepting the need to accommodate to the realities of foreign pressures and adopt new norms. The choice is cruel because either position can compromise the legitimacy of the existing authorities and leave a people without the effective performance of certain of the most crucial functions essential to the operation of the political system. The basic ingredient of leadership is a mixture of firmness and steadfastness on the one hand and innovation and guidance in change on the other; yet at any time what is seen as an improper blending of the mixture can undermine the magic of human leadership. In some situations an acute crisis of legitimacy may arise if long-standing leaders make concessions to the changing times while in other circumstances equally acute problems can arise for the legitimacy of the entire system if leaders fail to make concessions to the modern world.

The first type of legitimacy crisis was dramatically illustrated in the challenge to the Tokugawa leaders when Commodore Perry sought to open Japan to foreign intercourse in 1853. For the previous 250 years Tokugawa rulers had based their supreme authority on a feudal structure and the complete isolation of Japan from the rest of the world. Faced with the manifest superiority of the American warships and with Perry's demand for a commercial treaty that would have opened Japan to the world, the Tokugawa leaders called in the leading daimyos or feudal lords who owed allegiance to the shogunate and asked their advice as to what the national policy should be. There is evidence that the shogun thought that by this extraordinary act it would be possible to gain the universal consent of all his feudal supporters to the need of bowing to the inevitable. However, the shogun's enemies among the lords stepped forward and insisted that the Tokugawa regime had to maintain its own rules and that this was not the time for accommodation, but rather the moment for the shogunate to perform its basic obligation of protecting the entire country from foreign threats. The stage was thus set so that even the modest concessions demanded by Perry were enough to undermine the legitimacy of the Tokugawa regime.[27]

A similar process served to weaken and eventually destroy nearly all the traditional systems of authority in Africa. In some cases the confrontation involved the humiliation of outright military defeats,

[27] For analysis of the politics of the downfall of the Tokugawa and of the Meiji Restoration see E. Herbert Norman, *Japan's Emergence as a Modern State* (New York: Institute of Pacific Relations, 1940); W. W. McLaren, *A Political History of Japan during the Meiji Era* (London: Scribners, 1916); and Chitoshi Yanaga, *Japan Since Perry* (New York: McGraw-Hill, 1949).

but hostility and antagonism were not necessary ingredients; even when the foreign powers sought to cooperate with traditional authorities (in situations of indirect rule based upon treaty relationships, the legitimacy of the old system was invariably weakened). Indeed it would seem that the more the colonial power sought to maintain the precise nature of the traditional pattern of rule, the greater the likelihood that the old rulers would lose their appeal of legitimacy. Whenever, on the other hand, the European power significantly altered the practices of government to meet the needs of a changing world, the old rulers, in modified guise, generally had a better survival rate. For example, the Dutch sought to preserve much of the old pattern of traditional rule in Indonesia with negligible success, while the British drastically changed the system of rule in Malaya all in the name of the old rulers and even now the traditional Malay autocracy plays a significant role in a rapidly developing country, while the traditional Indonesian rulers have largely lost their powers.[28]

Yet at the other extreme we find that dogged attempts to resist all change and refuse to accommodate to foreign pressures may in time lead to a destructive form of the legitimacy crisis. Whenever the population becomes more aware of the potentialities of modern life than their leaders seem to be, existing patterns of authority are likely to be mortally weakened. This is as true of moderately reforming regimes as of the most tradition-bound isolationist governments. It is all too easy for the outside observer to recognize the dangers to governments of not trying to adjust rapidly to the demands of the modern world, largely because most observers tend to accept the legitimacy of cosmopolitan ways. History also supports this view; in our era the pressures of the modern world have in fact penetrated all societies in some degree. Yet in truth the record of history is not nearly so overwhelming nor so rapid in unfolding as most critics of traditionalist regimes would like to believe. Throughout the Middle East, Southern Asia, and Africa there have been a surprisingly large number of governments that students have been predicting will soon fall to the pressures of progress, but that have amazingly continued on their traditionalist course with as much stability as neighboring gov-

[28] For general discussion of the nature of indirect rule in Malaya and Indonesia compare Rupert Emerson, *Malaysia: A Study in Direct and Indirect Rule* (New York: Macmillan, 1937); and J. S. Furnivall, *Colonial Policy and Practice* (New York: New York University Press, 1948, 1956).

ernments that have sought much more actively to keep up with the times.

In short, in analyzing the dilemma of firmness and accommodation we may conclude that care needs to be taken not to underestimate the destructive consequences of a society losing its roots or its own traditions. Outside advocates of development are peculiarly inclined to see virtue in accommodation—which means the acceptance of their values —and little merit in firmness—which involves respect for someone else's traditions. This conclusion also suggests that the dilemma of firmness and accommodation is really a part of a larger dilemma of preserving or rejecting a society's history.

The Dilemma of Preserving or Rejecting the Past

The integrity of the leaders of any developing country is constantly being tested by the manner in which they treat the issue of history and by how transitional people view their past and their future prospects. This is a matter that was discussed in some detail with respect to the identity crisis, and here we need only observe that any government that seeks to turn its back completely on the past and concentrate only on development and modernization exposes itself to the charge that it has sold out to the foreign world of either the West or the Communists. Yet on the other hand any government that strives to revive memories of a distant past, while hoping to ignore the more immediate history of possible colonial rule with its humiliations of foreign penetration and control, is in the equally vulnerable position of trying to live with myths that have lost their potency. In this dilemma the issue of legitimacy between the past and the present overlap with the issue of identity between the foreign and the self, the "they" and the "we."[29]

[29] For an extremely sophisticated discussion of this problem from the point of view of the intellectual historian see Joseph R. Levenson, *Confucian China and Its Modern Fate* (Berkeley: University of California Press, 1958).

Levenson points out that the problem for the traditionalist is that ideas cannot remain the same once their historical context has been changed. Concepts and beliefs claim vitality because of not only what they assert but also for what they deny and ignore. With historical change, and the appearance of new ideas, traditional concepts can no longer deny what they once were able to do. Thus, the contemporary advocate of traditional ideals who must assert his beliefs in the face of the modern world is in quite a different position than the man of the past who could live securely with his beliefs and his comfortable ignorance of all alternative ideas. Thus it is that in many transitional societies the traditionalists who would strive to maintain deep roots in their old cultures are in fact driven to a shallow and affected position. In a very fundamental sense they are, in spite of their desire to assert a pride in native culture, like the xenophile whose understanding of the culture he would emulate can never be the same as those who were born to it.

Possibly the most successful attempts at resolving this basic dilemma occur when leaders claim that their radical programs represent only a restoration of historical conditions. This tactic is as old as Confucius, who denied that he was an innovator even as he held up to the Chinese people a vision of their earlier history that was as new to them as any utopian's vision of a futuristic society could have been. In more modern times we find that Ataturk continually asserted that the goal of a secular Turkey was nothing more than a return to the true historic Turkey.

The fact that politicians throughout history and in all cultures have found it useful to dress their innovational proposals in the guise of old practices, suggests that this dilemma is related to another fundamental problem—that of achieving a satisfactory balance between giving people only what they want and calling upon them to do things they are not really prepared to do. When leaders suggest that their new measures are really nothing more than a continuation of old traditions, they are in effect saying that they are not asking the people to do things that represent merely the whims of the leaders, but rather that they are only encouraging people to carry on with what were once the routine activities of the society. This takes us to another fundamental dilemma common to the legitimacy crisis.

The Dilemma of Satisfaction and Sacrifice

This particular dilemma involves a clash between the requirements that leadership respond to the desires and satisfactions of a people while at times compelling them to make sacrifices for goals unrelated to their immediate wishes. In any political system the demands of government on the resources of the society, both material and human or psychic, are always greater than the sum of the individual demands from the society for the political system to mobilize resources for special interests. This is because there is always the need for some additional resources to fulfill the tasks of maintaining and developing the political system as a more or less independent system. It is this gap that inevitably places the leaders in a position of seeming to demand more of the citizenry than they are prepared to give to the society. It is this gap that sometimes inspires cynicism on the part of both the people and the leaders themselves. The latter are aware that they are to some degree manipulating demands and dealing with problems that go well beyond what the people may immediately want.

If there is no legitimacy crisis and the people are prepared to trust their leaders, then there can be a broad acceptance of the right of the government to do more than merely process and aggregate into public policies those interests articulated by the public at large. In such a situation the people are ready to accept as reasonable the belief that if at the moment the rewards of the system must be more psychological than material, then they are, in a sense, practicing a form of "savings" so that the system will be able to make greater "investments," and hence the material rewards of "consumption" will be significantly higher at a later date. The outlook of the people is thus optimistic toward the future and the sense of loyalty will be high.

On the other hand, when there is a serious legitimacy crisis, particularly if it is related to a rise in the demands for equality, then the popular reaction may be that the elite lacks the authority to go beyond meeting the immediately articulated interests of the public. The plea of the leadership that it must mobilize resources in excess of such current public demands can make the people feel that their leaders are trying to exploit their power position for personal gain. Requests for sacrifice and delay in consumption under such circumstances may be seen only as the further tricks of a malevolent elite. In this view there is little room for optimism because there is no such concept as an expanding system with increased shares for all, only a closed system in which there must be a constant struggle to determine how the limited shares are to be divided. In a traditional society the spirit of hierarchy predominated, and people were prepared to accept the notion that some people are better off in both power and material terms. As long as people see virtue in the concept of hierarchy they can obtain high psychic rewards from such a traditional system and be effectively loyal to it. In the transitional system, however, the expectation of equality has destroyed the legitimacy of hierarchy, and thus conspicuous differences in the rewards of the elites and the masses can produce resentment and cynicism.

The spirit in which this dilemma of legitimacy is dealt with is critical in determining whether the elite political culture will be able to provide the necessary entrepreneurship for development. In many of the developing areas the elite has moved from an exaggerated sense of their own powers, and, hence, of their freedom to manipulate to a cynical view of the people and their mass culture, and they have finally arrived at widespread practices of personal corruption when they have confused the allocation of system maintenance resources with their own personal interests. In much of Africa there has recently been a tendency for this form of corruption to creep into public life. Leaders often feel that they must engage in such practices because even though they are currently members of the elite world they originally came from humble backgrounds and have no personal resources to fall back upon once they are through with public life.[30]

The manner in which the elite culture communicates a sense of time and of progress can often be critical in determining how well it handles the problem of this gap. If the elite culture is capable of suggesting that delay and postponement of "consumption" is not part of a trick to cheat the public of its deserved rewards, but rather a way of achieving even greater rewards, then of course it will be possible for the government to engage in more rational "investment" policies of nation building. The difficulty is that the suggestion of postponement can easily result in disappointments that can lead to forms of "privatization" in which everyone feels he must look after his own interests.[31]

The Problem of Alienation and the Function of Commitment Evocation

Our analysis of the dilemmas inherent in the legitimacy crises thus brings us finally to the basic danger that widespread alienation may make it impossible for the political system to perform one of the essential functions of commitment evocation. When the leaders can no longer appeal to the loyalty of the society and there is no longer faith in the value of the system itself, the process of development can produce the most serious form of breakdown of the polity.

---

[30] This problem was explicitly discussed by former Prime Minister Sir Abubakar Tafawa Balewa of Nigeria during the parliamentary debate which followed the filing of a censure motion against Chief Festus Okatie-Eboh, Minister of Finance and Leader of the House, in April 1963, *West African Pilot*, Lagos, Nigeria, April 24, 1963; *Daily Express*, Lagos, Nigeria, April 24, 1963.

[31] The problem of corruption which is often so casually discussed with respect to Asian, African, and Middle Eastern politics has not received the serious analytical treatment it deserves. Both simple moralistic attacks on the prevalence of corruption and facile defenses of such practices on the grounds of cultural differences seem equally to miss the point. With respect to the developmental problem there is a need to distinguish among different forms of corruption in order to determine (1) those forms which either inhibit or facilitate development, and (2) the kinds of corruption likely to be most widespread at different stages of development.

We cannot here treat in great detail the problem of political alienation except to point out, first, that our entire analysis of the legitimacy and identity crises has in fact been a discussion of this problem, and, second, that we must distinguish between two forms of alienation that stem from different patterns of relations between the general and the political socialization processes.

The first form of alienation or cynicism occurs when there are sharp conflicts or discontinuities between these two processes of socialization, for example, when the individual was given in early childhood a view of the universe and of social and human relations that is highly orderly, trusting, and just, but then, through the political socialization process, he is given a view of the political realm that is unregulated, malevolent, corrupt, and dishonest. It is the conflict between the optimistic view of what the world could be like and the way the political world is perceived that produces a kind of cynicism and alienation that will always remain slightly vulnerable to reformist appeals. This appears to be the kind of alienation that is the most prevalent in the American mass political culture.

Another form of alienation, however, occurs when the early socialization process provides the individual with a distrusting and suspicious view of all human relations, and then the later agents of political socialization leave him with conflicting and contradictory notions about the political realm. Some agents of political socialization may make exaggerated appeals to idealism, suggesting perhaps that a particular political movement has the magical capacity to change the world into a safer and happier place. The majority of the agents of socialization, however, teach that political life is as bad as, if not worse than, all other forms of social life. In such a political culture, of which Italy is a reasonable example,[32] people are distrustful of political institutions but no more than of other insititutions; and, while they are likely to be unmoved by moderate reformist movements—"you can't change human nature,"—they can be carried away by messianic revolutionary movements that make the promise of radically changing all of life.

In the developing countries one of the great difficulties is that alienation is more likely to be of the second than the first type. Most traditional cultures have not produced a favorable environment of attitudes for easy and constructive social life, and thus there

[32] Cf. Joseph LaPalombara, "The Italian Political Culture," in Pye and Verba, eds., op.cit.

are not likely to be deep reservoirs of positive sentiment that can be readily tapped by reformist movements which hold out the modest hope of merely giving order and integrity to a confused political realm. More often the basic socialization process has already implanted suspicion and mistrust of human relations outside the immediate family. The nonpolitical socialization may also be so out of tune with the times that it seems to be irrelevant for all that comes later in the political socialization process, and thus the individual's understanding and feelings about politics cannot rest on firm foundations.

In concluding this discussion of the identity and legitimacy crises, which are central in shaping the political culture, it is appropriate to note that while it is important for the analysis of transitional societies to understand that many of the difficulties in the developmental process may arise out of the problems in the socialization process, it is equally important to appreciate the possibility of forming a government to overcome these liabilities. It will be remembered that in concluding our analysis of the identity crisis and introducing the legitimacy crisis we observed that the actual performance of government can give people a stronger sense of new identities in time. So now in concluding our discussion of how the legitimacy crises can produce a sense of alienation unless the elite can overcome popular suspicions and distrust, we may appropriately turn to a detailed analysis of how the development syndrome can effect the performance of authoritative structures. For the relative success of the existing institutions of government in carrying out some of the essential functions of the political system is often the most decisive factor in determining the ability of a new nation to resolve its problems of legitimacy.

With an appreciation of these relationships in mind, we can turn from the crises of the political culture to a discussion of the crises of the political process and then of the governmental process.

CHAPTER 5

POLITICAL PARTICIPATION: CRISIS OF THE POLITICAL PROCESS

MYRON WEINER

MODERNIZATION generates pressures for political participation. One of the most disruptive crises in modern times has been caused by the efforts of those not in power to gain access to power or to influence decisions made by governing elites. The transformations from monarchy to republic, from colonial rule to independence, from no party to party systems, from limited to universal adult suffrage, and from dictatorship to democracy have all meant new relationships between the citizen and the state and new forms of political participation. This is not to say that the widening of political participation is inevitable in the modern world, for clearly there are forms of government that successfully resist sharing power and that have even narrowed the right to participate, but even authoritarian regimes have had to cope with pressures for participation either through repression or by creating institutions that permit or, more often, appear to permit certain forms of participation.

When modernization took place in 18th and 19th century Europe, few questions stirred more intellectual debate than the issue of the right of the masses to participate in government. Should the masses, that is those who are governed, be permitted to organize themselves to influence government or to select those who govern them? If the will of the masses is obeyed, what will happen to the common good? Should the masses be permitted to express opinions, or should government impose some limits for the good of society as a whole? Under what conditions ought men to have the right and the moral obligation to change their government? And will the proliferation of factions attempting to influence government destroy or preserve liberty, and destroy or preserve order? Questions such as these were raised not simply out of any abstract concern for political philosophy but rather because increasingly large numbers of people in Western Europe and in America sought to participate in public life, with the result that political institutions were being changed (or overthrown) to accommodate new forms of political activity.[1]

Today, in the last third of the 20th century, there are again sharp differences of opinion on the effects of mass political participation, particularly its effect on the larger public good now loosely defined in the modernizing areas as "development." Of its effects on economic growth, some believe that participation is a necessary condition for the essential attitudinal changes, while others argue that large-scale political participation will limit the capacity of government to extract resources (in the form of taxes) essential for capital accumulation and investment. Some argue that participation provides feedback to policy-makers, thereby improving their planning, while others believe that it encourages consumption-oriented allocations of resources. Some believe that participation, especially at the local level, restricts the growth of the centralized authority that appears to be needed to carry through modernization programs. Of the effect of participation on political stability, some postulate that participation is essential to establish responsive government, that responsiveness is necessary to legitimize authority, and that legitimacy is a precondition to stable and orderly government. Others argue that political participation can outrun institutionalization and lead to excessive demands, violence, and instability, particularly when established elites are undermined.[2]

These divergent views of the consequences of a growth in mass political participation are partly a reflection of the analysts' ideological predilections, but these differences also reflect a situation in the real world. An expansion of political participation seems to have one effect in a multi-ethnic society and another in a homogeneous culture. It seems to have one effect in a society with a weak bureaucracy and weak central government, and still another in a society with a strong, centralized bureaucratic system.

In this chapter we shall look at some of the causes and consequences of rapid changes in political participation. In particular we shall at-

[1] Along with new participation came a growing awareness of the link between citizenship and the character of modern man. John Stuart Mill's classic defense of representative government emphasized that it encouraged those qualities of intellectual, political, and moral excellence that *ought* to be cultivated by modern states. Mill attacked despotic regimes not simply because he distrusted benevolent despots but because despotism demanded obedience and passivity on the part of citizens.

[2] Although there have been many persuasive attempts to link variables in political systems to one another (see Samuel P. Huntington, *Political Order in Changing Societies* [New Haven: Yale University Press, 1968], Chapter 1), the precise relationship of political participation to both political stability and economic growth remains one of the most contentious areas of development analysis.

tempt to examine the varied effects of changing patterns of political participation as they relate to the form and timing of the participation and to the social structure and political institutions of the society in which participation is taking place. In Part I we shall discuss varied notions of political participation and suggest a working definition. Part II will examine the conditions under which there is a rapid rise in political participation. Part III will look at the different societies and political systems in which participation increases and explore the question of whether it makes any difference in political development if the demand for political participation occurs early or late in the development process. In Part IV we look at the effects of different sequences of political participation, that is, the order in which different social groups entered political life. Part V examines elite responses in order to see how and what kinds of crises arise. And in the concluding section, Part VI, we look at how, if at all, participation crises are resolved.

Part I. What We Mean by Political Participation

Since the term "participation" is normatively positive in virtually all contemporary political systems, including those governed by one-party dictatorships and military juntas (in itself an interesting phenomenon), it is important that we provide a precise behavorial definition that can be used for analytical purposes. A brief examination of the ways in which "participation" is used calls attention to how central the issue of participation is in many of the ideological controversies of modern times and how essential it is to be precise in this area.

1. Participation is often used to refer to acts of *support for* as well as *demands upon* government elites. Authoritarian regimes often sponsor referenda, plebiscites, and mass rallies as a justification for asserting that their authority rests upon popular support. Participation in this sense is meant to refer to popular legitimacy; it does not mean that those who provide support have the option of denying support or making demands.

2. Participation is often used to mean only *successful* efforts to affect the actions of government or to choose government leaders. Critics of democratic systems often describe participation as formal and ineffectual when the efforts of some groups to change policies or leaders are unsuccessful. Is it meaningful, for example, to speak of

mass participation if the majority will (as expressed in public opinion surveys or in voting) is thwarted?

3. Some people define as participation only those acts of citizens that are defined by law as legitimate—voting, demonstrating, petitioning, lobbying, etc.—excluding illegitimate actions. But in contrast, some radicals see illegal acts such as civil disobedience and other forms of mass "confrontation" as the only genuine acts of participation in a democracy.

4. One school of democratic thought views *representation* as an appropriate form of participation in large-scale complex societies, since millions of citizens cannot effectively participate in government directly. Others argue for direct democracy or participatory democracy to eliminate all intermediaries between the citizen and the state. The proponents of direct democracy argue that representatives invariably become part of the elite power structure and therefore cease to "represent" the interests of those who elected them. The representative system should either be eliminated (using referenda where possible or through decentralizing the government) or representatives should be required to act as their constituents wish them to act. Here we have the familiar conflict over different theories of representation—between those who view the representative as the agent of the voter acting in accordance with the will of the majority of his constituents against those who adopt the alternative Burkian theory that views the elected representative as a free actor voting for legislation in accordance with his own principles but periodically submitting himself to his electors for approval.

5. Alienation—as distinguished from apathy—is sometimes seen as a form of participation. Apathy suggests a lack of interest as well as a lack of action, while alienation suggests intense political feelings concerning the futility of political action. The inaction of the alienated and the apathetic may have quite different consequences for the performance and subsequent development of the political system, but how, in practice, do we treat one form of inaction as participation while excluding the other?

6. When we speak of participants, sometimes we mean only the activists who run for public office, attend public meetings, join political parties, and spend a substantial portion of their time on public matters. Sometimes we also include "lesser" forms of political participation such as voting (even when weakly motivated). Some definitions of participation include those who do not vote but talk about political

matters with their neighbors, express political opinions, and consume political information through the mass media. Since participation is clearly a continuum, where along the line should we draw a distinction between participant and non-participant?

7. Similarly there is a kind of "persistence continuum" along which participants can be scaled, ranging from institutionalized activities that are continuous and organized to episodic outbursts—riots, lynch mobs, and even political assassinations.

8. Participation, although generally used to refer to acts aimed at choosing political leaders and influencing public policies, might also include efforts to influence bureaucratic actions. Most discussions of political participation tend to exclude the efforts of peasants to influence the local bureaucracy and of businessmen to obtain permits and contracts, yet in many societies these are the most common ways in which citizens seek to affect a government's actions.

9. Some definitions of participation include only activities affecting national politics, while others include participation in local institutions as well. Observers may define peasants as nonparticipants even though they are deeply involved in tribal, caste, or village politics. "Mass" political participation may not involve a shift from nonparticipant to participant status, but a shift from participation on one level of public life to another.

10. Finally, there are different notions as to what constitutes a *political* act. What constitutes a political act in one society may be nonpolitical in another; similarly an identical action may be defined by most people in a society as nonpolitical at one point in time, but as political at another.[3] And frequently there are differences within a society as to whether a given act is political or not. A technician or scientist joining the brain drain may define his action as a personal one, but his countrymen may see his behavior as disloyalty. Similarly, the destruction of property in American ghettos may be seen by some Americans as simply a criminal act, while others perceive it as a political act.

We should also note that actions that are viewed in a society as highly political at one time later become nonpolitical private matters.

[3] Sidney Verba has also suggested that we distinguish between politicization (defining a problem as political) and participation (activity relevant to the solution of the problem); he concludes that political development is characterized not only by an increase in political participation but also by an expansion in the number and scope of problems that are perceived as political ("A Study of American Political Life and Political Development," unpublished, Stanford University, 1966).

Indeed, there appears to be a tendency in modern industrial societies to channel social conflicts from the political to the legal arena. Thus many worker-management conflicts are now handled through an elaborate network of judicial procedures and institutions created to settle disputes outside of politics. Similarly, political disputes between races and religious groups are often managed, if not settled, by the passage of legislation that permits disputes to be handled on an individual basis by the bureaucracy and the courts. Perhaps one measure of how successful a political system is in the management of group conflict is whether conflicts are moved from the political to the judicial realm where they can be treated not as conflicts between large social groups but as conflicts between and among individuals.

All these various definitions of political participation suggest that we are dealing with a continuum rather than a dichotomous concept, that societies and individuals differ in their conceptions of what constitutes a political act, and that most of these definitions have normative values associated with them. If, therefore, we want to use a definition of political participation that can cover the wide range of activities viewed as participation in different societies, then the definition must be somewhat comprehensive. For the purposes of this chapter I shall use the concept of political participation to refer to any voluntary action, successful or unsuccessful, organized or unorganized, episodic or continuous, employing legitimate or illegitimate methods intended to influence the choice of public policies, the administration of public affairs, or the choice of political leaders at any level of government, local or national.

Three aspects of this definition warrant comment. The first is that for our purposes participation is defined as *action*, including verbal action, not simply attitudes or subjective feelings. In all political systems people have attitudes toward government and politics, but unless there is some action it would be inappropriate to use the term "participation." Alienation is an act of participation only if it is verbally expressed. Second, we are using the concept to refer to *voluntary* activities by citizens. Involuntary acts, such as serving in the armed forces (through conscription) or paying taxes, are excluded. Belonging to organizations or attending mass rallies under government orders is also excluded. Third, the definition assumes that the citizen has a *choice* in the selection of public officials. We therefore exclude voting in elections in which there is only a single slate of candidates since citizens have not been permitted to make choices. Such "support participation" or, more accurately, coercive mobilization is important for authoritarian regimes, but it should not be confused with genuine political participation involving voluntary choices by citizens.

Part II. Conditions for Political Participation

The fact of increased political participation—first in Western Europe and America in the 18th and 19th centuries, and today in the developing areas of Asia, Africa, and Latin America—is by now quite familiar to historians and political scientists. Since the same phenomenon may have several causes, however, we have a number of theories, not necessarily conflicting, that attempt to explain why there is an increase in the numbers of people who participate or seek to participate in the politics of a political system.[4]

For centuries men lived in systems where few governed and many expected to be governed. In such political systems (Almond and Verba have called them "subject cultures"), each individual tended to accept his own position, and the children of governors became governors while the children of the governed assumed that they would continue to be governed by others. The socialization process, expressed through religious institutions, the educational system, the legal system, and the family, inculcated habits of compliance in some and the will to govern in others. Even in systems where rebellions occurred these rebellions were typically aimed at replacing one group of governors with another, not at enlarging the size of the governing class so as to give a greater share of power to those who were governed or to institutionalize procedures whereby citizens would have a greater voice in the selection of governors. Prior to the 18th century in Europe it can be said that rebellions (in the sense of attempts by citizens to influ-

---

[4] For a review of the literature on political participation, focusing particularly on individual behavior and individual motivation rather than on the macro-dimensions of political participation, see Lester Milbrath, *Political Participation* (Chicago: Rand McNally and Co., 1965) and Robert E. Lane, *Political Life: Why People Get Involved in Politics* (Glencoe: Free Press, 1959). There is an excellent bibliography in Herbert McClosky's "Political Participation," *International Encyclopedia of the Social Sciences*, Vol. 12, pp. 264-65. For a review of the comparative efforts to study political participation, see Stein Rokkan, "Comparative Cross-National Research," in *Comparing Nations*, Richard I. Merritt and Stein Rokkan, eds. (New Haven: Yale University Press, 1966) and Stein Rokkan, "The Comparative Study of Political Participation," in *Essays on the Behavioral Study of Politics*, Austin Ranney, ed. (Urbana: University of Illinois Press, 1962). For theories concerning the conditions under which political parties emerge, see Joseph LaPalombara and Myron Weiner, eds., *Political Parties and Political Development* (Princeton: Princeton University Press, 1966), Chapter 1.

ence or change a *particular* government through illegitimate means) sometimes occurred, but that revolutions (in the sense of attempts to transform the *system* of government) were rare. Indeed, as Gluckman has pointed out, rebellions have often strengthened the legitimacy of government by making it possible for discontent to be directed at specific men rather than at the political system itself.[5] Thus, many monarchies and bureaucratic empires persisted for centuries in spite of—and some might argue even because of—occasional rebellions that changed one set of rulers for another but left the legitimacy of the regime intact.

Considering the great durability of nonparticipant political systems and the strength of the institutionalized socialization processes that have sanctioned nonparticipation, why have the pressures for political participation grown in the modern and modernizing world?

SOCIAL MOBILIZATION

One theory, associated with the names of Karl Deutsch and Daniel Lerner, postulates that elements of the modernization process lead to participatory changes.[6] Lerner has focused on the impact of urbanization and exposure to the mass media, while Deutsch has suggested a more complex combination of characteristics of the modernization process that he has called social mobilization. Mannheim, in an earlier version of this theory, spoke of people being uprooted from their community and from their traditional ways of life to be mobilized into new modern institutions such as the army, urban life, and the factory. The process by which people are shifted from one set of attachments to another results, it has been argued, in new involvements in mass politics.[7] Deutsch has tried to quantify these notions by suggesting that there are clusters of social changes that tend to go together—exposure to mass media, changes in residence, changes in occupation, increases in education, and increases in income—and that these are associated with new forms of political participation.

The theoretical underpinning of this body of theory is that the

[5] Max Gluckman, *Custom and Conflict in Africa* (Glencoe: Free Press, 1959).

[6] Karl W. Deutsch, "Social Mobilization and Political Development," *American Political Science Review* 55 (September 1961), 493-514, and Daniel Lerner, *The Passing of Traditional Society* (Glencoe: Free Press, 1958).

[7] Social mobilization does not necessarily lead to increased political participation. It can also result in a situation under which large numbers of people become available for manipulation by elites. The availability of the masses is a central theme in the literature on mass society. See William Kornhauser, *The Politics of Mass Society* (Glencoe: Free Press, 1959).

modernization process affects the process of socialization, which in turn shapes political attitudes and behavior. This body of theory has given rise to a number of empirical studies and statistical analyses aimed at assessing the relative weight of one variable against others, singly or in combination. In a recent cross-cultural attitudinal study, for example, Alex Inkeles has attempted to demonstrate that exposure to the factory is a more powerful modernizing factor (with, presumably, political consequences) than either urbanization or education.[8] One merit of this theoretical approach is that it provides us with some readily measurable cross-cultural indices that many other systems-specific theories fail to provide.

SOCIAL STRATIFICATION

A second theory of political participation looks not at the various indices of modernization but at the impact of modernization on the system of social stratification. The theoretical argument is that the modernization process creates social groups that had previously not existed, that it changes the relationship of existing social groups with one another, and that these two types of developments within the stratification system determine who will enter politics. This theory is derived from the familiar notion that a social system consists of both the social differentiations (for example, occupational differentiations, biologically based differentiations of age and sex, etc.) necessary for the functioning of the system and a scheme for distribution of power and authority. The differentiations—say of age, income, or occupation—are important because they are the bases of rank assignment. Individuals show esteem, respect, or honor to other individuals, offices, and institutions based upon some scale of values. It is feelings and acts of deference that give effective meaning to social differences and that in the final analysis define social position.

Much of the literature on changing patterns of political participation in Europe has focused on changes in the system of class stratification. The desire by new middle classes for a higher social status commensurate with their new material gains has often been described as an important element in their quest for political power in 18th and 19th century England and France. We now understand that social groups may seek power not simply because they have specific policy or administrative demands that they wish to satisfy but because win-

---

[8] Alex Inkeles, "The Modernization of Man," in *Modernization: The Dynamics of Growth*, Myron Weiner, ed. (New York: Basic Books, 1966).

ning or sharing power is a mark of achieving social status. When status is the goal of contending groups, the issue becomes *who* will decide government policy rather than *what* government policy ought to be.

In many developing countries status struggles have often centered less around the system of class stratification than around the system of cultural and ethnic stratification. The fact that struggles are often along the lines of ethnicity in many developing countries (and in Eastern Europe, which has resembled the developing areas in this respect) rather than along class lines, as in Western Europe, has made a difference in the kinds of issues fought over. Where class is the issue, the struggles tend to be over welfare policies, taxation, and matters of economic policy; where ethnicity is the issue, the struggles are generally over language policy, state-church relationships, and, most important of all, educational policies.

The drive for status, however, is an element in both class and ethnic stratification. It has been an important element in the political behavior of many new participant social classes in European politics; it has been important in the drive for status and power on the part of ethnic minorities in the United States, in Eastern Europe, and in the developing countries; and today it is an important dimension in the behavior of the Black Power movement in the United States.

There are two related variants of stratification theory that are widely used to explain changing patterns of political participation. One is the concept of relative deprivation and the other is the concept of status reversal.

Relative Deprivation. The concept of relative deprivation examines the psychological dimensions of unfulfilled expectations. Some theorists emphasize the sense of inequality and deprivation that results when individuals or groups perceive that others have better access to the advantages of society. Other theorists focus on the unfulfilled expectations that result from an unsatisfactory want/get ratio. In either case the theory postulates that changes in a developing society lead to unsatisfied desires affecting one's sense of well-being. In examining psychological deprivation, rather than actual material deprivation, this theory helps to explain why social protest, politicization, and increased participation often accompany increasing income and improving living conditions—why rioters in American urban ghettos are often not the poorest and not the unemployed, why tensions rise when regions or groups in a country develop (i.e., increase their income) at different rates, and why countries with rising standards of living are the ones most likely to have large-scale protest movements.[9]

Status Reversal. The theory of status reversal calls attention to the psychological problems of those social groups who lose status as a result of the modernization process. In some developing societies, for example, certain tribes or castes who were once widely esteemed lost much of their status as new criteria for status became widely accepted. Men may no longer be given esteem simply because they are martial, or because of their family position, or because they are religious. Status is increasingly based on wealth and power, and both are more likely to be achieved by those who are educated and have a "modern" outlook and style of living. In East Africa, for example, the Masai tribes, a proud pastoral people whose status, wealth, and power diminished under British rule, are beginning to see political activity as a means of reasserting their historic position. Similarly in northern India, the Rajputs, who governed many of the princely states under British rule and lost power and prestige in relation to peasant proprietors and to the new urban middle classes after independence, have recently been attempting to reassert their political power through participation in mass electoral politics.

The notion of status decline is also used by students of European politics to explain the politicization of the social classes whose income was not declining, but who feared the rise of lower social classes into higher positions in the social hierarchy. Dahrendorf, Lipset, and other students of social stratification have pointed to status decline as an important element in the rise of radical right-wing movements in Central Europe during the interwar period.[10]

---

[9] Ted Gurr defines relative deprivation as the "actors perceptions of discrepancy between their value expectations (the goods and conditions of the life they believe they are justifiably entitled) and their value capabilities (the amount of those goods and conditions that they think they are able to get and keep)." ("Causal Model of Civil Strife: A Comparative Analysis Using New Indices," *American Political Science Review* 62, 4 [December 1968], 1104.) For a discussion of the conditions under which aspirations increase faster than achievements, see Daniel Lerner, "Toward a Communication Theory of Modernization," in *Communications and Political Development*, Lucian Pye, ed. (Princeton: Princeton University Press, 1963).

[10] For a social psychological study showing that downward mobility is correlated with prejudice against minority groups, see Joseph Greenblum and Leonard Pearlin, "Vertical Mobility and Prejudice: A Socio-Psychological Analysis," in *Class, Status, and Power: A Reader in Social Stratification*, Reinhard Bendix and Seymour M. Lipset, eds. (Glencoe: Free Press, 1953), pp. 480-91. Greenblum and Pearlin show that those who have lost status are more aggressive toward minority groups than even lower stationary classes. Two recent volumes provide new materials on fascist and

The social stratification approach to the study of political participation has, as we have suggested, the virtue of calling attention to the role which status struggles now play in the developing areas and have played historically in European and American political development. The approach calls attention to the fact that the demand for political participation is often not for distribution of the goods and services under the control of government but for the status that accrues to those who hold power. Indeed, in developing countries where government has not yet effectively penetrated the society and economy, where its capacity to extract and distribute resources is limited, politics of status may be particularly acute for, in a sense, that may be all there is to fight over. Social position may be more important than public policy, and the question of who governs more important than that of how power should be used.

THE INTELLIGENTSIA

A third theory of political participation grows out of concepts expressed by the school of historians concerned with development of nationalist movements and the impact of ideologies on political participation. This theory focuses primarily on the role played by the intelligentsia in spreading both equalitarian and nationalist ideas and, thereby, arousing the masses into political action. The intelligentsia, according to this theory, revive or generate historical memories, restore indigenous languages, and generate new national identities; the intelligentsia often introduce equalitarian ideas and diffuse them throughout their own country. These activities on the part of the intelligentsia arouse people to take part in political life—first in nationalist movements, then in the newly independent states. This

<hr>

right-wing movements in prewar Europe, Hans Rogger and Eugen Weber, eds., *The European Right* (Berkeley: University of California Press, 1966) and the issue on *International Fascism, 1920-1945, Journal of Contempoary History* 1, 1 (1966). Surprisingly, the social basis of European right-wing movements is not well documented. Among the notable exceptions are the following: Istvan Deak's article on Hungary in Hans Rogger and Eugen Weber, *The European Right*; Eugen Weber's article on Rumania in *Journal of Contemporary History*; Rolf Dahrendorf's analysis of the social basis of the Nazi movement in Dahrendorf, *Class and Class Conflict in Industrial Society* (Stanford: Stanford University Press, 1959); Stanley F. Payne's excellent study, *Falange* (Stanford: Stanford University Press, 1961); and Seymour M. Lipset, *Political Man* (New York: Doubleday, 1960), Chapter 5. The Lipset study brings together data on the social basis of fascism in Germany, Austria, France, Italy, the United States, and Argentina. Another recent comparative study, viewing fascism as a revolt against the modernization process, is Ernest Nolte, *The Three Faces of Fascism: Action Française, Italian Fascism, National Socialism* (New York: Holt, Rinehart and Winston, 1965).

theory emphasizes the role of the intelligentsia as the producers and disseminators of ideas capable of changing the attitudes and behavior of other social classes.

This viewpoint is well established in the literature of European and, more recently, Asian intellectual history. In political science, Rupert Emerson has emphasized this approach in his study of the development of nationalist movements, and Hugh Seton-Watson has utilized this approach to compare the patterns of political participation in pre-war Eastern Europe to those of contemporary Asia and Africa.[11]

Strong empirical support for this theory comes from the observations that substantial increases in political participation often occur before there is large-scale modernization, and that societies with similar levels of urbanization, mass media, and other elements of a social mobilization index have quite different levels of political participation. Moreover some systems ranking very low on a social mobilization index have more political participation than those with a higher rank. In short, it would appear that the ideas of a relatively small number of influential people may mobilize large numbers of people into political action before there has been much modernization. This theory stresses the independent role not of ideas alone but of ideas held by a socially esteemed class viewed by many people within the society as bearers of the tradition. Robert Redfield and Milton Singer have called attention to the presence in most traditional, particularly peasant, societies of such a class—the priests, teachers, bards, patrons, and men of learning who both transmit and transmute tradition.[12] Even without massive changes in the system of social stratification or the inroads of a modernization process these social classes may arouse the masses to struggle against colonial rulers and to seek greater equality in and access to the political process. Examples of this kind of stimulus to political organization would be the role played by the lower clergy of the Eastern Orthodox Churches in eastern and southern Europe in the late 19th century, the role of the Buddhist Sangha in Ceylon, Burma, and recently in Vietnam, and the role of modern

[11] Rupert Emerson, *From Empire to Nation: The Rise to Self-Assertion of Asian and African Peoples* (Cambridge: Harvard University Press, 1960) and Hugh Seton-Watson, *Neither War Nor Peace: The Struggle for Power in the Postwar World* (New York: Praeger, 1962).

[12] Robert Redfield, "The Social Organization of Tradition," *Far Eastern Quarterly* 15 (November 1955), 13-21 and Robert Redfield, *Peasant Society and Culture* (Chicago: University of Chicago Press, 1956). Redfield's concepts are developed by Milton Singer in "The Great Tradition in a Metropolitan Center: Madras," in *Traditional India: Structure and Change*, Singer, ed. (Philadelphia: American Folklore Society, 1959).

intellectual classes—lawyers, doctors, journalists—in the development of nationalist movements in India, Pakistan, and much of Africa.

New ideas about political equality may be independently created within a society, but in contemporary Asia and Africa the new ideas are often exogenous. Worldwide communication, travel abroad, and the movements of armies have led to a diffusion of ideas concerning political participation. The diffusion process may generate changes even when the factors internal to the system in which these ideas originated are not present elsewhere. Thus trade unions of the unskilled and semiskilled did not develop in England and America until there had been a long experience of craft unions and a substantial amount of industrialization; in Asia and Africa, by contrast, trade unions are organized by left-wing political leaders almost immediately after factories are constructed, and the percentage of the labor force in unions may be far higher in many developing societies today than was the case in England and America at a comparable stage of industrialization. Indeed, there are countries in the developing areas that have a larger proportion of their industrial labor force in trade unions than does France or several other European countries.

INTRA-ELITE CONFLICT

Intra-elite conflict is also often a critical factor in triggering mass political participation. A relatively unified governing elite in a developing country may be less inclined to arouse mass participation than a divided elite. In a competitive political system both governing elites and their opponents are likely to seek mass support to use against each other. But if there has been little social mobilization, if the governing elite is unified, and if the government suppresses dissenting leaders, it is often possible to keep demands for political participation to a minimum. It is striking, for example, to see how little political participation and how little demand for it there is in many new states that have one-party or military regimes, even though, as in many African states, the political system was open and competitive for a few years.

It is probably the case that relatively smaller amounts of force can keep down political participation in less-developed systems than in most modern industrialized societies, though modern industrial societies generally have a higher capacity to exercise coercion. In any event, elites in many newly independent states readily perceive that political organization, mass movements, and mass dissent are the creations of a handful of people whose repression would bring an end to the discontent. This is the case so often that governing elites in under-developed countries find it particularly tempting to use repressive instruments. The fact is that the amount of repression necessary to squelch dissent and eliminate opposition movements has been rela-tively modest in most developing countries compared to modern totalitarian dictatorships.

GOVERNMENTAL OUTPUT

Thus far we have emphasized the impact of environmental factors on the growth of political participation, that is, the impact of the so-cial system on the political process. We have noted the role of the social mobilization process, the importance of changes in the system of social stratification, and the role played by an elite as a kind of vanguard in precipitating mass political organization. A fourth explanation for political participation looks at the government's impact on the citizen. This theory emphasizes the output of government as a factor in chang-ing the rate of political participation. First of all, the expansion of the extractive and regulative capabilities of government brings hitherto untouched groups into contact with government. If taxes are collected, law and order enforced by police, and new regulations imposed, in-dividuals are likely to respond by organizing themselves to deal with government or to defend themselves against the state. Similarly, once the state begins to assume welfare functions and distribute incomes and services, people will often start organizing to press the state to accelerate distributive measures. By taking on new activities, the state has in effect redefined what is political. What individuals once per-ceived as activities in the private realm or as religious matters (such as divorce, marriage, or inheritance rights) may now be viewed as a public matter.

Moreover as long as conflict resolution is a matter to be handled within the tribe or caste, resolved through traditional judicial bodies, or pursued through blood feuds, these activities are not thought of as "political," at least not in any larger national sense. But once central authority establishes a uniform court system, codifies the law, forbids blood feuds, and establishes a police system, then competing groups may try to defeat one another through national political action rather than through traditional combat. The conflicts may not be new, but the arena in which the conflicts take place has been changed, and competition and conflict now require political action.

Moreover the establishment of universal adult suffrage, the establishment of rights to form associations, engage in free speech, and maintain a free press provide an incentive to individuals and social groups to enter the political process. In short, political participation may also increase when the opportunity to do so has been created by the state. Obviously political participation is likely to be greater in an open democratic society than in an authoritarian one, and one need not postulate differences either in social stratification or levels of modernization to account for the difference.

The varying conditions under which pressures for political participation grow, specified by these four theories, can all be seen as the consequences of the growth of equality, differentiation, or capacity in a political system; in short, as the consequences of the development process of which participation is itself a part. The social mobilization theory, for example, is a variation of the concept of the growth of equality; the stratification theory is a variant of the notion of increased differentiation; the elite theory, focusing on the impact of a vanguard social class, emphasizes the importance of the spread of the concept of equality; and the theory that focuses on the expansion of governmental activity is a variant of the concept of capacity. In short, changes in social structure, in the value system, and in the institutions and performance of government—all elements of the development process—account for a growing demand for larger political participation.

It is important to note, however, that all these factors need not be in operation, that there may be and generally is an imbalance in the development process so that one factor, but not the others, may be at work. Moreover it is likely to make a considerable difference whether political participation occurs as a result of a small elite's introducing ideas of equality in a society with low social mobilization and little governmental capacity or it comes about as a result of increased social mobilization, the development of a more complex system of social stratification, and an expanding governmental system. The stage in the development process at which political participation takes place can be critical in determining such matters as how fully institutionalized political participation becomes—whether political movements are status-oriented or policy-minded, ideologically diffuse or highly specific, and, most important of all, how much success large numbers of people actually have in influencing the formation and implementation of public policy. It is important then that we look more closely at the question of the timing of increased political participation and ask what the consequences are for the political system if participation occurs at one point in the development process rather than another.

Part III. Historical Dimensions of Political Participation

Since, as we have noted, a rather large number of different factors can cause an increase in political participation, this increase (or demands for it) can take place at any time in the development process. The growth of large-scale political participation and its relation to other kinds of changes in the political system have important consequences for how political systems develop.[13] Here we shall consider the growth of participation in relation to four other types of changes: the development of the institutional framework for participation; the growth of central authority in relation to politically autonomous local authority; the expansion of the bureaucratic system, its autonomy, and the degree of its penetration into the society and economy; and the growth of a sense of national identification. In terms of the general framework of this book, we shall be looking at the growth of political participation in relationship to the growth of legitimacy, penetration, and identity.

THE INSTITUTIONAL FRAMEWORK FOR PARTICIPATION

In France, England, and Western Europe generally the demand for increased political participation arose before the institutional framework that would permit large-scale participation existed. Indeed, in much of Western Europe, demands for political participation by the new middle classes undermined the authority of monarchs and led first to the creation of elective bodies, then to the gradual expansion of the suffrage. The range of social classes permitted to participate in elections was widened—from the propertied to the nonpropertied, from the dominant ethnic and religious group to minorities, from the

---

[13] This theme is discussed in much of the writing on developing areas. Gunnar Myrdal in his *Asian Drama: An Inquiry into the Poverty of Nations*, 3 vols. (New York: Pantheon, 1968) notes that "in Europe the strong independent state with a fairly effective government and a common pattern of law enforcement and observance preceded nationalism, and both preceded democracy" (Vol. 1, p. 119). In South Asia, he continues, nationalism came first, then democratic ideologies ("if not much democratic reality") prior to the creation of effective governments (Vol. 3, p. 774). Myrdal notes two differences between the historic European cases and the developing areas: (1) the different order in which these development processes occurred and (2) the cumulativeness and overlapping features of these processes in the developing areas.

educated to the uneducated (or less-educated) working classes. The decision to incorporate new participants into the system generally resulted in some major institutional changes in the political system. The most important were the establishment of elective institutions, the establishment of the system of universal adult suffrage, and the institution of legal changes permitting the right of association. Each of these changes was often preceded by intense political conflict as new groups seeking to participate in a political system demanded that there be these institutional changes to incorporate them into the political system. It is important to note that, once an institutional change takes place, the new institution may make it possible for the political system to incorporate more easily other new groups into the political system at a later time. Thus once it is established that all literates shall be given the right to vote, then the lower classes and migrants seeking to influence the political system know that they can take part in the system once they learn to read and write. Similarly, once the right to organize into associations is granted, then any new occupation, social class, or community that seeks to increase its political influence can do so without necessarily creating a political crisis.[14]

In much of Europe these institutional changes, particularly the expansion of the suffrage and the passage of legislation establishing freedom of association, generally took place as a consequence of a growth in demand for political participation. In most late-developing countries, in contrast, it has been common for such institutions to be created prior to the rapid expansion of demands for political participation as a consequence of elite imitation of European and American political institutions. Thus some Asian and African countries with small nationalist movements established elective bodies and universal adult suffrage immediately after independence even though there was often little mass popular demand for such institutions.

The establishment of political institutions permitting political participation prior to the growth of large-scale demands for participation can have important effects on the kinds of commitment or lack of commitment to these institutions among citizens. It is striking to see how easy it has been in many African and Asian countries to overthrow parliamentary institutions, to replace competitive political parties with

[14] For an account of the historical controversies over the definitions of citizenship and the rights to participate, see T. H. Marshall, *Class, Citizenship and Social Development* (Garden City, N.Y.: Doubleday, 1965) and Reinhard Bendix, *Nation-Building and Citizenship: Studies of Our Changing Social Order* (New York: John Wiley and Sons, 1954).

military juntas, and to suspend elections or even the right to form associations.[15] Had these institutions been the outcome of a combative
process in which political groups fought for and thereby became committed to the establishment of these institutions, then they might have
proven to be more durable. There is something to be said for the
argument that what is fought for is more highly valued.

NATIONAL PARTICIPATION AND LOCAL AUTHORITY

In the historical movement toward increased political participation,
two decisions have been particularly important. One was the decision
to extend citizenship rights to the adult population. The other was to
establish an electoral system based on equalization of votes. The result
of both these innovations was to establish a direct relationship between
the citizen and central authority, thereby reducing the political role
of such intervening institutions as feudal lords, tribal chiefs, or the
church. Political participation has historically been associated with the
growth of central authority. As individuals began to pay taxes directly to central authority and were affected by compulsory military
service and compulsory education, as individuals began to be affected
by the state, there was growing pressure for increased citizen rights in
national politics.

Paradoxically, the growth of mass political participation has been
primarily associated with the centralization of authority rather than
with the growth of local institutions. Indeed, there are many instances
of steps taken by national governing elites to encourage political participation as a means of undermining local institutions. In late 19th
century Germany, for example, the establishment of suffrage and the
creation of national parties was in part directed against local landed
authorities. Similarly, in Ghana the efforts of Nkrumah's government
to expand the Convention People's Party as a mass political organization was in part a means of undercutting the authority of the Ashanti
chieftains. One function of a mass "participant" party in the one-party
states of Africa is to strengthen the center against local authorities by
seeking to get people to identify with a national political institution.
In India too the expansion of the suffrage and the establishment of
democratic electoral processes in the former princely states was a way
of eroding the influence of maharajas and strengthening loyalty toward the state and central governments.

[15] For an examination of the tensions in political systems in which political participation is high and institutionalization is low, see S. P. Huntington, *Political Order
in Changing Societies, op.cit.*

But when traditional local authority continues to remain powerful, when landlords, for example, continue to wield economic controls (and often legal and coercive powers as well) over the peasantry, then the establishment of national suffrage and the creation of representative institutions can become an instrument for strengthening the hand of local potentates at the national level. Landlords are often able to use their command over peasants, tenants, and landless laborers to extend their power into the national political system, and political parties and elected representatives can become the instruments of the landlord class. In short, if large-scale mass political participation is permitted in an electoral system before there has been land reform and before legal authority is transferred from local potentates to a nationally controlled bureaucracy, then the effect will probably not be the liberalization or radicalization of the political system but, on the contrary, a growing conservatism. With local landowners and aristocrats in national power "supported" by the rural masses, reform may become more difficult than if the countryside had not become enfranchised. This has been the pattern of political development in many countries of Latin America, where the effects of political participation have been so different from that in systems where participation took place after the autonomous authority of local potentates had been eliminated.

POLITICAL PARTICIPATION AND BUREAUCRACIES

Does political participation take place before or after the development of a bureaucracy, and how does the development of new bureaucratic institutions affect the growth of political participation?

In recent years in the United States and in Western Europe there has been a growth of demand for the right to participate in the making of rules within the institutions in which people spend most of their working hours—factories, colleges and universities, hospitals, newspapers, television stations, etc., that is, the institutions of modern society. This type of demand is of course not new, since the Reformation centered precisely on a variation of this issue—to what extent did laymen have the right to participate in the affairs of the Roman Catholic Church. Today universities are in an upheaval over the respective rights of students, professors, administrators, trustees, and alumni; in France and many other European countries there have been debates over the respective roles of management, workers, and government in the internal management of factories.[16] As it becomes increasingly clear to citizens that their lives are affected not only by the state but also by the many institutions that make up a modern society, the concern over participatory rights is shifting toward these new non-governmental institutions.

But this new demand raises some of the same fundamental issues that existed earlier in the controversies over the rights of citizens in relation to the state. What are the appropriate spheres of activity for the bureaucrat (whether he be a government bureaucrat or a university official) as against the members of the society or institution? This question calls attention to an important dilemma in the political modernization process—there is a conflict between the demands of citizens for the right to participate in the making of decisions and the demand of the professional bureaucrat for autonomy in the making of appointments, promotions, and decisions that in his judgment require "professional" expertise. This dilemma arises in countless public and private institutions—in universities between faculty who believe that they alone are competent to make appointments and to formulate curriculum policy and students who seek student power; between school teachers who want to be protected against parental interference in matters in which they consider themselves to be professionally competent and parents who want to influence the way schools educate their children; between bureaucrats in national, state, or local governments who believe they have the expertise to implement and even formulate policies aimed at accelerating production or improving transportation or rehabilitating slum housing and citizens who are unwilling to accept a doctor-patient definition of their relationship to government officials.

To what extent is the balance between the bureaucrat and the citizen affected by the timing of the development of bureaucratic institutions in relation to political institutions? Max Weber was very much concerned that the early development of a powerful bureaucracy when political institutions were still weak would lead to a system under which bureaucrats would follow their own private interests and values and not be responsive to political leadership. Weber feared that the

[16] Charles de Gaulle, in an address, promised that participation would become the guiding principle of a "renewed France." He defined participation as a system in which all those working in any organization—business or university—must be "associated directly with its functioning, with the results it achieves, and with the contribution it makes to the nation" (*New York Times*, June 30, 1968).

[179]

early bureaucratization of Prussia and Germany would enfeeble the democratization process. A number of historians have similarly argued that political parties became a more powerful political force in Britain than in France or Germany in part as a result of Britain's relatively late bureaucratization. And recently, in a similar vein, Fred Riggs has suggested that a "premature" development of bureaucratic structures, coming before parties and interest groups have had an opportunity to develop, could slow the democratization process in the developing areas and could lead to the development of unresponsive bureaucratic systems.[17]

A politically responsive bureaucracy, according to these arguments, is more likely to develop in a country in which parties, voluntary associations, and some form of representative institutions exist prior to or at least at the same time as the bureaucratic structure is being created than in a state in which an autonomous powerful bureaucracy is first created. If these arguments stand up after further historical investigations, we would be in a better position to predict the patterns and possibilities of democratization in many of the developing nations.

POLITICAL PARTICIPATION AND NATIONAL IDENTITY

In most Western European countries the growth of national sentiment took place prior to the democratic revolution. Frenchmen, to take the most obvious case, clearly thought of themselves as Frenchmen even before the French revolution. It is difficult for us today to consider France as a country with great cultural diversity, but prior to unification and centralization under the French kings, the area was in fact quite diverse. In language, the country was divided by the *langue d'oc* and *langue d'oil*; in art, between the predominance of early Romanesque traditions in the south and later Gothic styles in the north; in law, between the new royal codes of the north and the persistence of Roman law in the south; and in religion, between the religious orthodoxy of the north and the heterodoxies of the south. In spite of these cultural differences the French kings, aided by a war with England and by the spread of internal trade, were able to mold

[17] Fred W. Riggs writes "The merit system (in the bureaucracy) cuts at the root of one of the strongest props of a nascent political party system, namely spoils" ("Bureaucrats and Political Development: A Paradoxical View" in *Bureaucracy and Political Development*, Joseph LaPalombara, ed. [Princeton: Princeton University Press, 1963], p. 128). See also Fred W. Riggs, *Administration in Developing Countries: The Theory of Prismatic Society* (Boston: Houghton Mifflin Co., 1964) and *Thailand: Modernization of a Bureaucratic Polity* (Honolulu: East-West Center Press, 1966).

not only a single nationality but also a single cultural tradition. Had there already existed a stronger sense of local sentiment in the various regions of France and, more importantly, had political participation been high, then the task of building both a single nationality and a single culture would have been far more formidable.[18]

This already heightened sense of the right to participation is why nationality building is more difficult today in the developing areas than was the case in premodern Europe. Today's multi-ethnic political systems must bring diverse ethnic groups together at a time when there is often already a considerable amount of ethnic self-awareness and a considerable amount of political participation. Today the kinds of choices available to governing elites attempting to create a sense of national unity are, therefore, quite different from the alternatives available to Western European monarchs in the 16th or 17th centuries. Historically there have been at least two distinct patterns for relating culturally different groups to a single national polity.[19] One is a policy of incorporating an ethnic group into the political system while permitting the ethnic group to maintain its cultural distinctiveness. This policy assumes that there can be a single national *civic* culture without a single national general culture. Among the more developed countries this pattern has been followed by the governments of Switzerland, Belgium, Yugoslavia, and Canada. This approach has important policy consequences for the character and control of educational institutions and for the distribution of power within administration and within the legislature, and it also affects the choice of national symbols. The alternative pattern is one of assimilation aimed at destroying the cultural individuality of ethnic minorities. This approach obliterates the distinction between a general culture and a civic political culture. At one extreme of course this approach may lead to genocide and the expulsion of minorities, but more typically it means using the "national" language in the schools and discouraging those institutions that maintain the cultural distinctiveness of minority groups.

There are many factors that determine whether an assimilationist

[18] For an account of the process of state-building in western and central Europe from a geopolitical point of view, see W. Gordon East, *An Historical Geography of Europe* (London: Methuen, 1966), Part 2.

[19] For a discussion of these alternative policy choices, see Myron Weiner, "Political Integration and Political Development," *The Annals of the American Academy of Political and Social Science*, 358 (March 1965), 55-57, and Clifford Geertz, "The Integrative Revolution: Primordial Sentiments and Civil Politics in the New States," in *Old Societies and New Nations*, Geertz, ed. (New York: Free Press, 1963).

rather than an incorporationist policy can be pursued with any success by governing elites: the relative size and distribution of the ethnic groups, the extent of outside support enjoyed by ethnic minorities, and the degree of distinctiveness, complexity, and strength (not easily operationalized notions) of the minority cultures. Among these variables one should surely include the degree of politicization of the ethnic minority. An ethnic group that is politically passive and whose members do not participate in political life may more easily be assimilated or, for that matter, incorporated into political life than an ethnic group that is already self-conscious of its own identity and is already politically organized to deal with the political system in which it lives. In short, where ethnic minorities are already self-conscious participants in the political system, then the option of assimilation as a means of building national sentiment is generally not feasible.

The same political decisions that have a unifying effect under conditions of low political participation can have a distintegrating effect when there is large-scale political participation. It would have been easier, for example, for the British to have chosen Hindi as India's official language in the early part of the 19th century (when the decision to adopt English was made) than for the government of India to make a national language decision in the 1960's when all regional groups, each with its own language, are represented and active in parliament. Had Hindi been taught in the schools throughout the country and used as an official language for 100 years, the issue of a national language would not have been so divisive in the postindependence period. In contrast, the Dutch established Bahasa Indonesia, an adaptation of Malay, as an official language and as a language of instruction in the elementary schools so that in spite of the linguistic differences within Indonesia where approximately 25 major languages are spoken, the issue of a national language has not been divisive, as it has been in India.

In short, in systems with a high rate of political participation the policy options for a government involving the development of a sense of national identity must be different from those in political systems in which citizens are politically more passive.

Part IV. Sequences of Political Participation

Thus far we have considered the timing of new participatory movements in relation to other processes or crises of political development. We have explored the interaction of participation with the penetration of bureaucracy, the growth of national identity, the centralization of authority, and the institutionalization of participation. In terms of the framework of this book we can say that we have been particularly concerned with the relationship of the crises of political participation with other crises of political development.

A second way to look at the timing or sequences of political participation is to examine the order in which new participants enter the political system. We look at sequences *within* the process of political participation itself. Many of our theories describing the process of democratization, the spread of nationalism, and the establishment of a sense of national identity contain some elements of a sequence model of political participation: that is, they postulate that the order in which certain social groups began to participate in political life has had systemic consequences for the development of democracy or for the development of stable and legitimate authority.[20]

One theory of democratization in European history, for example, emphasizes the gradual unfolding of political participation as monarchies and aristocracies were challenged by the "rising" bourgeoisie who in turn were challenged by lower classes and by a growing industrial labor force. A sequence theory of political participation is often used to explain historical cleavages and alliances in political systems.[21] If, for example, the peasantry is brought into politics before there is large-scale industrialization and urbanization and before the power of the aristocracy has been broken, there may be an alliance of the peasantry with the landed aristocracy against the city dweller, against industrial entrepreneurs, and against the industrial labor force.[22] But

[20] For another sequential model of political participation, see T. H. Marshall, *Class, Citizenship and Social Development, op.cit.* Marshall provides a brilliant account of the history of the development of three notions of citizenship: civil, or the rights necessary for individual freedom; political, or the right to participate in government; and social, or the right to security, a reasonable standard of living and education. Marshall suggests that civil rights developed in 18th century England, political rights in the 19th, and social rights in the 20th. Using the crisis framework of this book, we might speak of the three sequences as legitimacy, participation, and distribution.

[21] For a penetrating discussion of the conditions under which a political system acquires the allegiance of the working class to democratic institutions without alienating the middle and upper social strata, see Robert A. Dahl, ed., *Political Opposition in Western Democracies* (New Haven: Yale University Press, 1966), p. 361.

[22] This was the case in several Latin American countries. Applying this notion, some historians of the French revolution have suggested that the absence of working class and peasant representation in the Third Estate in 1789 permitted greater militancy than probably would have occurred if they had been represented, since the French lower classes—at that time—were much more influenced by the aristocracy than by the bourgeoisie. See Charles Tilly, *The Vendee, A Sociological Analysis of*

if, on the other hand, there is no landed aristocracy or the power of the larger landholders has been broken, then industrial entrepreneurs may successfully forge an alliance with peasant proprietors (another "classic" conservative pattern) against a radical middle class and/or an industrial labor force. Or if the church has allied itself with conservative landholding elements, when the modernization process begins one can expect tensions within the church as the lower clergy begins to work with an increasingly politicized peasantry and urban labor force.

The typical Western European sequential pattern of political participation involved a shift in power from the countryside to the cities as urbanization and industrialization increased. Thus in Western Europe power was successively widened to incorporate demands for political participation by social groups as they became modernized.[23] The industrial entrepreneurs and the modern urban middle classes sought and generally won power first. Then the most educated sections of the working class—the skilled craftsmen—formed unions. Only later was this followed by the organization of the unskilled labor force. There is some evidence to suggest (although this generalization like those we have just made needs more precise historical investigation) that the peasantry who were most active politically were first those engaged in commercial agriculture rather than those engaged in subsistence farming. Suffrage was often extended on the basis of educational or at least literacy qualifications, thereby depriving the least modernized, or at least the uneducated, the right to participate.

Theories of the development of nationalist movements also generally imply a kind of sequential development of political participation. Some theories postulate that, although the first interest in displacing colonial government comes from a literary or cultural elite— intellectuals, priests and monks, writers and journalists—who are concerned with the preservation of a cultural heritage against Western cultural imperialism, nationalist movements are soon supported by urban entrepreneurs and the lower middle classes in urban centers

---

the Counterrevolution of 1793 (Cambridge: Harvard University Press, 1964). The rapid extension of the suffrage to the lower classes during the early phases of modernization can serve to strengthen the role of the most conservative elements in the countryside and cast therefore a politically moderate tone upon the entire modernization process.

[23] Robert R. Palmer, *The Age of the Democratic Revolution*, 2 vols. (Princeton: Princeton University Press, 1959-1964).

and shortly afterward win support from the working classes and the peasantry. This colonial model postulates the prior politicization of urban centers, followed by the politicization of the countryside. The implication of this latter model is that the spread of political participation in underdeveloped, former colonial societies generally means an increase in the power of what is typically described as "traditional" social groups as opposed to more "modern" elites.[24]

For example, many newly independent countries achieved independence through the efforts of the most modern, educated, urban elites. Once in power, however, under the influence of their own populist commitments, these elites often expanded suffrage immediately without imposing literacy qualifications. Some recent studies in elite change in developing areas show that new participants and younger elites are often less educated than those they replace, are more likely to represent the interests and outlook of peasant proprietors, and, in general, are more rural than urban oriented. As a consequence, their commitment to modernization may be less and their capacity to act in ways that will accelerate modernization may be (though by no means necessarily) less. In Ceylon the rise of rural participation in national politics and the growing political involvement of Buddhist monks, local Sinhalese-speaking school teachers, and traditional medical practitioners meant that religion and language displaced economic development issues as the most salient ones in politics. A similar pattern occurred in Turkey when the rural-based, more traditional-minded Justice Party took power.

There is some evidence to suggest that large-scale peasant participation during early phases of modernization also imposes significant constraints on the kinds of policies that modernizing governments can pursue. Since the state cannot readily impose high taxes on the rural sector, there is often a greater emphasis on more easily disguised, but less equitable, indirect taxes than on clearly visible land taxes or taxes on agricultural income. It has also been suggested that in a highly participant system the state will be less able to give attention to using its scarce government resources for developmental activities but will have to give more attention to welfare and distribution programs, and that the expansion of education will be dictated more by the demand of peasants for the opportunity to move

[24] For an analysis of the sequence of participatory changes in India, see Myron Weiner, "Political Development in the Indian States," in *State Politics in India*, Weiner, ed. (Princeton: Princeton University Press, 1968), pp. 37-40.

their sons into bureaucratic posts than by the need for the development of an educational system that can produce the skills necessary for a modern industrial society.

On the "positive" side (positive from an economic-development point of view), however, it should also be noted that large-scale peasant participation leading to heavier governmental attention to the development of the agricultural sector can be a more profitable use of capital resources, and that the resulting increase in the ability of peasants to buy consumer goods can also be a major stimulus to industrial development.

The issue of whether large-scale political, especially rural, participation slows or accelerates economic development is probably a false issue. What is more relevant is that large-scale political participation imposes constraints upon policy-makers, and, although the *speed* of economic growth may not be determined by the pattern of political participation, the *kind* of economic growth which takes place may be. Certainly the character of those who govern at the early phases of the modernization process and of the groups that subsequently come to share power has important consequences for economic development, but to explore these consequences in a rigorous fashion would require a systematic and empirical examination of the demands made by different social groups, the effects these demands have had upon economic policy, and, most important and often neglected, the impact these policies have actually had on the rate and patterns of economic growth.

Part V. Crises of Participation

In a predominantly black neighborhood of New York City a group of parents has fought for a larger part in the running of city-managed schools. In Paris, Berlin, Tokyo, and Berkeley students have demanded a position in the decision-making institutions of their universities. And in Czechoslovakia, Russian tanks moved in to halt a liberalization process that had permitted broader citizen participation.

In both modernizing and modern societies people seem inclined to create voluntary associations—partly for conviviality, partly to exchange information, partly to regulate their own activities, but often to influence government. Much of the time these new associations, which may be interest groups or political parties, local associations or national bodies, simply take a place in the political system alongside other groups, but often they create a national crisis of political participation. A participation crisis can be defined as a conflict that occurs when the governing elite views the demands or behavior of individuals and groups seeking to participate in the political system as illegitimate.[25] A participation crisis can occur under a variety of conditions.

First, the government elite may believe that it alone has the right to govern and therefore rejects demands for political participation by other social groups as illegitimate. For example, Western European monarchs and aristocrats, feeling that they had a right to govern by virtue of religious sanction, historical right, and their moral quality, were antagonistic to sharing power.

Also, an elite may feel that power is the prerogative of certain well-defined social classes whose minority position in the total population does not inhibit them from believing that power ought not to be shared with other groups who do not share the same values. Such a situation exists when a political system is dominated by a single ethnic group that bars political power to other ethnic groups demanding power. Among recent examples are the Watusi in relation to the Bahatu in southern Africa, the Arabs in relation to Africans in portions of northeast Africa, the French colons in relation to the Algerians before independence, and the Afrikaans of South Africa in relation to the Bantu people. In each of these circumstances a minority group controlling the political system fears that any sharing of power on the basis of equality would lead to their loss of control over the political system.

The conditions for a participation crisis can also exist when the elite has majority power and denies a share of the political power to minority groups seeking it. This crisis existed in parts of the American south when blacks were denied participation in the electoral system. And prior to the second world war there were participation crises in Central and Eastern Europe when governing elites sought to keep power away from geographically concentrated ethnic minorities in order to prevent secessionist movements.

A second reason for a participation crisis is that the groups that make demands may be organized into institutions that the governing

[25] It is necessary to distinguish between demands for political participation and the content of political demands. New participants, for example, may demand a greater share of governmental resources or may demand that their own language be taught in the schools, thereby creating a distribution or identity crisis simultaneously with a participation crisis. What distinguishes a participation crisis from other developmental crises is that the demand, whatever the specific content, also includes the right to share power.

elite view as illegitimate. The governing elites of many underdeveloped countries, for example, while accepting the principle that their citizens may organize to influence public policy, nonetheless view ethnic associations as illegitimate types of political groupings. Political elites of different political systems have remarkably diverse responses to the same types of political groupings. One elite may view a religious, caste, or tribal association as the "legitimate" expression of a community's identity and interest, while another political elite may view the same type of association as "exclusionist," "separatist," "communalist," and, therefore, as illegitimate. In Tanzania, for example, the governing elite does not view tribal associations as legitimate institutions for political activity, while the governing elite of neighboring Kenya is far more tolerant of tribal associations.

Third, governing elites may view demands for political participation as illegitimate because they view the methods of making demands as illegitimate. Many authoritarian political systems, for example, are prepared to share power but only with those who enter politics through narrowly prescribed channels. Governing elites of one-party systems, for example, may permit individuals to participate, but only if they join the party or institutions controlled by the party. In Tanzania and in Yugoslavia political participation has been encouraged and certain types of dissent permitted so long as they take place within the party organization. But in both countries political party participation outside of the one-party apparatus is not permitted, and in Yugoslavia efforts to form an official opposition have thus far been squelched.

All governing elites view certain forms of political participation as illegitimate. No governing elite views violence and civic disobedience as legitimate forms of political behavior. Most governing elites react sharply to participatory demands of a mass character that imply threats of violence or coercion, mass demonstrations, general strikes, and the like. Governing elites are typically reluctant to be responsive to demands made through methods that they define as being coercive for fear that the result will be a widespread disrespect for the established procedures which alone they consider legitimate.

A fourth possible condition exists when the types of demands made by political participants are viewed as illegitimate. A governing elite may view some demands as so illegitimate that it will not tolerate their acceptance as public policy, nor will it tolerate the entrance into power of groups that have as their goal the carrying out of what the elite perceives as illegitimate policies. A demand, for example, that the government establish an official state religion may be viewed with such anathema by a governing secular elite that it will not tolerate the rise to power of those who would implement such a demand. Similarly, some elites in Western Europe have felt as strongly on the question of state support for religious schools.

In the latter part of the 19th century many governing elites in Europe viewed demands for the establishment of a socialist state as being so illegitimate that groups that made such demands were declared illegal. The reverse situation exists today in most Communist states where governing elites view as illegitimate all claims for the restoration of private property.

Most Asian and African governments view demands for secession as illegitimate, have not permitted secessionist groups to publicly seek wider support, and would not permit such groups to take power unless they gave up their demands. The Indian government, for example, declared that parties advocating secession would not be legal, thereby forcing the largest opposition party in the state of Madras to give up its secessionist objective rather than go underground.[26] However, some governments do permit secessionist movements to participate in electoral politics for fear that repression would only create martyrs and support for the movement among the very groups whose national loyalty is sought by the government. It should be noted, incidentally, that secessionist movements are by no means confined to the multi-ethnic newly independent states of Asia and Africa. There is a small but violent Breton secessionist movement in France, an active Scottish nationalist party, a movement among the Basques of Spain, and an active nationalist movement in the French-speaking provinces of Canada.

The demand for special corporate representation on the part of certain ethnic minorities is another kind of demand, both in the developed and developing areas, which many governing elites view as illegitimate. Most colonial governments permitted some form of corporate representation, allowing each caste, tribe, or religious group to have exclusive control over the selection of its own representatives

[26] The Indian Criminal Law Amendment of 1961 is quite explicit. "Whoever by words either written or spoken, or by signs, or by visible representation or otherwise, questions the territorial integrity or frontiers of India in a manner which is, or is likely to be, prejudicial to the interests or safety or security of India, shall be punishable with imprisonment for a term which may extend to three years, or with fine or both." A similar law exists in Pakistan.

to some legislative body or advisory council. Moreover, there were often provisions for reserved appointments to the bureaucracy and even quotas for admission into schools and colleges. Some newly established governments in the developing areas have viewed such corporate forms of representation as contrary to the principles of national equality and national identity, since corporate representation serves to strengthen parochial identification. Corporate representation also runs contrary to the "modern" principle of equality of opportunity. But in many underdeveloped societies weak social groups pressed for some kind of corporate representation on the ground that equality of condition is the objective, and that if equality of opportunity alone were followed then weak social groups would fall behind even faster. Following this reasoning, the government of India reserves posts in the state and national administration for ex-untouchables, provides lower grade requirements for administrative appointments and for admissions to college, and in general utilizes a quota system. In contrast, Americans are so committed to the notion of equality of opportunity and so oriented toward achievement rather than ascriptive norms in public employment and university admissions that the demand for quotas has created a value crisis, especially among those committed to the achievement of social and economic equality.

Another demand causing a participation crisis—a variant of number four—is that made by new participants for decentralization of power so that they may share or control power at some level of the political system. The demand by ethnic minorities in a multi-ethnic society for control over their own territory is often viewed with considerable alarm by governing elites who fear that such decentralization will erode both national power and a sense of national loyalty.[27] Many newly established central regimes in the developing areas, unsure of their own command of national power, have directed their energies

[27] In France as elsewhere, there has been a long struggle between the centralists who were impatient of regional minorities and the decentralists, or, in French terms, between Jacobinism and Girondism. Though centralism in France predated Jacobinism, the Jacobin ideology provided a model of the centralized state for much of 19th century Europe and is still subscribed to by sections of the French government opposed to giving more power to the provinces. See "Paris Turning Its Attention to Poor and Disaffected Brittany," *New York Times*, February 1, 1969, p. 3. It's an ironic footnote to history that the Jacobins who played such an important role as ideological centralists were originally composed of deputies from Brittany and that one of their most prominent leaders, Michel Gerard, was a peasant proprietor from Brittany whose waistcoat and plaited hair were to become the model for Jacobin fashion. The centralized state, however, predated the revolution. Alexis de Tocqueville noted that "Under the Old Regime, as nowadays, there was not a town, borough, village or tiny hamlet . . . that could freely administer its own affairs. Then, as today, the administration held the French in tutelage."

toward the centralization of authority. Thus, in spite of the multi-ethnic character of many of these states, which would suggest the need for some kind of federal system, new regimes have often resisted demands for any decentralization. The postindependence Indonesian government, for example, was opposed to the establishment of a federal system and resisted demands on the part of political groups in the outer islands, especially in Sumatra and in the Celebes, for greater autonomy.

The fear of autonomy at the local level is especially acute when the demand comes from ethnic groups close to national boundaries. In such cases a central government fears, often rightly, that autonomy can be the first step toward the development of a secessionist movement. For this reason the government of India was reluctant for many years to grant autonomy to the Naga tribes and to the tribes in northern Assam.

In modern industrial societies the demand for local autonomy or, as it is sometimes referred to in the United States, "community power," seems to be particularly associated with regions or groups of people not sharing in the opportunities that an industrial society has provided other elements of the population. It is no accident that the Breton region of France, the French region of Canada, and the Scottish region of Great Britain, all economically backward areas of these countries, have had growing nationalist movements.

Since the historic thrust of political development virtually everywhere in the world has been toward the centralization of authority, the demand for political autonomy or decentralization is typically distrusted by most governing political elites. In the United States, for example, the demand by Black Power groups for community control, with blacks running their own schools, operating their own businesses, controlling their own welfare programs, and even managing the local police station is often viewed as an illegitimate demand by the governing power structure of most large cities, including of course the police departments, teachers' unions, and many businesses that operate in the ghetto areas.

The demand for the transfer of power to local groups often grows out of one or both of two considerations. One is that the local group, especially when it is a distinct ethnic group, believes that it is numerically too small and socially too weak to share power effectively in the larger political system.[28] Second, the local group may have a

[28] This feature of the demand for community control is caught humorously by Victor S. Navarsky in his definition of "participatory democracy" as "a practice

strong sense of community that creates a desire to set the group apart from others. In this case, the demand for community power may also be a device for preserving or strengthening the sense of community on the part of the ethnic minority.

Fifth, a participation crisis can also arise when the group that seeks participation does not want to share power with the existing elites but instead wishes to replace the governing elite and thereafter deny that elite the right to hold power. In short, we can have a crisis of participation when those who seek power view the holders of power as being totally illegitimate, without any historical right, religious sanction, or moral qualities that entitle them to govern or even share in the processes of government. The typical version of this pattern in the contemporary world is the demand by nationalists for the end of colonial government. The comparable situation in European history was the attack by revolutionaries on monarchies and aristocracies, particularly in France and Russia. Earlier we defined a participation crisis as one in which the governing elite viewed the demands of new participants as illegitimate. Here we have enlarged the definition to include the reverse situation in which new participants view the holders of power as illegitimate.[29]

Part VI. On the Prevention and Resolution of Participation Crises

How do political systems or, more precisely, governing elites respond to demands for political participation? And what are the consequences of their responding one way rather than another? Why does one political elite respond in a way that permits an orderly increase

---

whereby a community (usually black Northern) controls its own affairs in politics, economics and education without interference from the government. To be distinguished from 'states rights,' a practice whereby a community (usually white Southern) controls its own affairs in politics, economics and education without interference from the government" ("Word Game," *New York Times Magazine*, February 9, 1969, p. 14).

[29] All political crises involve a divergence in views between governing elites and portions of the participant masses. Professor John Montias, at an S.S.R.C. conference on historical sequences of political development, at which the papers in this book were discussed, suggested that a supply-and-demand framework could be used for the analysis of crises. Participation and distribution are demands made by the masses upon elites that control the supply; identity, legitimacy, penetration, and extraction are demands elites make upon the population. Thus citizens may try to increase participation and distribution while resisting governmental policies for extraction and penetration. Within limits citizens may accept both extraction and penetration, and within limits the elite may accept both participation and distribution. When the elite and mass are highly divergent in their valuation of the respective claims of each, then the country is likely to be faced with a formidable political crisis.

in the amount of political participation in the system while another elite responds in a way that creates a political crisis? It is fascinating to observe the varied responses that the governing elites of different political systems make to the same type of participation demands. In fact one useful research exercise would be to examine both historical and contemporary examples of these phenomena.[30] The aristocracy in one political system, for example, may refuse to share power with participants, while in another system the aristocracy may be willing to enlarge the circle of participants in government. A possible result in the first instance may be an intensification of conflict and a revolution overthrowing the aristocracy, as in France; in the second, the power of the aristocracy may decline but many of its values may be adopted by the new participants, as in Great Britain. In the developing areas it is striking to observe the different responses of governing elites to the efforts of tribes to take part in political life as tribal associations—to ban them in some systems, to incorporate them in others. What will be the long-term effect of these alternative responses on the ultimate development of a greater sense of national identity?

INSTITUTIONAL ADAPTATION

As Huntington and Verba have pointed out, the critical question in a participation crisis is not to ask simply how does the elite respond to demands for political participation, but to ask what new institutions emerge from the crisis. The establishment of new electoral procedures and institutions and the creation of new party organizations and interest groups have historically been the ways in which political participation has been institutionalized. These structures have typically provided a framework for new groups in each successive generation to enter the political system without necessarily creating a crisis. Citizens can learn to redress their grievances through established, legitimized political procedures only if these procedures do in fact offer them a reasonable chance of satisfying their demands—if there are, in effect, appropriate rewards for using these procedures and, by implication, punishments for failure to use them.

[30] The sudden expansion of new participatory demands is one factor that warrants systematic attention. A very rapid large-scale increase in political participation often creates a crisis situation because it frightens the existing elite so that it responds with repression; it strains the resources of the state, particularly of newly formed political systems with limited administrative capabilities and financial resources; and because there is a tendency for new participants, who have not been socialized into a civic order with established rules for influencing public authority, to use violence and civil disobedience.

But we cannot speak of electoral procedures or party structures as being institutionalized unless those who participate in politics value these procedures and structures. One of the most difficult and important issues in the study of political development is precisely this: how and under what conditions do procedures and institutions become valued in and for themselves, not simply for how they perform? After all, institutions often perform badly and we may continue to value them. This is what we mean, of course, when we say that an institution is legitimate. We value electoral procedures even when candidates we oppose are elected. In much of the developing world today electoral procedures, legislative bodies, and the system of choice-making through competitive political parties are not seen as having any intrinsic value; therefore, they are easily cast aside when at some point they are not working well.[31]

A crisis of participation therefore can be viewed as resolved when there is a new agreement among governing elites, contending elites and political participants on the legitimacy of demands and on the value of certain institutional procedures created to meet the demands. As a result of a crisis, for example, the working class may have won the right, legitimized in legislation, to form associations and to strike. In another crisis the governing elites may have agreed to expand the suffrage or allow representation to groups hitherto excluded from the political system. In still another crisis the government may accept the right of tribes or castes to organize into ethnic associations or, alternatively, the tribal or caste members may have come to accept the notion that tribal or caste associations are not legitimate, although as individuals they may participate in political life through multi-tribal national political parties. Finally, in another crisis the governing elites may accept the legitimacy of the demand for the nationalization of property, while socialist parties who have made the demand may now agree that they should use only established legal procedures and provide compensation for nationalized property.

Once a political system has resolved a participation crisis—that is, once there is a greater consensus or congruence among those who have power and those who seek it as to procedures, institutions, and demands, then the political system has a new capacity for coping with a

---

[31] Some people accept the democratic system because it seems like a useful system for solving problems; others because they feel it is the only legitimate form of government. Those who have an instrumental view of democracy will easily turn against it when the system "fails" to solve problems.

new range of problems. The first trade union strike, for example, may have provoked a political crisis, but thereafter union strikes may occur in greater numbers without necessarily creating a major crisis in the political system. Moreover, once workers are given the right to organize and to strike, governments generate the capacity to develop procedures for the management of industrial conflict.

In practice, of course, participation is not an all-or-nothing affair, and no institutional settlement is ever necessarily final. The choice for a governing elite confronted with a demand for new political participation is rarely between complete repression or complete equality of participation. In between is a wide range of institutional arrangements. Precisely how much political participation is permitted in a political system is central to the whole question of how participatory demands are resolved and why they are in practice almost never permanently settled. This question of how much participation is permitted centers around two theoretical issues—the question or theory of representation and the theory of access.

THE THEORY OF REPRESENTATION

The notion of representation has both structural and sociopsychological dimensions. From a sociopsychological point of view the concept implies that people feel represented by someone whom they have chosen and that the person chosen feels that he is "responsible" or "responsive" (two notions with quite different meanings) to those whom he represents.[32] There is also the structural issue, so central to the question of representation, of whether representatives to elected bodies are chosen by equal numbers of people so that votes and voters are weighed equally. In most political systems some groups of voters have more relative strength than others. As a result of this, in the United States there have been conflicts over apportionment, the issue of gerrymandering, and, more recently, the issue of rural overrepresentation in an increasingly urban society. Federal systems deliberately provide unequal representation on a regional (and what is often the same thing, on a linguistic, tribal, or religious) basis in order to maintain the loyalty of certain participants. But since populations move and demographic changes take place, the system of representation established at one point in time to satisfy some groups is no longer

[32] See Alfred de Grazia, *Public and Republic: Political Representation in America* (New York: Knopf, 1951) and Anthony H. Birch, *Representative and Responsible Government* (London: Allen and Unwin, 1964).

satisfactory to a later generation. Recent disputes in Canada and Belgium, as well as in the United States, illustrate this point.

THE THEORY OF ACCESS

In no political system do people have equal access to power. As David Truman has pointed out, those who participate have different degrees of resources.[33] The variables of organization, information, status, wealth, and social affinity to those whom they are trying to influence all affect the success of political participants in having access to political power. Though they may have equality in votes, in no political system do the richest men and the poorest have equal access. It should be noted again that individuals and groups participating in the political system may become dissatisfied with their limited access. A group of villagers or tribesmen with a long-established pattern of access to local administration may come to feel that the important decisions affecting their lives are now being made at the national and not the local level, and, therefore, they may seek access into the national political system. Similarly, a group of voters may come to feel that voting is no longer sufficient for exercising influence and may organize themselves to improve their access to the decision-making levels of government.

Since both the amount of influence people want and the amount they actually have vary, no pattern of political participation is ever fixed in a political system. When the gap between the two is very great, the political system is likely to be in considerable turmoil. When both are low (as in a traditional-subject culture) or both are high (as in some modern industrial societies), the political system is more likely to be stable. However, the main point is that in modern and in modernizing societies where the amount of influence people want changes no institutional arrangements have yet been found which automatically adjust to the changing relationships and changing demands of individuals and groups.

AUTHORITARIAN RESPONSES

Thus far we have considered some of the ways in which elites choose to permit greater participation in a political system. As we look more closely at patterns of political development in Asia and

[33] David Truman, *The Governmental Process: Political Interests and Public Opinion* (New York: Knopf, 1951). The concept of access is also a central theme in Robert A. Dahl, *Who Governs? Democracy and Power in an American City* (New Haven: Yale University Press, 1961).

Africa, we see that most governing elites in the developing areas have chosen to restrict rather than enlarge political participation. Most developing countries do not permit free elections, or have representative legislatures; they impose restrictions on opposition parties or ban them completely; they limit freedom of the press and assembly. Open party systems have been replaced by one-party states, patrimonial dictatorships, or praetorian rule. Initial attempts to reproduce the institutions of former colonial rulers have almost all ended, and while none of the new states has lapsed back into what can be called by any stretch of the imagination "traditional" political systems, very few regimes resemble that of their former colonial masters in any respect. The Indonesians have not reproduced the Dutch political system, the Tanzanians have not followed the British model, and the Congolese have hardly replicated the Belgian system. Moreover only a handful of newly independent countries have been able to preserve democratic institutions and practices for any extended period of time —India, Ceylon, the Philippines, Malaysia, Singapore, and Kenya are among the few. Almost everywhere else authoritarian dictatorships reign.

Though the new regimes are authoritarian, they often have little authority. Their ability to suppress opposition politicians may be high, but their capacity to enforce compliance upon a predominantly illiterate, nonindustrial, rural population is low. Were these elites simply concerned with maintaining the status quo, they might be satisfied with mere suppression. But they are in the main transformative elites who need public support to carry out their goals. Indeed, their object is typically to transform the attitudes and behavior of their citizens. Therefore most of the authoritarian elites governing the developing areas seek active rather than passive support and view some forms of political "participation" as desirable. Such governing elites often try to find new forms of political "participation" of the sort that will encourage or even mobilize citizens to support the regime and its goals without allowing them to make any demands upon it.

A governing elite may seek support participation for any one or several of the following reasons: it may seek some form of political participation as a means of creating or strengthening a sense of national identity; it may view support as necessary for increasing the regulatory and especially the extractive capabilities of the government—in short, support is needed for building an army, collecting more taxes, and imposing and enforcing new laws; the governing elite may view participation as a necessary step toward generating public involvement in economic development activities; finally, the elite may want expressions of popular support in order to strengthen its international capabilities—in order to be a force in world affairs and to influence its neighbors, the elite may want and need to demonstrate that it has popular support at home.

Building public support can substitute for developing certain institutions and it can be a substitute for other kinds of incentives. A government may try to increase its capacity to collect taxes by building a political party or by holding mass rallies instead of (or along with) developing an efficient administrative apparatus with a high extractive capability. Similarly, in order to increase economic growth, government may use popular support as a substitute for economic incentives as a means of getting people to invest more, work harder, or innovate.

Some of the most interesting institutional innovations in the developing countries in the past decade have been made by authoritarian regimes seeking ways of involving the public in development activities without at the same time allowing an increase in the demands made upon the regime. For example, the Pakistan government, after the military takeover in 1956, created a system of "basic democracies" that provided for maximum participation in the election of local bodies but which also provided for the indirect election of the president and the national and provincial assemblies, thereby leaving the national elite pretty much free to do as it pleased.[34] Generally, fostering participation at the local level has proven to be a useful device of authoritarian regimes for encouraging support for development activities without encouraging the growth of political demands.

A number of African states, however, have been reluctant to encourage political participation at the local level for fear that traditional tribal authority might be strengthened; they have chosen instead to encourage participation in a single national political party. Several authoritarian regimes in Africa have chosen to use the single mass party as an instrument to mobilize the populace into development activities and, in general, to encourage compliance with government

---

[34] In practice it meant that President Ayub Khan could make arrangements directly with Pakistan's established powers, from the officers of the armed forces down to the village headmen and landowners.

policy.[35] Few of these mass parties, however, have lived up to the expectations of the elite.[36] Moreover, in spite of the rhetoric, the age of mass political participation has hardly touched much of Africa. Few people are affected by the so-called mass parties, and political passivity rather than political involvement is still the typical pattern in much of rural Africa.[37] But as urbanization, mass communication, and industrialization take place, and government administration increasingly penetrates and affects the countryside, then political participation will grow and the stability of many authoritarian regimes is likely to be threatened. Moreover, many of the new authoritarian regimes have not found a satisfactory way of sharing power with the younger generation, and as the elites age they are likely to be challenged by younger men.[38]

ENCAPSULATION

While both the democratic and the authoritarian responses to participatory demands can in their own way lead to an increased capacity to govern, there are possible elite responses that allow increased participation but have a negative effect insofar as increasing governmental capabilities is concerned. For example, although an elite may consider a group's demands as illegitimate and make it clear that it will continue to view the demands as illegitimate, it may

[35] Other voluntary or quasi-voluntary institutions, such as trade unions and co-operatives, are also used by authoritarian regimes to affect citizen attitudes and behavior; indeed, even nonauthoritarian regimes in the developing areas often attempt to influence or control voluntary associations in order to restrain them from making demands upon government. See Willard A. Beling, ed., *The Role of Labor in African Nation-Building* (New York: Praeger, 1968).

[36] For a critical examination of the mythology associated with the so-called mobilizing role of one-party states, see Aristide R. Zolberg, *Creating Political Order: The Party Systems of West Africa* (Chicago: Rand McNally, 1968).

[37] Though coups and revolutions have been endemic in Africa, there are few if any instances where one could say that a change in regime occurred as a result of a popular uprising. The same point, incidentally, could be made for most of the coups elsewhere in the developing areas. As Manfred Halpern points out, there have been no peasant rebellions in the Middle East in the 20th century; nor have any governments in South or Southeast Asia been overthrown by a mass upheaval (Manfred Halpern, *The Politics of Social Change in the Middle East and North Africa* [Princeton: Princeton University Press, 1963]).

[38] In this brief survey of strategies used by authoritarian elites to respond to demands—or anticipated demands—for political participation we should also note the role of material rewards. The government may take measures to provide portions of the citizenry with a greater share in the fruits of economic growth, a policy often pursued by revolutionary left-wing governments. The elite may also co-opt potential participants into the political system, a strategy pursued by the Iranian monarchy. In short, authoritarian regimes often pay off potential political participants with government jobs or higher income.

permit the group to organize and to take part in public life—only, however, with the understanding that the group will not be admitted into the corridors of national power. Many Western European governments have permitted Communist parties to take part in national parliamentary elections and allowed them to take power at the local level but have made it clear that they would not permit the Communists to take national power. Similarly, in the developing areas some governments permit ethnic minorities to organize but consider illegitimate and unacceptable any demands that might result in increasing the minority's control over a portion of the nation's territory. In addition, certain groups in many democratic countries are permitted to take part in political life even though their demands— for church-supported schools, or for secession, or for the expropriation of private property—are viewed as illegitimate by the governing elite and by a large proportion of the population.

If a substantial proportion of the population belongs to groups making unacceptable demands, then there are certain kinds of actions that government cannot take and certain dissatisfactions that simply cannot be met. The government, for example, may not be able to reform and modernize the educational system if it is not willing to negotiate the question of state involvement in church-supported schools or the choice of languages to be used in the schools. The government may not be able to pursue an accommodating policy toward a minority group even when prudence dictates that accommodation may be the only alternative to civil war, a conclusion many outsiders drew on observing the response of the Nigerian government to the Ibo demand for greater regional autonomy.

There are thus some political systems in which political groups are permitted limited forms of political participation. They are allowed to organize and seek supporters; they may even put up candidates for public office but they are not permitted to affect public policy. In such political systems some political groups do not communicate with one another. One might say that they are encapsulated in the political system but not incorporated by it.[39]

[39] Some writers would describe such systems, which allow powerless participation, as unintegrated, based on the definition of integration that refers to the regularization of structures and processes whereby the discrete elements in a given national territory are brought into meaningful participation in a political system. We can describe this form of integration as process integration. France, for example, has national integration—in the sense of a shared national identity—but not process integration. Therefore we can say that countries like France and Italy, which have encapsulated certain political groups, have a low degree of process integration.

DILEMMAS OF NEW PARTICIPANTS

Thus far we have discussed participation crises from an elitist point of view by focusing on the alternative strategies available to elites for coping with new demands. But it is also important to consider the kinds of strategies available to new participants who seek greater access into the political system. Since there is a vast social science literature describing and explaining different types of political movements, it is not necessary to enumerate the enormous range of political demands and types of political organizations that men have created.[40] We should note, however, that irrespective of the type of political movement or the content of the demands being made, there are certain characteristic choices or dilemmas faced by new participants as they deal with governmental authority.[41]

Should they, for example, work within the existing legal framework set by governmental authority, thereby increasing the possibility of winning the support of moderate sections of the elite but also increasing the possibility of losing support from more militant groups? Should they make moderate demands that are relatively easily negotiable? Should the demands be extreme in order to solidify loyalty among followers even at the risk of bringing a coercive response from those upon whom the demands are made?

Should a group work alone so as to maintain purity of purpose, program, and ideology at the risk of being isolated and ineffective, or should the group work in coalition with others in order to increase its strength but at the price of compromising its program and ideology?

Should demands be explicit and precise, offering therefore the elite a clear possibility to bargain but also thereby setting a ceiling to what can be obtained, or should the group be deliberately imprecise in its demands to see how far it is possible to go? Similarly, should de-

[40] For a review of types of political movements, see Neil Smelser, *Theory of Collective Behavior* (Glencoe: Free Press, 1963). See also the articles on "Social Movements" in *International Encyclopedia of the Soviet Sciences*, Vol. 14, by Rudolf Heberle (pp. 438-44) and Joseph Gusfield (pp. 445-52), including an extensive bibliography.

[41] In choosing among alternative strategies it should be noted that new participants do not feel the same constraints experienced by those groups that already participate in the political system. Old participants can lose influence; new participants often feel that they have nothing to lose "but their chains." Moreover, since new participants haven't yet used the rules prescribed by the governing elite, they often haven't begun to value these rules. For an excellent discussion of the conditions under which new participants in a political system develop a sense of political community, see Reinhard Bendix, *Nation-Building and Citizenship: Studies of Our Changing Social Order* (New York: John Wiley and Sons, 1964).

mands be directed at the weakest, most vulnerable institutions in the political system where success is most likely but where the consequences are also likely to be limited, or should demands be directed at the strongest institutions where victory would be more difficult but where the long-term impact might be greater?[42]

How these questions are answered by new participants will obviously determine the kinds of challenges faced by governing elites. And, in turn, how governing elites respond to demands will influence which of these choices will be made by new participants. There is thus a feedback relationship between demands and response. If a moderate demand receives a negative response, a political group may adopt illegitimate methods that in turn may result in a repressive response by government. Or a political group whose demands are moderate but whose methods are militant can often increase its popular support by provoking government into a repressive response.[43] In these ways small disputes between a few citizens and government can often be escalated into a participation crisis.

PERSISTENCE OF PARTICIPATION CRISES

While the crises of identity and legitimacy, or what Pye has called the crises of the political culture, can be resolved for rather long periods, the crises of political participation seem destined to be recurrent in modern democratic systems. Although any particular participation crisis may be resolved through structural changes in the political system—by opening access to the electoral process, for example, or by the organization of political parties and interest associations—nonetheless crises are likely to recur. The recurrence is a result of two kinds of changes that constantly occur in modern societies and that lead citizens to be dissatisfied with the program, ideology, style, and organization of existing political parties and interest groups. These changes may also make citizens dissatisfied with the existing

[42] For a study of the use of mass protest as a strategy for relatively powerless groups to increase their bargaining ability, see James Q. Wilson, "The Strategy of Protest: Problems of Negro Civic Action," *Journal of Conflict Resolution* 3 (September 1961), 291-303. The theme is further developed by Michael Lipsky's "Protest as a Political Resource," *American Political Science Review*, 62, 4 (December 1968), 1141-58. Lipsky also describes the way in which protest can be used to build a political organization.

[43] Provoking government into repressive action is a favorite strategy among revolutionaries. Among American new-left radicals such action is an attempt to cope with what Herbert Marcuse has called the "repressive toleration" of the American political system; it is a system, he argues, that readily makes concessions in order to avoid radical change.

pattern of representation or with the degree of access they have to individuals with the authority to make political decisions affecting their lives.

The first of these changes is a shift in the socioeconomic pattern of society. For example, new occupations may appear and old ones may be eliminated as a result of technological advances. People may move from one part of the country to another. The status and incomes of farmers and workers or of ethnic minorities may change. There may be shifts in the industrial importance and prosperity of some regions of the country. This type of change is an enduring part of a modern industrial society and it tends to lead one or more groups of people to be dissatisfied with the amount of power they have.

The second type of change leading to a recurrence of participation crises is generational change. New generations are often dissatisfied with the patterns established by those who preceded them. Institutional structures created by one generation to meet its needs may not suit the needs of the next generation.[44] Postwar Austria and Germany, for example, needed a coalition government of centrist parties, but the elders who created the pattern responded to dissensions and dangers that had little meaning or reality to a younger generation. Similarly, the civil liberties by which one generation sought to protect itself against reactionary and authoritarian forces may later be dismissed by a younger generation eager to remove conservative or even liberal elements from power.

There appears, moreover, to be a tendency in all modern industrial societies for a portion of the younger generation to be dissatisfied with all institutions. While modern complex societies create and need institutions and rules to make orderly life possible, a segment of each new generation feels that all institutions destroy human spontaneity by imposing restraints and establishing rules. Those who hold this view therefore use their political participation to undermine the whole process of institutionalization. This anti-institutional mood can exist in opposition to authoritarian regimes and to civil demo-

---

[44] For an historical analysis of the role students have played in revolutionary movements, see Lewis S. Feuer, *The Conflict of Generations* (New York: Basic Books, 1969). "If historical materialism is the ideology of the working class," writes Feuer, "then historical idealism is the ideology of student movements. If 'exploitation' is the master term for defining class conflict, then 'alienation' does similar service for the conflict of generations." (Feuer, "Conflict of Generations," *Saturday Review* [January 18, 1969], 53). For a critique on the literature on political generations, see Marvin Rintala, "Political Generations," *International Encyclopedia of the Social Sciences*, Vol. 6, pp. 92-95 (with bibliography).

cratic orders. To those who view institutions, rules, and conventions as an enemy the distinction between a political system that is closed to political pressures and one that provides open access to those who seek change is irrelevant. The modern revolutionary mood therefore differs from the old; while older revolutionaries sought to reconstruct the old order and replace old institutions with new ones, modern youthful revolutionaries are often more concerned with bringing an end to all institutions. Thus, ironically, at a time when modern democratic societies have become more successful than ever before in creating open participant political institutions revolutionary movements have now arisen that question the very notion of institutionalized political participation.

CHAPTER 6

PENETRATION: A CRISIS OF GOVERNMENT CAPACITY

JOSEPH LA PALOMBARA

~·~

Part I. Introduction

THE CRISIS OF penetration, like that of distribution, relates primarily to certain changes in governmental performance and to certain kinds of outputs of the political system. Although these changes also involve psychological dimensions—and certainly bear directly on more psychologically rooted crises like identity and legitimacy—they turn our attention to more specific institutional arrangements and their modification (or lack thereof) through time. In the broadest sense all crises, conceived as sharp breaks with traditional processes, challenge the capability of an existing governing elite, and indeed such challenges in each of the crisis areas we discuss place pressure on the elite to modify old institutions and/or to create new ones.

Such pressures to effect change and/or to modify or adapt institutions seem ubiquitous among political systems. We know however that the intensity of the problem often can and does lead to civil strife—indeed to a form of internal war. We refer here not merely to the kinds of violence that attended the national unification of Western nations like Germany and Italy, or non-Western nations like Japan, India, and Nigeria. We allude to all those examples of resistance to national policies—they number in the thousands—where those who sought to avoid effective national penetration were willing to resort to violence on a large scale and to risk life and limb. Where such events occur or threaten, a crisis as opposed to a "normal" problem of penetration is present.

Similarly, a penetration crisis exists when the proportion of resources a nation must devote to penetration itself greatly limits or imperils its other activities. This would tend to cause a chain reaction wherein the legitimacy of the national government, however fragile or secure, is threatened in its turn, thus compounding crises.

What distinguishes the crisis of penetration analytically is that it may be associated with pressures on the governing elites to make institutional adaptations or innovations of a particular variety. It is in this sector of change, for example, that problems of public administrative organization become preeminent. This is so not merely with regard to the need or desire to maintain a given physical territory intact and differentiated from the "outside," but, perhaps more importantly, to the need for "penetrating" aspects of the sociocultural system which have remained nonidentified with, nonparticipating with, immune from or indifferent to the political system for which the crises are relevant.

To state this somewhat differently, the crisis of penetration introduces in the human environment either purposeful or unanticipated changes that test the organizational, technological and/or diplomatic capabilities of an existing governing elite. Examples of such changes abound in the historical or contemporary world. The elite, for whatever reasons, may be faced with the desire or the need for governing greatly expanded territory. When Jefferson more than doubled the size of the United States through the Louisiana purchase, he and his associates confronted a penetration crisis purposefully induced. When a Pakistani elite confronted a postpartition situation involving a vast nation-state whose two parts were physically separated by over a thousand miles, a similar though less purposeful crisis was created. When changes in political participation confront an elite with extreme difficulties—such as those associated with communalism in India or tribalism in Africa—a penetration crisis of unanticipated dimensions and proportions is set into motion. Indeed when in any political system a ruling elite seeks to modify the prevailing authority system, the elite itself has both created and must confront a penetration crisis, the resolution (or failed resolution) of which will offset whatever equilibrium other historical crisis management may have established.

The penetration crisis also brings dramatically to the surface problems of institutionalization, in the sense intended by Huntington.[1] For it is apparent on the one hand that those political systems and governmental arrangements most readily able to respond to the changes we are suggesting are those that manifest the greatest institutionalization and the least fragility. This is a matter of considerable importance since some of the literature on social change tends to

[1] S. Huntington, "Political Development and Political Decay," *World Politics*, 17 (April 1965), esp. 394-403. See his much more detailed treatment of this problem in his *Political Order in Changing Societies* (New Haven: Yale University Press, 1969).

associate the most deeply and firmly institutionalized sectors of society with the greatest capacity (and predisposition!) to resist change. Yet, as Apter[2] and others have noted, it is exactly certain kinds or forms of "traditional" (read "deeply institutionalized") authority that may in fact be best suited for handling the kinds of problems created by the crisis of penetration. As a matter of fact, certain tensions growing out of a particular sequencing of crises—as, for example, when successful demands for greater participation precede or run ahead of effective penetration crisis management—will be the most severely felt and most damaging to political stability when the capability of dealing with penetration problems is low or inadequately developed. These and other developmental problems will become clearer as our discussion proceeds.

Part II. The Meaning of Penetration

Before we can proceed to a discussion of various aspects of the penetration crisis however it is necessary to clarify the matter of definition as well as certain misconceptions regarding the relationship between "modernity" and the ability to respond to the environmental changes we include in the penetration crisis category. All too often we misleadingly come to associate the ability of political leadership to resolve penetration crisis problems with the degree of economic and technological "modernity" characteristic of a particular society. For when we speak of penetration "demands" or "requirements," we generally refer to the *effective presence* of a central government throughout a territory over which it pretends to exercise control. From this vantage point the easiest test of "bad" crisis management would be the ability of a political elite to hold the real estate together. Good examples of politics falling at one end or another of this implied continuum would be, say, Nigeria and the Congo at one extreme, Switzerland and the United States at the other.

The rub here is that this conceptualization stresses the ability of a central government to keep a given territory *physically* united; it tends to an overemphasis on formal organizational means to achieve this particular end; and it may very well obscure several quite important respects in which penetration may be achieved or in any event greatly buttressed in its formal organizational dimensions by

[2] David E. Apter, *The Politics of Modernization* (Chicago: University of Chicago Press, 1965); *The Political Kingdom in Uganda* (Princeton: Princeton University Press, 1962).

[207]

the way in which other crises, particularly those of legitimacy, identity, and distribution, have been handled.[3]

Where the attitude toward capability focuses narrowly on penetration as a matter of boundaries and real estate, it is very easy indeed to commit the technological fallacy. More than one observer of the developing countries has associated the weakness of central government with the lack of organizational and technical means to extend control over the outlying reaches of the polity or nation-state. Wherever one finds rebellion, secession, or armed truce between central and regional political elites, or competition with the central government in international affairs, it is correct (in the truistic sense) to conclude that the penetration crisis has been inadequately resolved. It is *not* however correct to infer from such events that the problem is primarily organizational-technological or that such problems tend to be more frequent at lower than at higher stages of economic development. In this regard it should suffice to point out that, as of this writing, both Nigeria and Canada are experiencing quite similar penetration crises and that neither technological nor organizational considerations would suffice in any effort to understand their bases or the probable ability of either central government to resolve the crisis it faces.

We shall discuss in a moment the sense in which levels of organizational skill and technology may or may not be theoretically associated with penetration crisis management. In order to separate the strictly geographical from the sociopsychological aspects of this phenomenon, however, it is necessary to define what it is we mean by "penetration." In its broadest sense penetration means conformance to public policy enunciated by central governmental authority. The degree of penetration in any polity may be viewed as the probability that governmental policies regarding the polity as a whole, or any of its subdivisions, will be carried out—at least with regard to the spirit of such policies and the regulations that ensue from them.

Differently put, for any political elite, penetration refers to whether

[3] We are aware that this discussion, even though somewhat recast conceptually, is not radically different from a vast literature dealing with force, consent, or contract, or natural evolution as the basis for the organization of the "state" and the basis for the state's legitimacy. Our discussion is perhaps justified by the fact that we are not seeking here definitive answers regarding the "origins" or indeed the "nature" of the state so much as we are seeking to elucidate what patterns of stimulus and response that can be empirically observed and measured seem to be associated with particular lines of political evolution.

they can get what they want from people over whom they seek to exercise power. Such power clearly refers to areas of governmental policy that go considerably beyond taxation, conscription, and control of deviant behavior. It would include as well the full range of social welfare activities, programs of animal husbandry, agricultural modernization, shifts in forms of productive activities, demographic management, new modes of political participation, and so on. As we shall note below, the problem of gaining compliance with such policies refers not merely to geographic sub-divisions of a polity but to social, ethnic, linguistic, racial, and other subdivisions as well.

The penetration phenomenon has two important and closely interrelated dimensions. The first may be thought of as the capability of the central government to achieve penetration regardless of what may be the views, desires, attitudes, or predispositions of those who are the objects of governmental policy. The second dimension has to do with the existing or modified ability and predisposition of the objects of policy to receive information regarding policy accurately and to *wish* to conform to such policies voluntarily. Varying degrees of such ability and predisposition are obviously inextricably tied to what we mean by legitimacy. Consequently a particular choice of means for resolving a penetration problem may in certain political cultural contexts result in successful penetration crisis management, but it may also recreate or aggravate legitimacy problems.

When one comes at this problem normatively, as most writers about politics have done for two millennia or more, the question of means looms large, quite apart from what may be the elite's ability to force conformance to its wishes. In our theoretical and historical formulation, considerations of means as they refer to patterns of differentiation and capacity are value free; they do not raise troublesome normative questions; and they may be evaluated in the most restrictive kind of ends-means framework, such as the need for holding together, or expanding, the territory constituting the existing polity.

Normative as well as empirical-operational reflections are introduced by our discussion of equality. For if we are correct in assuming that the thrust or motivation for equality is a generalized condition, everywhere to some degree discernible in space and time where societal organization is present, it is clear that we must conclude that certain *means* of resolving penetration crises are undesirable. Whether they are also untenable or inefficacious over time depends, we believe, on the intensity of the need or desire for equality in its several dimensions.

In the strict sense of the definition of penetration we have suggested, no nation-state has ever succeeded for long in achieving total geographic or sociopsychological penetration. This is true not only of societies that are often described as systems of overwhelming consensus, like the United States and Great Britain, but also of countries like the Soviet Union and China to which the label of totalitarian has been attached. Even today, there are relatively vast areas in the Soviet Union where what is enunciated as national policy at Moscow may or may not be implemented at the geographic periphery. Closer to home it is increasingly apparent that federal policies will have a problematical outcome not merely in the remote regions of "Appalachia" but in some of our major urban centers as well.

On this score, the developing nations are not so much different in kind as they may be different in numbers. Manila is in a touch-and-go relationship to the outer islands of the Philippines as far as implementing central policies or administrative regulations is concerned. The geographic boundaries of the Congo are fuzzy and uncertain from the standpoint we are discussing. Whether there exists a central governmental authority in Mao's China today is open to considerable doubt. How many of the states on the vast Indian subcontinent are meaningfully penetrated by New Delhi is a matter of equal concern to leaders of the Congress party and international peacekeeping organizations. Furthermore, everywhere that there exist large, restive ethnic or racial minorities, the efficacy of the central government's penetration capacity is continually brought into question. One need not look to the newer nations to note this; a glance at recent events in Northern Ireland, Quebec, the Basque country, and the American South would suffice.

Wherever one looks, then, it is necessary to ask whether and why penetration crisis management in both the geographic-controlling and sociopsychological-conforming sense seems to be working well or badly. In raising such questions it is essential that we clarify both the theoretical efficacy of *means* available to the central authority and the predispositions to conform apparent in the extant political culture.

Part III. Technology and Penetration

It is far from clear that capacity in the management of penetration crises is positively and directly related to the degree of technology available in a particular society. This seems to be true irrespective of what may be the predisposition to conform to central authority, or to accept change, on the part of the objects of central authority. Where, as in Thailand, social-psychological structures tend to lead the Thais peaceably to adapt to considerable changes in both the patterns and content of central authority and its policy output, this predisposition is evidently deeply rooted in cultural patterns that are not in turn tied to given levels of technology. The instabilities of Thailand seem to have been much more closely associated with intra-elite struggles at the center than with changing problems of penetration. The tautologous observation here evidently is that challenges of development confronting elites at the nation's center (that may require modifications in organization and indeed in life style), are readily met where the political culture and broader society evince marked willingness to adapt to new conditions. Whether future changes in technology, patterns of work, and economic organization will someday modify that tendency to adapt is an interesting question, but it in no way suggests that level of technological development independently and systematically affects penetration.

Our point can be best illustrated, perhaps, if we think of contemporary and historical situations where the Thai pattern is obscure, or where for various reasons geographically, ethnically, socially, religiously, or geographically based segments of the society are not willing to adapt or where they actively oppose the very changes associated with a penetration crisis.

One might begin by noting that both aspects of the penetration crisis were resolved by a number of nation-states long before anything like a modern industrial technology was available to centralizers or nation builders. This pattern is true not only of the classic case of Great Britain but also of such countries as France, Switzerland, Brandenburg-Prussia, and Japan. Indeed, it is in part because of historical examples such as these that we shall want to discuss later in this volume the significance of the sequencing and clustering of the various crises of political development.

In the case of England, history will show that the Normans and Angevins succeeded in establishing central control during the twelfth and thirteenth centuries. To be sure, the penetration crisis was not thereby permanently resolved, and in the ensuing decades and centuries the central authorities were compelled to respond to penetration crises that reemerged both internally, as regions resisted expansionist tendencies from London, and externally, as "outsiders" sought to wrest control from central power holders. In recent months, of course, Great Britain is experiencing a major penetration crisis, growing out of the ethnic conflict between Protestants and Catholics in Northern Ireland.

Moreover, penetration in the earliest decades was at best approximate, limited to a small number of fiscal and military powers exercised from the center and implemented by a combination of contractual arrangements on the one hand, and relatively primitive means of transportation and military capability on the other. These facts alone would lead one to want to draw some careful and seemingly important distinctions between twelfth-century England and later nation-building eras in France, Brandenburg-Prussia, and Japan, when gunpowder, new concepts in military organization, and a much improved system of transportation and communication were at hand.

To note that penetration crises materialized and were resolved in some places before the era of industrialization and technological revolution is not meant to dismiss completely the importance of either in assessing the capability of nation-building political leadership. It would be simplistic and antihistorical to obscure the fact that in absolute terms the Industrial Revolution greatly changed the potential for control available to both existing and aspiring central political elites. However, as we are viewing the concept of penetration here, it seems to us all too easy to see the modern means of transportation, communications, and physical coercion as resources available primarily to the centralizers (i.e., to those who confront the penetration crisis from the vantage point of established power) and therefore to obscure the fact that varying amounts of the same technology are available to resisters, those nonpredisposed to conform—the system wreckers.

The relevant question to ask about technology, and indeed about organizational skill, at any point in time when a penetration crisis arises is who has how much or can utilize how much of the available technology. For the nation builders or centralizers or crisis managers of many developing countries there are two important ironies to note here. The first is that in some circumstances the availability to would-be centralizers of the most modern technology, particularly its instruments of force, are irrelevant. What good, one might ask, are some modern highways, armored columns, massive airpower, improved identification methods, and instantaneous communications systems where those who resist penetration are located in inaccessible places, or in places where the psychological predisposition to resist is little weakened by the use of force? Fidel Castro and a few hundred of his comrades remained essentially immune from the sophisticated military technology Battista sought to use against them on the small island of Cuba. Short of atomic saturation, the immensely superior technology of the United States is insufficient to permit the leaders of South Vietnam to gain effective penetration even of that portion of the Vietnamese peninsula that lies south of the seventeenth parallel. Somehow the difficulties confronted by the twentieth-century centralizers seem immensely greater than anything confronted by the Normans or Angevins seven centuries ago, or the Prussians and the French at Paris in the seventeenth century.

The second irony is that an advanced technology itself can work against the management of penetration-crisis problems. For the critical question about technology is its *relative* availability to contending forces in the power struggle. Although this has always been the case, in the contemporary world it seems to have complicated greatly the problem of geographic penetration where force must be used or is elected as a major instrument. Thus those who unified Nigeria or prevented its disintegration, face problems of effective resistance through the use of modern weapons far greater in magnitude than was the case, say, in seventeenth-century France or nineteenth-century Japan.

Such examples abound in the developing areas, and they suggest that we proceed with considerable caution in any attempt to relate the variables of industrialization and technology to the resolution of the penetration crisis. It would seem necessary first to assess the relative access to technology or its products available to the would-be centralizers as opposed to those population segments or to those outlying geographic regions with separatist and autonomous views. Where the technology of warfare is involved, such a calculus seems obvious enough. But the procedure is important to follow even when resistance to penetration falls short of terror, violence, or open warfare. For example, just as the same mass medium (like the cheap transistorized radio) can free man, it can enslave him; the same instrument for diffusing information and winning support for the central government's policies can and is used to thwart the central government's efforts to create new loyalties or to gain widespread conformance to its policies.[4]

Such an assessment would also have to include estimates of the amounts and kinds of technology that would be forthcoming to contending groups from outside of the nation-state involved in crisis confrontation. Consider the case of the United States, where during the short space of a half-century its territory was extended from the Appalachian Mountains to the Pacific Ocean. Some of the expanded territory was acquired by purchase, some by treaty, some by military conquest. In more than one place these changes encountered resistance from local inhabitants, the Indian tribes. More than one B-grade motion picture has hinted at what might have greatly complicated geographic penetration had Europe's great powers provided the Indians with vast supplies of the most sophisticated weapons of that era and with technological assistance regarding their effective use.[5]

Another important element in such a calculus would require some attention to the "crisis load" and to how well or badly any of the other five crises we are treating are being managed. For example, the mere clustering of several crises over a greatly restricted time period may not represent a serious or unmanageable problem if the intensity of each crisis is relatively low (e.g., mild demands for greater participation; threats to legitimacy that do not affect central governmental institutions; identity crises that involve relatively small or greatly isolated segments of the total population; non-compliance with governmental policies that are marginal from a nation-building perspective, etc.). Similarly, a strong, deeply rooted, stable sense of national identity will provide the centralized rulers much greater latitude in responding to changes associated with the penetration or, as we shall later see, with the distribution crises. Nor should we overlook the possibility that the relative distribution of the instruments of

---

[4] This important point is partly obscured in Wilbur Schramm's otherwise excellent volume, *Mass Media and National Development* (Stanford: Stanford University Press, 1964). Schramm, it seems to me, is overly sanguine in his calculation of the nation-building efficacy of rapid means of information diffusion. Although he notes more than once that national development must be a balanced process, he fails to be explicit about the kinds of circumstances where, say, the centralizers or nation builders might want to slow down the tempo of information diffusion and, perhaps, the dissemination of cheap transistorized radio receivers.

[5] Karl Marx touches on this type of problem in a series of articles for the *New York Herald Tribune* where, with typical Victorian or Prussian arrogance, he discusses the "natural" inability of the Chinese or the Asian Indians to organize themselves into anything like the "modern" military systems of colonizing powers. See Shlomo Avinieri, *Karl Marx on Colonialism and Modernization* (New York: Doubleday and Company, 1968).

coercion may be so overwhelmingly favorable to the central power holders that this advantage will permit effective control by force over a time span during which penetration efforts of the sociopsychological variety can proceed with little serious interruption. It is essentially this type of crisis management that writers refer to when they note how, over time, central leaders of the Soviet Union, say, have been permitted to rely less on terror and coercion, more on other more voluntaristic patterns and institutions in maintaining a penetration balance in both of the senses intended by our definition.[6]

Finally, in concluding this section on technology, we must concede that in theory at least the chemical-electronic-psychological means exist whereby a very high degree of conformity can be assured without overt resort to the more traditional instruments of force and violence. We are thinking of a wide range of instruments, including such things as tranquillizers, truth drugs, subliminal communication, computerized intelligence systems, and political volatility analyses that in the hands of central powers may be used for "good" or "ill," but which in any case may eventually compel some modification of what we say here about the relationship between technology and the crisis of penetration.[7]

Part IV. Penetration and Institution Building

It is tempting to argue that for most of the developing countries—certainly for almost all of them in Africa and Asia—existential conditions associated with the crisis of penetration are the ones requiring paramount attention. This seems true first because where these problems remain ill-attended or unresolved, the resolution of other nation-building crises is impeded and changes wrought by many of the latter are greatly exaggerated. New forms of participation, including mass elections, introduced in areas where problems of penetration remain severe quickly threaten the stability, even the geographic integrity of a new nation. Whatever normative judgments one may have made of the Diem regime in South Vietnam in the mid-fifties, for example, it

---

[6] Whether the shifts in control patterns discernible in the U.S.S.R. support the so-called convergence theory of political development need not detain us here, although this meta-developmental formulation probably deserves more than the summary dismissal it now receives from Sovietologists and Sinologists.

[7] We are referring to something more real than the realm of science fiction and potentially as plausible as the system of control depicted in George Orwell's *1984*. See, for example, Harold Lasswell and Daniel Lerner, eds., *World Revolutionary Elites* (Cambridge: M.I.T. Press, 1965). Cf. the excellent critique of Dankwart Rustow, "The Study of Elites," *World Politics*, 18 (July 1966), 690-717.

is reasonably clear that his resistance to holding free elections was based on the certain knowledge that that kind of participation would greatly aggravate penetration problems. Somewhat similarly, it is apparent that the particular sequencing and clustering of crises in postindependence India has created participation and penetration crises in great tension not only in states like Kerala and Bengal but also in other major regional subdivisions of the country. In Kerala the government at New Delhi has achieved a degree of effective penetration that in some striking cases permitted it to negate the outcome of electoral participation. In Calcutta and Bengal the apparent prudent strategy has been to recognize how much less capacity for penetration in the same sense the national government possesses. Against the advice of some of her own advisors in central administrative agencies, the Prime Minister has wisely preferred to search out strategies and techniques of penetration that involve not so much the national institutions of administration as they do a set of institutions much more closely identified with changes in patterns of participation themselves.[8]

We can also surmise that the widespread limitation or demise of competitive party politics in the newer nations does not necessarily reflect an ideological bias against "free" elections. Rather, such developments suggest the judgment that these polities are not yet sufficiently well penetrated (or do not yet possess a strong enough overriding national political identity, or do not possess sufficient legitimacy) to warrant the "luxury" of open party competition as a form of participation.

An important underlying reason for the apparent paramountcy of penetration problem-solving implies something about developmental sequence. The management of all other crises seems to be more affected by the penetration-crisis profile than it is by any of the others. It is worth suggesting several reasons, beyond historical analogies, why this is so. For any polity and those who would maintain stable control of it certain base-line conditions are not merely "givens" at any point in time, but they may be thought of as the least readily established and least readily changed of these conditions. Two of these, concerning which crises may occur, are identity and legitimacy.

---

[8] Our reference here is to Prime Minister Gandhi's choice of the party system and the regional legislative system—as opposed to the military, police, and central bureaucracy—as instruments for dealing with the severe problems that have characterized Calcutta and West Bengal in recent years and months. Her reliance on party politics seems overwhelmingly rewarded in the elections of 1971.

The factors that account for the amount of either of these two qualities that any polity possesses are usually deeply rooted in history. They are, as we have already noted, greatly affected by questions of race, language, religion, and community. In the case of legitimacy an existing pattern of human organization or behavior is usually the result of slow, incremental changes spanning decades or centuries. We have more than once characterized the identity-legitimacy problem by citing a famous aphorism uttered by one of Italy's Risorgimento leaders shortly after the country's unification: *"Fatta l'Italia, bisogna fare gli Italiani"* (Having made Italy, we must now make Italians).

Dealing with problems of identity and legitimacy is not merely a matter of policy output but almost always also a matter of organization or of institution-building. If effecting change in patterns of identity involves socialization, the latter in turn requires the construction or transformation of schools, the creation of a national military apparatus, and the modification of systems of transportation and communication to make the nation-state something more than an abstract symbol with little relevant meaning in the beliefs or value systems or the daily lives of elites and masses. If legitimacy is a problem, existing legitimacy-bearing institutions must be more strongly associated with the governing elites, or ways must be found to create and manage organizations (e.g., political parties, armies, clubs, bureaucracies, etc.) that will garner higher legitimacy response from those who are the objects of policy. Changes associated with demands or opportunities for participation or distribution are also crises that often tax the institutional-organization skills of an existing or aspiring political elite.

When we speak of excessive crisis loads in the developing countries, we are usually referring to an imbalance between demands on governing elites on the one hand and the capacity or capability of elites to respond to such demands with new or modified policies and organizations on the other.[9] In no other crisis sector are the relationships over time between the phenomena of capacity and differentiation better illustrated. What accounts for stability in a governmental system

---

[9] On this particular way of characterizing the political development process, and the varying but always critical role in it of public bureaucratic organization, see S. N. Eisenstadt, *The Political Systems of Empires* (London: Free Press, 1963). For a briefer statement of his theory, see Eisenstadt, "Bureaucracy and Political Development," in the volume by that title edited by Joseph LaPalombara (Princeton: Princeton University Press, 1963), Chap. 4.

over an extended time period is best described in our terms as the achievement of a new level of governmental output such that the government is shown to be capable not merely of responding efficaciously to a configuration of demands manifested at a previous point, but is also prepared to adapt to a new level of demand—and of possibly complicated crises in some sectors—that the most recent adaptation to change or crisis entailed. Everywhere in human history such adaptations, whether or not successful or optimal, have required and involved major efforts to modify or to create organizations.[10] The central salience of organization is perhaps most aptly put by Carl Friedrich who once wrote, in commenting on popular demands for limited government, that before government can respond to such demands, there must first exist a government with powers to circumscribe.[11]

We take the view, then, that any adequate resolution of the penetration crisis rests primarily on the ability of national political leadership to create and to institutionalize organizations. These organizations, as we noted in previous chapters, need not be only governmental or political, restricted as it were to such things as legislatures, bureaucracies, or political parties. They can and often do include secondary associations, of whatever degree of voluntary character,[12] that are tuned to create, or to adapt to otherwise induced change.

[10] We do not wish to neglect or to obscure that one pattern of response by governing elites that may be characterized as "symbolic" rather than organizational. Patriotic speeches, appeals to extra-human sources of legitimacy, "bread-and-circus" strategies would fall under the symbolic category. Regardless of what may be the degree of efficacy of such responses to crisis problems, or for how long efficacy persists, it is striking that these patterns too require organizational apparatus and innovation. Goebbels, unlike Marc Antony, required considerable organizational and technological assistance in order to use symbols as an instrument of control and conformance. So do the leaders of the developing nations who seek to (or must!) substitute rhetoric for policies.

[11] C. J. Friedrich, *Constitutional Government and Democracy*, rev. edn. (Boston: Little, Brown, 1946), p. 37. It might be added here that one of the most striking qualities of the governing elites of the developing nations is how limited is the scope of power they command; how fragile their control of their own or their nation's destinies; how problematical their capacity for coping meaningfully even with changes or demands involving relatively low crisis-load intensity, when the latter is judged not relative to imminent capacity but relatively across space and time.

[12] The degree of voluntarism associated with organized group affiliation is, of course, a matter of considerable theoretical significance. Until recent years, Western social science notions of such group affiliations were (and remain for many!) strongly influenced by the formulations of F. Tonnies, *Gemeinschaft und Gesellschaft* (1887) and E. Durkheim, *De la division de Travail Social* (1893). A quite radically different sociopsychological theory of group affiliations in the modern world, one which denies voluntarism and individuality, is suggested by Lucio Mendieta y Nuñez, *Theorie des Groupements Sociaux* (Paris, 1937), and is discussed in an important paper by Peter Kodzic, "Political Penetration Defined," Institute of Social Studies, The Hague, 1968 (mimeo.).

It should be made clear that organizations created to cope with penetration crisis problems need not be "modern" in the absolute, contemporary sense. For any polity at any point in time many such organizational arrangements appear to be the most "modern" in their modified or innovated forms because they seem most closely and immediately connected with the management of change. However, it requires little historical reflection to note that in many instances "traditional" structures have been successfully utilized to weld together a viable national polity. Indeed, one important dimension in successful management of such crises is the extent to which the structures are institutionalized, not fragile, and therefore flexible enough to adapt to changes in the environment.[13] It is more than a little ironic, therefore, that some scholars and many political leaders of developing nations have often assumed an irreconcilable dissonance and conflict between the institutions and organizations of "traditional" and "modern" society. If history has anything at all to teach us here, it is that successful penetration or adaptation to change, always involves an admixture—sometimes a smooth blending, sometimes an abrasive juxtaposition—of old and new institutions.

To return to an earlier point, it is necessary to understand that organizational skill relating to coping with a penetration crisis must include private secondary associations as well as formal governmental arrangements. Indeed one critically important capability of the political power holders is that relating to the kind of blending of public and private organizations without whose integrated cooperation most of the specific tasks of nation building and economic and social development will be gravely impeded. Nevertheless, the crisis of penetration is usually a direct challenge to governmental institutions, and here, sooner or later, the most important organizational innovations and adaptations must occur. Today both the widespread impulse to national development and the conditions of the contemporary world require that central governmental authority be capable of ruling— at least of exercising a minimal amount of power—throughout the domains encompassed by the would-be nation-state. Without it we are certain to experience, as Cyril E. Black[14] gloomily predicts, a period of nation building not markedly unlike that of war, violence, crime, and human suffering and degradation that characterized the developmental histories of the so-called modern world.

[13] See S. Huntington, *op.cit.*
[14] Cyril E. Black, *The Dynamics of Modernization* (New York: Harper and Row, 1966).

Part V. Types of Penetration Crisis and Their Resolution

In suggesting how central governments might approach some of the penetration problems we have touched on more or less abstractly it will be convenient to delineate several examples of specific crises and then to say some things about ranges of response to them. We shall deal with the crises of empty territories, regional differences, communal autonomy, and peasant communities.

CRISIS OF EMPTY TERRITORIES

This crisis has two principal subtypes. The first and perhaps most apparent type in the histories of the developed nations involves attempts by a particular political system to expand its physical boundaries. Such expansionist ambitions are as old as recorded history. The problems of penetration they create have remained markedly constant over time.

One may also perceive the empty-territory crisis where a central government decides to effect more than ephemeral control over territories that are formalistically a part of the system but that have retained a high degree of local autonomy and an equally high degree of immunity from direction from the center. This situation too can be found in history and in the contemporary world. Thus, for example, territorial descriptions of vast empires of the past often obscured how little effective penetration emanated from the center to the outlying reaches of the empire. To be sure, both the Chinese and Roman imperial systems sent troops to remote regions, but the facts will show that such organizational devices were rarely sufficient to secure more than a minimal conformance to imperial wishes or policies.

The Romans experimented with various organizational innovations designed to cope with this problem. Praetorian prefects, specifically posted to the most remote imperial regions, were dispatched to assure the authority of Rome; the prefects themselves often became independent power centers—so much so in fact that additional officials, such as the military and judicial magisters had to be invented in order to correct the slippages in control that occurred under the praetorian system of field administration. By and large, such efforts were fruitless. As Morstein Marx correctly notes, these historic systems "reflected little experience in combining great size with close control."[15]

[15] Fritz Morstein Marx, *The Administrative State* (Chicago: University of Chicago Press, 1957), p. 36. Cf. K. A. Wittfogel, *Oriental Despotism* (New Haven: Yale

However, the problem is not necessarily limited to historical situations. Much more recently, the French have attempted to create more effective regional administrative units, in part to assure more effective penetration from the center for such national policies as economic planning. Initial efforts to create "super-prefectures" simply ran afoul of the deeply entrenched interests of the Napoleonic prefectorial system. The traditional prefects, who have long exercised enormous political influence over the *départements* were not enthusiastically cooperative. Later efforts on the part of Paris to create regional governmental jurisdictions were defeated in popular referendum. What is quite fascinating and revealing about these experiences is that not only the old-line prefects, but also the local elites with whom the prefectorial system has to some degree become identified, strongly and successfully opposed these proposed changes. It is not merely historic or "less-developed" political systems, then, that have experienced often considerable difficulty in extracting closely conforming behavior over all or most of a national territory.[16]

The first form of the same problem has been massively documented in the administrative histories of several Western nation-states. The most fascinating among these are Brandenburg-Prussia and France. In each case, the rulers of a particular polity sought to expand the geographic areas over which they could exercise control. What motivated these ambitions and attempted changes need not detain us here, although both of these histories, I believe, raise very serious doubts about developmental theories that hold that political innovation or change usually follows from, rather than promotes, changes in the economic and social spheres.[17] The point is that Paris, as a governing center, did not become anything like a reality until the organizational genius of a Colbert was put to work in favor of the ambitious, centralizing monarch, Louis XIV. *"L'etat c'est moi!"* while providing a significant psychological-religious rationale for absolute rule, would have remained a hollow concept had organizational

University Press, 1957), who spells out a provocative and controversial theory of despotic control exercised by empires organized around major river systems.

[16] French scholars like Michel Crozier, Jean Pierre Worms and Pierre Gremion have researched various aspects of these phenomena. See, for example, Gremion's "Introduction à une étude du système politico-administratif local," *Sociologie du Travail* (January-March, 1970), pp. 51-73.

[17] One of us has treated in some detail the motivations underlying major administrative transformations in the evolution of several Western nations. See Joseph LaPalombara, "Values and Ideologies in the Administrative Evolution of Western Constitutional Systems," in Ralph Braibanti, ed., *Political and Administrative Development* (Durham: Duke University Press, 1969), pp. 166-219.

innovations not been available to transform the theory into an impressive instrument of control. Similarly, the history of Brandenburg-Prussia which brought a German "new nation" of the 19th century so quickly to prominence as a major power is first and profoundly a history of administrative organization, beginning in the 17th century with the innovations of the "Grand Elector" and extending through the work of Frederick the Great, and vom Stein after Prussia's defeat by Napoleon at Jena.[18]

For the developing nations, the present penetration crises they confront contain aspects of both the imperial and the nation-state expansionist patterns summarized above. Where the people encompassed by a developing nation generally concede that they are Indians or Filipinos, Indonesians, Bolivians, or Brazilians, the problem resembles that of empire—extending some or more effective control to areas of polity until now relatively immune from it. Where, as in the Congo or Nigeria, there is strong resistance to accepting even the generic or blanket national label, we find situations similar to those that confronted the expansionist Prussian or French centralizers.

However, the developing nations' centralizers are faced with newer and greater pressures relatively unknown to their predecessors in the West. In the present, the greatly improved technologies of transportation, communications, and warfare impel leaders at the center to devise effective means of ruling over their whole territories. Where boundary changes can be effected with lightning swiftness, where resistant or separatist population segments can just as quickly create debilitating insurgency or carry through their national-disintegrative ambitions, it greatly behooves the central ruling authorities to fill any vacuum of rule within their formal domains. Where the insurgent or separatist movements are concentrated in economically richer areas, the pressure not to lose control, to penetrate, is all the more urgently and painfully felt.

A second important way in which developing nation rulers feel

[18] Some of the details of these important experiences in managing penetration crisis problems in several European countries, can be gleaned from the following: H. Rosenberg, *Bureaucracy, Aristocracy and Autocracy; The Prussian Experience, 1660-1815* (Boston: Beacon Press, 1966); R. A. Dorwart, *The Administrative Reforms of Frederick William I of Prussia* (Cambridge: Harvard University Press, 1953); T. F. Tout, *Chapters in the History of Medieval England*, 6 vols. (Manchester: Barnes and Noble, 1920-1923); G. Hanotaux, *Origines de l'Institution des Intendants de Province* (Paris, 1884); P. Viollet, *Histoire des Institutions Politiques et Administratives de la France*, 3 vols. (Paris, 1903); C. Cole, *Colbert and a Century of French Mercantilism* (Hamden, Conn.: Archon Books, 1964); O. Ranum, *Richelieu and the Counsellors of Louis XIII* (Oxford, 1963).

greater pressure is when the origin of a penetration crisis involves the level and kind of demand for services emanating from the provinces. It matters little whether the revolution of rising expectations is a spontaneous groundswell or clamor fabricated by counterelites. The fact is that subjects demand of their central governments today not only a right to participate but a spectrum of services, benefits, opportunities and amenities unheard of in the West on a mass scale until well into the nineteenth century. One certain consequence of this situation is that the central elites will not be permitted the luxury of leaving certain territories "empty" until they feel they can and should deal with them, as the central elites would wish. From the Chinese and Romans onward for many centuries, such authorities bothered about empty territories when they were confronted with the need for curvée labor, soldiers to fight wars, or revenues to support an aristocracy at court or expensive military expeditions. That situation is now radically changed in developing nations, not only for ambitious leaders who are filled with avaricious or idealistic nation-building fervor but who are also confronted with subjects who can generate a level of demand that the center is ill equipped to satisfy.

CRISIS OF REGIONAL DIFFERENCES

Related to, but not coterminous with, the empty-territory problem is that of gross regional differences. These differences can and do run the full gamut of human organization and behavior. They can refer to language, dress, religion, occupational patterns, family structure, authority patterns, literacy, temporal-spatial orientations, ambition, discipline, physiological characteristics, race, ideology—in short, an enormous number of dimensions along which compatability or incompatability with the centralizing power might be measured. We know from Western history exactly how extreme can be the gap between the center's cultural and economic configuration and what one finds at the periphery.

In the less-developed areas, the very categories defining uneven development will often signal how great may be such gaps. If Western history is any teacher, we also know not merely how difficult is the task of narrowing or closing such gaps but, indeed, how much resistance to such efforts regionally differing sectors can generate. As a matter of fact, there is no so-called developed country that can claim to have resolved this problem completely and, therefore, claim to have achieved a level of penetration (or identity or legitimacy) where all geographic regions of the country are essentially undifferentiated from any other.

Our newspapers and literature often focus on nations like India as extreme examples of this problem. Yet, if countries like the United States and Italy have not succeeded in eliminating instabilities induced by regional differences, why should we expect that the penetration crisis will be any the more readily resolved in Brazil regarding the Northeast, in Indonesia or the Philippines regarding the outer islands, or in Peru and other developing countries where we find such marked contrasts between people of the coastal plains, the higher mountains, and the jungle.

More often than not, what occurs in such situations is that both the central political elites and the people in the highly different regions persist in an enormous lack of mutual empathy. Almost all policies emanating from the center are interpreted primarily in terms of how they threaten regional customs or culture; almost all reactions from the regions are interpreted at the center as manifestations of a primitiveness or traditionality that must be removed, by force if necessary, in order to push along the nation-building or nation-developing enterprise. In this sense, the regional resistors are viewed from the developing-nation centers much like the American Indians were viewed by Washington, or Washington's pioneering adventurers.

As we shall note below, the problem here must not, as sometimes happens in developing countries, be distorted to mean that all regional differences must be obliterated, or all regional or "nonmodern" institutions destroyed. A moment's reflection will show that there are still strikingly identifiable Welshmen in Britain, Burgundians in France, Sicilians in Italy, and Bavarians in Germany to say nothing about persisting senses of identity much below the geographic areas that such regions suggest. The aspect of the penetration crisis that regional differences highlight is rather that of discovering (1) what it is that can and should be modified or homogenized, and (2) what organizational means are available for permitting marginal regions to function as a contributing factor in a national system, notwithstanding the persistence of certain atypical patterns.

CRISIS OF COMMUNAL AUTONOMY

This crisis, too, is related to what has been said above, but it involves its own unique characteristics that should not be obscured. It is conceivable, for example, that this particular kind of penetration crisis can—and indeed does—occur quite apart from how different from the rest of the polity a particular segment may be. Where we encounter regional differences, we may also find a strong tradition of communal autonomy. India, Ceylon, and any number of African states will provide many examples of this phenomenon.

However, many of the developing nations also evince examples of a kind of "sociological federalism," wherein traditional political arrangements assumed that various minority ethnic groups would rule themselves. Whatever central authorities existed in such systems limited themselves to dealing with the leaders of such communities. The Ottoman *millet* system would be a good example of this arrangement, as would certain aspects of British colonialism vaguely defined as "indirect rule." In Southeast Asia it was the practice of most colonial governments, for example, to encourage *separate* Chinese communities, relying for intracommunity order maintenance and education on the political leadership that these communities themselves produced. Similar examples, not involving colonialism, can be found in European and Japanese feudalism and in patterns of central control that characterized several European nations for some centuries following the breakdown of feudalism. What we call the clientelistic structure of political loyalties in Southern Italy or the caudillo pattern of political loyalty in Latin America is not significantly different in its dynamic political consequences from the format we are discussing.

A penetration crisis occurs whenever the central authorities decide that such a communally (or personalistically) based autonomy is inconsistent with national developmental aspirations. What the contemporary centralizers have discovered is that these ancient patterns readily lend themselves to patterns of political organization and intervention that are communally based. Such patterns appear irrational and retrogressive in developing countries where, as we have noted, processes of modernization tend to follow commercial as opposed to communal lines. In such situations, and especially where it becomes apparent that political parties and organization can best be organized and mobilized along communal lines, the central government experiences pressure to break down and eliminate such lines, to penetrate these communities, and to make them more readily and instrumentally available for the ends-in-view of the central authorities. The antipathy for the Chinese communities that one finds in Southeast Asia must be interpreted in this context. War or no war, the centralizing elites would probably find it intimidating and intolerable to be confronted within their own nation-state borders with communal groups evincing the degree of autonomy and integration (and potential capacity to resist centralizing policies) that is characteristic of such communities. The greater the degree of integration or self-sufficiency one finds in such communities, the greater the probability that they will and can resist penetration attempts from the center.

CRISIS OF PEASANT COMMUNITIES

In the developing areas today the most widespread and fundamental form of the penetration crisis is that which requires that central governments come into closer touch with their rural populations. This problem is not merely one to be identified as involving elite and mass relations. Much more significantly, it involves the urban-rural dichotomy, and in this form it has distressed and plagued central authority and modernizers of the more developed countries well into the twentieth century.

Marx and Lenin had a feeling for this problem when they speculated about and warned against the fundamentally "reactionary" character of the peasantry. The modernizers of the U.S. Department of Agriculture's extension service confronted this problem in recent decades, as have those representatives of Mexico's PRI who have sought to modernize agriculture. This kind of crisis is neither one of identity nor of legitimacy. Resistant peasants are perfectly willing to acknowledge their citizenship in a particular nation-state and to acknowledge that those who rule from the center have a right to do so. Indeed, the same peasants who will support and welcome a revolutionary regime as they did in France will then fiercely resist efforts aimed at changing their style of life.

There is both great irony and great challenge here, for peasants are likely to manifest their fiercest opposition to center-determined programs designed to improve their lot. Generations of agricultural field administrators or community development agents have marveled at the obstinate refusal of the peasant to have his material condition improved. The language of animal husbandry, or of agronomy, or of public health is alien to him—an outside, hostile force, considered hostile simply by reason of communicated symbols that are completely outside his ken. Lacking both knowledge and empathy,[19] he can only

[19] Empathy here is used in Lerner's sense. See D. Lerner, *The Passing of Traditional Society* (Glencoe: Free Press, 1958).

react to outsiders with suspicion and fierce hostility. He represents in this sense the most ubiquitous aspect of the crisis of penetration.

Part VI. Responses to Crisis

Early in this chapter we noted that the penetration crisis involves both a strictly organizational and a strictly sociopsychological dimension. As with the other crises we have been discussing, we can think of them as forcing political elites to give consideration to structure, process, and attitudes. We have also sought to demonstrate, however, that the penetration crisis, like that of distribution which we will treat in the next chapter, forces our attention to considerations of structure—to organizations and how they can be most rationally and efficaciously institutionalized. Very few of the problems or changes we have discussed in this chapter can be confronted, much less resolved, unless one gives considerable thought to the relationship between public ends-in-view and the organizational wherewithal for making those ends something more than wishful aspirations.

When we make this general problem specific to the developing nations of Asia and Africa, there is an additional consideration to bear in mind, namely, that for most of these countries most of what development is perceived as involving will require or demand *public* intervention on a most unusual scale. This commitment to the centrality of the public sector is critically important not only to the crisis of distribution but in this case to the crisis of penetration as well. To put it very summarily, the range of problems for which additional penetration capacity is required in the developing nation seems much greater than any such demand experienced in the history of the West. These newer nations require not only administrative generalists, capable of managing law-and-order problems in the best tradition of district officers of the British Colonial Service; they require as well a fantastic range of administrative specialists, who can handle everything from the organization of consumer or marketing cooperatives to the training of pilots to fly jet airplanes and the specialized personnel to maintain the latter. In many cases, the problematical status of nation-state boundaries is such that significant military forces are required as well.

One perfectly reasonable reaction to all of this is to conclude that reasonably efficacious crisis management is unlikely or impossible, that chaos is the most probable outcome of most existential situations, and that one should simply wait and see what, if anything, emerges from chaos. Such a view is unduly pessimistic. The unprecedented magnitude of the problem and of its attendant penetration crisis is no reason for assuming that historical or contemporary experiences are devoid of guidelines.

The first and most important point to make, we believe, is that generalizations alone about meeting the crisis of penetration with *specific* patterns of organization will simply not do. For example, if some idealized conception of the modern polity requires a Weberian system of public bureaucratic organization, it is certain that in some countries such patterns of public administrative organization will have to be much later in materializing than in others. As an operating organizational axiom it is probably much more pertinent to note that all administrative systems partake of all three of the Weberian authority configurations and that it may be fatal, say, to insist on legal-rational organization where the only hope for adaptation to change must rest on the kinds of administration associated with traditional or charismatic authority. The important lesson here is that no pattern of economic, social, or political change is inextricably tied to a close empirical approximation of a Weberian ideal-typical construction or to a particular configuration of the Parsonian pattern variables.[20] It is important to begin by asking not what existing structural arrangements impede adaptation to change but, rather, which of them are more rather than less susceptible to such adaptation.

A second general point would be that the problem of geographic penetration is overriding for most developing countries. Such penetration may be achieved through the instrumentality of military organization, but even when this is possible more organizational innovation is required. There is considerable debate whether such innovation should stress the administrative functional specialist as opposed to the administrative generalist, particularly in those situations where administrative talent of any variety is in extremely short supply. As a general operating principle, greatly buttressed by evidence from

[20] The mischief implicit in any other formulation of this statement is limitless. The extent to which, notwithstanding disclaimers, social scientists have made Weberian notions of legal-rational authority or Parsonian notions of achievement, functional specificity, community orientation, universalism and affective neutrality, necessary conditions for modernity is amazing, both in its antihistorical aspect and in its failure to appreciate what a wide range of behavioral patterns traditional institutions can tolerate. In this regard, see, Joseph LaPalombara, "Public Administration and Political Change: A Theoretical Overview," in Charles Press and A. Arian, *Empathy and Ideology: Aspects of Administrative Innovation* (Chicago: Rand McNally, 1966), Chap. 4.

both the developed and developing areas,[21] it would seem that the first requirement is that of producing a corps or supply of administrative generalists, not only at the center, where their utility is obvious, but also in the field, where they will not bring to their tasks the narrow orientation, the insensitivity, and the potential for negative popular response that is so characteristic of the specialist. If historical examples are of any value here it is that efforts to achieve effective penetration were concentrated in administrative areas that appear specialized now (in countries of great administrative differentiation) but which were of a general administrative configuration, not only in 17th-century France and Prussia, but in England as well in earlier periods.

One important difficulty in this recommendation is that administrative generalists in postcolonial countries tend to manifest an attitude to the masses that was typical of colonial administrative generalists but that now tends to aggravate a number of the crises we have discussed. The solution to this acknowledged problem, however, is not that of substituting public health or agricultural specialists for district officer-type generalists as it is that of training generalist field administrators to new patterns of attitudes toward and interaction with the masses, and particularly the local and regional elites.

A third point, which conditions but does not supersede what is said above, is that responses to a penetration crisis should be based on a highly particularized "profile" of the nation involved. Such a profile would measure such things as public policy needs and goals, existing human, physical, and organizational resources that might be mobilized for goal achievement, unequivocal obstacles that are also present within the system and, on the basis of these factors, some estimate regarding what can be done and over what period of time.[22]

This type of profiling would help us to identify what probable proportions to set between administrative generalists and specialists. To cite two extreme examples. India is well supplied with a competent, elite corps of general administrators descended from the high-status apparatus and tradition of the Indian Civil Service. The Congo, on the other hand, is abjectly disadvantaged by comparison. Stress in the

---

[21] See R. Braibanti, "Civil Service of Pakistan: A Theoretical Analysis," in Inayatullah, ed., *Bureaucracy and Development in Pakistan* (Peshawar, 1963), Chap. 9; Fritz Morstein Marx, "The Higher Civil Service as an Action Group in Western Political Development," in J. LaPalombara, ed., *Bureaucracy and Political Development* (Princeton: Princeton University Press, 1963), Chap. 3.

[22] For a detailed elaboration of this approach, see J. LaPalombara, "Alternative Strategies for Developing Administrative Capabilities in Emerging Nations," *CAG Occasional Paper*, 1965 (mimeo.).

former should be on functional specialists in administration; stress in the latter should be on trained administrative generalists.

Profiling would also be a vitally important way for breaking down a penetration crisis into one or more of the specific categories we delineate above. Some of these crises require military intervention, or administrators specialized in law and order. Empty territories, for example, are generally penetrated by the military, followed by generalist administrators hard on the heels of the latter. The crisis of peasant communities, on the other hand, may require administrators who are specialized primarily in adapting central governmental programs and policies to the deeply rooted social-cultural psychological structures one encounters in peasant societies.

Such an approach would also be salutary in the sense of inducing the central authorities to determine which existing traditional structures—public or private—might be integrated into the overall organizational effort to respond to changes related to problems of penetration. History again offers the most striking example of such a strategy. The sheriff and the justice of the peace, for several centuries the key figures in Norman and Angevin penetration of England, were *Saxon* institutions, not something imposed from the outside.

Histories of successful nation-building abound with other examples as well. Soviet officials at Moscow quickly learned that "penetrating" Soviet Central Asia necessitated working through indigenous institutions. Nomadic and village-dwelling persons in these remote, rural sectors were not as readily available to Soviet political and administrative institutions that might be created in urban centers. New institutions were bypassed for traditional means of dealing with governmental outputs; when traditional institutions were suppressed, traditional authorities often continued in their former roles under newer guise as Communist or Soviet officials. The story is much the same for post-revolutionary Mexico where PRI at Mexico City, if it governs remote villages at all, does so through the indirect instrumentality of indigenous structures and institutions.

If central leaders are inclined to use indigenous structures where they can, this inclination will almost certainly involve the implication that for most developing countries a highly centralized administrative apparatus is neither desirable nor possible. When we think of centralizing organizational crisis solutions of the past, we tend to exaggerate the extent to which such centralization occurred in fact—in

England, Brandenburg-Prussia, France, or elsewhere. The truth is that centralization efforts frequently failed because, for example, the same counts, dukes, or intendants in France who were designed to make Paris paramount also developed centers of countervailing power in their local territories. The Ottomans who sought to reduce this tendency by making slaves and eunuchs their chief administrators soon found that family or locally centered interests found their way around this practice. A more expedient and realistic arrangement would be that of reaching contractual agreements with centers of local or regional power, even if to do so implies achieving less than desired by way of central control. Such arrangements often produce more than would otherwise have been possible.

We can conclude this discussion by referring briefly to three important problems that greatly affect the management of penetration crisis problems. The first of these has to do with what Eisenstadt[23] describes as the necessary balance between the free-flowing resources of a bureaucracy and its dependence on political or social groups within the political system. Where those who staff bureaucratic organizations are merely abject instruments of a dominant social-political class they are not likely to contribute much to successful crisis resolution except insofar as sheer force will achieve that end. On the other hand, an extreme independence of the bureaucracy from social and political controls will usually lead it to pursue expediency interests apart from what may be the interests of the system they serve.

It is vitally necessary therefore that those who hold political power at the center and must respond to crisis be able to set a wide range of standards for those who will man administrative organization. Such standards move from abstract considerations of the relationship between citizen and administrator or criteria of professionalization to the more mundane considerations of what kinds of "arrangements" are or are not acceptable with local or regional elites.

Second, it is worth emphasizing that while the crises of penetration tend to have a distinct and, in a sense, inevitable *geographic* dimension, there are clearly other important dimensions to look for, only some of which have been treated in this chapter. The "crisis of peasant community" may well be the "crisis of peasant mentality" where the deep fissure over nation-building policies is between urban and rural dwellers. Similarly, a penetration crisis that reflects a central government's inability to persuade, induce, or force a racial mi-

[23] S. N. Eisenstadt, *Political Systems of Empires,* op.cit.

nority to adhere to national policies may be only accidentally or superficially a geographically limited problem. The same holds true of penetration problems pertaining to chronological age. Contemporary difficulties that Western national governments encounter with the young, and the extremely difficult problems that Britain and the United States experience with non-white minorities clearly illustrate these last two points. In this sense, the social-psychological dimension of penetration can and usually does persist long beyond the time when the geographic dimension has been adequately disposed of by centralizing authorities.

Finally, it is necessary to acknowledge that most of the penetration problems we have been discussing are of the law-and-order variety. The government must make its presence felt in outlying regions, and this need will produce responses in the form of armies, tax collectors, judges, police, and similar administrative authorities, or it will be confronted with demands for greater participation that may necessitate not merely the fostering of political parties but also the creation of village-level deliberative bodies as well.

For a great many of the developing nations, however, we have noted that the demands on the central government far exceed claims for law and order or participation, but spill over into the broad area of social and economic equality. Indeed, the political leaders themselves, as a matter of public policy, will set goals that involve fundamental economic and social transformations. Such demands, or public policies, are generally described as planned change. They create as intense a range of problems of a penetration-crisis variety as do considerations of territorial integrity and law and order. More than the latter, they bring the government face to face with that aspect of penetration that is primarily sociologically based. We have named this particular crisis "distribution," and we turn now to an examination of it.

CHAPTER 7

DISTRIBUTION: A CRISIS OF RESOURCE MANAGEMENT*

JOSEPH LA PALOMBARA

Part I. Introduction

IN THE BROADEST sense all of the problems of governance may be considered distribution problems that may or may not reach crisis proportions. This would certainly be suggested by Easton's definition of the political process, indeed of the "political system" as the "authoritative allocation of values."[1] Easton, like Parsons and others, seeks among other things to distinguish politics from economics, and he notes that while political allocation may have to do with the full range of values in a society, it is the "authoritative" aspect of certain decisions regarding such allocations that places them in the sphere of politics. Harold Lasswell, in a classic earlier work, suggested much the same thing when he entitled his volume: *Politics: Who Gets What, When, How.*[2] David Apter, in an initial formulation of his structural scheme for elucidating the political system, defines political behavior as demands aimed at modifying the existing stratification system,[3] and it is clear that what places such demands in the sphere of politics is that the decisions and authority of government stand behind such modifications.

* Revisions of this chapter were written while I was on research leave of absence supported by the Ford Foundation and by Yale University's Concilium on International Studies. I am indebted to Garry Brewer, Ron Brunner, and Theodore Schultz for cogent criticisms and suggestions offered regarding an earlier version of this chapter.
[1] The political process, or political system, conceptualized in terms of the mechanisms, patterns, institutions, norms, procedures, etc., associated with the *authoritative* allocation of values derives, of course, from Max Weber. David Easton's initial elaboration of this definition is found in his *The Political System* (New York: Knopf, 1953), pp. 129-34. Cf. Gabriel Almond's definition of a political system in his "A Functional Approach to Comparative Politics," in G. A. Almond and J. S. Coleman, *The Politics of the Developing Areas* (Princeton: Princeton University Press, 1960), pp. 7-9.
[2] Harold D. Lasswell, *Politics: Who Gets What, When, How* (New York: Meridan Books, World Publishing, 1936).
[3] David E. Apter, "A Comparative Method for the Study of Politics," *The American Journal of Sociology*, 64 (November 1958), 221-37.

More recently Easton succinctly summarized what he means by "authoritative allocation," and his words provide us with a guide for specifying the narrower sense in which we shall be dealing with problems of distribution in this chapter. Easton says, "Briefly, authoritative allocations distribute valued things in one of three ways. An allocation may deprive a person of a valued thing already possessed; it may obstruct the attainment of values which would otherwise have been obtained; or it may give some persons access to values and deny them to others."[4] It is clear enough that the range of "things valued" may well encompass every facet of man's needs and desires in organized society. Lasswell's well-known and extensively explicated roll call of human values[5] alerts us to the fact—often dramatically attested by revolution, war, and other forms of political violence—that man neither lives nor dies for bread alone. His desires for respect, deference, status, love, association, and the like take us into realms where the material may be marginal at best and where challenges to political elites involving such valued things may be far removed from the material/economic realm.

We might take as an example here the crisis of participation treated by Myron Weiner or the central value of equality discussed by James Coleman in this volume. The demand to participate, to achieve equality as a citizen, may be and often is motivated by a great range and complexity of aspirations, from the calculated desire to exercise power in one's own material interest to the moral insistence that each citizen be accorded one vote in the selection of those who will govern. Political elites confronted with such demands are therefore not necessarily taxed with the need for modifying the distribution of the *material* resources of the community. Crises of legitimacy and identity are often even more telling examples of situations in which the demands upon the political elites are overwhelmingly psychological and symbolic rather than material in their implications.[6] By the same

---

[4] David Easton, *A Framework for Political Analysis* (Englewood Cliffs, N.J.: Prentice-Hall, 1965), p. 50. There are several problems with this particular definitional specification but they need not detain us here.

[5] See Harold D. Lasswell, *The Analysis of Political Behaviour: An Empirical Approach* (Hamden, Conn.: Shoe String Press, 1966), esp. Part I.

[6] Lucian Pye, who has written extensively on the notion of an emerging "world culture," puts this matter quite nicely: "It is still possible to discern," he says, "in the movement of world history certain conventions and even social norms that have increasingly been diffused throughout the world and that people generally feel should be recognized by any self-respecting government. Many of these standards do trace back to industrial society and the rise of science and technology, but most of them have by now a dynamic of their own. Mass participation, for example, reflects the sociolog-

token, what the leaders of national polities require from the broader population is not merely material and physical support but the kind of support or cooperation that reasonably well-resolved identity and legitimacy crises would imply.

Having acknowledged the broad range of concerns that may lead to political demands, we must also recognize that many demands are indeed material. A psychologist like Maslow establishes a *hierarchy* of human needs that accords the highest priority to physical and safety requirements and the last priority to the need for self-realization and growth.[7] At each end of his five-category hierarchy one can find the basis on which people make demands on political leaders that test the latters' willingness and ability to modify the extant material configuration of society.[8]

We intend then to narrow the definition of distribution problems

---

ical realities of industrialized life, but it has also been taken to be an absolute right in the spirit of current world views. Other ideals, such as the demand for universalistic laws, respect for merit rather than birth, and generalized concepts of justice and citizenship, seem now to hold a place above any particular culture and thus reasonably belong to some universal standards of modern political life." See Lucian W. Pye, *Aspects of Political Development* (Boston: Little, Brown, 1966), p. 36.

[7] Abraham H. Maslow, "A Theory of Human Motivation," *Psychological Review*, 50 (1943), 370-96.

[8] We might note here that economists, too, have encountered a similar problem in trying to distinguish between and among kinds of "welfare." In his classic formulation, long followed by economic theorists, A. C. Pigou distinguishes "economic welfare" from the broader category of "social welfare." Economic welfare is defined by him as "that part of social welfare that can be brought directly or indirectly into relation with the measuring-rod of money." Pigou goes on to acknowledge that this distinction is defensible notwithstanding that "no precise line between economic and non-economic satisfactions" can be drawn and notwithstanding the economists' understanding that economic welfare is not the only satisfaction that the individual desires to maximize. See A. C. Pigou, *The Economics of Welfare*, 3rd edn. (London: St. Martin's Press, 1938), Chaps. 1 and 2, and esp. pp. 11ff.

More recently, economists interested in measuring growth have acknowledged the limitations or handicaps implicit in Pigou's distinction, particularly when "growth" comes to be equated with changes in total or per capita national product. A strikingly thoughtful treatment of this problem is offered by Moses Abramovitz, "The Welfare Interpretation of Secular-Trends in National Income and Product," in M. Abramovitz, et al., *The Allocation of Economic Resources* (Stanford: Stanford University Press, 1959), pp. 1-22, esp. pp. 1-10.

It is also necessary to add that the matter of modifying the material conditions of society is always hedged in by one or more of the following considerations: First, what people want or elites wish to do may not be easily accomplished. Second, effecting particular changes may not be "best" for society given certain contextual configurations. Third, goals are generally myriad and it may not be correct to emphasize one or two of them to the exclusion of others. Fourth, it may be essential to look at alternative goals, given the complex, multiple, changing and ill-defined nature of social goals. Last, the demands or goals may not be realizable given the costs of information gathering and the necessary component of uncertainty. On several of these points, see R. A. Dahl, *A Preface to Democratic Theory* (Chicago: University of Chicago Press, 1956), pp. 48-50.

to include those that imply that the political elite take a hand to increase the material goods available to a society or to redistribute such goods as may be available at any given time. It is necessary to recognize that *two* dimensions to this kind of demand exist and that either dimension can reach crisis proportions, not merely in early stages of national development but later, and recurringly, as well. The first dimension may be understood as implying the imperative: Find the ways and means of producing more of the material things that are valued! The second dimension involves a quite different imperative: Regardless of what may be the society's capability of producing more, *change* the bases upon which things valued are distributed among society's members! Historically it has been the second of these dimensions that has overtaxed elite capability and sometimes led to revolution and the destruction of existing political regimes. Marie Antoinette's alleged terse response to peasant demands for bread is a rather arresting example of a frivolous and suicidal reaction to a redistribution demand. The first of these dimensions is typically illustrated when governmental officials, or economic elites who feel threatened by redistribution demands, insist, for example, that wage increases be closely tied to and conditioned by the *productivity of labor.*

It will be necessary to distinguish analytically between these two dimensions if we are to understand fully how it is that distribution demands can reach crisis proportions in relatively affluent countries.[8a]

[8a] Note that H. Lasswell and A. Kaplan, *Power and Society* (New Haven: Yale University Press, 1950), pp. 264-65, provide an important clarification of value *potential, expectation,* and *reality.* "The standard of living," they note, "may be the 'highest in history' or the 'highest in the world' but still not high enough when it is compared with that of the elect, or with the demands made by the self on the self—basically when it is compared with the value potential" (p. 265). The problem can be put schematically as follows:

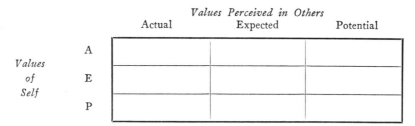

| | | Values Perceived in Others | | |
		Actual	Expected	Potential
Values	A			
of	E			
Self	P			

Each of the above cells then becomes a basis for comparison on the basis of which demands may be triggered where the discrepancies are felt to be too great and/or unacceptable. It is worth adding, however, that history shows us that on the mass side, persons will remain passive in the face of great levels of relative deprivation.

The distinction will also be useful in permitting us to highlight the dilemma that confronts developing country elites who are ideologically committed to redistribution but who are faced by certain realities—or "Iron Laws"—in implementing economic policies aimed at increasing the size of the available pie. In no other sphere perhaps are the abilities of political elites to deal with underlying impulses of equality, capability, and differentiation more severely or decisively tested.

We will now turn to a discussion of a number of factors that greatly impinge on elite capability to deal effectively with distribution crises. These include ideology, material and human resources, psychology, and the international arena in which the nation-state must operate.

Part II. Ideology and Distribution

For the greater part of human history, problems of distribution (or redistribution) confronting political elites might be viewed primarily as problems *en famille*. Roman emperors seeking to extract the maximum in goods and services from outlying provinces had to contend not so much with organized subjects as they were compelled to make deals with generals, consuls, and prefects sent to tame and administer these provinces in the name of Imperial Rome. King John confronted with restive barons at Runnymede found himself pressured by regionally based elites whose insistence on bargaining before paying laid the groundwork for the development of legislative representation. Centralizing French monarchs, some centuries later, discovered that even their personal agents could and did levy a fee as compensation for their efficiency in extracting goods and services from reluctant subjects. The pattern was not markedly different at the height of Chinese administrative centralization during the T'ang Dynasty or in Japan during the centuries of Tokugawa administration. Who got what was for a long period decided by considerations of ascription and by the generally accepted axiom that the few got much of what was available and the many got very little indeed. Mass passivity in the face of such exploitive behavior by government was greatly facilitated in the West by St. Paul's admonition, "The powers that be are ordained by God." In short, problems (or crises) of distribution were largely defined and determined by interactions *among* political elites.

It is necessary to recognize that this pattern persists into modern times and that one must be careful not to confuse the onset of mass politics, or greater participation, with a decline in the elites' role in creating and resolving problems of distribution. As Myron Weiner points out in his discussion of participation, many forms of its expansion may not in reality appreciably expand the number of persons who exercise salient or determining influence on public policy outcome. Indeed, in the industrialized West we must now interpret widespread restiveness on the part of youth and others to mean that those who have been enfranchised reject the vote or representative institutions as adequate arrangements for assuring broadened participation in the policy process. Demands for different, more effective forms of political participation represent not merely a rejection of certain claims of liberal democratic theory, but also a very severe problem for political elites in democracies who begin to perceive that some previously passive and supportive segments of the population seem *really* to want to leverage decisions.

The essentially elitist character of most crises of distribution is immediately apparent when we note the role that ideology plays in such crises. Masses do not make ideologies but are more or less activated or mobilized by them. Revolutions of rising expectations are rarely groundswells but rather represent the ability of elites or counterelites to diffuse new demands or expectations among otherwise passive objects of public policy. Where mass participation in various aspects of the political process has not been institutionalized (e.g., in the form of suffrage or voluntary associations), existing elites confronted with distributive demands need worry only about limiting circumstances of revolutionary upheaval or of regionally based pockets of resistance that may be removed through further negotiations or bargaining among elites. Where forms of mass participation have been institutionalized, however, the threats to elite stability are different and the probable nature of negotiations and bargaining is radically modified. To cite only the most obvious example of this, we might note that votes are a form of currency potentially available to counterelites in proportions that may constitute as much of a threat to an established elite as guns, bombs or guerrilla bands.

As a conditioning factor in distribution crises, ideology may be important in circumstances of limited political participation; it becomes extremely significant in circumstances where the propensity to risk revolution is high, or when forms of mass political participation potentially threaten the continuity of an existing elite. Ideology is also a strikingly important conditioning factor where it operates, as it often has, to limit the ability of political elites to respond to either of the dimensions of distribution demands we have noted above. Although these remarks seem to be self-evident, it may be useful to explore them in some further detail.

Ideology involves something less encompassing and perhaps more specific than belief system. As we are using the term here, it includes a philosophy of history, a view of man's place in it, some perception and estimate of probable directions of societal development, and a set of prescriptions regarding how such development may be hastened, retarded, or modified.[9] As such, ideology is not likely to be generated by the masses or to be understood by many of them in all of its nuances and refinements. It emanates rather from intellectuals or political elites (or counterelites), and it tends to be communicated to mass audiences in extremely simplified forms, amounting in many cases to slogans.

An ideology takes on particular importance for a political elite under several different circumstances. First, ideologies may be responsible for generating demands that require action (or inaction) on the part of political role occupants. Second, ideologies may greatly impinge on the ability of political elites to effect changes they wish to bring about in the society. Third, ideologies may become necessary instruments whereby the elites themselves can mobilize the masses and justify their own policies which, though they may be labeled "modernization," will often involve radical breaks with tradition.

Indeed, Matossian suggests that modernizing elites in countries of delayed industrialization are often "assaulted" individuals who are compelled to reorient themselves regarding their relationship to the West, their own peoples' past, and the masses of their own countries they propose to lead. Ideology, created by intellectuals, becomes in these circumstances one means of coping with the contradictory pressures and great tensions that such circumstances create.[10]

[9] See Joseph LaPalombara, "Decline of Ideology: A Dissent and an Interpretation," in C. I. Waxman, ed., *The End of Ideology Debate* (New York: Funk and Wagnalls, 1968), pp. 320ff. Cf. L. H. Garstin, *Each Age Is a Dream: A Study in Ideologies* (Portland: Old Oregon Bookstore, 1954).

[10] See Mary Matossian, "Ideologies of Delayed Industrialization: Some Tensions and Ambiguities," *Economic Development and Cultural Change*, 6 (April 1958), 217-28. A fascinating proposition of the author here is that *all* ideologies of delayed modernization are essentially revolutionary. Considerable, but not conclusive evidence for this surmise is offered from a number of historical examples of late modernization.

We might summarize this general point by referring back to Easton and noting that ideology enters the political system and may generate crisis when it implies, requires, or otherwise impinges on *changes* in existing patterns of authoritative value allocation. In making the point precisely in this way, we wish to recognize the validity of what Dahl, among others, has noted—namely, that the same issues or problems may or may not have ideological "potential." Much would depend on the intervening factors of cognition and affect. That is, where both of these factors are present and intense, the ideological potential of the issue or problem is also very high and may quickly create crisis conditions for the elite.

We shall limit our discussion here to those aspects of ideology that relate to or affect problems of distribution.[11] The ideology of nationalism, for example, was a strong and critical force underpinning anticolonial movements, and its powerful thrust toward national independence has led to the creation of an impressive number of new nations—many of them "mini-states" of problematical viability. In many of these same states nationalism carries with it a demand for greatly expanded political participation or for symbolic evidence that a freed people have achieved equality as citizens. Nationalism as an ideology, however, impinges on problems of distribution only when it subsequently leads to demands that the political elite in a postcolonial setting alter the existing resource base or modify the criteria according to which valued goods and services are distributed.

Insofar as nationalism implies such things as full independence or sovereignty and a more effective resolution of "penetration" problems, it tends to carry with it certain implications regarding the allocation of goods and services. One obvious area of resource allocation is to police and military establishments, generally felt to be essential to nation builders for symbolic or other reasons. More than one writer dealing with recent nationalism in Africa and Asia has stressed that for some time following the achievement of independence, national-

Regarding this proposition, much of what R. I. Sinai, *In Search of the Modern World* (New York: World Publishers, 1967), has written contrasting China and Japan, Mexico and Turkey is extremely fascinating and, I believe, essentially supportive of the Matossian thesis. See especially Chaps. 3 and 4.

[11] It is obvious that ideological motivations may underlie demands for altered political participation that do not necessarily imply distribution or redistribution problems. Indeed, the 19th-century English parliamentary debates in favor of an expanded suffrage are striking because of the extent to which those who favored the reforms sought to reassure reluctant elites that *nothing* substantial would change as far as the political power structure was concerned. On this point, see Myron Weiner's discussion in this volume.

ism can be an effective symbol around which delayed redistributive reforms can be justified by political elites. If, as we have suggested in the preceding chapter, the matter of holding the real estate together is recognized and accepted as a prime need, it is possible to dull the cutting edge of ideologically based demands for greater equality in the economic sphere and for the greater capability in the organizational sense that increasing the amount of material goods available would imply.

It is also necessary to recognize that nationalism generally implies economic self-sufficiency, which easily spills over into the often unfortunate notion that "modernity" means industrialization. We shall have something more to say about this particular problem in the next section of this chapter. For the moment it is sufficient to observe that even where a commitment to industrialization is not the overwhelmingly central national policy, improving the nation's economic base, or its capacity to produce more goods and services, implies investment. Investment, in turn, implies capital accumulation through savings, borrowing, foreign aid, or a combination of all three of these devices. The first of these methods affects taxation policies and the denial of other "consumables" often creating great dilemmas for existing political elites. Such dilemmas take on great magnitude and easily reach crisis proportions where national identity is a fragile matter and where the scope of effective central governmental power is extremely limited.

In conditions of extreme economic scarcity it is probable that ideological commitment to nationalism will create or exacerbate already existing, zero-sum or constant-sum public orientations toward governmental policies. No one has described this problem better than James Scott, who characterizes an important aspect of Malaysian politics as the "competition for a constant pie." Scott says, speaking of Malaysian civil servants, "They have what could be called *a 'constant pie' orientation, an orientation that assumes a fixed scarcity of desired material goods.* The 'pie' cannot be enlarged that all might have larger 'slices' but rather is constant so that much political and economic life is seen as constituting struggle of one individual, family, group or nation to expand its slice at the expense of other individuals, families, groups or nations."[12] Scott's study is full of rich quotations documenting how pervasive this orientation is in Malaysian society.

[12] James C. Scott, *Political Ideology in Malaysia* (New Haven: Yale University Press, 1968), p. 94. (Italics in the original.)

This essentially Hobbesian or Darwinian view of society and politics is echoed in an earlier study by Banfield where the system observed was Montegrano, a small community in Italy's economically backward Mezzogiorno. Banfield describes the dominant ethic of the community as "amoral familism," an ethic for which the central precept is "Maximize the material, short-run advantage of the nuclear family; assume that all others will do likewise."[13]

Both Scott and Banfield go on to describe the political and economic consequences of such an orientation; both note that the orientation itself is not necessarily pathological if one can show, for example, that for long periods of time a zero-sum or constant-sum, dog-eat-dog pattern of economic interaction represented a fair description of reality. Moreover, distributive policies from time immemorial have almost always led to systems of stratification where those at the lower end, whether among India's "untouchables" or Italy's "braccianti," lived in conditions of seemingly perpetual poverty and insecurity.[14]

More than one writer has associated the zero-sum or constant-sum orientation toward public policy with peasant societies of low technology and scarce economic resources. Only two of the areas (i.e., Greece and Spain) in which Foster finds this phenomenon may be considered somewhat "developed" countries, and it is striking that the list of other such places directly observed by Foster includes only countries from Asia, Africa, and Latin America.[15] It is important to recognize, however, that the list is certainly not restricted to the less-developed countries, but that the psychological phenomenon may be found in more developed countries long after industrialization and, indeed, even among entrepreneurs living in the most urbanized regions of such countries. Italy and France are typical examples of such countries.[16] And if Oscar Lewis is correct, then the "culture of poverty," which certainly encompasses this psychological trait, can be found not

[13] Edward C. Banfield, *The Moral Basis of a Backward Society* (Glencoe: Free Press, 1958), p. 85.

[14] The most persuasive analysis in Banfield's study is that dealing with the impact of poverty and degradation over long periods of time on the formation of Montegrano's ethos.

[15] George M. Foster, "Peasant Society and the Image of the Limited Good," *American Anthropologist*, 62 (April 1965), 293-315.

[16] For Italy, see Franco Ferrarotti, "L'Evoluzione dei rapporti fra direzioni aziendali e rappresentanti operai nell'Italia del dopoguerra," in *Atti del IV Congresso Mondiale di Sociologia: Aspetti e problemi sociali dello sviluppo economico in Italia* (Bari, 1959), pp. 133-48. For France, see John E. Sawyer, "Strains in the Social Structure of Modern France," in E. M. Earle, ed., *Modern France* (London: Russell and Russell, 1951), pp. 293-312; and David S. Landes, "French Business and the Businessman: A Social and Cultural Analysis," in *ibid.*, pp. 334-53.

merely in an underdeveloped Mexico or Puerto Rico but also in the heart of the world's capital of modern industry—New York City.[17]

We will say something more below about the relationship between a zero-sum or constant-sum view of public policies and the challenge of economic development. What we must stress here is that the ideology of nationalism inevitably runs head-on into this particular obstacle when an aspiring new nation proposes either to shift the distributive (and redistributive) power from village and city to national capital, or where the amount of such power already exercised at the center is to be amplified. Nation building occurs at someone's cost. Resistances to paying that cost will be forthcoming from all groups that are adversely affected in the short-run by the policies of nationalism.[18]

The ideological dimension of distribution crises is today further complicated by widespread attachment to something called "socialism." It is extremely difficult to generalize about the relationship of socialist ideology to the resolution of distribution problems, for much depends on what aspects of a more-or-less vulgarized Marxism are emphasized, and by whom.

In the hands of some mass-manipulating leaders, "socialism" may become nothing more than a "nationalistic populism," of considerable importance and efficacy in an anti-colonial phase, but of possible dis-

[17] See the following by Oscar Lewis: *Life in a Mexican Village: Tepoztlan Restudied* (Urbana: University of Illinois Press, 1951); *La Vida* (New York: Random House, 1968).

[18] For present purposes, it is necessary to distinguish the ideology of nationalism typically found in underdeveloping nations today from its 19th and 20th century variant in the West. It may well be that the distinction, fuzzy at best, will disappear as nationalisms born of anticolonialism give way to aggressive inter-nation behavior among developing countries. In this regard, one should soberly assess the pessimistic predictions offered by C. E. Black, *The Dynamics of Modernization, op.cit.*, Chaps. 5 and 6. Black's comment that political modernization "need not" be associated with violence is a hope we can share, but not a very realistic expectation for the future.

It is also noteworthy that the 19th and 20th century variants of nationalist ideology *were* able to move some people to considerable sacrifice in the interest of long-term (even if spuriously reasoned) gains. The cases of Nazi Germany and Fascist Italy are noteworthy. The particular turn that Chinese propagandizing and international behavior have taken is ominously reminiscent of these historical episodes. We are unable to say, however, how much of this kind of sacrifice was induced by strong *previous* resolutions of identity problems or crises.

Rupert Emerson, *From Empire to Nation* (Cambridge: Harvard University Press, 1960), gives us the most thoughtful analysis of the Western taproots of the ideologies of nationalism now evident in Asia and Africa. Among the points he makes is that we must expect vehement nationalism despite the fact that "Time has dealt harshly with the optimistic dream that the principle of nationality is the avenue to peace." (p. 388) Moreover, Emerson insists (p. 382) that the vehemence itself is a product of the "Imperial arrogance and racial discrimination" practiced by Western colonial powers themselves.

tribution-crisis difficulty in a post-independence phase of development. Expectations of equality, of redistributive justice, created during the euphoria of anti-colonial political agitation can lead to crisis situations where independence involves the granting of universal suffrage and freedom of political organization, and masses (through their leaders) begin to insist that existing political leaders deliver on the expectations created. These "sobering" moments, as we now well understand, lead elites severely to restrict the freedom of political organization. Participation then takes on new forms and certainly new meaning as harassed political leaders seek to "moderate," "channel," and "control" the level of demand forthcoming from the "outside."

Other variants of socialist ideology, however, can also become instruments for moderating or disciplining "excessive" distributive demands, for engendering the degree of sacrifice on the part of the masses elites feel is necessary to economic development, and for creating a stronger sense of identity and legitimacy than may at first exist in a particular developing nation. Both the Leninist-Stalinist and the Maoist versions of Marxism are excellent examples of how ideology can affect all three of the above ends that may be central to political elites. Ideology explains why short-term demands must be delayed in the interest of a "larger pie" later; why persistent "excessive" demands may legitimately be construed as crimes against the worker state; and why fragile, unsteady young socialist nations are constantly menaced by class enemies in both the domestic and international environments. Along with myths and doctrines like "The Divine Right of Kings," "Volk," and "Manifest Destiny," the ideology of socialism in the hands of skillful political elites can be used to legitimate distributive policies that are not immediately or apparently in keeping with demands for equality.

Socialism as an ideology is of course a two-edged weapon, almost equally available to nation-building elites and to the counterelites who would replace them.[18a] Those who strongly feel that distribution demands require increased capability to enlarge the amount of goods and services available are met by the opposition of others who, in the name of the same ideology, argue for more redistribution now. Where the latter reach out for a mass following, threatened en-

---

[18a] Lasswell and Kaplan, *op.cit.*, p. 125, suggest a possibly useful distinction to be drawn between *ideology*, which would pertain to entrenched elites, and *utopia*, which would describe certain aspects of the belief systems or doctrines of counterelites. The distinction strikes me as immensely more meaningful in empirical research than those confusing distinctions drawn by Karl Mannheim in his celebrated *Ideology and Utopia*.

trenched elites in developing countries look to strong men—or "heroes" in the felicitous model A. W. Singham offers us—to protect their positions and to somehow reconcile existential conditions with purported ideology.[19] It is a tension-inducing, problematic mission for nation-building leaders who accept such a challenge today.

We must emphasize therefore that the nature of extant ideologies today greatly complicates the ability of elites to respond to distribution crises. Western nations industrialized at considerable expense to rather large segments of their pre-industrial and early-industrial populations. The dominant ideologies (including religious ideologies) their elites confronted (or created!) tended to enshrine inequality. The Protestant ethic provided not merely reinforcing canons of work and thrift but also the concepts of predestination, election, and eventually, social Darwinism. All of these factors served to reinforce policies that either ignored redistribution demands or made it possible to tie them to a particular theory of economics associated with capitalism and implying somehow that individual man could get more only if he produced more. Developing elites today are not so fortunate.

There is one additional sense in which ideology strongly influences how elites today can respond to problems of distribution.[20] We refer to the pervasive expectation that problems of economic development—as well as of distribution and redistribution—will be overwhelmingly the responsibility of the public, as opposed to the private, sector. This expectation is not restricted to those countries that might be characterized as influenced by socialist ideology of whatever variety or mutation. Nation-states currently defined as "new," "developing," or "emergent" find themselves located in history at a time when the concept of extensive public-sector intervention is very widespread. It is striking that the intervention may be demanded either as a socialist-based conception of economic planning and public ownership of the instruments of production or as the modern conception of the

[19] A. W. Singham, *The Hero and the Crowd in a Colonial Polity* (New Haven: Yale University Press, 1968), esp. pp. 192-95, 315ff.

[20] The dimensions of ideological impact we are discussing here are meant to be purely illustrative. There are other dimensions that could be explored, as for example how national elites can encourage savings and capital accumulation for industrial investment in countries where the Muslim religion includes severe strictures against the charging of interest. One may shrug off this obstacle by noting that there is historical evidence that religious squeamishness can be overcome. Western industrial development, for example, would probably have lagged—in any event would probably have taken quite different structural form—if the Christian ethic were a matter of serious and widespread practice, or too rigid in its interpretation by the clerical elite. Dostoevski's "Grand Inquisitor" spoke an all-too-universal message.

broad human responsibilities of welfare capitalism. In either case such demands place burdens on government that are unprecedented in terms of the scope of governmental activity and the range of talent required in order to perform such activities at a minimum level of efficiency and rationality. Such demands immediately raise unavoidable questions about the relationship between things desired and the kinds of physical and human resources nation builders can bring to bear in their satisfaction.

Part III. Physical and Human Resources

The literature on political development stresses the commitment of political elites in the new nations to the central goal of economic development. The so-called "ideologies of mobilization" presumably imply highly disciplined forced marches to bring an economy up to and beyond the "take-off" point of self-sustaining growth.[21] Whether the regime is described as essentially democratic, as in India, or totalitarian, as in China, the omnipresence of the problem of economic modernity is perhaps the most striking aspect of national policy.

Perhaps the greatest irony and tragedy regarding this widespread impulse is that most of the developing nations (as well as many of those that are presumably "developed") will never reach that stage of modernity and affluence associated with some Western nations and Japan. The popular press, a great many visionaries, and some scholars speak of atomic energy and technology as the available means for eradicating most of man's social, psychological, and economic ills. Presumably, on such reasoning, the historical striving for equality and capacity we have theorized about in this volume has never been more possible of fulfillment.

Much as we can sympathize with such humanitarian hopes, it is necessary to describe them as illusory and national policies that are based on such projections or expectations as dangerously unrealistic. It may well be that the material condition of mankind will improve in absolute terms. But it is also highly probable that both within many

[21] The "stages" theory of economic growth is attributed to Walt W. Rostow, *The Stages of Economic Growth: A Non-Communist Manifesto* (Cambridge: Harvard University Press, 1960). Cf. the important work suggesting the limitations of Rostow's theories, Albert O. Hirschman, *The Strategy of Economic Development* (New Haven: Yale University Press, 1968). For an excellent discussion of the phenomenon of "mobilization," see S. P. Huntington, *Political Order in Changing Societies* (New Haven: Yale University Press, 1968), pp. 433-60. See, also, Milton J. Esman, "The Politics of Development Administration," in J. D. Montgomery and W. J. Siffin, eds., *Approaches to Development: Politics, Administration and Change* (New York: McGraw-Hill, 1966), pp. 59-112.

nations and among extant nation-states the poor are destined to get poorer vis-à-vis the affluent populations or nation-states.[22] No one has put this depressing fact more persuasively than Joseph Spengler. He notes, for example, that the present state of international income disparities is such that developing nations are between ten and twenty times better off than the underdeveloped countries. Assuming (not always realistically!) that future rates of economic growth in the latter countries will be between 50 and 100 percent better than in the developed nations, Spengler points out that it would take between 100 and 200 years for the income averages to begin to catch up. He expects therefore that the absolute spread between the economic condition of rich and poor nations will actually increase.[23]

We note this problem not to offer solutions or indeed to settle controversies concerning it,[24] but rather to describe the broad existential background against which the elites of developing nations must make decisions affecting distribution and redistribution. More specifically, such decisions have to do with physical and human resources and their management. As two students of economic development put it, the maintenance of economic growth involves the factors of technological progress and capital accumulation, natural resources, population, and resource flexibility.[25] Exactly what "mix" of policies is "best" for any single country is the subject of a vast and growing literature that cannot be treated here.[26] We will call attention to cer-

[22] It is striking for example that in a relatively more "developed" nation like Italy two decades of "emergency" governmental intervention in favor of the depressed, underdeveloped South has not closed the "amenities gap" between that region and the rest of the country. Indeed, on most indicators, the gap has actually widened. See Joseph LaPalombara, *Italy: The Politics of Planning* (Syracuse: Syracuse University Press, 1967). For a broader view of this problem see L. J. Zimmerman, *Poor Lands, Rich Lands: The Widening Gap* (New York: Random House, 1965), esp. Chap. 2.

[23] Joseph J. Spengler, "Economic and Political Development: Some Interrelations," in Ralph Braibanti, ed., *Political and Administrative Development* (Durham: Duke University Press, 1969).

[24] See the thought-provoking and controversial recent work by Gunnar Myrdal, *Asian Drama: An Inquiry into the Poverty of Nations*, 3 vols. (New York: Random House, 1968). There is much in this controversial book that all students of the developing countries must ponder with the utmost care. Not the least interesting aspect of Myrdal's study is his discussion in Vol. I, pp. 5-35, of the need for greater understanding of the biases and inappropriate theories and concepts Western scholars have displayed in their attempts to understand complex processes like political and economic development.

[25] G. M. Meier and R. E. Baldwin, *Economic Development: Theory, History, Policy* (New York: John Wiley and Sons, 1962), Chap. 24.

[26] Wilfred Malenbaum and Wolfgang Stolper, "Political Ideology and Economic Progress: The Basic Question," in J. Finkle and R. Gable, eds., *Political Development and Social Change* (New York: John Wiley and Sons, 1966).

tain aspects of this problem that seem to us to impinge strongly on the management of distribution crises.

NATURAL RESOURCES

At first blush it would appear that the natural resource base of a country severely and perhaps absolutely limits the economic potential of a nation-state. But the economic history of Great Britain or Japan would surely call such generalizations into question. Even more important for our purposes is the growing realization that some of the "laws" of development emanating from the "classical" school of Western economics may simply not be tenable. From Ricardo onward, economists have asserted that land (and other natural resources) serve to set limits on economic growth potential.[27] At the other extreme we have models or theories like those of Harrod, where the "law" of diminishing returns from land is self-consciously omitted and where indeed land is not included as a significant variable in economic growth models.[28]

Theodore Schultz has brought great wisdom to this debate, and his strictures to economists and contemporary nation-building elites are worthy of the most serious consideration. In a recent collection of his eminently readable essays Schultz notes that "The postwar dogma, so widespread among the less-developed countries, that modern economic growth is dependent wholly on industrialization has done much harm."[29] He notes that the only present exceptions to this dogma are Taiwan, Mexico, Israel, and, more recently, Pakistan. He goes on very strongly and cogently to contest the widely held view of professional economists that primary production in agriculture and mining is essentially a drag on economic growth in poor countries. Where nation builders believe that the level of marginal return to be derived from additional investment in these sectors is essentially near or at zero, it is a short, seemingly inescapable step to emphasis on investment for industrialization.[30]

Schultz's message, carefully developed in an early study, is simple and straightforward. Inputs into economic growth should be based

[27] For a first-rate theoretical treatment of classical dynamics, see William Baumol, *Economic Dynamics* (New York: Macmillan, 1951).

[28] R. F. Harrod, "An Essay in Dynamic Theory," *Economic Journal*, 49 (March 1939), 14-33.

[29] Theodore W. Schultz, *Economic Growth and Agriculture* (New York: McGraw-Hill, 1968), p. 21.

[30] *Ibid.*, p. 48.

on a careful examination of the expected rate of return per unit of capital invested. He insists that in many countries it may well be that the rate of return per unit invested in agriculture may be as large as or larger than the return realized in any other sector.[31] Rather than pursue development policies that rest on assumptions regarding the decreasing marginality of land, Schultz would insist that the natural resource situation is for any underdeveloped nation an important guide to its economic growth potential. This position would seem to be persuasive even if, as some economists will argue, it is difficult or impossible to quantify alternative development (e.g., investment) strategies in comparable units. Schultz seems to be driving at the more basic economic assumptions about land.[31a]

The matter of population is another factor that requires more careful attention than it is usually accorded, and certainly a less Malthusian treatment than is too often the case. Schultz himself notes that population projections are frequently handled much too mechanically. He insists that man "is not a mechanical reproductive robot, as has been shown by the declining birth rate of the Japanese. Simple long-range projections are all too mechanical."[32] Almost thirty years ago Joseph Schumpeter put this matter with characteristic terseness. "Forecasts of future populations, from those of the seventeenth century on, were practically always wrong. For this, however, there is some excuse. There may be even for Malthus's doctrine. But I cannot see any excuse for its survival. In the second half of the nineteenth century it should have been clear to anyone that the only valuable things about Malthus's law of population are its qualifications."[33]

More striking than the accuracy or inaccuracy of population projections are economic growth theories that are clearly anti-Malthusian in the sense of identifying growth in population as a positive factor. Spengler, for example, adheres to the classical notion that change is

---

[31] Theodore W. Schultz, *Transforming Traditional Agriculture* (New Haven: Yale University Press, 1964).

[31a] On this point, however, cf. Hirschman, *op.cit.*, pp. 33-34.

[32] T. W. Schultz, *Economic Growth, op.cit.*, p. 19. To be sure, relative to other time-series data (e.g., consumption levels, investment levels, etc.), population data and the governing parameters are relatively fixed, representing slowly changing or fixed elements in the culture. Thus, for some purposes and for shorter rather than longer periods of time population projections may be unobjectionable.

[33] Joseph A. Schumpeter, *Capitalism, Socialism and Democracy* (New York: Harper and Row, 1942), p. 115n.

at a minimum in a society that is declining in size, that the opposite proposition is probably untenable, and that the ideal situation is one where there exists slow, gradual increase in population.[34] But along comes a thoughtful, imaginative, and careful scholar like Ester Boserup whose central thesis is that agricultural production *and productivity* tend to increase where there is strong population pressure. It is precisely this pressure that causes differentiation of occupational roles, raises the efficiency of agricultural labor, and leads to increased productivity. The fascinating and challenging implication of her treatment of historical data is that underdeveloped countries with persistent, sustained growth in population represent higher probabilities of successful economic development than countries with stagnant or declining populations.[35]

What does all of this have to do with distribution crises in contemporary nation-building?

The most obvious and striking inference is that nation-building elites, terribly harassed as they are to perform an often incompatible set of social and economic miracles, may be greatly wasting extremely limited resources. The pressures on these men and women, which we have described as "crisis loads," are so great that one would assume an instinctive preference for investment inputs that would produce the greatest gains and therefore the greatest satisfaction of distribution demands. But if scholars like Schultz are correct, we may be witnessing a pattern of self-defeating national policies wherein inputs produce relatively less productive, possibly even negative, results. In previous nation-building experiences elites could perhaps afford to be less concerned with such a problem, for reasons we touched on in the previous section of this chapter. But where political participation is widely extended in the population, where discontent can be rapidly generated and widely diffused through modern system of communication, where ideologies explicitly require that egalitarian norms

---

[34] J. J. Spengler, *op.cit.*, p. 5. (Mimeographed copy of chapter cited above.)

[35] Ester Boserup, *The Conditions of Agricultural Growth: The Economics of Agrarian Change under Population Pressure* (Chicago: Aldine Publishing, 1965). Garry Brewer and Ron Brunner, in personal communications to the author, have objected to this conclusion, noting that "growth in population goes to economic development; stagnation or decline in population growth goes to economic stagnation and decline." If one accepts that both of these elements are operating, then it is the "mix" or the relative values and interactions of each that is important. They go on to say that "a reduction in population pressure both depresses consumption and stimulates investment." Depending on the *magnitude* of these two effects, income may decrease or increase. It depends on the context.

be directly and immediately implemented—in these circumstances the luxury of wasteful economic policies is at the very least a politically destabilizing factor. This caveat is crucial even where we know that, by and large, political decision-makers operate at the margins and in circumstances of uncertainty.

A less obvious observation is that precisely that segment of developing nations—the agricultural sector—is in most instances least able to lobby for its own (and, incidentally, for the national) interest. Such secondary associations and interest groups as do develop in such countries tend to be concentrated in urban centers. Traditionalistic, agricultural sectors of the society neither encourage nor easily lend themselves to organizational changes that lead to efficacious political intervention. We thus find anomalous situations where national policies emphasizing industrialization (probably doomed to failure) are determined and executed at the expense of exactly that sector of the economy that might, as Schultz would put it, make the most significant contribution to economic growth. It is little wonder therefore that nation-building elites look to the rural sectors as consisting of uncooperative, "backward" populations that must be "mobilized" behind other national developmental goals.

When one reflects on Western development and the price that agriculture paid to further it, it is possible in many instances to conclude that the results obtained were worth the sacrifice it involved. One cannot assume, however, that similar outcomes will characterize most of the now less-developed nations, where the monolithic pursuit of industrialization involves deliberately depressed agricultural prices as well as artificially augmented prices for the kinds of goods and services that the agricultural sector consumes.[36] It is more than probable that such policies will be counterproductive, for sooner or later they must serve to intensify rather than to alleviate problems of distribution.[36a]

[36] One of the most arresting allegations that Theodore Schultz makes is that U.S. assistance policies under Public Law 480 have unhappily served to discourage agricultural modernization in exactly those countries that most definitely need and would be greatly benefited by such transformations. See T. W. Schultz, *Economic Growth*, *op.cit.*, pp. 37-39.

[36a] We are aware of the enormous complexity of this problem and of the efforts of contemporary economists to cope with it. For example, for a rigorous treatment of the issue of dualism, see J. Fei and G. Ranis, "Agrarianism, Dualism and Economic Development," in I. Adelman and E. Thorbecke, eds., *The Theory and Design of Economic Development* (Baltimore: Johns Hopkins Press, 1966), pp. 3-41. Cf. R. Nurkse, *Problems of Capital Formation in the Underdeveloped Countries* (New York:

An additional complicating aspect of rigid and dogmatic insistence on industrialization involves what we shall call spurious urbanization. This pattern is present where population movements from countryside to city are not in reality motivated by employment opportunities that can absorb the masses of semiliterate or illiterate peasants who move to cities in search of opportunities to improve their material situations. As many Latin American situations attest, industrial investments frequently involve financial inputs into industrial enterprises that are not labor intensive and/or that require semi-skilled or highly skilled labor. Unlike the industrialization patterns of Western Europe, such structural conditions do not make it possible to employ in industry persons who have recently abandoned agricultural cultivation. As a consequence, the urban centers of developing countries are often characterized by a restive unemployed lumpenproletariat on the one hand and by equally restive unemployed intellectuals on the other. These two groups then combine to form a catalytic set of demands that precipitate a distribution crisis.

What all of this suggests is that quite apart from ideological considerations it may now be necessary for nation-building elites to rethink with great care the relationship between natural resources and the nation's potential for responding to distribution demands. It matters very little whether the prevailing ideology is capitalist or socialist, whether public- or private-sector oriented, if the calculus of economic growth leads political elites to obscure developmental opportunities that could, if wisely and systematically pursued, remove many pressures having to do with the size of the economic pie or with the tempo at which its availability for consumption is programmed. This necessity seems to be particularly relevant for political leadership greatly hampered by the amount of effective power it can exercise, by degrees of national identity that often fall below the minimal level required by political stability, and by mass responses that keep the problem of political legitimacy very much in question. If so-called developed nations were blessed with a more extended time period over which a sequence of nation-building crises could be confronted and resolved, this suggests all the more reason why political elites not so favored historically must be even more creative in relating resource endowments to developmental capabilities.

Oxford U. Press, 1953); J. Fei and G. Ranis, *Development of the Labor Surplus Economy* (Homewood, Ill.: R. D. Irwin, 1964); Benjamin Higgins, *Economic Development* (New York: Norton, 1959).

HUMAN RESOURCES

This leads us to comment on the human resource variable in distribution demands. As we noted above, Western nations were permitted to pursue patterns of economic change in which essentially unskilled workers recruited from the countryside could be gradually absorbed into the urban-industrial sector. In a very critical sense the improvement of the human-resource base tended to follow and to be guided by the exigencies of industrial development. Furthermore the economic transformations we associate with the spectacular development of Western countries beginning in the 18th century were not restricted to industry and urban centers but also involved striking advances in agriculture, and here, too, upgraded human skills tended to follow somewhat gradual change. We know that this circumstance is now the exception as far as contemporary nation building is concerned. The range of aspirations and demands confronted by the less-developed countries is not merely unprecedented historically, it brings immediately and distressingly to the surface the shortage of qualified manpower in these newer nations.

As in the case of the physical/natural resource problem, the manpower problem has many more facets and dimensions than we can explore here. There are, however, two facets that warrant some discussion: (a) the quality of leadership required in the formulation and execution of national or regional economic plans and (b) presumed psychological obstacles to economic growth.

(a) Planning and its human exigencies. Economists are often, and perhaps not fully justifiably, accused of excluding noneconomic variables (particularly certain "values") from their economic growth models and from their analyses and recommendations regarding public policies.[37] Lindblom, for example, acknowledges that economists are not frequently concerned with "resultant psychic states" of policy implementation; that economists will often—even if uneasily—neglect the income distribution implications of their recommendations; that they rarely choose among values underlying policy; and that a "good policy" for an economist "is often not the level of want

---

[37] It must be noted that central concern for the state of the economy's well being can and often does bring economic theorists directly into those areas of public policy that have social or ethical, as well as purely economic implications. A striking example for the United States would be James Tobin's argument for a "negative income tax." Other examples from leading economists like Friedman and Samuelson could be cited.

satisfaction directly achieved," as for example in those cases where the satisfaction of want "reduces the demands upon the individual to exert himself within the framework of conditions arranged through public policy."[38]

Lindblom goes on to say that the weighting and aggregating of conflicting values is a *political* and not an intellectual process and that in the United States at least the weighting takes place when public policies are enacted and as a result of interactive processes that he calls "fragmentation."[39] Where such patterns are present, economists need not be concerned with alternative or conflicting values since their aggregation or reconciliation occurs within the political sphere of policy-making. In this formulation economists are not so much social engineers as they are recognized experts deliberately working on only one portion of a complex human and institutional mosaic.

The difficulty with this formulation is not merely that it is inapplicable (as Lindblom concedes) to "monolithic government" but also that it is contrary to precisely the thrust toward centralized policymaking that is so typical of many of the developing countries. However one may evaluate the desirability or empirical validity of pluralistic incrementalism as a system for reaching economic development, distribution and redistribution decisions, it seems not to be consonant with the intentions of contemporary nation builders. It also seems to imply the availability and diffusion of more high-talent manpower than the typical developing nation can muster.

Harbison and Myers put the human resource problem quite laconically: "The building of modern nations," they say, "depends upon the development of people and the organization of human activity."[40] Or as Theodore Schultz would put it, the resolution of problems of distribution or redistribution requires unprecedented "investment in man" by nations still in the pre-industrial or early industrial stages.

It has always been thus, although as we have already noted in many Western societies investments in man for more than immediately relevant production occupations came rather late, uncompelled by

[38] Charles E. Lindblom, "The Handling of Norms in Policy Analysis," in M. Abramovitz, et al., *op.cit.*, pp. 169-71. The quoted material is from p. 169.

[39] One limiting type of aggregation involved in "fragmentation" Lindblom calls "bargaining." The other limiting case has no name but seems to me to involve a corporativistic delegation of power over segments of policy. *Ibid.*, pp. 174-75.

[40] F. Harbison and C. A. Myers, *Education, Manpower, and Economic Growth* (New York: McGraw-Hill, 1964), p. v.

commitments to certain levels of technology that require considerably more than the gradual removal of illiteracy. Nevertheless the history of the West is quite instructive at certain points, and particularly where the state (i.e., government) itself assumed major responsibilities to further economic growth. To cite but one important example, the transformation of public administration associated with the growth in power and affluence of Brandenburg-Prussia from the Great Elector in the mid-17th century to the unification of Germany two centuries later was clearly furthered by inputs into the training of administrators in the area of public management.[41] Thus, a wide range of demands with distribution implications greatly challenged the political elite's organizational and innovative capacities. On one hand, as we pointed out in the last chapter, the overriding need for effective administrative penetration had to be met as a problem of high priority in the sequence of nation-building chores. On the other hand, needs and demands extending into the area of material well-being and reflecting impulses to equality clearly required that governments extend their capabilities in other sectors as well. In each of the cases of successful Western industrialization one will locate the men, often great men of state, whose energies were devoted to finding the best possible fit between demands on the political system and the human talent required to satisfy them.

As we noted early in this chapter, distribution demands imply that government should see to it that the size of the pie is increased and/ or that it should be differently shared. We must now add that the aggregate of such demands has until now been greater than society's capacity to supply them. Where, for whatever set of reasons, the gap between demand and supply reaches excessive limits, system-disintegrating forces are brought into play. When we then ask what sorts of things governments can do to keep the relationship within acceptable limits, we may quickly be led to consider such instruments as charismatic demands for sacrifice, symbolic output in the form of propa-

---

[41] On the evolution of administrative change in Brandenburg-Prussia see Hans Rosenberg, *op.cit.*; Reinhard A. Dorwart, *The Administrative Reforms of Frederick William I of Prussia* (Cambridge: Harvard University Press, 1953). Merle Fainsod, "Bureaucracy and Modernization: The Russian and Soviet Case," in Joseph LaPalombara, ed., *Bureaucracy and Political Development* (Princeton: Princeton University Press, 1963), pp. 233-67, provides a fascinating overview of Russian attempts to gear administrative manpower to developmental—often redistributive—tasks. For an extended treatment of certain aspects of the view we are propounding here, see Joseph LaPalombara, "Values and Ideologies in the Administrative Evolution of Some Western Constitutional Systems," in R. Braibanti, ed., *op.cit.*

ganda about nation, the use of repressive physical force (where it is available), etc. Manning Nash quickly disposes of the subject of this entire volume when he notes that elites will be best able to react to distribution crises in those nations where the greatest, effective national sovereignty is present; the elites are well organized; there is considerable allegiance of masses to the nation and the central government; and the society itself is not seriously rent by ideological cleavage.[42]

Let us assume, however, that the elite itself is predisposed at least to encourage growth in the pie's size—possibly even major policies of redistribution. What can or must it do in order to handle such an assignment?

Economists more or less agreed on how one would answer this query. Eckstein, for example, lists five areas of state intervention to further growth. They are: (1) the provision of social overhead capital in the form of such things as laws, health, contracts, and education; (2) the provision of such items of economic overhead capital as central banking, roads, and transport; (3) the development of a wide range of instruments designed to control economic behavior in both the areas of investment and consumption; (4) the direct governmental operation of economic enterprises; and (5) the provision of centralized planning.[43] Spengler provides a similar list of political prerequisites, although he, like Eckstein, recognizes that there can be serious disagreement regarding specific items in such enumerations.[44] Thus Spengler would insist on a degree of "sub-system autonomy" that would clearly not be readily acceptable to Marxian or indeed even to some neo-Keynesian economists. That such differences of opinion are not strictly intellectually based but spill over into the area of ideological preferences is one reason, perhaps, why economists prefer the orientation to professional roles that Lindblom describes.

In any event, one can conceive of Eckstein's list as one that neces-

[42] Manning Nash, "Some Social and Cultural Aspects of Economic Development," in J. Finkel and R. Gable, eds., op.cit., pp. 285-95. This argument is a bit like saying that elites are best able to handle distribution crises in those places where such crises are unlikely to occur.

[43] Alexander Eckstein, "Individualism and the Role of the State in Economic Growth," Economic Development and Cultural Change, 6 (January 1958), 81-87. Regarding control of consumption and investment, it is well to point out, as does Hirschman, op.cit., pp. 33ff., that very little is known about how to do this so that the resolution of the problem itself is far from facile.

[44] See J. J. Spengler, op.cit. Cf. his "Bureaucracy and Economic Development," in J. LaPalombara, op.cit., pp. 204-12.

sitates increasing supplies of high-level manpower in both the private and public sectors where economies are "free" or mixed, and overwhelmingly in the public sector where central planning and state ownership of the means of production characterize the system. To say that for most developing countries such talent is in extremely short supply is an obvious understatement. To add that many of these same countries are oversupplied with disaffected unemployed intellectuals largely untrained in the occupational specializations required by the Eckstein or Spengler lists is one way to describe the frustrating dilemmas political elites confront. We might then also note that the shortage of human resources extends to skilled labor and also to the entrepreneurial personality whose importance in any theory of growth has been apparent to us at least since Schumpeter's formulations.[45]

This situation must then be assessed in a developing-nations context where perhaps the most pervasive ideological commitment is to centralized economic planning. As Myrdal describes it, "The basic principle in the ideology of economic planning is that the state shall take an active, indeed the decisive, role in the economy: by its own acts of investment and enterprise, and by its various controls—inducements and restrictions—over the private sector, the state shall initiate, spur and steer economic development. These policy measures shall be rationally coordinated, and the coordination be made explicit in an overall plan for a specified number of years ahead."[46]

As Myrdal sees it, the ideology of planning is intimately associated with the ubiquitous commitment to "modernization" in today's developing countries. The "ideals" encompassed by modernization include rationality in the identification of problems and prescriptions set for their resolution; the improvement of a wide range of human conditions felt to be undesirable; increases in productivity in all branches of the economy; rises in what Myrdal calls "levels of living"; greater social and economic equality; inculcation of attitudes

[45] A very nice treatment of this problem is found in Bert Hoselitz, "Economic Growth and Development: Non-Economic Factors in Economic Development," *American Economic Review*, 47 (May 1957), 28-41. Hoselitz notes that in Europe many of the laws and the legal institutions that facilitate economic growth existed long before European economies reached the take-off stage. He adds that this was not the case in Japan where large-scale Samurai merchants served as quite effective substitutes.

[46] G. Myrdal, *op.cit.*, Vol. 2, p. 709. Myrdal, who has more than one reservation about the ability of Asian nations to modernize, notes that the widespread commitment to planning is historically unprecedented. "Its appearance in this Rip Van Winkle world," he observes, "among people still drowsy with the slumber of centuries, makes the challenge of state economic planning all the more dramatic." (p. 710)

and creation of institutions more readily attuned to creating and accepting change; national consolidation; effective national independence; political democracy of one variety or another; greater participation and autonomy at the "grass" roots; and social discipline within a context of democratic planning.[47]

This is a tall order for any country, "developed" or otherwise. Where the countries involved in trying to fill it are underdeveloped, filling that order clearly requires enormous inputs into education, or to what Schultz and others have called "investment in man."[48] Inputs into education are now to some extent intellectually facilitated by economic growth theories that recognize that education and health, like some other social amenities, must be in part viewed as investment rather than consumption.[49] Nevertheless, education as an investment

[47] *Ibid.*, Vol. 1, pp. 58-73.

[48] Myrdal finds the neglect of factors like health and education in earlier postwar economic growth models quite astonishing. He is quite derisive about the fact that "investment in man" is treated as a new "discovery"; he is not at all convinced that recent econometric models treat either health or education as more than residuals; and he remains greatly skeptical that even such improved models can be validly or usefully applied to underdeveloped countries, at least those in South Asia. See *ibid.*, Vol. 3, pp. 1533-51; 1956-68ff.

[49] See, for example, H. P. Gideonse, "Economic Growth and Educational Development," *College and University*, 38 (Summer 1963), 425-26; A. O. Hirschman, *op.cit.*, esp. Chap. 5; H. Correa and J. Tinbergen, "Quantitative Adaptation of Education to Accelerated Growth," *Kyklos*, 15 (1962), 776-86; G. Myrdal, *op.cit.*, pp. 1540-45; Everet Hagen, *On the Theory of Social Change* (Homewood, Ill.: Dorsey Press, 1962), Chap. 3. The latter notes that "Economists writing about growth, being sensible men, usually acknowledge the influence of non-economic factors." Hagen then cites several examples, and adds, laconically, "But virtually without exception, the economists who make such acknowledgements in passing then proceed to present economic theories of growth as though they were the full and sufficient explanations." (p. 37n) It is the movement away from this parochialism, as difficult as it will be for theorists and practitioners, that the more recent group of growth theorists has happily furthered. Thus we can and should note that such expenditures are often routinely accounted for in the following manner:

$$Y = C + I + G + F$$

where

Y = GNP
C = consumption
I = investment
G = government expenditures
F = net foreign contribution to GNP

and

$$G = G_1 + G_2 + G_3 + R$$

where

G_1 = gross government investment
G_2 = government expenditures on health, education, and welfare
G_3 = other government expenditures (wages and administrative costs)
R = transfer and subsidies

sector in nation-building cannot remain a lumped residual variable, for it is clear that nation-building elites faced with competing demands will as a practical matter have to make decisions about how, where, and how much of the national product will go into education.

The general guideline that Myrdal would provide for the poorer countries is that "no independent value attached to education is considered to be valid if it conflicts with the value of education as an instrument in development."[50] For obvious reasons Myrdal and others would stress the instrumental rather than the consummatory aspect of education on the grounds that the poor nations can ill afford educational "frills" and that the most immediate contribution to economic growth will come from educational policies broadly gauged to improve the productivity of most semi-literate or illiterate labor forces. Moreover it is clear that such policies have the additional attraction of satisfying the redistribution demand for economic and social equality and are therefore likely to be widely accepted and supported.

If one turns to the nation-building experience in the West, we find that much education was of this instrumental variety when it became available to more than a tiny segment of the population. Indeed, one way to depict the greatly augmented problem here for the leaders of non-Western nations is to note, as we suggested above, not merely the instrumental gradualness of extended educational opportunities in Western societies but also that spurts in educational reform tended to be in direct response to severely felt needs (e.g., the reform of French education after the defeat of France by an immensely superior, technically trained German army; or the reconstruction of the Brandenburg-Prussia bureaucracy after the devastation of the Thirty Years War); and that universal compulsory education of any kind generally followed the Industrial Revolution.

More than ever before in history, then, problems of distribution and redistribution confront political elites with the need for rationalizing systems of education, for guaranteeing that whatever the physical resource base of a nation steps be taken to assure the kind and amount of skilled manpower that can maximize the material and related things the nation can produce. As Harbison and Myers put it, "Human resource development is the process of increasing the knowl-

[50] G. Myrdal, op.cit., p. 1621. Chap. 31, "Education: The Legacy," Chap. 32, "Literacy and Adult Education," and Chap. 33, "The School System" (all in Vol. 3) strike me as the best synthetic treatment of this problem currently in print.

edge, the skills and the capacities of *all* of the people in a society."[51] They return to Alfred Marshall, seemingly neglected by early post-war theorists of economic growth, for the postulate that the most important capital investment is that which is dedicated to the training of human beings.[52] They are also careful to agree with Myrdal that education cannot be considered merely a "human right" (or we might say here a redistributive mechanism) but must be carefully assessed in terms of what varying forms of it, as well as what particular investment costs, will contribute to production.

The advice from Harbison and Myers would be that inputs be concentrated in the direction of increasing the available supply of high-level manpower. In their scheme such manpower would include: entrepreneurial, managerial, and administrative talent in the public and private sectors; professionals; qualified teachers with at least twelve years of education; subprofessional technicians such as nurses, agricultural assistants, and certain kinds of skilled workers; and top-ranking political, labor, judicial, and military leaders. These are the people who in their view must fill the "strategic positions" in modern societies. Their training requires secondary education at least.[53]

Others like Myrdal might stress the benefits to be derived from concentrating on small educational increments in the larger population. But if it is recognized, as we suggest above, that centralized economic planning does in fact raise to maximum levels the number of high-level manpower units required, the empirical data furnished by Harbison and Myers are both arresting and discouraging.[54] How is one to find some points or sectors of hope in developmental crisis situations where the overwhelming number of persons lack even primary education and where many of the university educated elite are specialized in areas that are far removed from the technical and scientific exigencies of planned economic growth.

[51] F. Harbison and C. A. Myers, *op.cit.*, p. 2. The central issue here is of course that groups are identified and rank-ordered, often on the basis of assumptions about pay-offs from investment. Given resource constraints, the wish to benefit *all* may be untenable, at least in the short-run.

[52] See Alfred Marshall, *Principles of Economics* (New York: Macmillan, 1930), pp. 216, 564, who is treated by both Myrdal and Harbison and Myers. Evidently, the "discovery" of education as an important input is associated with the gradual understanding among students of American economy that the fantastic economic growth of the U.S. could not be adequately explained by models that were in fact too narrowly tied to classical economic formulations.

[53] F. Harbison and C. A. Myers, *op.cit.*, Chap. 3.

[54] See, for example, the table, *ibid.*, p. 55. Their discussion of the use of foreign manpower and the most economical way to educate future skilled manpower is also worthy of careful reflection. See *ibid.*, pp. 55-69.

One important sector in which educational programs must produce not only more but also different skilled manpower is public administration. As we pointed out in our previous chapter, the crisis of penetration places severe demands on political elites to produce the kinds of law-and-order administrators who are able to make of new or expanded *national* control more than a fond, abstract hope. Some former colonial areas, such as India, Pakistan, Ceylon, and Malaya, had a considerable advantage since they inherited indigenous law-and-order administrative personnel of astonishingly "modern" capabilities. These men were often not merely highly skilled to perform central or field general administrative functions; they could also serve roles of great importance in the resolution of identity and legitimacy crises. Along with political party leaders, they could and did do much to diffuse and to inculcate a new sense of nationhood and of the role of citizens within these new systems.[55] Presumably, too, such broadly trained public service personnel could also serve as a talent pool from which the vital services of coordination might be provided as political elites moved toward centralized planning as a means of responding to distribution and redistribution demands.[56] In this sense, one might say that such administrative generalists were available for nation-building and/or "crisis-management" roles not unlike those that arose in comparable periods of Western national development.

For most developing nations, however, even large or in any case sufficient members of law-and-order administrators are in short sup-

---

[55] There is now a considerable literature on this topic. See, for example, Ralph Braibanti, "Reflections on Bureaucratic Reform in India," in R. Braibanti and J. J. Spengler, *Administration and Economic Development in India* (Durham, N.C.: Duke University Press, 1963), pp. 3-68; Ralph Braibanti, "The Civil Service of Pakistan: A Theoretical Analysis," in Inayatullah, *Bureaucracy and Development in Pakistan* (Peshewar, n.d.), pp. 189-249; Robert Tilman, *Bureaucratic Transition in Malaya* (Durham, N.C.: Duke University Press, 1964).

[56] It cannot be overemphasized that the ambitions of central planners generally greatly outrun the capacity of existing administrative talent to turn plan aspirations into concrete reality. The coordination of a great number of highly related, planned activities is one of the most taxing organizational and behavioral problems, as the experience of the Soviet Union has clearly shown. For some indication of how perplexing this problem can be even in a developing nation *not* overwhelmingly committed to economic growth largely dominated by the public sector, see Ralph Braibanti, *Research on the Bureaucracy of Pakistan* (Durham, N.C.: Duke University Press, 1966), esp. Chaps. 2, 3, 4. Cf. Bela A. Balassa, *The Hungarian Experience in Economic Planning* (New Haven: Yale University Press, 1959), Chap. 3; J. M. Montias, *Central Planning in Poland* (New Haven: Yale University Press, 1962), pp. 294-333. Although neither of these last two books is primarily concerned with political/administrative problems per se, they serve to demonstrate much about this matter, as well as to dramatically highlight the pressure for a wide range of human skill that planned economic change requires.

ply. For all of them the supply of administrators with training that fits the technical-scientific requirements of central planning is even more strikingly low or essentially nonexistent. Thus, whether motivated by nationalistic ambitions to improve the country's relative economic standing or by internal demands to produce and distribute more, the elites of new nations generally feel considerable pressure for administrative change or "reform." Invariably such reforms require decisions regarding education. The problem of designing the educational apparatus that is attuned to this particular need is only one example of the generally crucial role the nation-building literature now ascribes to education. As Coleman rightly notes, "In modernizing countries, education may achieve a central role precisely because it is one of the principal instruments for change available to the polity."[57]

We shall not be detained here by questions regarding how any particular nation can provide the public administrative resources essential to meeting problems arising out of distributive demands. Whether one is thinking of improved systems of planting and marketing rice or collecting taxes, highly complex decisions must be made regarding *who* should be educated, by *whom*, in what *sequence* or *phasing* of educational opportunities, with what particular *outputs* in mind, with what particular type of *curricular content* in mind, in what kind of general-technical *educational mix*, and against what overall place educational investments should occupy in the total resource outlay for economic growth.

Questions such as the above suggest that not merely the economic but also the political consequences of the "investment in man" must be carefully taken into account. That is, if our interest extends to some way of relating something as specific as educational inputs to the *political* crises of nation-building, we cannot accept the notion that the prime concern of the economist (i.e., the greatest output per unit of investment, given certain economic growth policy commitments) should or can remain the only one. Furthermore, even when economists are presumably dealing with the purely economic effects of investments in man, their conclusions are often not in accord with each other and almost as often imply *political* capacities that may not

[57] James S. Coleman, ed., *Education and Political Development* (Princeton: Princeton University Press, 1965), p. 521. It should be stressed that Coleman cites three strong motivations for improved education, not all of which are necessarily reflections of distribution problems. These are: (a) elite ideologies that may require expanded educational opportunities; (b) mass demands; and (c) a combined elite-mass demand not to be dependent for education on the facilities or the human resources of foreign countries. *Ibid.*, pp. 521-22.

be feasible or realistic for many nation-building elites. A few illustrations will have to suffice.

As we noted above, growth economists are not of one mind regarding how to treat population density and the rate of population growth. Similarly, there is considerable disagreement about how many of what kinds of persons should be educated to do what at particular stages of economic development. Harbison and Myers clearly favor a "middle-level" strategy that would eschew both massive efforts at the primary level and highly expensive inputs into university education.[58] They view costly university education as something to aim for in the long run and increased primary education as insufficient to meet the skilled manpower needs of improved agriculture and the break-through into industrialization. Depending on available manpower configurations, they would tailor educational strategies to these specific national profiles. In each of the strategies chosen however, the production of high-level manpower would be a prime consideration.[59] Myrdal, who holds that the major problem of South Asia is the under utilization of illiterate labor, would urge a massive input into the matter of bringing great numbers of peasants to the point where they can work immediately to improve their level of living.[60] He is also insistent that educational opportunities aimed at providing nothing more than greater equality would actually accelerate rather than impede economic growth.[61] His is an eloquent plea that the failure to ask probing questions about who should be educated how to do what is a very useful device for justifying the perpetuation of inequality in the developing nations. Our inference is that he would certainly place the "model" offered by Harbison and Myers and by a host of Western econometricians, in this category.[62]

Close to the Myrdal notion of educating large numbers of persons as quickly as possible are the views of W. Arthur Lewis. Lewis is not worried about glutted markets, nor would he be overly concerned about overproduction of basically educated persons. He assumes that an oversupply of any particular group is a short-run phenomenon and that over longer periods of time both the skill requirements of employers and status and compensation expectations of the educated will

[58] F. Harbison and C. A. Myers, *op.cit.* Cf. F. Harbison, "The Prime Movers of Innovation," in C. A. Anderson and M. J. Bowman, eds., *Education and Economic Development* (Chicago: Aldine Publishing, 1963), pp. 229-39.

[59] F. Harbison, *op.cit.*, pp. 234-35. [60] G. Myrdal, *op.cit.*, Vol. 3, 2068.

[61] *Ibid.*, Vol. 1, p. 572. [62] *Ibid.*, Vol. 3, pp. 1959-60.

change.[63] On the other hand, while Hoselitz favors investments in man, he cautions that how many should be educated and when depends largely on a careful examination of other factors. He notes that theories regarding investments in man involve overly simplified extrapolations from past and present Western national experiences to present and future experiences in developing nations. He concludes that "Although some returns from investment in education may be expected at all stages of economic development, investment in educational facilities may produce much lower returns at certain earlier stages of economic growth than the application of equal amounts of investment in other forms of capital, especially capital constituting the material infrastructure of an economy."[64] Foster adds that education may be a necessary but not sufficient condition for development, and that lack of attention to oversupply can create unemployment.[65] Like Hoselitz he is aware of the possibility that educational policies can greatly exacerbate *political* problems confronted by harassed elites.

What guidance can contemporary nation-builders extract from such seemingly contradictory advice? How can central planners who must at least strive to produce a larger pie find the proper "mix" of policies that will represent the optimal (but not necessarily effective for securing political stability!) response to a variegated set of demands? What does one do, for example, when it might be demonstrated, as Hoselitz suggests, that in stressing the production of administrative manpower capable of dealing with problems of economic growth (i.e., distribution) one may evolve policies that increase the social and political inequalities that result in increasing the gap between people whenever (as it usually does) it is both a cause of and

[63] W. A. Lewis, "Education and Economic Development," *International Social Science Journal*, 14 (1962), 686-88, cited in J. Coleman, ed., *op.cit.*, p. 525. This view of Lewis' seems somewhat inconsistent with Harbison's claim, *op.cit.*, p. 235, that Lewis has "repeatedly" criticized African nations for emphasizing wide diffusion of primary education and for investing too much in higher education at the expense of secondary education.

[64] Bert F. Hoselitz, "Investment in Education and Its Political Impact," in J. Coleman, ed., *op.cit.*, p. 543.

[65] Philip J. Foster, "The Vocational School Fallacy in Development Planning," in C. A. Anderson and M. J. Bowman, eds., *op.cit.*, pp. 153ff. We should add that Foster takes a dim view of specialized education, stressing that generally educated persons will respond to a range of incentives provided by the market and by governmental policies. His data from Ghana in this regard are very persuasive. In any event, he seems to be essentially in agreement with Myrdal that social scientists have greatly overdrawn the peasant's refusal to adapt to new patterns of life. (See *ibid.*, pp. 148ff.)

effect of differentials in educational achievement, and in denying strongly articulated demands for political participation.[66]

Because both the configuration and hierarchy of demands will differ from country to country, it is difficult to escape the conclusion that each situation must be treated in many respects as if it were (as in many ways it must be) unique. Such a conclusion would indeed seek to profile each country at a particular point in time and seek to relate the total capacity of a political system to the developmental ends it may set itself.[67] Furthermore, a profiling of specific national conditions *through* time would permit alternative specifications and projections of possibly very high policy utility, thereby minimizing the biases that are often introduced by cross-sectional analyses.[67a] In any event, some generalizations about policy "mixes" and about the nature of inputs into particular kinds of education are warranted, we believe because as many of the works we have cited suggested broad base-line or parametric conditions are similar in subgroupings of developing nations. It is necessary to recognize that just as land/man ratios served as rough guidelines for a number of economic development generalizations, similar generalizations can be adduced where one seeks to associate physical and human resource conditions, economic developmental aspirations, and the probable political consequences of elites reacting in one way or another to mass demands that reach one degree or another of intensity. In seeking to achieve such a primitive calculus, we have thus far emphasized certain factors that may be associated with the stimulus side of developmental problems. Demands are made on elites from other elites or aspiring elites or from the mass sector of society; available indigenous physical and human resources can be brought to bear in their satisfaction. Alternatively, national elites themselves set certain goals, often ideologically postulated, and the same mixes of physical and human resources can be mustered in efforts to achieve their satisfaction. Where such de-

[66] Bert F. Hoselitz, in J. Coleman, ed., *op.cit.*, pp. 559-60. Hoselitz adds some other unwanted political/economic consequences of badly drawn educational policies. These include: (1) excessive competition for high-level manpower jobs with the resultant reintroduction of ascriptive criteria of selection; (2) retardation of widespread political participation; and (3) the possible "export" of high-level manpower through out-migration.

[67] For a discussion of the utility of the use of "profiles" in assessing the matter of improving public administrative capacities, see Joseph LaPalombara, "Alternative Strategies for Developing Administrative Capabilities in Emerging Nations," in F. W. Riggs, ed., *Frontiers in Development Administration* (Durham: Duke University Press, 1971).

[67a] See, on this point, James Brown *et al.*, *Overview of Land Use and Transportation Models in Planning* (New York: National Bureau of Economic Research, 1969), pp. III, 2-3 (mimeographed).

mands or goals imply distributive policies, they almost invariably imply that much deeply-rooted behavior associated with the production of goods and services will have to be modified. No discussion of this intricate process would be adequate without some reference to cultural or psychological factors that impinge on the processes involved.

b. Psychological obstacles. As we look backward in time and observe which nations have been more or less successful in entering "advanced stages" of economic modernity, it is greatly tempting to go in search of what is "different" about such nations and then to translate what may be spurious correlations into critical factors of causation. We have a vast literature which even when it does not reflect unsophisticated assertions about "national character" tends to boil down to our saying that developmental crises are well managed when there exist able governmental elites or when the nonelites themselves develop certain character traits that are conducive to "rational" problem-solving and problem-posing. Such views are without doubt fortified by the presumed Iron Laws of economic growth, by which it can be reasonably well demonstrated that not all goals and desires are compatible, that not all of them can be satisfied in the short-run, and that above all, future improvements can be obtained only at the expense of immediate sacrifices—generally described as savings or the accumulation of capital. A somewhat harsher, perhaps more realistic way of putting this matter is that future long-term improvements occur at the short-term expense of someone. When this problem is treated at the total systemic—or macro-economic—level, questions regarding who is paying what relative cost for such long-term benefits tend to be set aside. The general assumption is that economic growth will be desired by everyone because it will benefit everyone more or less.

Where reasonable consensus can be obtained, as it usually can, that a larger pie is a generally desired goal, it is reasonable to expect that some appeal to the willingness to sacrifice will have a positive effect. Further, where on other grounds the governmental elite can have more than marginal faith in its own legitimacy and coercive resources, policies that are likely to be unpopular can also be enunciated and rationalized on the basis of future expectations of greater gains. Where a significant portion of the population is available for mobilization behind national developmental goals, another asset of considerable exploitive possibilities is available to the national elite.

Once there is a minimal agreement that the resolution of distribution demands involves sacrifice in the interest of a future larger pie, however, elites generally face the grim prospect of finding the ways to modify human behavior. It is at this point that considerations regarding culture and behavior are potentially of great significance.

How does one get people to save and to enter the exchange economy who have been accustomed for centuries to a subsistence or barter economy? What must be the nature of the inducement that will lead farmers to use chemical fertilizer who have never done so; to plant rice or use land in a way that would involve breaking with tens of generations of traditional workways; to save in a pattern that associates what is saved with broad economic change rather than merely to hoard precious metal? How can one persuade certain individuals to take economic risks never before contemplated; to willingly pay taxes on the assumption that public investments in infrastructure will benefit everyone? One might ask a host of similar questions that finally bring abstract notions of economic change (or changes in distribution) face to face with what many writers have called the patterns of tradition or tranditionalism. Surrounding and reinforcing these patterns are presumed to be certain sets of attitudes and predispositions that will either facilitate or be inimical to change.

Once again we find that the relevant social science literature is on the whole not very encouraging. The "models" of "traditional society" we are offered depict structural, attitudinal, and behavioral conditions that are presumed to be hostile to change and certainly not easily attuned to the kind of economic modernization that distribution crises resolution would seem to require. Sociologists and anthropologists in particular have provided the roll call of characteristics that serve to impede economic transformation. These characteristics would include: rigid systems of social stratification that prevent the kind of occupational mobility that modernization implies; limited "spatial" reference that makes the diffusion of change-inducing information quite difficult; lack of "empathy"; emphasis on spiritual as opposed to material values; the absence of a tradition where the written word is highly valued; great pressures and predispositions to conform to age-old patterns of human interaction; strong deferential systems based on considerations of age, sex, and ascriptive roles; lack of knowledge of or interest in the scientific outlook; the almost total absence of entrepreneurial personalities; narrowly defined social solidarity; and systems of religion that greatly reinforce all of the above.[68]

Apter sums it all up by noting that "Cultures never give way completely to the new, no matter how ruthless the impact of innovation. The varied responses of tradition to modernization account for many of the differences in political forms among the new nations."[69] Elsewhere Apter has stressed that while industrialization is not the probable developmental outcome for many new nations, "modernization" will probably occur everywhere.[70] If we can agree with Apter that one important ingredient of modernity is the capacity of society to innovate without distintegrating, we can then go on to understand why the particular configuration of a given traditional society will tend to limit elite options in problem solving and to dictate the particular mix of policies and the tempo of their implementation that elites can follow. In many places, as Apter argues, development itself will become a central precept of a "political religion"; in many others some of the ideologies we have discussed in this chapter will be seen as the instruments for overcoming psycho-cultural barriers to change.

Whatever may be the environmental factors that impinge on the degree of freedom available to elites, a number of critically important transformations appear to be universally required if problems of distribution are to be adequately resolved.

First, the evidence seems overwhelming that little can be done to increase the size of the pie unless levels of literacy are dramatically raised over a relatively short time span. In no other sector, we believe, is the "big push" argument regarding nation-building problems more

[68] Among the more interesting treatments of this problem are the following: D. E. Apter, *The Politics of Modernization* (Chicago: University of Chicago Press, 1965), Chap. 3; R. N. Bellah, "Religious Aspects of Modernization in Turkey and Japan," in J. Finkel and R. Gable, *op.cit.*, pp. 188-93; W. N. Brown, "Traditional Culture and Modern Developments in India," *Report of the Eleventh International Congress of the Historical Sciences* (Stockholm, 1960), pp. 129-62; Robert Redfield, *Peasant Society and Culture* (Chicago: University of Chicago Press, 1956); Clifford Geertz, ed., *Old Societies and New States* (London: Free Press, 1964), esp. the essays by McKim Marriott (pp. 27-56), David Apter (pp. 57-104), Clifford Geertz (pp. 105-157), and Lloyd Fallers (pp. 158-219); E. E. Hagen, *On the Theory of Social Change* (Homewood. Ill.: Dorsey Press, 1962), Chap. 4.

[69] D. E. Apter, *The Politics of Modernization, op.cit.*, p. 81.

[70] D. E. Apter, "Political Religion in the New Nations," in C. Geertz, ed., *op.cit.*, pp. 59ff. This faith in the probable ubiquitousness of modernization is open to some doubt, particularly if one means to imply that once the chains of "tradition" are broken, unilinear progress or in any case no retrograde steps back to traditionalism will occur. History is full of examples of modernizing societies that subsequently slipped "backward."

persuasively made. Increases in literacy that are more than merely incremental seem to be essential, as Myrdal and others have noted, both to improved patterns of agriculture and to new demands for consumption that will in turn spur growth. As contradictory as it may appear, this method of managing distribution crises requires taking steps that would in the short run tend to intensify distributive demands.[71]

It is surely literacy that will be vitally instrumental in bringing peasants to understand that they can achieve greater control of their physical environment than they have believed for tens of generations; that social relationships are not necessarily immutable; that the activity of exchange and commerce is not necessarily spiritually degrading or morally reprehensible; and that activities other than owning and/or working marginally productive land can provide security for self and family. It is literacy that may eventually endow the peasant with "empathy," make him more self-reliant in reaching decisions affecting his occupation and level of living, encourage him to be mobile as far as employment opportunities are concerned, and lead him to question the hierarchical patterns of power and authority that characterize family life and the broader society. Where such personality transformations lead to "rising expectations," distribution demands are likely to escalate. Without such escalation, however, it is improbable that any new demands can be adequately met and so the traditional system will remain stagnant.

Second, it is unlikely that much can be done to resolve distribution crises unless elites themselves, or salient segments of the elite, also modify their own psychocultural patterns. As Hagen persuasively argues, the elites of developing countries are often subject to the same anxieties, the same fear of the environment, the same incapacity to innovate, the same reluctance to venture into the little known that is characteristic of the peasant. Hagen says:

> To a member of the elite, in short, as to one of the simple folk, the phenomena of the physical world are a limiting and a

[71] For an extremely provocative theoretical essay on the relationship of general education to development, see Harvey Leibenstein, "Shortages and Surpluses in Education in Underdeveloped Countries: A Theoretical Foray," in C. A. Anderson and M. J. Bowman, eds., *op.cit.*, Chap. 3. Cf. Harvey Leibenstein's *Economic Backwardness and Economic Growth* (New York: 1957), which, along with contemporary writings of Paul Rosenstein-Rodan, is closely associated with the theory of the "big push" in economic development. The relationship of literacy to subsequent potentialities and directions of development is treated by Daniel Lerner, *The Passing of Traditional Society* (Glencoe: Free Press, 1958).

threatening force against which he is almost helpless. No more than the peasant does he think that his reason and the logical instrumentalities at his disposal can prevail against them. This is the great contrast between the elite of traditional societies and the middle and upper classes of technologically advanced societies, a contrast which it is difficult for a member of the latter to appreciate fully.[72]

Both this shared anxiety and the elites impulse to feel different from the peasant serve as impediments to economic growth. Earlier in this volume Lucian Pye explores varieties of identity crises that relate to the more specific nature of a dominant elite, and it is clear that one must probe beyond the most abstract level of generality in any attempt to elucidate the crisis configuration of a single nation. Nevertheless it is certainly striking that similar attitudes exist in Europe in precisely those countries that were late economic modernizers (e.g., Italy and France) or that have yet to make a strong break-through toward modern technological growth (e.g., Spain and Portugal). Entrepreneurial activity, so desperately needed in the resolution of distribution problems, is therefore wanting for a wide variety of reasons, some of them religious, some of them social-structural, but some of them deeply psychological as well. It may be, as McClelland has argued, that the distribution of n-achievement among the entire population is an important index of potentiality for creative historical spurts in technological change.[73] Nevertheless we may stress here that while the motives of all men can help to facilitate or to impede change, the motives (and related capacities) of some men are more important than those of others. If we are to conclude, as Hagen does, that social change will not occur without changes in personality and that the ability to produce and sustain technological advance is a particularly complex example of this phenomenon, we must also conclude that personality changes in elites are prime desiderata.[74]

[72] E. Hagen, *op.cit.*, p. 75.

[73] David C. McClelland, *The Achieving Society* (Princeton: Van Nostrand, 1961).

[74] E. Hagen, *op.cit.*, Chap. 5. See esp. pp. 88-97, for a most illuminating exploration of certain psychological characteristics of the "innovational personality." Both Hagen and McClelland lay great stress on the implications for later personality structure of the role of the mother in the family and of the relationship of children to her. See D. C. McClelland, *op.cit.*, pp. 341-62. Cf. D. C. McClelland, "The Achievement Motive in Economic Growth," in J. Finkel and R. Gable, *op.cit.*, pp. 139-56. Whether, as E. Hagen, *op.cit.*, pp. 97ff., claims, a heavy distribution of "authoritarian personalities" in a population is consistently an inhibition to economic growth may be open to some question. The cases of Germany and Japan, for example, immediately come to mind.

The work of McClelland and Hagen might at first blush suggest that personality traits cannot be modified until fundamental changes have occurred within the institution of the family. Yet closer examination reveals that other institutional changes can encourage greater receptivity to economic change. Moreover, a number of factors (several of which we have discussed in this volume) may very well serve to accelerate change even if we are not prepared to say that they cause it. The ideologies of mobilization or nationalism are cases in point. Urbanization, changes in patterns of political participation, the appearance of "political religions" or the modification of existing religious dogma, the creation of economic infrastructure, and the organization of more efficient markets—all of these are factors, often open to public policy manipulation, that can run counter to traditional impediments to economic growth.

Furthermore, as we have noted in our discussion of other crises, the context in which crises occur, and in what particular sequence, must be taken into account. Hagen in the empirical studies he explores in his fascinating book, notes the extent to which status displacements or interruptions will be conditioned by preexisting institutional psychological factors.[75] It seems important to add that "traditional society" is not a monolithic or homogeneous concept for which empirical referents are always and everywhere the same.[76] This point is brought forth with great cogency by Bert Hoselitz, who insists on a conceptual differentiation be drawn between "traditional" and "traditionalistic" societies, and that differentiation be measured by such factors as whether traditional values are consciously or unconsciously held; formalized or nonformalized; normative or nonnormative; and a matter of habit, usage, or ideology.[77] More recently Apter has taken some of these dimensions and along with others established a typology of traditional societies specifically aimed at suggesting their probable receptivity to change and particularly to economic changes that would respond to distribution demands.[78] One must at any rate avoid theo-

---

[75] E. Hagen, *op.cit.*, Part V.

[76] It is striking that not even village life located in a single geographic region, indeed in a single nation, can be easily abstracted. Hugh Tinker, for example, cautions that the universe comprising something called the "Indian village" comprises some 500,000 units, concerning which some ascribed characteristics would not hold across the board. See his "The Village in the Framework of Development," in R. Braibanti and J. J. Spengler, eds., *op.cit.*, pp. 94-133.

[77] Bert F. Hoselitz, "Tradition and Economic Growth," in R. Braibanti and J. J. Spengler, eds., *Tradition, Values and Socio-Economic Development* (Durham, N.C.: Duke University Press, 1961), pp. 83-113.

[78] D. E. Apter, *The Politics of Modernization, op.cit.*, Chap. 3.

retical formulations that imply excessive pessimism or permanent stasis in nation-states unless the empirical evidence strongly supports such a formulation. Thus, although we have tried to be cautious in this volume in extrapolating from past Western experiences, it is instructive that great economic and technological changes did occur in a variety of Western nations, some of which displayed (and still display!) patterns of hierarchy, ascription, low mobility, strength of custom, and a wide range of other characteristics associated with the psycho-cultural structure of peasant or traditional society.

Thirdly, we would suggest that no adequate response to distribution crises is likely to be found unless it is conceded that not only the masses but also the more privileged social strata as well must be encouraged to develop patterns of savings for investment, of delayed gratifications in the interest of future gains and satisfactions. Spengler is explicit about this and suggests that one of the great problems in responding effectively to distribution exigencies is the excessive tender mindedness of contemporary nation builders.[78a] Insofar as some of the obstacles to economic growth we have discussed are real, removing them will not easily occur, says Spengler, if the political elite relies on man's essential goodness and rationality or on the notion that democratic procedures will produce the desired results.[79] Myrdal also underscores this weakness, holding that the creation of conditions that will permit satisfying distribution (and redistribution) demands requires far less attention to liberal democratic values and practice and much more attention to inducements and coercions that are instrumental for planned change. Myrdal would want obligations placed on persons everywhere in the social system, accompanied by rigorous enforcement. His bluntly put indictment is that "The absention from compulsion has thus been permitted to masquerade as part of the modernization ideals."[80]

The demand for forceful leadership puts the emphasis largely on the role of the elite in economic and political development, which is where we believe it should be. Although we have not treated the masses as inert in our formulations, we have certainly conceptualized the developmental crises as involving largely elite interactions, elite

---

[78a] It is laconically pointed out to me by Garry Brewer that what the social scientist calls "tender-mindedness" may really be political-mindedness or survival-mindedness.

[79] J. J. Spengler, "Economic and Political Development: Some Interrelations," *op.cit.*, pp. 12-17.

[80] G. Myrdal, *op.cit.*, Vol. 1, p. 67.

aspirations, elite initiatives, and elite responses to signals from the mass environment. The vital role of political elites raises in turn the nagging issue of power, and our persistent observation has been that the most striking aspect of political power in developing nations is how little of it most elites have at their disposal. It is for this among other reasons that we have stressed the necessity of confronting nation-building crises sequentially where possible,[81] and why we suggest above the need for responding to demand within the context of existing institutional arrangements whenever possible.

How much space or elbow room a given elite will enjoy in responding to distribution demands will depend not merely on internal conditions but on external factors as well. In concluding this discussion, we can turn to a brief discussion of the impact of several of these latter factors on elite crisis management capability.

Part IV. The International Environment

For many of the developing nations the international environment is a major cause of nationalism. It is also the cause of ambivalence Westernized elites of former colonies experience when they seek on the one hand to create "modern" national polities and recognize on the other hand that both the philosophical and institutional models for such polities are derived from the West. As Myrdal notes, essentially all aspects of what is now considered "modernity" are alien to the cultures that are striving to be modern.[82] One of the vital nation-building requisites the elites of these cultures must satisfy is that of finding the ways and means of rendering these aspects "indigenous." In most places, this is no easy chore, particularly when internal considerations make extremely complex and hazardous the particular cultural level at which to pitch the new goals of modernity.[83]

Of much greater potential difficulty, however, is the tendency of all contemporary nation builders to want to copy the West—to assume as it were that modernity means in many ways becoming the mirror image of highly industrialized and affluent societies. The ubiquitous urge to industrialization, the neglect of agriculture, and the assumption that traditional lifeways are essentially incompatible with the modern state are manifestations of this tendency to copy.

[81] See Sidney Verba's concluding chapter in this book.
[82] G. Myrdal, *op.cit.*, p. 73.
[83] See McKim Marriott, "Cultural Policy in the New States," in C. Geertz, ed., *op.cit.*, pp. 27-56.

Where it finds its way into major governmental policies having to do with economic development or institutional change, the results of this tendency, to put it mildly, can be clamorously counterproductive.

Examples of such policies could be multiplied. Modern steel works or major power dams are introduced at great cost into situations where little else about such cultures can warrant or support such investments. As a host of writers have now underlined, to be "modern" often means to collect the trappings of national sovereignty, from expensive embassies abroad and delegations in the United Nations to expensive hotels and a large-industrial façade at home. Aided and abetted by bad technical assistance advice, some of these nations have plunged into quixotic industrial development endeavors where it is apparent that the complex range of complementary social, economic, commercial, and psychological arrangements necessary for such enterprises will be long in materializing—if they materialize at all. The emphasis we have placed on the need to be governed by the steps forward that existential circumstances will permit is a reflection of the overdiffusion of information about how the developed world lives. When the urge to keep up with the Joneses moves into the international realm and gets out of hand, the results for a developing nation can often be as catastrophic as they often are for upward striving middle-class Americans.

If McClelland is correct, the compulsion to copy is greatly spurred by what he finds to be the gambler's instinct in people of low n-achievement.[84] Such persons tend to lack the cold rationality and the minimax orientation of the entrepreneur. Rather than key investments to reasonably delineated pay-off expectations, such persons tend to gamble on the excessive pay-off, the get-rich-quick gamble, the all-or-nothing wager. When those who play the long shots are national leaders their undoing affects millions of other persons who know little or nothing about the precarious development game and who, if they did, would probably not wish to play it at all. Where it becomes apparent that national leaders, charismatic or otherwise, have pretended to do more than they can achieve, it is natural that disillusionment and frustration should result.

Although such gambles are frequently primarily economic, it is clear that they are also political. This is so, first, because the major players are likely to be political and bureaucratic leaders. It is true also because the game itself will test the capacity of leaders to create

[84] D. C. McClelland, *op.cit.*, pp. 221-25.

or transform political and administrative institutions. It is also the case because governmental policies will reveal just how effective the elite can be in impinging on the attitudes and the organizational and behavioral proclivities of the community as a whole.[85]

Closely related to the above problem is the fact that the international environment now provides various amounts and forms of assistance to contemporary nation builders. Where that advice is bad —for whatever reasons—the international financial and technical assistance touts can have extremely unfortunate impacts on problem-solving in developing nations. Where the kinds of assistance provided are ideologically determined by extraneous considerations in the international arena, the consequences of such programs can be equally mischievous.[85a]

We are thinking here of more than Myrdal's apt remark that international advice to developing countries is likely to be fallacious on the ground that social science "models" more or less appropriate to Western experience are uncritically applied to non-Western developmental situations. One important protection contemporary nation builders have against such advice is that it probably cannot be readily turned into effective policies anywhere.[86] We have in mind, for example, decisions of major powers, or of international financial agencies, that reflect both ideological conflict and attempts to win the support of developing nations behind one ideological clustering or another. Even where nation-building elites deliberately use such conflicts to have their own way regarding technical or economic assistance, the results of such investments are not necessarily those of improving crisis-management capabilities.

Another example of the possibly unintended consequences of international assistance is provided by Theodore Schultz. He argues quite cogently that the shipment of agricultural surpluses to poor countries under Public Law 480 has often had the wholly unsatis-

---

[85] See Montgomery's treatment of this point in his "A Royal Invitation: Variations on Three Classic Themes," in J. D. Montgomery and W. J. Siffin, eds., *op.cit.*, pp. 259-69.

[85a] I have tried my hand at some guidelines that political scientists might follow in providing better guidance, and I assume the formula could be equally applied by other social scientists. See J. LaPalombara, "Political Science and the Engineering of National Development" (New Haven, 1970), mimeographed.

[86] See Ralph Braibanti, "Transnational Inducement of Administrative Reform: A Survey of Scope and Critique of Issues," in J. D. Montgomery and W. J. Siffin, eds., *ibid.*, pp. 133-83. Cf. Joseph LaPalombara, "American Higher Education and Political Development," in D. C. Piper and T. Cole, *Post-Primary Education and Political and Economic Development* (Durham, N.C.: Duke University Press, 1964), pp. 95-127.

factory and unfortunate consequence of permitting nation builders to slight or to ignore the need for inputs into agricultural development at home. When the provision of agricultural surpluses and military aid is combined with the dominant U.S. assumption that to develop means to industrialize, we have all of the ingredients that add up to misguided planning and eventually to extremely inadequate responses to distribution demands.[87] Thus, while foreign assistance does increase the amount of resources available to a developing country, its longer range impact may well be that of perpetuating underdevelopment.

Whether or not influenced by ideological or international conflict considerations, the foreign aid programs have pointed primarily to the matter of assisting developing nations in the management of penetration and distribution crises. The United Nations, the Ford Foundation, and the U.S. Agency for International Development have stressed improving the public administrative resources of many developing countries. Large sums have been expended in creating educational or training institutions abroad, in bringing several thousand political and bureaucratic officials to the United States or other countries for training purposes, and in providing consultants and advisors on administrative reorganization and reform programs in developing countries. The overwhelming proportion of such assistance has gone to Asian, African, and Latin American countries.[88] Such "institution-building" efforts have aimed at long-run transformations of elite capability in managing some—not all—of the crises of nation building. They have often been marked by the absence of a full understanding that the process of responding to distribution demands is eminently political *before* it is purely economic and that in any case institutional transformations and changes in elite skills and attitudes will have assuredly and unmistakably political consequences. Insofar as aid-receiving nations have accepted the notion that "reforms" can be abstracted from broader political contexts, no appreciable service has been accorded indigenous elites. Among other things, emphasis on the technocratic aspects of elite capability may run counter to other impulses we have discussed in this volume. Braibanti makes the point nicely:

[87] This line of argument runs through Schultz's *Economic Growth, op.cit.*, but see esp. pp. 21-36.

[88] See R. Braibanti, "Transnational Inducement," *op.cit.*, pp. 137-61.

Neglect of the ideological factors is destructive of the total program of administrative reform. In the long run it is impossible to achieve and maintain technical adminstrative efficiency unless there is deep belief that it is a means of securing justice in the whole social order. This is the logical outcome of belief in human dignity. Inculcation of a dogma of efficiency for its own sake is not likely to have continuing regenerative impulse. . . . An efficient bureaucracy which is lacking in humane purpose is, in the last analysis, worse than a bureaucracy that is inefficient but consciously directed to humane objectives.[89]

In this observation, Braibanti reminds us that problems of creating viable nations are not manifested or resolved in mutually exclusive compartments. Even where problems of distribution seem to be overwhelmingly pressing, the successful building of a nation requires that those responsible for its policies have a broader view of the subtleties and the instruments of statecraft.

The reminder holds as well for those who provide foreign assistance to developing nations. The Western nations themselves have provided economic and technical assistance with one hand and extracted an imposing technical reimbursement with the other hand. Titmuss, for example, asserts that since 1949 the United States had absorbed 100,000 scientists, doctors, and engineers from developed and developing countries. He alleges that the United States gets more medical assistance (in the form of foreign trained doctors) from abroad each year than it gives. He estimates that in the last twenty years the U.S. has, through such brain-drain devices, saved more than four billion dollars in educational costs.[90] Whatever may have motivated such high-talent manpower to desert their home countries, it is apparent that the international mobility of labor supplies tends to aggravate distribution problems confronted by developing nations.

Although both the giving and receiving of international economic and technical assistance imply to some degree a reciprocal surrender of sovereignty, neither donor nor recipient today is easily disposed to accept this elemental postulate.[91] The recipient increasingly insists on "no strings attached"; the donor chaffs under the impossibility of

---

[89] *Ibid.*, p. 179.

[90] R. M. Titmuss, *Commitment to Welfare* (New York: Pantheon Books, Random House, 1968), p. 126. See, also, p. 36, note 4, for documentation of this allegation extracted from American publications and from the testimony of a number of U.S. scholars.

[91] J. D. Montgomery, "A Royal Invitation," *op.cit.*, p. 290.

controlling actual purposes to which assistance is put. Where this view prevails, it is unlikely that those who provide assistance can call into examination what Montgomery calls the purpose of state-craft and particularly that aspect of it that might be labeled "political morality."[92] National pride, particularly in former colonial areas, makes it difficult or impossible for political elites, no matter how pressed with developmental problems, to accept conditions that seek to strike a balance among the impulses to equality, differentiation, and capacity that are associated with the urge to modernize. Where choices have to be made, capacity will loom large in a hierarchy of priorities. It is easier to mobilize, one surmises, than to permit participation; easier to coerce than to seek to induce; easier to silence opposition by force than to permit it relatively free reign in suggesting policy alternatives and to compete for political power in societies where alternative occupations are scarce; easier to apply constant-pie orientations to political as well as economic choices and to assume that in politics, as in all of life, the other man's gain is one's personal loss.

To be sure, such orientations to problem-solving are encouraged by nation-building crisis loads that are historically unprecedented. They tend nevertheless to perpetuate rigidities of elite response, so often fortified by ideology, fed by envy, and nurtured by psycho-cultural residues that the probability of responding well to distribution crises would seem to be very low indeed.

Early in this chapter we noted that distribution crises tend to recur, that they are less permanently resolved than crises of identity, legitimacy, or participation. Every so-called developed country is currently experiencing such problems in one form or another, and in several countries they have reached extremely intense or crisis levels.[93] The difference between most of these latter countries and the developing nations is that the problems recur at a time when most of the other problems of nation building have been resolved. No such luxury is available to those who lead developing nations. Demands for distribution and redistribution in such places clearly place the nations' survival in a state of jeopardy and raise questions about the appropriate mix of equality, differentiation, and capacity for which

[92] *Ibid.*, pp. 285-94.

[93] The "poverty problem" in the U.S. involving both black and white Americans is a good example. The nature of "welfare" and the ends to which welfare policies should be directed is another example. In this regard, see R. Titmuss, *op.cit.*

Western national development is at best a hazardous and approximate guide.

Part V. Conclusions

We have sought to explore in this chapter a range of factors that seem to impinge on the ability of nation-building elites to deal with demands that have distribution implications, and particularly with those distributions (or redistributions) that are material in nature. Such demands are always present in political systems. Just as certainly, the total of such demands will be greater than the ability of political elites to accommodate all of them. Where governmental response does not carefully weigh relative intensities of demand, the danger of crisis and political instability arises. Yet weighing intensities is anything but a precise mathematical operation. It has much to do with arbitrariness in evaluating the ideological underpinning of particular demand and the power resources of those who make them against competing demand and power resources and the physical-human resource capability of the political elite itself.

In the simplest situation distribution demands may be understood to refer to the imperative that those who govern increase the amount of goods and services available to the total system. Viewed from this vantage point, the more "developed" polity is one that demonstrates the greatest capacity to respond to such demands with new or modified patterns of differentiation and capacity. This implies, for example, new ways of producing wealth, increasing the productivity of labor, establishing and coordinating complex national economic plans, making the most parsimonious choices regarding the investment of limited resources, training administrative personnel with the necessary skills pertaining to an economically innovating role for the public sector, and so on.

But we have also insisted in this volume that a third impulse in political development is the desire for equality. This desire when manifested in the arena of distribution demands, almost always implies redistribution. Those who are guided by considerations of equality not only want more of what is currently available but also aim at more or less profound changes in systems of stratification. In the short run equality motivated distribution demands create great dilemmas regarding investment and consumption. From a long-run vantage point such demands tend to threaten the vested, entrenched position of exactly those relatively insecure nation-building elites who are expected to satisfy the demands themselves. It is possible, in short, to argue that crises of distribution dramatically reveal that impulses toward equality, capacity, and differentiation are not always compatible and that maximizing only one of these may sometimes require slowing down or minimizing the others.

If we may be permitted the assumption that the three impulses we speak of are empirically real and not merely a projection of the normative orientations of the authors of this volume, then it is possible to conceive of political development as measured by the ability of political elites to optimize all three of them. Doing so as a practical matter requires, we believe, a willingness to avoid clichés about economic growth, to look open-mindedly at highly abstracted models of traditional impediments to change, and to search for solutions that do not easily shelve considerations of equality for some hazy future reference when other prior problems of nation building have been resolved. To cite the most obvious example, the undeniable postulate of economic theory that growth requires savings and sacrifice does not often specify who will have to save and who sacrifice.

It should also be clear from what we have said in this chapter that our major concern is with a particular subgroup in society—those who govern. It may very well be that a society's general capacity to modernize economically depends on the amounts of energy and information available to it. Forays into the industrial development of the West would reveal at first glance a very high correlation between these two variables and subsequent economic growth. It is equally possible that the psychocultural variables we have touched on in this chapter will help us to understand why Japan industrialized before China, France before England. Our central concern, however, is with the role of government in these processes, and particularly with its demonstrated capacity to respond—well or badly—to demands that affect its place in the total dynamic processes of change. A nation that is well on the way to industrialization (e.g., Russia or France), but nevertheless experiences violent revolution, may be said to have been grossly underdeveloped in the sense in which we are using that concept in this volume. The striking feature we have sought to emphasize in this chapter is that *governments* have been brought into the process of guiding and affecting societal change as never before in human history. In Italian peasant culture there is an adage which goes: "*Piove. Governo ladro!*" This translates: "It is raining, and the corrupt government is the cause." A quantum change in orientation involving a challenge to political capacity occurs, we believe, when the adage becomes: "It is raining, and the government must do something about it." At any point in time therefore the extent of political development can be assessed only by comparing the level of demands elites confront with their ability to deal with them. Not simplistically or arbitrarily, however, for we return to our assumption that beyond the impulses for capacity and differentiation there exists historically and empirically the impulse for equality.

It is only when capacity is measured against the impluse to equality that one can begin to make judgments about how much of it is present. As we suggested in the previous chapter, force and coercion may resolve the penetration crises but, perhaps, only at the expense of maintaining a tenuous hold on real estate in the short run and building up a reservoir of revolutionary counterforce in the longer run. Where governmental capacity is used essentially to deny the existence or the acceptability of the impulse to equality, we postulate that the developed state of such a system may be spurious. In doing so we leave unresolved the problem whether equality everywhere and necessarily includes the demand to participate in decision-making, although we believe that this is probably the case. The point is simply that, for a host of historical and contemporary reasons, people who are the objects of political power today expect it to be used to modify a wide range of life-chance distinctions that have persisted for millennia in human society.

We must also recognize that problems of distribution or redistribution become particularly salient for nation builders when they rise above an inchoate level of discontent and become demands incorporated or created by members of the elite system itself. As we noted above, masses do not make ideologies, but intellectuals do. "Revolutions of rising expectations" are more often than not simply weapons created and then used by elites or counterelites who desire to share power, and possibly to change radically existing patterns of public policy. Resistant political elites may succeed, as Weiner suggests, in squelching such counterelites, but they will be less able to extract conformance from great masses of individuals once the latter have been successfully politicized as recalcitrant oppositional forces. Indeed, it is exactly such circumstances which require that elite policy decisions seek to optimize all three developmental impulses rather than any one or two of them.

Problems of administrative penetration and of distribution directly challenge the ability of existing elites to adapt existing institutions to new demand situations or to create new ones. Where it is expected that governmental intervention will be paramount in both of these problem sectors, institutional innovation will involve primarily the sector of public administration. Nevertheless it is necessary to understand that such problem-solving capability is not necessarily restricted to the public sector and that political elites can take and have taken steps to incorporate elements of the private sector in this dynamic process as well. Whatever else one might say about the sale of public office or of tax farming in European countries, it is fair to argue that such devices did serve nation-building purposes. That central authority eventually lost touch and control of such arrangements is warrant for a specific rather than a highly generalized judgment regarding the political efficacy of such arrangements. The more important consideration is whether the institutional arrangements the elite select are likely to satisfy the combination of performance demands it confronts or sets itself. And these arrangements, we assume, must necessarily be guided by the nature of the "crisis load," or by how well or badly the other crises of nation building have been or are handled.

These considerations suggest, finally, that while crises of distribution ideally occur at the end of a developmental sequence, reality rarely conforms to ideal considerations. For the typical contemporary developing nation, indeed, responses to distribution demands greatly escalated by mass participation may well determine how and how well the problems of identity and legitimacy may be resolved. In these circumstances, the pressures to resort to coercion or to mobilization ideologies may become overwhelming. The burden of this chapter has been in part to suggest that "models" for rapid economic change must be skeptically scrutinized lest their uncritical acceptance lead to aftermaths that turn out to be nation disintegrating rather than nation building.

CHAPTER 8

SEQUENCES AND DEVELOPMENT

SIDNEY VERBA

THE CHAPTERS in this volume have presented a framework for the study of political development.[1] It is a framework that the present authors have found most useful as a way of giving order to what often seems an inherently disorderly subject—the historical processes by which nation-states (or political systems, if one prefers a more abstract formulation) have developed over time. The chapters intend to illustrate the usefulness of the framework. It is, however, a framework for the study of political development, not yet a theory; that is, it directs one's attention to certain significant phenomena and the relationships among them without presenting a coherent and interdependent set of propositions.

If the latter is our goal (albeit, given the complexity of the subject, a most distant one), one can ask: What is the next step in that direction? Substantively, the next step from the present work would involve a focus on *sequence* rather than on crises or critical problems. The current chapters have spelled out a set of crises or problems faced by political systems as they change over time. In this volume these crises have been considered one by one—as is indicated by the book's organization. What is required next is a consideration of the relationship among these crises or problems over time. If the crisis model is to become a theory of development, it seems likely that the propositions in it or the hypotheses generated by it will have to do with the sequence by which crises arise: the consequences, for instance, of one crisis emerging before the other, of the simultaneity of crises, and the like. Or, if one were seeking descriptive generalizations, the most interesting ones would involve consideration of the paths that nations have followed (through what sequence of crises?) to their current positions. Is there a uniform path followed by all nations? Is there a uniform path followed by all those that have reached some terminal state such as democracy? What is the range of variation in alternative sequences?

[1] This chapter was originally written as an "internal" memorandum for the Committee on Comparative Politics commenting on the crises scheme. Its purpose was to raise questions and suggest the directions from which answers might come. It was not intended to answer the questions raised. It is reprinted here with the same intent.

Though the chapters in this volume tend to focus on one crisis or another, all address themselves to this problem. Each of the crisis chapters is filled with interesting discussions of the relationship of its particular crisis and others. Nevertheless, the full consideration of sequences requires that one consider all the crises at the same time.

There are a variety of ways in which one might move to a consideration of the question of sequences. One way would be to take the crisis notions as they now exist and turn to the material of history, refining the concepts and deriving generalizations out of the confrontation with historical materials. This will be the approach adopted for a further volume.[2] There the focus will turn from the individual crisis to the individual nation—that is, from single crises considered on the basis of examples from many nations as in this volume, to single nations considered in terms of all the crises.

An alternative approach involves an attempt to refine the model before applying it. This concluding chapter will begin—but only begin—that attempt. We will deal with some additional questions that would have to be raised if one were to operationalize more precisely the concepts used in the volume and develop a more generally applicable sequential model. And to do so, we will step back a bit— away from the historical data. We shall, in a sense, merely present some notes to a beginning. Perhaps this is inappropriate for the concluding chapter of a volume that is, in turn, a concluding volume of a series on political development. Then again, maybe it is not.

There are a number of reasons why sequential models are attractive to students of political development.[3] Sequential models represent a way of systematizing patterns of historical change, of dealing with the paths from one type of political system to another. They are a way in which causal and genetic models of change can be linked. The student of political development finds that he must study a wide sweep of history in order to understand the nature of political change in any particular society. But attempts to study development in his-

---

[2] A volume on a number of countries organized around the theme of the crises of development will be edited by Raymond Grew.

[3] See, among others, G. A. Almond and G. B. Powell, *Comparative Politics: A Developmental Approach* (Boston: Little, Brown, 1966); A.F.K. Organski, *Stages of Political Growth* (New York: Knopf, 1965); D. A. Rustow, *A World of Nations* (Washington: Brookings Institution, 1968); Talcott Parsons, "Evolutionary Universals in History," *American Sociological Review*, 29 (June 1964), 329-57; Cyril E. Black, *The Dynamics of Modernization* (New York: Harper and Row, 1966); and Eric Nordlinger, "Time Sequences and Rates of Change," *World Politics*, 20, No. 3 (April 1968), 494-520.

torical depth can become mere narrative with little explanatory power. A sequential model of development can give order to historical understandings of change and development by providing a framework within which causal statements can be made about development patterns that extend over a long period of time. And, by providing a sequential ordering of "stages" or events, such a model can provide us with the tools to deal comparatively with developments in many different societies. Such models do not have to be deterministic; they may allow predictions of probable paths of change and estimations of the consequences of alternative paths.

This paper will deal with four questions that can be raised about sequential models of development. These are:

I. *What is a sequential model?* Is it a causal model of development, an evolutionary model, or what? Or is it merely a set of rubrics for the writing of narrative history in a more orderly fashion?

II. *Sequences in relation to what?* This question asks about the underlying dimension or problem for which the sequence is relevant. What is it that is developing during our developmental sequence?

III. *Sequences of what?* What are the items that appear in sequence? Is it a set of events, a set of institutions, a set of decisions, of crises, or what? In many cases, a set of "stages" of development is postulated with one stage presumed to follow another. What do we mean by these "stages"? Can they be observed and distinguished one from the other?

IV. *What is the relationship among the items in the sequence?* How does one event or stage relate to the next within the model? Does one follow the other with some regularity? Does it always follow the other? Does it "cause" the other? Is it a necessary precondition of the other? Or what?

I believe that these are useful questions to be asked about sequential models, and questions not always or often asked. I shall discuss each of these questions generally, and then discuss the questions in relation to the particular sequential model implied in the notion of the critical problems or crises of development embodied in the present volume. My purpose is not to construct a particular sequential model out of the crisis approach. Rather, I raise some issues that would need consideration in attempting such construction.

Part I. What Is a Sequential Model?

In most social research that attempts to deal with problems as complicated as "nation building," we usually face a dilemma. We can use fairly precise models that do not fit the empirical material or fairly loose formulations that fit reality better, but only because they are loose. This dilemma can be seen in relation to sequential models. A sequential model might merely refer to a set of loose descriptive categories of events or problems that exist in societies. We might then allow for alternative sequences without indicating the likelihood of one ordering of events rather than another or the consequences of one ordering rather than another. Under such circumstances, a sequential model becomes merely a set of convenient rubrics for narrative history. Most sequential models aspire to something more, but many are in fact of this sort.

On the other hand, if one were to attempt to define a set of sequences more precisely—indicating clearly what the sequences referred to, defining the stages precisely with clear cutting points between them, and hypothesizing paths that are more likely than others (or hypothesizing a necessary path)—one would have a sequential model that was quite precise, but that probably would not apply to reality. One would have trouble finding the data to test the hypothesis. (One advantage of looser formulation is that one can more easily find some appropriate evidence—but this, of course, has its dangers.) And if tested, it would probably not hold up.

In short, a sequential model may represent a loose framework for narration in which case it is more useful than no framework at all—but not much. Or it can be a more precise model of social change—in which case it would be terribly useful if we could achieve it, but quite hard to achieve. The rest of these remarks will be based on the assumption that we aspire to the latter model, but are often forced, in fact, to operate closer to the former.

What kind of explanation is implied by a sequential model that aspires to be more than a framework for description? It is a dynamic explanation in that the relationship between the initial and resultant conditions is ordered over time. Harsanyi differentiates between static and dynamic explanations in the following way: "We shall speak of static explanation when a social variable is explained exclusively in terms of variables belonging to the same time period; and we shall speak of dynamic explanation when at least some of the explanatory variables used belong to an earlier period than the variables to be explained."[4]

Sequential models take this dynamic form. But—if there is any meaning to sequential models as distinct from other models—they probably have the following characteristics as well. The resultant condition that one is trying to explain (the existence of democracy, the development of a "modern" state, the growth of a bureaucracy) is explained in terms of a number of initial conditions. Futhermore, the initial conditions are not necessarily treated as if they occur simultaneously. The crucial concern is with the effect on the resultant condition of the order in which the initial conditions occur—this may include simultaneous occurrence, but that is only one possible pattern. It is this stringing out of conditions over time that makes the model a sequential one.

In this sense, sequential models can take a logical form not unlike that employed in the causal modelling appearing in much current political science literature.[5] But in much of the literature using causal modelling, the time sequence of the variables is uncertain since the data are cross-sectional in time. The assignment of an order to the variables is the task of the researcher guided by a variety of plausible assumptions about them.[6] Sequential models using historical data allow the ordering of items without any such—sometimes dubious—assumptions. The result may be that, though the overall logical shape of the relationship is the same, the significant analyses of the relationships within the sequence will be different. Whereas the causal modeller working with cross-sectional data will often look for the sequence that best fits the data and best accords with plausible assumptions about the items being sequenced, the causal modeller looking at the actual sequences of historical development in societies finds the sequence given to him by the data. He will, therefore, look further.

---

[4] J. Harsanyi, "Explanation and Comparative Dynamics in Social Sciences," *Behavioral Science*, 5 (April 1960), 136-145, 137.

[5] See, for instance, H. M. Blalock, Jr., *Casual Inference in Nonexperimental Research* (Chapel Hill: University of North Carolina Press, 1964); D. J. McCrone and C. F. Cnudde, "Toward a Communications Theory of Democratic Political Development: A Causal Model," *American Political Science Review*, 61 (1967), 72-79; and H. A. Alker, Jr., "Statistics and Politics: The Need for Causal Data Analysis," in S. M. Lipset, ed., *Politics and the Social Sciences* (New York: Oxford University Press, 1969), pp. 244-314.

[6] Often an attempt is made to infer the ordering from the pattern of statistical relation among variables. But the procedure does not get around the need for the researcher to choose an ordering. See D. Forbes and E. Tufte, "A Note of Caution in Causal Modelling," *American Political Science Review*, 62 (December 1968), 1258-1264.

The type of question asked might take the form: What are the alternative sequential patterns one finds in different units? And, given different classes of sequential patterns, how do they differ in terms of the impact on some resultant condition?

The causal model as the framework within which to place sequential models of historical development is useful, not because we are yet in a position to test such models—certainly not in relation to such broad characteristics as crises. It is useful to consider causal modelling since sequential models, if explanatory, will take some such causal form. Furthermore, the causal model framework allows one to avoid the often unfortunate organic metaphors that can be associated with sequential development models—references to growth and decay and their focus on inevitability. But much more processing of the current crisis model is required if it is to be developed in such a causal form.

Part II. Sequences in Relation to What?

Sequential models link a series of conditions or events stretched out over time. In this sense, a sequential model makes the dependent variable of the first proposition the independent variable of the next. One has a series of statements about the relation over time of A to B, and B to C, and so forth. The important point about sequential models is that the focus is not on any single link but on the entire chain of events. But if the series of conditions is to have any internal coherence—the chain of events is to have some meaningful referent—they must be all related to some underlying developmental problem.

Coherence can be given to a sequential model in either of two ways. One can select some resultant condition of a system and ask questions about the sequence of changes by which that resultant condition is approached. Or one can select an underlying dimension and relate each change in the system to a movement along that dimension. The first way of conceptualizing the problem might lead us to choose democracy as a resultant condition and to ask questions about the sequence of changes by which systems that are nondemocracies become democracies—or about the consequences for the likelihood of achieving democracy of alternative sequences. An alternative procedure would be to talk of democratization as a dimension and relate the sequence of changes to the movement of the system along this dimension. Either is legitimate. The latter approach to choose a dimension is useful in that it allows one to deal with societies that may never reach the specified resultant condition and with societies that are not moving in that direction. Furthermore, the use of the two ends of a continuum as the states from which and to which a society may move (from *Gemeinschaft* to *Gesellschaft*; from primitive to modern; from autocracy to democracy) without specification of the nature of the continuum that links them makes it difficult to talk of transitions or of the processes by which a system moves from one end to the other. Unless we know the ordering dimension that links autocracy and democracy (is it the amount of popular participation, the extent of legitimate opposition, the regularity of elections, or some combination of these and others?), it is difficult to talk of transitional patterns.

On the other hand, the choice of a resultant condition as the "anchor-point" of one's sequential model may have certain advantages. Certain important resultant conditions of a political system may not be preceded by a linear transition along some analogous dimension— the path to democracy may not entail a steady movement of democratization but some more circuitous path where the pattern of change could best be described by other dimensions. Or the shortest path to democracy might entail a movement backwards in some dimension of democracy.

The selection of a particular dimension of development or terminus of development is difficult as the long fruitless debates about what political development "really is" suggest. Sequential models tempt us to use organismic analogies about growth, maturation, or decay as the underlying dimension, or to talk about the mature society or the developed society as the resultant condition of the development process. When a psychologist such as Erik Erikson talks of stages of psychological development, he, too, may have problems in specifying the stages of development, but there is least the clear linkage that can be made with physiological patterns of maturation through which human organisms proceed. But there is no clear developmental process of this sort when one deals with social institutions.

Given the lack of organismic development to which we can link our sequential models, the choice of any particular underlying dimension of development can be subject to two criticisms: that it is teleological or that it is normative and arbitrary. On the first point: one can be interested in how societies democratize without assuming either that movement in that direction is inevitable or that the attainment of that end explains the pattern of development of the societies that have reached it. Rather, if we are interested in how democracies develop, the degree of democracy or the attainment of democracy becomes the dependent variable. Systems may or may not move in that direction. This is what we attempt to explain.

If the selection of some underlying dimension we want to explain does not necessarily make us teleologists, it does still raise the problem of the arbitrary nature of the dimension or resultant condition and the values implicit in choosing it. This cannot be avoided. In this sense a choice of any underlying dimension depends upon the extent to which it is of general interest. If the dimension is one for which upward movements represent a value, this does not make the choice invalid. If we prefer democracy, why not study the conditions under which it grows? In the sense, all theories have a normative element.

Having said this, we must add that the choice of underlying dimension ought still to be guided by criteria of usefulness. Several such criteria can be suggested:

1. The dimension ought to be an important one, both in terms of the interests of the researchers and in terms of the extent to which it differentiates societies in ways that are of significance. This implies that the underlying dimension of development ought to be a dimension that is correlated with many other changes in society: if you know its position on the dimension, you know quite a bit about it.
2. The dimension should be one upon which all relevant units (in our case, nation-states) can be placed.

These general considerations of the choice of an underlying dimension of development can be applied to the various chapters in this book. There could be at least as many sequential models of development as there are dimensions of development—one could have a sequential model of democratization, of bureaucratization, of national integration, and so forth. And, of course, more than one model could be associated with any developmental dimension.

This can be related to this collection of chapters on the "crises of development." When a society successfully passes a crisis—say of legitimacy or participation—is it more developed? And what is meant by that? It cannot simply be that successful solution of a crisis of participation makes the society more participatory; or that passing a crisis of legitimacy makes the society more legitimate; for that specifies no link between participation and legitimacy crises. What would make the two crises part of the same model of development is that they both relate to some underlying dimension of development.

The five crises of development are related in this book to a variety of outcomes, but the underlying dimensions of development most consistently referred to are equality, capacity, and differentiation. These are clearly dimensions rather than resultant conditions; one more easily conceives of societies being more or less equalitarian, capable, or differentiated, not of some society that is equal, capable, and/or differentiated. Thus, it should be possible to link the successful "passing of a crisis" with a movement along these dimensions.[7] "Success" in this sense would mean more equality, or capacity, or differentiation, or all three of them.

But the use of the multiple dimensions raises a problem in this respect—if one is looking for an underlying developmental continuum. Equality, capacity, and differentiation may not vary together. Indeed, in many circumstances they would seem to be negatively related; certainly an increase in differentiation often implies a lowering of equality. And though an increase in governmental capacity might be used to increase equality, there is no inherent reason why it cannot be used to reward advantaged groups more and thereby decrease equality. This can be seen further if one relates these three dimensions to the various crises. The links are not always clear in the discussions, but the successful passing of a crisis is often related to a change in the position of a society on these developmental dimensions. The successful passing of a participation crisis usually implies an increase in equality in the political sense—access to the vote is more equally distributed or individuals come to participate in new ways, such as in the administration of poverty programs. But this also implies a reduction of the differentiation between those who rule and those who do not rule, between those who have access to legitimate channels of participation and those who do not. The ideal of political rights (or economic rights, if we want to consider parallel problems of distribution) on the basis of citizenship is essentially an ideal opposed to differentiation. Or, to take another example, the successful completion of a penetration crisis would seem to imply an

[7] The relationship between the notions of equality, capacity, and differentiation on the one hand and the five crises of development on the other is not completely clear. An alternative relationship is suggested at various points in the volume whereby unbalanced changes among equality, capacity, and differentiation lead to the crises. But my interpretation of E, C, and D as the underlying dimensions of development affected by the crises seems consistent with the main connections made between these two sets of terms.

increase in governmental capacity,[8] but it might also imply a reduction in equality.

An alternative to using all three—equality, capacity, and differentiation—as the underlying developmental dimensions would be to select one dimension (from among these three or from elsewhere). Each of the three dimensions has some advantages and limitations. Capacity is the most obvious candidate for *the* underlying dimension of development, not because it is the "essence" of development, but because of its centrality and importance in relation to political change. If capacity were selected out of the developmental triad of equality, capacity, and differentiation, "development" would refer to the growth in the capacity of governmental institutions to make and enforce decisions.

The dimension of capacity is found at the heart of many developmental models; it is general and important enough to warrant close attention (and it is ambiguous enough to illustrate some problems in sequential models). Almond and Powell talk of the development of various system capabilities (all apparently relevant to the general ability of the society to manage its environment);[9] the chapters in this book talk of "capacity" as one of the major characteristics of the modern system; and Halpern talks of political modernization as the general ability of a system to constantly innovate and to handle new pressures for change.[10] Let us consider how the notion of capacity might form the basis of a sequential model of development.

The notion of general capability (to adapt and manipulate) is not adequate for the characterization of the relevant patterns of change that form the dependent variables of the sequential models. One would still have to face some problems of distinction and of measurement. For one thing, if we are considering "political" development, it might be useful to distinguish governmental (or political) capacity from more general societal capacity. This would involve distinguishing between the capacity to adapt to and manipulate the environment that involves the relatively central coordination of societal resources and activities and the capacity that does not. Thus, there may be

[8] Indeed, it is a bit difficult to distinguish between the successful passing of a penetration crisis and the increase of governmental capacity. There may be some overlap between the ECD typology and the five crises—in particular when it comes to penetration as a crisis and capacity as a dimension of development—which makes the relation of one of the other difficult.

[9] Almond and Powell, *op.cit.*

[10] M. Halpern, *The Politics of Social Change in the Middle East and North Africa* (Princeton: Princeton University Press, 1963).

within a society a high level of ability to manipulate the environment (a high level of technology, an efficient economy, etc.), but insofar as this does not involve the central coordination of societal activities, it would not reflect "political development."

The distinction between general societal capacity and the capacity of political institutions would allow us to separate the component of political development from other forms of development. In addition, it would help make clear the ambiguous normative implications of this sort of development. In the first place, it becomes clear that political capacity is not the same as general societal capacity and that, at certain times, the two may be antithetical. Too much governmental capacity for controlling the economy may reduce the overall economic capacity of the society, and governmental capacity may be used for purposes we evaluate positively or negatively.

But even if one could isolate political capacity as the underlying dimension of development (or perhaps decide that one was interested in more general capacity), the problem of measuring such capacity remains. And here one is caught on the horns of a dilemma. That which seems most important to measure may be difficult, if not impossible, to measure, while that which can be measured may not seem interesting or relevant. Let us consider this from the point of view of political capacity—how capable is the government in coping with the environment and satisfying the demands and needs of the citizenry? In the first place, "capacity" suggests an ability to perform, not actual performance. But can the former be measured without using the latter? Or assume we take the easier task of using performance rather than potential performance as the measure of capacity. Problems remain. On the one hand, we may want to measure capacity in the relative sense—that is, relative to the types of pressures generated in the environment and the types of goals held by members of the society. Different environmental conditions (and we include in the environment the general social setting of the polity and its external setting in addition to its natural environment) as well as different sets of goals create different levels of pressure for political adaptation and manipulation. For a variety of reasons industrialization creates pressures for greater political coordination in the manipulation of the environment—both because it creates a set of objective problems that require centrally coordinated solutions (coordinating the functionally differentiated parts of the economy, providing for welfare when traditional institutions fail) and because it creates a set of values that places pressures on the central coordinating agencies. An "adequate" performance level, therefore, would be different in industrial and nonindustrial societies, in societies with a politicized citizenry and societies with a politically uninvolved citizenry. Such a consideration of the alternative demands for performance that political decision-makers face means that we would deal with something similar to the Almond and Powell notion of responsive capability.[11] Since governments can (and do) deal with all sorts of problems and since societies differ greatly in the problems they face, it is attractive to avoid an arbitrary definition of governmental performance and to relate that performance to the demands made upon the government. Indeed, one could extend the notion to make governmental capacity a measure of "how well" governing elites do in coping with the demands made upon them by the citizenry and the environment relative to the resources they control.

The problem is, of course, that such measures are difficult, if not impossible. It may be possible to measure what the government does—how much it spends on various items—but difficult to relate that to pressures for such performance. The tendency is to measure capacity by the success or failure of the performance—does the system survive, is there internal violence? But this represents the result of capacity or incapacity rather than a measure of it.

The alternative is a simpler measure—perhaps the proportion of the GNP that is accounted for by the government account or some other measure.[12] The advantage is that this is (relatively speaking) a measurable dimension. It may not be an interesting one in terms of a more comprehensive view of development. In any case, an attempt to limit the developmental dimension to capacity would have to face these issues. (And, of course, an attempt to use all three developmental dimensions simultaneously would have to face these problems —as well as others.)

The measurement problems associated with equality as the underlying dimension of development are probably less severe than are those inherent in the notion of capacity. There are many ways to measure equality.[13] And one would have to decide what was to be considered equal—wealth, political access, opportunity, and so on. But

[11] Almond and Powell, op.cit.

[12] See Karl de Schweinitz, Jr., "On Measuring Political Performance," *Comparative Political Studies*, 2 (January 1970), 503-11.

[13] See Hayward Alker and Bruce Russett, "On Measuring Inequality," in R. Merritt and S. Rokkan, eds., *Comparing Nations* (New Haven: Yale University Press, 1966).

the problems seem less inherently insoluble. And equality as the underlying developmental dimension represents a normatively sanctioned goal in most societies. One limitation is that it is a much more limited notion than general capacity. One might not want to limit the underlying dimension of the model to such a "partial" outcome.

Differentiation—the last of the developmental triad—represents a particular type of structural change in society with crucial significance. It represents a structural change that is likely to be closely related to capacity, and one that might be amenable to more precise measurement, simply by observing the creation of new organizations or institutions to deal with particular types of problems. In the following sections of this chapter I will focus more heavily on this aspect of the developmental triad—particularly where I emphasize the important role of the creation of new institutions in response to a crisis.

But I do not want to suggest that there is a single answer to this question of the most useful underlying dimension of development to which to tie the sequential model. There are many possible answers. And indeed the weakness of E or C or D by itself might argue for a combined measure of development. But this would require both the solution of the measurement problems associated with each of the dimensions as well as some consideration of the various developmental combinations that could be generated by countermovements on these dimensions. One might, for instance, want to differentiate between increases in capacity that did not increase inequality and those that did.

Part III. Sequence of What?

Earlier it was pointed out that there are a variety of questions that can be asked about sequential models. The first question had to do with the logical structure of such models, and the second had to do with the underlying dimension against which one considers the sequential statements. The third question one can raise is: Sequence of what?

It is on the question of "sequence of what" that many sequential models founder. A sequential model involves saying something about a set of items: x must precede y which much precede z; or x is likely to precede y which is likely to precede z; and so forth. But often the sequential items—the "x's" and "y's"—are only vaguely specified. Sometimes they are particular events (independence or an internal revolution); or they refer to the creation of institutions (political parties, bureaucracies, various electoral mechanisms); or they represent the attainment of a threshold value on a variable (a per capita GNP above a certain value, a particular rate of growth, a rate of voting turnout). More often than not, the sequential items are more vaguely specified: the stage of "national integration" must precede the stage of "national maturity" or something of that sort. In a recent work on the "stages of political development" of the American party system, three stages of development of American parties are listed: the stage of invention, the stage of erection of enduring forms, and the derivative stage.[14] Each stage is given a precise set of dates. And though each stage does seem somewhat different and the notion of stages does offer a good framework for a narrative history of American parties, there is no clear indication of what differentiates one stage from another.

The same might be said for Cyril Black's four phases of modernization: the confrontation with modernity, the transition to modernizing leaders, socioeconomic transformation, and the integration of society.[15] On the one hand, they represent critical problems that persist in all societies; on the other hand, they must come in some order or one could not talk of them as separate phases. The concepts are useful, but it would be very hard to identify clearly one phase and distinguish it from another. Yet if one cannot do this, there is little about which one can develop sequential propositions.

Defining stages of development is difficult if one is dealing with changes in continuous variables such as per capita GNP or voting turnout. If one is dealing with such continuous variables, it may be a quite arbitrary decision when one places the cutting points that divide one stage from another, unless one finds some discontinuity. Certain values of variables may have threshold effects—above a certain value they behave differently in terms of their effect on other variables (Deutsch has suggested such thresholds with respect to rates of literacy),[16] but for most of the variables in political development models, such thresholds are hard to specify. If the variable does not change in a straight linear way, however, it may be possible to set cutting points that differentiate one stage from another. If there is a kink in the curve of some variable (as Gerschenkron discovers in

---

[14] W. N. Chambers, "Party Development and the American Mainstream," in Chambers and W. D. Burnham, *The American Party System: Stages of Political Development* (New York: Oxford University Press, 1967), pp. 3-32.

[15] Black, *op.cit.*

[16] K. W. Deutsch, "Social Mobilization and Political Development," in H. Eckstein and D. Apter, *Comparative Politics: A Reader* (New York: Free Press, 1963), pp. 582-603.

relation to industrial production in Europe or as Chambers finds in relation to voting rates in the early 19th century when they jumped from 26.9 percent in 1824 to 57.5 percent and 57.8 percent in 1828 and 1832), one can more legitimately label the points on either side of the discontinuity as different stages.[17]

It may, therefore, be easier to talk of stages if one is talking, not of changes in the values of continuous variables, but of the more discrete patterns of change connected with such events as major changes in institutional structure. Thus, one can perhaps talk of the pre-independence stage and the post-independence stage; or of the pre-party stage and the post-party stage; or of the stage before party competition and the stage after it. But, even if this specification of stages is easier, the important point is that it may be trivial unless one has some clear notion of the significance of a particular stage in relation to stages before and after it.

A SEQUENCE OF CRISES?

This brings me to the question of sequences from the point of view of the model developed in this volume. When we talk of sequences in relation to the five problems or crises of development—identity, legitimacy, participation, penetration, and distribution—what are we referring to? Are these sequences of levels of performance, or sequences of the development of institutions, or sequences of "crises" (and if so, what are they?) or what? Perhaps, by explicating what some of the alternative meanings might be of sequences of these sorts, we can shed some light on the uses of the particular model developed here and on some of its ambiguities.

The five "crises" or critical problems which form the basis of the chapters in this volume seem in some respects difficult—without further specification—to place into a sequential model. This is so for two reasons. In the first place, there is some ambiguity as to what exactly the crises or problems are. In part, the issue is whether they are *crises* (some special kind of event that comes and goes) or persistent problems that political systems face. And, whichever conception of the item is used, they are difficult to place in a sequence because the five items seem to come together. This is to be expected since the five crises or problems are different types of items and not mutually exclusive. Thus, a particular governmental innovation at a

---

[17] W. N. Chambers, *op.cit.*; and A. Gerschenkron, *Economic Backwardness in Historical Perspective* (Cambridge: Harvard University Press, 1962).

moment of stress—perhaps the passage of a new type of welfare program or a governmental commitment to a redistributive tax program in response to public demand—is an action that addresses itself to the problem of distribution, the success of which may depend upon the government's ability to "penetrate" the society (to get people to comply with the new system), which in turn may depend upon the extent of legitimacy in the system (or, conversely, the way in which the new welfare program works out may affect the legitimacy of the system), and the measure itself may have grown out of some process of participation. Thus, at almost any point where one talks of a political system as faced with a problem of one of the five sorts discussed in this volume, one finds traces of the other four problems. Indeed, one of the hallmarks of a "crisis" (and I will return to a discussion of that term in a moment) seems to be the coexistence of a problem of legitimacy with one or more of the other problems.

The fact that, at first glance, the items that we wish to sequence do not seem to come in a sequence is not so crucial if some further "processing" of these items is carried on. There are two aspects to this processing. We must decide on the nature of the items that we are trying to arrange in a sequence, and we must deal with the problem of the assignment of any particular item to one of the categories. The first issue is: are we talking of crises or problems or what? The second issue is—assume we have decided the answer to the first—how do we decide that a particular event is a participation crisis rather than a distribution crisis? This latter question requires for its answer some consideration of the rules that tell us what kind of a problem or crisis we have and, secondly, from whose perspective the crisis or problem is assigned to a category. Let us look at these two issues in order. The following comments are not meant to be prescriptive nor to suggest that the meaning of the crisis scheme suggested here is the only one possible (or even preferable). I merely want to illustrate the kind of consideration that would be useful for the five-crisis scheme.

WHAT IS A CRISIS?

If we are to put different crises in a sequence, we must decide what they are. The five crises or problem areas discussed in this volume may be thought of as having a close relationship to the process by which the government makes and enforces decisions. Identity, legitimacy, participation, penetration, and distribution may be thought of as aspects of governmental decision-making that may (under circumstances to be discussed below) become problems or lead to crises when they become arenas of conflict. One could define these five-problem areas (and I believe the term "problem area" is better than the term "crisis," a concept I would prefer to reserve for a narrower purpose) as follows:

1. The *penetration* problem is the problem of how much effective control the central government has.
2. The *participation* problem is the problem of who takes part (who has some influence over) the making of governmental decisions.
3. The *legitimacy* problem refers to the basis on which and the degree to which the decisions of government are accepted by the populace of a society because of normative beliefs on the part of the populace as to the "rightness" of the ways in which decisions are made.
4. The *distribution* problem refers to the extent to which the decisions of government are used to distribute or redistribute material benefits and other benefits in the society.
5. And the *identity* problem refers to the definition of the set of individuals whom it is believed appropriately fall within the decision-making scope of the government, i.e., to the question of the appropriate members of the system. If some members of the populace do not consider themselves as appropriately falling within the domain of the government or, conversely, feel that some other group not within that domain belongs within it, one can talk of an identity problem. (This definition is more restrictive than others that take a more psychological form. It has the advantage of having a more precise political referent.)

The five problems would thus seem to be important in relation to governmental capacity to make decisions. They may not be the only problems—and I can find no clear logical structure among them nor any warrant for considering the list exhaustive—but one cannot doubt their importance as problems.

As five aspects or potential problems about governmental decision-making one can see that they do not easily or naturally form a sequential pattern. They are problems or questions that exist at any point in time: all government action may or may not be effectively carried out (the problem of penetration). All imply questions of legitimacy: are they accepted because of normative beliefs as to their rightness? All imply questions of participation: who took part in making the decision? And so forth.

Since the five problem areas coexist at any point of time, we must make some further distinctions if we are to talk of sequences. We might, thus, distinguish the five items in the following way: at some points they are merely aspects of decisions; at others they become *problems*; at others they become *crises*. If a particular aspect of the decisional process is not in question at some point in time—there are, for instance, generally accepted rules as to who should participate in decisions and how—we can say that there is no "problem" in that area. But there is a problem in relation to one of the aspects of decision-making as soon as it becomes "problematic"—i.e., some do not accept the way things are done in relation to that aspect of decision-making; it becomes an issue or an arena of conflict.

The five aspects of governmental decisions are potentially problems at any point of time. This makes clear that there is no necessary ordering or sequence to the five potential problems; they may arise, be solved, and arise again in a different form. One sequence with which we might deal would be the sequence with which particular problem areas become salient. More important might be the sequence with which institutions are created to handle problems in each problem area. (By institutions, I refer to more than formal institutions—to generally accepted regular procedures for handling a problem and to normatively sanctioned behavior patterns.) Within each problem area it should be possible to list those institutions that would be most relevant. For example: in relation to problems of penetration one could look for the date of the development of a national administrative service able to enforce decisions from the center to the periphery or for other administrative innovations; in relation to identity one could look for institutionalized solutions to linguistic controversies, school controversies, political boundaries, and the like; in relation to participation one could index the development of the franchise, or political parties with mass bases; in relation to distribution one could index the development of welfare administrations, or of a redistributive tax system, and the like.[18] These patterns of institutionalization

[18] See S. Rokkan, "Sequences and Development," unpublished paper presented to World Congress of Sociology, Evian, 1966.

may be the most useful way of locating particular nations in their sequential positions. This is so for the following reasons:

a. The creation of such institutions represents the kind of discontinuity that makes the distinction between stages both operationally easier and intuitively more meaningful.

b. Institutions have a tendency to persist. Therefore the development of one may involve an irreversibility; once it is created it develops its own dynamic. In this sense, also, the development of such institutions represents a significant change in the system.

c. Institutions represent major innovations. Once they are created they may have the internal flexibility to handle new problems within the general problem area in a fairly routine manner.

d. If we focus on institutionalization as the result of a crisis, we are very close to the third dimension of the developmental triad—differentiation. The development of institutional means to deal with the particular problem areas does not necessarily imply differentiation or the development of a new organization specializing in that function. It might be possible for the institutionalized means to involve the taking on of a new task by an older organization. But, in general, new institutional means to deal with problems of the sort we have been discussing involve the development of differentiated organizations to deal with them. If the crises are thought of in these terms, the result is that (at least) one of the underlying dimensions of development will be differentiation.

As the basis for a set of sequences, the pattern by which various institutions are created has much to recommend it. Merely to consider the pattern by which various problems become salient would be difficult—how does one know when a problem is a salient problem—and perhaps trivial? New institutionalized ways of handling a particular problem area create the *historical trace* of the salience of any particular problem at some point in time; it remains relevant the next time the same type of problem arises and may be relevant for the handling of other problems. Furthermore, the particular configuration of the problem that leads to the institution may shape important aspects of the institution. As Lipset and Rokkan indicate, the nature of the conflict out of which a party is created may structure political cleavages long after the conflict itself has faded.[19]

[19] S. M. Lipset and S. Rokkan, *Party System and Voter Alignments* (New York: Free Press, 1967), pp. 1-64.

Concentration on institutionalization also focuses attention on what can legitimately be called "crises" in a political system. In almost all cases, what are discussed as crises in the present volume are situations in which the basic institutional patterns of the political system are challenged and routine response is inadequate. We may define *a crisis* as a situation where a "problem" arises in one of the problem areas (that is, members of the society are discontented with one of the five aspects of the decisional process), and some new institutionalized means of handling problems of that sort is required to satisfy the discontent.

The definition needs explication. It represents an attempt to distinguish between ordinary governmental performance and responsiveness and particularly crucial periods of governmental innovation. Crises arise when there is an increase in pressure for change in one of the five aspects of the decisional process. (There may, of course, be other crises as we ordinarily use the word. I am here trying to relate the term "crisis" to the five problem areas discussed in this volume.) Not all pressures for change in the handling of the aspects of decisions can be considered crises. A crisis is a change that requires some governmental innovation and institutionalization if elites are not seriously to risk a loss of their position or if the society is to survive. This implies the following:

a. Whether an environmental change will generate a political crisis will depend in part on who is affected by the change. The closer a group is to the central communications channels, the more organized it is, the more it controls significant resources, the more likely is a particular problem to be converted into a political crisis. In this sense, it becomes clear that crises are more likely to start within the governing elite than out of it.

b. Whether or not a crisis develops depends on the routine flexibility of the system. As defined, a crisis can only lead to innovative behavior on the part of elites that changes the institutionalization pattern of the society or to replacement of the elites. If the system has a great deal of routine flexibility—if, for instance, it has previously institutionalized means of dealing with problems of the sort that are raised—it may be able to respond to the new demands without any change in the institutionalized pattern.

The distinction between innovative response that changes the institutional pattern of the system and routine response that meets a particular set of demands within the established pattern of institutionalization helps us specify which sequences are most relevant. The five problem areas—identity, legitimacy, penetration, participation, and distribution—represent a set of continuing problems for any society. They are never solved in a final sense. One can study a society at any time to see how it is dealing with each problem. Crises represent stages in the solution of these problems that require new patterns of institutionalization to deal with them. Thus, crises do not necessarily persist, but may come and go. It is possible to say that a particular crisis has passed, but not that a particular problem has passed.

The incorporation of a marginal group into political participation may be a routine act for the government if the principle of incorporation had been established at some earlier time; but the shift of a system from one that is institutionalized around the exclusion of significant groups from politics into one that is organized to incorporate new groups would represent an innovative change in institutionalization.

c. The crisis model does not imply a constant movement toward greater political capacity.[20] Not all crises are solved by innovative decisions. Some may lead to the collapse of other institutions or to general societal collapse. And though crises, unlike critical problems, can come and go, they may persist either because a system is forced to undergo, over an extended period of time, constant re-institutionalization or because it is incapable of institutionalizing a response to a new pressure and, therefore, rests at the brink of violence or dissolution.

d. The fact that crises can be solved and followed by routine activity within the problem area ought not to be taken to imply that once a society has passed a crisis in a particular area, another crisis within that area may not arise at a later date. As societies change and as more individuals are mobilized into politics, recurrent crises of distribution or participation are possible. Changes may create pressures for entirely new kinds of distributive activities or new types of participation that involve something more than the expansion of the previous patterns of institutionalization. Thus, a society may resolve a crisis of participation by adopting a system of suffrage. After that it may be possible to handle demands for participation with routine expansions of the electoral base. But at some later date, demands for participa-

[20] Nor, to repeat a point made earlier, would such a movement necessarily be a "good thing."

tion above and beyond the electoral system may arise and create pressure for new institutionalized patterns. An example might be the demand that those affected by the welfare programs in the U.S. have an opportunity to participate in the administration of these programs. Those who want this new mode of participation already have access to the ballot, but now are defining the participation problem in a new way. The case would be the same in a society in which a welfare system that guarantees to all some minimum level of life has been institutionalized, but is challenged by a new definition of the range of governmental responsibilities.

Several sources of crises may be suggested:

a. A continuing source of potential crisis is environmental change that increases the relevant population for political activity. As processes of social mobilization take place, more and more people define more and more problems as political. Thus, if one could accurately measure some of these dimensions over time, one would probably find in most of the developing nations that the proportion of the population defining issues as political is constantly rising. If the response to these rising expectations requires a new pattern of institutionalization, a crisis exists; but if the rising set of demands on the government can be met by routine responses, there can be constant governmental expansion and innovation without any concomitant crisis. To take another example, problems of identity may receive relatively long-term solutions when the boundaries of a nation are established. But at some later time when, perhaps, new ethnic groups are politically mobilized, the identity problems are likely to reemerge.

b. Another source of potential crises in any particular area of governmental performance is governmental performance in other areas. Thus, the successful routine incorporation of new groups into political participation may create potential crises in distribution or in identity as the numbers for whom these are relevant issues rise. Or, the institutionalization of flexible responses in relation to one of the areas of social benefit creates potential crises in other areas where such institutionalization of flexibility is missing. A successful creation of a flexible system of welfare allocations may enable the government to handle demands for further welfare allocations through routine decisions. But the expansion of welfare may create pressures for greater political participation. And if the pattern of institutionalization is less flexible in the area of participation, the likelihood of a crisis in that area will grow. Thus, it may be that crises of development often arise out of unbalanced growth. These considerations have implications for the sequence of crises or problems, and I shall return to them later.

c. The above sources of potential crises derive from the sector of mass-elite relations. In addition, crises may arise because of a re-definition of political goals on the part of political elites. Elites are exposed to ideologies of change from abroad and from intellectuals in their own countries; they are constantly faced with stimuli that might lead them to raise the number of goals that they want to achieve through political activity. In some sense, one would not expect elite-generated goals to carry the same crisis potentiality as mass-generated goals. A crisis exists when re-institutionalization within a performance area is needed if elites or the system are not to risk dissolution. If the pressure for re-institutionalization comes from the elites themselves, the price of failure would seem to be less severe. But elite dissatisfaction with governmental performance may lead to crises in any of the following ways: (1) Elite re-definitions may be communicated to nonelites. Insofar as elite goals are communicated to the masses and the elites are incapable of fulfilling them, they may suffer the consequences of the expectations they arouse. (2) If elites cannot achieve the goals they set for themselves, this may result in various kinds of behavior that are dysfunctional for the system: apathy and internal conflict among competing elites are the two most likely forms. (3) Elite dissatisfaction, if successfully met through new institutionalization, may create the imbalances alluded to in the previous section. A system of participation may create environmental pressures for changes in the distributional system.

It should be clear that the distinction between routine problem-solving within an established pattern of institutionalization and crisis problem-solving that involves the creation of some new institution is not a clear one. The patterns of institutionalization we are talking of involve not only formal governmental structures—e.g., the passage of a law allowing access to politics for new groups—but the development of accepted systems of norms as well. Thus, a change on the part of elites in the direction of the acceptance of the legitimacy of political participation of some previously inactive group may represent an institutionalization of an innovative sort. Perhaps the incorporation of Southern blacks as political participants is a noninnovative routine expansion of political participation for the United States, but it represents a new level of institutionalization for Alabama.

Thus, crises represent situations in which the society moves in a new direction. They are the major decisional points at which the society is redefined, and are therefore relevant to sequential changes.

One last point about crises: They would seem always to involve problems of legitimacy as well as one of the other problem areas. This is another reason, perhaps, for the coexistence of crises as described in the various chapters of this volume.

IDENTIFYING CRISES AND CRISES SOLUTIONS

If we are to develop models of change applicable to a large number of societies—models that hinge on the order in which crises arise and institutions are created—one of the first items on the agenda should be the development of rules for deciding when a crisis exists, which problem area it is related to, and what the nature of the solution is. The task is by no means easy: the many specific crisis situations involve multiple problem areas. And the institutions created in response to a crisis may not always directly relate to the problem area that generated the crisis (a distribution crisis is met by an institutionalization of greater police power—i.e., a penetrative answer).

There is another reason why it is sometimes hard to assign a particular problem or crisis to one of the five problem areas. This is the question of the perspective from which a particular problem is assigned to one of the problem areas. Different actors in a situation will define a problem differently—largely in terms of the solution they consider appropriate for it. Consider the present urban crisis in the United States: to some it is a problem of penetration (to be solved by further extension and strengthening of the police powers of the state); to some it is a problem of distribution (to create new and better jobs, schools, housing, and the like); and to some it is a question of identity and/or legitimacy (perhaps to create a new and separate black society). In some sense there is no answer to the question of what kind of problem or crisis it "really" is, nor is it likely to be helpful to suggest that this is a special problem that can be viewed in different ways. It is quite likely that most problems—especially those involving conflict—are problems to which there are alternative perspectives that would lead to different "codings."

In addition to the above tasks, one can add the task of assigning particular institutions to particular problem areas. How do we decide that a particular institution relates to a particular problem? Do we assume that the creation of a party system always represents a pattern of institutionalization relevant to a participation problem? A national bureaucracy relevant to penetration? Probably not (though that often seems to be the tendency) because particular institutions do many things. But if the sequence of institution building is to involve propositions about building institutions in one problem area rather than another, we have to know into which area they fall.[21]

There are clearly many tasks to be accomplished before the present scheme can be a precise guide to research (though, of course, there is value in suggestive though less precise guides). As indicated above, these notes are directed more at specifying some of these tasks and less at performing them. The task of specifying how one recognizes a crisis or problem when one sees one and how one knows what kind of a crisis or problem it is, is both the most important and the most difficult task in moving further with the scheme.

Part IV. The Relationship among Stages

This is the last general question that one can ask about sequences of development. Merely to divide the history of a society into stages or to talk of a sequence of events is to do very little unless one can make some statements about sequential ordering and about the consequences of various orderings. As pointed out earlier, one may be faced with a dilemma. If one makes strong statements, one is likely to be wrong. If one allows flexibility—"there is no necessary ordering of stages, all sorts of variations are possible"—one will not easily be shown to be wrong, but one will not say anything of much interest.

We will assume that—much as we might like things to be otherwise—we can only deal with probabilistic statements and (what is essentially the same thing) can only link stages in a sequence in terms of "everything-else-being-equal" propositions.

What are some of the models of the connection between stages in a sequence that can be developed within these constraints:

---

[21] There is another problem in the observation and measurement of crises. As defined here, a crisis vis-à-vis a problem area exists when there is a need for institutionalization to avoid the overthrow of the political leaders. But there are all sorts of ambiguities here. The evidence for a crisis becomes indirect. It might consist of the fact that a new institution was created or it might consist of the fact that the leaders were overthrown. But new institutions can be created without the threat of displacement of leaders. In order to distinguish that situation from what we have called crises, we would have to be able to assess the extent of "threat of overthrow" —by no means an easy task. Conversely, leaders could be overthrown for reasons other than one of our crises.

If one uses institutionalization as the measure of crisis and if institutionalization is really the central issue involved, it may be that the crisis notion will become less useful.

a. The one outcome, one path model: We might assume that there is a particular order of development that all nations have followed and that all will follow in the future. This, if phrased in its most extreme way, would assume that all societies will end at the same place and pursue the same path to get there. This is a very useful model if applicable. It is not.

b. The one outcome, many paths model: This postulates that all societies will end at the same place, but that there are many roads there. This is also not very useful.

c. The many outcomes, one path to each outcome model: This assumes that there can be many types of political systems (or at least more than one), but there is a determined sequence by which one moves toward one or another outcome. This would be a most useful model in that we could predict where nations would wind up by seeing where they stand in relation to a particular sequence.

d. The many outcomes, many paths model: This may be realistic, but it allows for almost any sequence and does not tell us much.

e. The necessary condition (functional prerequisite) model: This may be one of the more useful models connecting items in a sequence. It does not imply that any particular stage always follows a particular kind of stage. But it implies that in order to attain a particular stage, some other specified stage must be attained first. I believe that many of the stage models take this form. The model can be loosened by making it probabilistic—i.e., that it is *unlikely* for a particular stage to be reached until a specified earlier stage is reached.

f. The branching tree model: This conceives of a sequence of choice points (not necessarily points of conscious decision, but points where development can go one way or the other). At any point in a sequence of development, there may be alternative next stages. But which one is chosen closes the options for others. Closely related to this is the notion of irreversibilities—choices of one branch which once chosen does not allow backtracking. The development of certain kinds of governmental programs may be of this sort—the choice to set up a program in relation to a particular problem area may lead almost inevitably to the maintenance and even expansion of the program because of the vested interests it creates. The study of these irreversibilities might be most useful for the development of sequential models.[22]

[22] See Alker, *op.cit.*, pp. 267-70, for an example.

SEQUENCES AMONG THE CRISES

Until the previous questions of "sequences in relation to what" and "sequences of what" have been answered—that is, until there is some underlying dimension for which the sequence is relevant and some clear definition of what it is that is coming in sequence (and how one recognizes it when one sees it)—it is difficult to link the five crises or problems into some sequential ordering. The propositions in the various chapters in this book often take the form of the necessary condition model: one type of institution cannot be achieved or one type of crisis avoided until some other institution has already been created or some other crisis passed. Or, more often, it is suggested that the creation of one kind of institution or a particular crisis before some other will have particular consequences. But most of the sequential statements tend to be pairwise statements, that is, they link a pair of problems or crises rather than developing an extended sequence linking all five problem areas.

Under the circumstances, it would be foolish to attempt such an overall sequential model here. Rather, I would like to make a few general comments on how one might link the items in the sequence. Let us assume, as suggested above, that the items in the sequence are crises in the five problem areas as well as the moments at which institutionalized capacity to deal with these problem areas is developed. And the underlying dimension of development is the degree to which there are differential institutions to deal with the various problem areas. What is the relationship between the order in which crises and institutions in the problem areas arise and the likelihood that later crises will be met by successful institution building?

It may be possible to suggest reasons why the successful meeting of a crisis in one of the performance areas and the consequent development of institutionalized performance capacity in that area is necessary or (more weakly) useful for further development in other areas. To do this we can look at the problem areas in terms of three possible consequences of successful institutional development in each —its direct effect on the members of the society (its beneficial effects); its effect on pressures for further governmental performance; and its effect on the ability of the government to meet the problem. Thus, for example, the achievement of a certain level of institutional performance in relation to distribution represents a beneficial output to the members of the system but it also may trigger new demands in other areas or lead to facilitative inputs for the government (it increases the likelihood of system legitimacy, for instance).

If one looks at the relationship among all five problem areas, the situation resembles the problem of growth among sectors of the economy. In the long run, one can argue that there is likely to be pressure for some kind of balanced growth—i.e., more institutionalized capacity in all five of the problem areas. This is true for two reasons: On the one hand, institutional performance in any one area is facilitated by performance in the others. Unless performances in all the areas keep pace, performance in any particular one will slow down. Thus, systems may be unable to reach certain levels of distributive performance if legitimacy lags too far behind. In the long run, unless there is some balance in the growth pattern among the performance areas, there will be stagnation. In addition, the pressure toward a balanced growth pattern is a more positive one. Institutionalized performance in any of the performance areas is likely to generate demands for performance in the others. Thus, successful performance in the distributive area (leading to higher physical welfare, education, etc.) may generate pressures for performance in other areas—participation or identity, for instance.

But balanced growth is a long-run phenomenon. It may be possible for systems to develop in an unbalanced manner in the short run. Thus, the development of institutions to deal with the problems of identity may rush ahead of other performances—(as in the wake of a nationalistic revolution). And such imbalances may represent ways in which performance in other areas can be stimulated. Thus, elites who rely on a heavy dose of symbols of identity to mobilize their society for social change may indeed generate the kinds of secondary effects they want. But they also generate a potential problem if the rise in the identity level is not matched by concomitant performance in other areas.

In order to speculate about various sequences of the development of institutional capacity among the five performance areas, it is also useful to look at institutions in the five problem areas in terms of the demands they are likely to generate (i.e., what kinds of performance demands are likely to be generated by performance in a particular area) and in terms of the facilitative inputs they generate (i.e., in what way does successful performance in an area facilitate governmental performance in another). This is outlined in Table I. In general (but only in general) institutional performances of the kind mentioned at the top of the table facilitate performance in items listed below. This happens directly or indirectly: identity directly affects legitimacy which in turn affects others below it. Thus, the creation of institutionalized capacity to generate a sense of identity (norms of nationhood or manipulable symbol systems) facilitates the institutionalization of legitimacy, and legitimacy in turn facilitates penetration. There is some reciprocal effect from the bottom of the chart upwards—distribution and participation performance facilitate legitimacy and perhaps identity. But, in general, the items above tend to be more useful for the performance of items below than vice versa.

TABLE I

Performance Area	Facilitative Inputs to Government	Secondary Demands for Performance Triggered
Identity	Legitimacy, Participation	Participation (Distribution?)
Legitimacy	Extraction, Penetration	
Penetration	Legitimacy, Extraction	Distribution (Participation?)
Participation	Legitimacy	Distribution (Identity?)
Distribution	Legitimacy	Participation, Penetration (Identity?)

The listing of identity first is in accord with the argument in the present chapters as well as the work of Rustow who argues that an ordering (in his terms) of unity-authority-equality facilitates growth and development.[23] There are several reasons why the establishment of institutions to further a sense of identity facilitates performance in other areas. For one thing, it increases the legitimacy of the governing elites—insofar as they are defined as members of the same system, it becomes less ego challenging to accept their directives and one is more likely to assume that they are acting in one's interest. (And since legitimacy in turn increases the potentiality of effective penetration, the relationship between identity and the other performance areas

[23] See Rustow, op.cit.

becomes clear.) Identity, thus, makes it possible for elites to mobilize resources and coordinate societal activities—i.e., a sense of identity may raise the government's general capabilities.

Furthermore, the affiliative needs served by performance in the area of identity may be the kind of needs that have to be satisfied if energies are to be available for other activities. It is not that the government of the nation is the only entity that can satisfy these needs. Indeed, in most situations other agencies—families, communities—may perform most heavily in the area of affiliative needs. But in situations of rapid change when other institutions are losing potency and when nationalistic ideologies are available for transfer from nation to nation, there may be small choice for elites not to try to solve the problem of identity first. If it is not solved, it will be hard to direct the attention of members of the system to other problem areas.

The development of some sense of affiliation may be particularly important before high levels of performance are reached in the distributive and, especially, in the participation area. Governments that are active in the distributive area and in which participation has been institutionalized (or at minimum, in which participation has been defined as a political right by the members of the system) will have to deal with the problems of the allocation of resources among competing interests, each with some political power and political resources. The management of conflict and competition can take place in many ways, but the existence of some overarching set of common commitments or identity—a we-feeling that overarches the issue conflicts in the society—may be a most useful way of minimizing this conflict. Allocational conflicts among participating groups may take place in societies with little sense of common community, but they are likely to be more severe and potentially more disruptive to the system.

The above section illustrates the way in which the requisite level of institutional performance in any one of the performance areas changes as demands in other performance areas change. The absence of a sense of national identity may be of little importance (have little effect on the performance of the government) in societies in which the government is not active in distribution and there is no participation. But where there are demands for participation and distribution, the potentialities of political divisiveness grow if some prior institutionalization of identity has not taken place.

This does not mean that it is impossible to develop a participatory system with a high level of distributive performance at low levels of common identity. But if this is the case, it may be necessary to have a higher ratio of coercion in the society and more extreme means of managing intergroup conflict.

One could speculate further about the extent to which the degree of institutionalization in one performance area facilitates performance in others. But the argument remains too abstract and vague until the problem areas and institutions are given more precise definition. Once this is done, however, it should be possible to test hypotheses about the consequences of the emergence of, say participatory problems before firm institutionalized solutions of identity.

Similar linking statements might be made about the secondary demands generated by performance in one issue area. Institutionalized performance in one area is likely to generate demands for performance in others. The questions one can raise are: What are the consequences of a sequence of development in which distributive institutions precede participatory ones? What difference does it make if the welfare state precedes democracy rather than vice versa? The questions may be moot in the developing nations since both are demanded at once. But the historical study of development may suggest some answers. In some sense, the Bismarkian policy for Germany represented an attempt to schedule distribution first and postpone participation. As Marshall suggests, the pattern in Britain was the opposite. Political rights were the product of the 19th century while social rights (distributions) are the product of the 20th.[24]

The relationship among the performance areas of the secondary demands generated is not clear. In general, the items at the bottom of Table I tend to be demand generating while the items at the top tend to be support generating. (Items in the secondary demand column in parentheses are items for which the suggested secondary demand is tenuous.) In general, this suggests that a satisfaction of the problem areas at the top before the ones at the bottom may allow a smoother and less stressful change, but that once the demand level starts to grow in relation to the items at the bottom of the table, there may be an upward spiral of performance demands.

One of the more interesting areas of study in relation to this kind of sequential model would be the impact of effective institutions in one of the problem areas on demands for institutionalized performance elsewhere. Under what circumstances does a successful dis-

[24] T. H. Marshall, *Citizenship and Social Class* (Cambridge, Eng.: Cambridge University Press, 1950).

tributive program generate more demand for participation, and vice versa? In general, it may be that institutionalized capacity in one area is one of the major sources for demands for capacity elsewhere. The more the government is capable of penetrating the society or the more the government distributes benefits through its activities, the higher are the stakes of political participation (there is something to participate *about*). Conversely, participants are likely to use their participation to further their distributive shares.

Another aspect of sequential patterns that can be explored is the demand for new institutionalized capacity in more than one area at the same time. Much has been written about why problems accumulate and what is the consequence of this accumulation. It is a commonplace to remark on the accumulation of problems in the developing nations. What Britain took centuries to do—solve the problems of identity, legitimacy, participation, and distribution—the new nations have to do in the briefest span of time. The various institutions have to be created all at once.

What are the consequences of the accumulation of problems? The major proposition is that the overlapping of any two problems makes each harder to solve. Why is this so?

1. A simple reason is that time, energy, and span of attention are limited. Governing elites may have difficulty managing several problems at the same time. Furthermore, some problems tend to be more salient and emotion laden than others. Identity may be one of these. Unless questions of identity are solved—boundaries set satisfactorily, independence achieved—it may be difficult to concentrate on other problems.[25]

2. More important is the fact that the problems raised in the various performance areas interrelate with each other. Several examples can be given of the ways in which a pair of problems, if arising simultaneously, exacerbate each other. The examples will be limited to pairs of problem areas, but extension to the ordinary situation of three or more problem areas arising at the same time should be clear.

a. Distribution and participation: The difficulty of the solution of a participation problem may depend upon the way in which those who have political power (and are being called on to share it with new groups) estimate the effects of that sharing. They may oppose participatory institutions per se in the belief that lower orders ought not

[25] See Rustow, *op.cit.*

to interfere in matters that do not concern them. But they are less likely to oppose participation if they perceive that the introduction of participation will not have adverse effects on their share of the distribution of goods, services, and statuses in the society. Disraeli may have discerned the deferential conservative in the British working class and therefore felt free to give him the vote; but elites who believe that those demanding participation are likely to use that participation to overthrow nonpolitical privileges are less likely to allow that participation.

Conversely, reforms in distribution are likely to be more palatable to elites if there is some belief that they can thereby obtain relief from participatory demand. Probably elites who believe they can buy a reduction of distributive demands by participation are, in the long run, wrong. As suggested above, either type of performance creates pressures for the other. But in the short run, the elites may believe (and perhaps correctly) that they are buying time in terms of the other set of demands by performance in response to one. But if the demands are simultaneous, a buying time tactic is not viable and elites may be unwilling to accede to any demands.

b. The problem is greatly exacerbated if an identity problem exists at the same time. If the very identification of the system is in doubt, the distributive demands and the participatory demands have the potentiality of fragmenting the system. It is not merely that a common identity does not exist to mitigate conflict, but that the conflict aroused by the distributive and participatory crises may lead to withdrawal from the system (in the sense of the creation of separatist movements) by those who feel disadvantaged. This is especially the case where the conflict among those demanding distribution or participation comes from members of identifiable subcommunities. In cases of this sort, the elites may perceive the demands for participation and distribution as challenges not only to the status system, but to the cultural integrity of the system—as if foreigners were demanding a voice in, and benefits from, the operation of politics.

c. The clearest example of how simultaneous problems compound each other is the existence of a problem of legitimacy coincident with a problem in some other area. The compounding is well enough known to require mere mention here, and is indeed what seems to characterize most of the "crises" discussed in this volume. Successful performance in any of the other areas depends upon the legitimacy of the government, and the legitimacy of the government depends to some extent on its performance in other areas. If its legitimacy is challenged at the same time as there is demand for some new level of performance in some other area: (1) it will not perform well in the other area, and (2) the challenge to the legitimacy will be reinforced. A challenge to governmental legitimacy is a serious challenge at any time. But if it is not accompanied by demands for performance in other areas at the same time, a government is more likely to survive the legitimacy crisis. Conversely, of course, if governmental legitimacy is not challenged, its ability to meet other performance crises is enhanced.

SPECULATION about the consequences of alternative sequences among the five problem areas and about the consequences of a cumulative pattern of crises or problems illustrates the usefulness of such an approach to the study of political development. If we could convert these speculations into testable hypotheses, we might have a powerful tool indeed for dealing with developmental histories in comparative perspective. Furthermore, such an approach might produce findings of great relevance to those interested in applying the findings of developmental studies to policy choice situations. It might not be in the power of developmental planners to schedule developmental problems or crises (though under certain circumstances that might not be impossible), but the planner would be armed with important information if he knew something of the consequences of various orderings of the problems or crises.

But the usefulness of such studies of developmental patterns based on hypotheses about alternative orderings of the problems or crises and the consequences of such orderings should also underscore the need for furthering "processing" of the "five crises" model of development for the purpose of further studies. This discussion has not represented an attempt to specify the precise ways in which that "processing" might be done but rather an attempt to suggest some of the issues with which the "processors" would have to deal. The latter task is, of course, much easier than the former. It is hoped that the potential usefulness of this approach to development will lead to attempts to deal with the more difficult task of converting the "five crises scheme" into a more precise model of political development. Until that processing is done, discussions of sequence—as exemplified, I am afraid, by the present chapter—may remain quite vague.

CONTRIBUTORS

LEONARD BINDER, born in Boston, Massachusetts, in 1927, is professor of political science at the University of Chicago. He has specialized in the study of Middle Eastern politics and Islamic thought and has done field research in Pakistan, Iran, Egypt, Lebanon, and Tunisia. His publications include *Religion and Politics in Pakistan, Iran: Political Development in a Changing Society*, and *The Ideological Revolution in the Middle East*.

JAMES S. COLEMAN, born in Provo, Utah, in 1919, is a specialist in African affairs and at various times has been director of the African Studies Center, University of California, Los Angeles; head of the department of political science at Makerere University College, Uganda; member of the advisory committee for Africa, National Academy of Science; vice-president of the International Congress of Africanists; associate director and representative for East Africa, Rockefeller Foundation; and director, Institute for Development Studies, University of Nairobi. His publications include *Nigeria: Background to Nationalism*, and he has served as both editor and contributor for *Politics of the Developing Areas* and *Education and Political Development*.

JOSEPH LAPALOMBARA, born in Chicago, 1925, is Wolfers Professor of Political Science at Yale University. He was formerly chairman of the department of political science at Michigan State University. He has been a visiting professor at the University of Florence, Columbia University, and the University of California at Berkeley. In 1971-72 he spent a year in western Europe as a Guggenheim Fellow. His main field of interest is comparative political institutions and behavior. He is author of *Interest Groups in Italian Politics*, *The Italian Labor Movement: Problems and Prospects*, *Italy: The Politics of Planning*, and other works; editor of *Bureaucracy and Political Development*; and co-editor of *Elezioni e Comportamento Politico in Italia* and *Political Parties and Political Development*.

LUCIAN W. PYE, born in China in 1921, is professor of political science at the Massachusetts Institute of Technology and a senior staff member of MIT's Center for International Studies. He is chairman of the Social Science Research Council's Committee on Comparative Politics, and a former Fellow of the Center for Advanced Study in the Behavioral Sciences. He is author of *Politics, Personality, and Nation-Building, Aspects of Political Development, Guerrilla Communism in Malaya*; co-author of *The Politics of the Developing Areas* and *The Emerging Nations*; editor of *Communications and Political Development*; and co-editor of *Political Culture and Political Development*.

SIDNEY VERBA, born in New York, 1926, is professor of political science at the University of Chicago. A former research associate, Center of International Studies, Princeton University, and Fellow of the Center for Advanced Study in the Behavioral Sciences, he specializes in cross-national study of political attitudes. He is author of *Small Groups and Political Behavior: A Study of Leadership*, co-author (with Gabriel A. Almond) of *Civic Culture: Political Attitudes and Democracy in Five Nations*, and co-editor of *The International System: Theoretical Essays* and *Political Culture and Political Development*.

MYRON WEINER, born in Brooklyn in 1931, is senior research associate of the Center for International Studies and professor of political science at MIT. He has done extensive field work in India and has held fellowships from the Ford Foundation, the Rockefeller Foundation, the Social Science Research Council, and the Guggenheim Foundation. He is author of *Party Politics in India: The Development of a Multiparty System, The Politics of Scarcity: Pressure and Political Response in India, Political Change in South Asia*; co-author of *The Politics of the Developing Areas*; editor of *State Politics in India*; and co-editor of *Indian Voting Behaviour* and *Political Parties and Political Development*.

Abramovitz, Moses, 235n, 254
accumulation of problems, consequences of, 314-15
Adelman, I., 251n
administration, 261-62; bureaucratic-administrative sphere, 89ff; influence of foreign aid on, 276-77
Africa, equality in, 93-94. *See also* developing countries
agricultural sector, role in economic development, distribution crisis, 248-51, 253; effect of "surplus" aid on, 275-76
alienation, 4, 36-37, 164; and legitimacy crisis, 156-58; as form of participation, 167
Alker, Hayward A., Jr., 287n, 294n, 308n
allocation, 233-34; resource, 240
Almond, Gabriel A., 58, 79n, 103n, 165, 233n, 284n, 292, 294
Anderson, C. Arnold, 98, 263n, 264n, 269n
Anderson, Charles W., 143n
Andrain, Charles F., 94n
anthropological development, *see* cultural development
Apter, David E., 39n, 82n, 86n, 87n, 92n, 94n, 99, 207, 233, 268, 271, 296
Arian, A., 228n
aristocracy, *see* elite
Aristotle, 4ff, 8, 16, 54
Asia, *see* developing countries
assimilation, rate of, 117; of minorities, 182
Ataturk, 121n, 126, 127, 154
authority, central, and participation, 177; disenchantment with, 145-46; and legitimacy crisis, 138-41, 143-47; local, 178. *See also* decentralization, elite, leadership
autonomy, 59; demand for bureaucratic, 179; local, 191-92, 224-26
Avinieri, Shlomo, 214n
Azikiwe, President Nnamdi, 94

Balassa, Bela, 261n
Baldivin, R. E., 247n
Balewa, Abubakar Tafawa, 156n
Banfield, Edward C., 242
Battista y Zaldivar, Fulgencio, 213
Baumol, William, 248n
Beling, Willard A., 199n
Bellah, R. N., 268n
Ben Bella, Mohammed, 71

Bendix, Reinhard, 169n, 176n, 201
Binder, Leonard, 70n, 146n
Birch, Anthony H., 195n
Bismarck, Otto von, 115
Black, Cyril E., 219, 243n, 284n; phases of modernization, 296
Black Power, 168, 191
Blalock, H. M., Jr., 287n
Bondurant, Joan V., 146n
Boserup, Ester, 250
Bowman, M. J., 263n, 264n, 269n
Braibanti, Ralph, 144n, 221n, 229n, 247n, 261n, 271n, 275n, 276-77
Brown, James, 265n
Brown, W. N., 268n
bureaucracy, 14, 34-35, 80; as it affects crisis management, 231; and political participation, 178-80
bureaucratization, as aspect of modernization, 34-35
Burnham, W. D., 296n
Butwell, Richard A., 131n

capacity, 78, 79n; as element of development syndrome, 78-80; as dimension of development, 291-94; legitimacy crisis, 57; distribution crisis, 61; participation crisis, 59-60; penetration crisis, 63, 209
Castro, Fidel, 71, 213
causal models, 287-88
centralization, 62, 139-41, 160, 190-91, 230-31. *See also* decentralization
Chambers, W. N., 296n, 297n
change, 45, 52-53, 106ff; administrative, in Brandenburg-Prussia, 255; conflict of tradition and, 267; role in crises, 52-67, 302ff; of elite personality, 270-71; environmental, as source of crises, 304; generational, 203-04; historical/intellectual threshold of modernity, 12ff; ideological, 240; institutional, 175-77; political, as distinguished from political development, 16-17; social, 166; social, and identity crisis, 118-23; as viewed by Western man, 3-17
charisma, *see* leadership
Chiang Kai-shek, 130
Ch'ien Tuan-sheng, 131n
Church, R. J. Harrison, 112
church-state relations, as cause of legitimacy crisis, 139

citizenship, 77-78, 160n; rights, and relation to central authority, 177
Civilization and Its Discontents, 40
Cnudde, C. F., 287
Colbert, Jean Baptiste, 221
Cole, C., 222n
Cole, T., 275n
Coleman, James, 73n, 75n, 88n, 90n, 92n, 94n, 96n, 97n, 98n, 233n, 234, 262, 264n, 265
colonialism, corporate representation, 189-90; effect on egalitarianism, 94-95; role in forming identity, 122-23; limitation as agent of nation building, 117-18; parochial elites in ex-colonial countries, 131; and penetration crisis, 225; synthetic elites in ex-colonial countries, 131-32
Comte, Auguste, 15, 19, 43, 55
Confucius, 154
Congress Party (India), 89, 94, 210
consciousness, 18-20, 38-40, 47; of change, 10, 52-53
Convention People's Party (India), 177
Correa, H., 258n
corruption, 156n
coup d'etat, 136-37, 142
crises, 22, 192n, 298-307; definition, 302-04; identifying, and solutions, 306-07; resolution, 69-70; sequence of, 297-98; sequences among, 309-16; sources of, 304-05. *See also* capacity, differentiation, distribution, equality, identity, legitimacy, participation, penetration, political development
crisis management, 227-28, 231ff, 266ff; distribution, 248ff; elite, 207ff, 273ff; institutionalization in, 69-72
Crozier, Michel, 221n
cultural development, 37-49; goal orientation as opposed to traditional ritualism, 46ff; science as opposed to magic, 44; tradition as opposed to innovation, 41-44
cultural relativism, 40-41
culture, 6-7; consciousness of, 47; psychologization of, 39-40; politicization of, 48-49. *See also* cultural development, political culture
Curle, Adam, 96, 97n

Dahl, Robert A., 183n, 235n, 240
Dahrendorf, Rolf, 77n, 82, 169, 170n
Darwinism, social, 14-15, 245
Deak, Istvan, 170n
decentralization, of authority, 189-92
De Gaulle, Charles, 66, 179
de Grazia, Alfred, 195n

demands, distributive, 279-80; leading to identity crisis, 129-31; political participation, 161; for voice in institutions, 178-80
Dennis, Jack, 145n
de Schweinitz, Karl, Jr., 294n
Deutsch, Karl W., 110n, 117, 165, 296
developing countries, demands from different groups, 95-96; development syndrome, 83-84; differentiation in, 84-93; education in, 97-98; equality in, 93ff; geographic penetration in, 228; identity crisis in, 119ff, 128-33; integrative problems of, 86; legitimacy crisis in, 139ff, 151-52; participation crisis in, 171-72, 196-97; penetration crisis in, 212ff, 222ff. *See also* Western impact
development, imbalance in, 97-98. *See also* change, cultural development, economic development, political development
development syndrome, 21ff, 74; in developing areas, 83-84; and distribution crisis, 279-81; legitimacy crisis, 135-36; overlap between crises and, 292; and participation crisis, 174-75; penetration crisis, 209-10, 217-18; relationship between elements, 80-83; underlying dimensions of development, 291. *See also* capacity, differentiation, equality
differentiation, 81, 85n, 87n, 92n; definition, 75; distribution crisis, 61-62; as element of development syndrome, 75-76, 84-93; and elite politics, 89-93; imbalance resulting in malintegration, 89-93; and legitimacy, 57-58; and participation, 60; and penetration, 63-64; underlying dimension of development, 291-92, 295
differentiation model, irrelevance for developing countries, 85-86
Dilthey, Wilhelm, 19, 43
Disraeli, Benjamin, 114, 315
distribution crisis, 60-62, 233-37, 299; and ideology, 237-46; and international environment, 273-79; role of leadership in, 253-66; psychological obstacles to economic growth, 266-79
  resolution of: 246-73; role of education in, 268-69; elite role in, 269-71; of human resources, 253-73; of natural resources, 248-52
  See also crises, economic development, ideology, political demands
divine right, 140, 187, 244

Doob, Leonard W., 118n
Dorsey, John, 95
Dorwart, Reinhard A., 222n, 255n
Dostoevski, Fedor, 245n
Drescher, Seymour, 51
Durkheim, Emile, 19, 42, 76, 218n

Earle, E. M., 242n
East, W. Gordon, 181n
Easton, David, 58, 144, 233, 234, 240
Eckstein, Alexander, 100n, 256, 257
Eckstein, Harry, 82n, 83n, 147, 296n
economic development, 245-46, 258n;
    distribution crises, 246-73; and elite,
    89-90, 272-73; integration, 25; lead-
    ership, 253-66; orientations, 241-43;
    participation, 186; political develop-
    ment, 22-27; state intervention, 256-
    57; in Western nations, 252ff
education, 34, 78, 81, 185-86, 190, 259,
    262n; distribution crisis, 268-69; and
    developmental process, 97-98; leading
    to nationalism, 14; role in nation
    building, 258-65; Western model of,
    94
Eisenstadt, S. N., 60, 75n, 81n, 83, 84,
    86n, 87n, 90n, 92n, 93n, 95-96, 97n,
    109n, 217n, 231
elite, crisis management, 207ff; dealing
    with political demands, 235ff; of de-
    veloping countries, 218n; and differ-
    entiation, 89-93; dissatisfaction, 305,
    and distribution crisis, 237-40, 256-
    57; and egalitarian demands, 95-97;
    and identity crisis, 124-33; impact of
    international environment on crisis
    management capability of, 273-79;
    legitimacy crisis, 155-56; penetration,
    206; political development, 103-05;
    political participation, 314-15; re-
    sponses to participation crises, 192ff;
    resolution of distribution crisis, 269ff;
    and revolution, 193; and socialism,
    244-45. See also authority, identity
    crisis
Emerson, Rupert, 106n, 152n, 171, 243
Engels, Friedrich, 55
Enlightenment, 19, 52
environment, capacity to cope with, 79;
    political community and its, 62
Epsilon, Book, 4
equality, 54, 76-77; in Africa, 93-94;
    as dimension of development, 291-95;
    and distribution crisis, 61; as element
    of development syndrome, 76-78; and
    legitimacy, 57, 135; in modernization
    process, 93-98; and participation crisis,

59, 170-72, 189-90; and penetration
    crisis, 62
Erikson, Erik H., 123n, 133, 148n, 289
Esman, Milton J., 246n
Ethics, The, 4
ethnic groups, 125-26, 128, 190; assimi-
    lation of, 117; and national identity,
    115-16, 181-82. See also minority
    groups
Etzioni, Amitai, 85n
Etzioni, Eva, 85n
Europe, identity crises in, 119; legitimacy
    crises in, 139-40; political participa-
    tion in, 171-72; penetration crises in,
    211-12; social stratification in, 167-68
exploitation, 237-38

Fainsod, Merle, 255n
Fairbairn, G., 128n
Fallers, Lloyd, 77n, 87n, 91, 93, 98n,
    268n
family, influence on development, 30-31
Farouk, King, 137
fascism, 170n
Fei, J., 251n
Feldman, Arnold S., 82n, 83, 86n
Ferrarotti, Franco, 242n
Feuer, Lewis S., 203n
Finkle, J., 247n, 256n, 268n, 270
Fisher, Margaret W., 146n
Fontenell, M., 3
Forbes, D., 287n
foreign aid, 275-78
foreign pressure, see international en-
    vironment
Foster, George M., 242
Foster, Philip J., 97n, 264
Fox, Richard, 147n
France, penetration crisis in, 221-22
Frederick the Great, 115, 222
Frey, Frederick W., 93n, 140n, 145n
Friedrich, Carl J., 141, 218
functionalism, 18ff, 27-28
Furnivall, J. S., 152n

Gable, R., 247n, 256n, 268n, 270
Gandhi, Mahatma, 110n, 216
Garstin, L. H., 239n
Geertz, Clifford, 38, 77n, 79n, 86, 95n,
    96n, 99n, 181n, 268n, 273
generational change, 203-04
Gerard, Michel, 190n
ghetto, American, 163, 191
Gideonse, H. P., 258n
Girondism, 190n
Glanvill, Joseph, 3
Glazer, Nathan, 126n
Glukman, Max, 166

Goebbels, Joseph, 218n
Greenblum, Joseph, 169n
Gremion, Pierre, 221n
Grew, Raymond, 284n
Grossholtz, Thelma Jean, 127n
Gurr, Ted, 169n
Gusfield, Joseph, 201n

Hagen, Everett, 122n, 258n, 268n, 269-71
Halpern, Manfred, 199n, 292
Hanotaux, G., 222n
Harbison, F., 254, 259, 260, 263
Harris, Dale B., 85n
Harrison, S. E., 88n
Harrod, R. F., 248
Harsanyi, J., 286, 287n
Heberle, Rudolf, 201n
Hegel, G.W.F., 4ff, 19-20, 55
Henderson, A. M., 138n
Higgins, Benjamin, 251n
Hirschman, Albert O., 246n, 249n, 256, 258
historical orientation, and identity crisis, 119-23; in viewing crises, 66-67
history, 20-21; and social science, 16; theory of, 3-17
Hobbes, Thomas, 7-8
Hodgkin, Thomas, 94
Hope, Richard, 4n
Hoselitz, Bert F., 75n, 257n, 264, 265, 271
Huntington, Samuel P., 106n, 139, 140, 142, 160n, 177n, 193, 206, 219n, 246n
Husserl, E., 3
Hyman, Herbert, 149n

identity crisis, 53-56, 110-34, 299; authority and, 109-10; in developing countries, 119ff; and legitimacy, 102; in Malaysia, 132; and performance, 311-12; political nature of individual, 54; in Turkey, 126-27
  resolution of: 75, 123-33; by assimilation, 117; by accommodation, 117-18; with closed elite, 128-29; in England, Japan and U.S., 125-26; with exclusive elite, 127-28; with expanding elite, 124-27; without a model elite culture, 132-33; with parochial elite culture, 129-31; with synthetic elite culture, 131-32
  types of: 111-23; and class, 114-15; national, and ethnic divisions, 115-18; national, and territory, 112-14; and social change, 118-23
  See also Western impact
ideology, 100, 143, 240n; in developing

countries, 108-09; and distribution, 237-46; of economic planning, 257-58; public sector intervention, 245-46; of nationalism, 240-43; role in cultural development, 38-39; socialism, 243-45; Protestant Ethics, 245
Inayatullah, 261n
industrialization, 36, 241, 293; and distribution crisis, 251-52; and political participation, 184-85
Industrial Revolution, 212, 259
Inkeles, Alex, 167
institution building, foreign aid and, 276-77; and penetration, 215ff
institutionalization, 310ff; accumulation of problems, 314-16; basis of sequences, 300-05; crisis management, 69-72; participation crisis, 193-95, 203-04; penetration crisis, 206-07, 218-19, 227-28
institutional changes, and political participation, 175-77
institutional development, effect on performance, 309ff
integration, 46-48, 76, 86-87, 200n; economic, 25; dimension of modernizing capacity, 98-100

Jacobinism, 190n
Jansen, Marius B., 126n
Jefferson, Thomas, 206
John, King of England, 105, 237
Jones, Stephen B., 133n
Justice Party (Turkey), 185

Kant, Immanuel, 19-20
Kaplan, A., 236n, 244n
Karens, 128
Kautsky, John H., 121n
Khaldun, Ibn, 6-7, 16
Khan, President Ayub, 198n
Kilson, Martin L., Jr., 142n, 143n
Kodzic, Peter, 218n
Kolakowski, L., 57n
Kornhauser, William, 166n

Landes, David S., 242n
Lane, Robert E., 165n
LaPalombara, Joseph, 70n, 90n, 95n, 98n, 108, 157n, 165n, 180n, 217n, 221n, 228n, 229n, 239n, 247n, 255n, 256n, 265n, 275n
Lasswell, Harold, 215n, 233, 234, 236n, 244n
leadership, building authority through, 147-50; charismatic, 99, 137, 148-49, 274; collapse of leading to legitimacy crisis, 143-44; and competence, 133-

34; and economic development, 253-66; and identity problems, 109-10; and legitimacy crisis, 143, 147-56; and zenophobic nationalism, 99-100
  dilemmas of choice: 150-56; firmness and accommodation, 150-53; preserving or rejecting the past, 153-54; satisfaction and sacrifice, 154-56
  See also authority, elites, identity crisis
legitimacy crisis, 56-58, 299; alienation, 156-58; and authority, 136-37, 143-47; compounded by other problems, 315-16; definition, 136; in developing countries, 151-52; goal fulfillment as related to, 90-91; and identity crises, 135; in Japan, 151; link to other crises, 136ff; resolution of, 75, 147-56
  causes of: conflicting/inadequate basis for authority, 138-41; disfunctional socialization processes, 144-47; excessive and uninstitutionalized competition, 141-43; collapse of leadership, 143-44
  See also leadership
Leibenstein, Harvey, 269n
Lemarchand, Rene, 88n
Lerner, Daniel, 93n, 165, 169n, 215n, 226, 269
Levenson, J. R., 120n, 153
Levin, Donald, 129n, 226
LeVine, Robert A., 93n
Levy, Marion J., Jr., 67
Lewis, Oscar, 242, 243n
Lewis, W. Arthur, 263, 264n
Lifton, Robert J., 119n
Lindblom, Charles E., 253n, 254, 256
Linebarger, Paul M. A., 131
Lipset, Seymour Martin, 82n, 109n, 170n, 301
Lipsky, Michael, 202n
Louis XIV, 221
Louisiana Purchase, 206
Luttwak, Edward, 142n

McClelland, David C., 270, 271, 274
McClosky, Herbert, 165n
McCrone, D. J., 287n
McLaren, W. W., 151n

Mahadevan, T. K., 146n
Mahdi, Muhsin, 6-7
Maine, Sir Henry, 41-42
Malenbaum, Wilfred, 247n
Mannheim, Karl, 165, 244n
Mannoni, O., 118n, 122n
Marc Antony, 218n
Marcuse, Herbert, 202n

Marriott, McKim, 268n, 273n
Marshall, Alfred, 260
Marshall, T. H., 77n, 78, 176n, 183n, 313
Marvick, Dwaine, 124n
Marx, Fritz Morstein, 220, 229n
Marx, Karl, 214n; on development, 27; on history, 19-20; theory, 14-15
Maslow, Abraham H., 235
Matossian, Mary, 120n, 239, 240n
Mazzini, Giuseppe, 95n
Meier, G. M., 247n
Meiji Restoration, 126, 151n
Mendieta y Nunez, Lucio, 218n
Merritt, Richard I., 165n, 294n
Merton, Robert K., 18
Metaphysics (Aristotle), 4
Milbrath, Lester, 165n
military, intervention, 35, 90, 142; rise of associated with modernization, 35
Mill, John Stuart, 160n
minority groups, identity crises of, 116; political participation of, 199-200; in U.S., 232. *See also* ethnic groups
modernization, 50-51, 101, 268n; capacity, 98-100; equality, 93-98; differentiation, 84-93; integration, 87-88; orientation toward, 67-72; phases of, 296; variety in, 82-83. *See also* cultural development, economic development, political development
modernity, historical/intellectual threshold?, 12-17; influence in development, 17-52; and integration, 46-48
Montgomery, J. D., 246n, 275n, 277n, 278
Montias, John, 192n, 261n
Moore, Wilbert E., 75n, 82
Morgenthau, Ruth Schacter, 94n
Moynihan, David P., 126n
Myers, C. A., 254, 259, 260, 263
Myrdal, Gunnar, 175, 247n, 257, 258n, 259, 260, 263, 264n, 269, 272, 273, 275

Nash, Manning, 256
Nasser, Gamal Abd, 71, 137
nation building, and distribution crises, 250ff; and sequential model, 286; elites and international assistance, 275
nation-state system, 116
national identity, and ethnicity, 115-16; in France, 180-81; nationality building, 181; and political participation, 180-82; and territory, 112-14, 133; in Western Europe, 180-81. *See also* ideology

nationalism, 63, 273; European, 116; and identity crisis, 110
nationalist movements, effect on activist politics, 106; and political participation, 170-72, 184-85
Navarsky, Victor S., 191n
Nietzsche, Friedrich W., 55
Nkrumah, Kwame, 137, 177
Nolte, Ernest, 170n
Nordlinger, Eric, 284n
Norman, E. Herbert, 151n
Nurkse, R., 251n

Okatie-Eboch, Chief Festus, 156n
one-party system, participation in, 188
Organski, A.F.K., 284n
Orwell, George, 215

Palmer, Robert R., 184
Park, Richard L., 146
Parsons, Talcott, 19, 42, 78n, 79, 80n, 82n, 138n, 233, 284; pattern of variables, 228
participation, political, 161-65, 215-16, 238, 240, 244
See also participation crisis
participation crisis, 58-60, 186-92, 299; in Africa, 198-99; definition, 187; in developing countries, 169, 175n, 176-77; and development syndrome, 174-75; dilemmas of new participants, 201-02; elite action giving rise to, 187-92; minority groups, 187-92; ideology, 170-72; and institutional changes, 175-77, 193-95; sequences of, 182-86
conditions for rise of: 165-75; government output, 173-74; role of intelligentsia, 170-72; intra-elite conflict, 172-73; social mobilization, 166-67; social stratification, 167-70
historical dimensions of: 175-86; bureaucracy, 178-80; institutional framework for, 175-77; national participation and local authority, 177-78; and national identity, 180-82
prevention and resolution of: 192-204; authoritarian responses, 196-99; encapsulation, 199-200; persistence of, 202-04; theory of access, 196; theory of representation, 195-96
See also social stratification
Payne, Stanley F., 170n
Pearlin, Leonard, 169n
peasant, participation in modernization, 183-86; in penetration crisis, 226-27
penetration crisis, 62-64, 205-10, 299; in developing areas, 210, 213, 222-

23; development syndrome, 217-18; in England, 211-12; in France, 221-22; geographic, 228ff; in historical situations, 220-22; and institution building, 215-19; and other crises, 214-15; minority groups, 231-32; role of national identity in, 214; participation effecting, 215-16; rising expectations in, 223; and technology, 210-15; responses to, 227-32; in Soviet Union, 230; in South Vietnam, 213ff; in Thailand, 211
types of, and their resolutions: 220-27; empty territories, 220-23; regional differences, 223-24; of peasant communities, 226-27; communal autonomy, 224-26; in developing countries, 227-30; institutionalization in resolution, 218-19
performance, governmental, 125, 304-05; institutional, 310ff; in relation to capacity, 98-100, 293-94
Perry, Commodore Oliver Hazard, 151
Pigou, A. C., 235
Piper, P. C., 275n
Plamenatz, John, 118n
Plato, 8
political culture, divisions among people as result of political socialization, 106-07; elite, 103, 127ff; mass, 48-49, 103, 126-27; role of traditional values in changing societies, 107-08
in developing countries: authority as it affects role playing in, 109-10; common problems of in, 102-10; differences between early and late, 104-05; ideology in, 108-09
See also culture, cultural development
Political Culture and Political Development, 108
political demands, 95-96, 187n, 190-92, 236n; concerns which lead to, 233-35; distribution in response to, 234-35n; material, 235-36; material rewards, 199n
political development, 6ff, 98; evolutionary, 73-83; role of identity in, 117-18; ideological factors in, 276-77; philosophical inquiry into, 3-17; in Latin America, 178; relation of mass political culture to, 103-04; sequential models of, 284-85; theories of, 68-69; underlying dimensions of, 291-95; West European influence on, 12
crises of: 52-67, 298-99; modernization syndrome and, 65; patterns of

resolution, 67-72; sequences and, 137-38
See also crises, economic development
political identity, 56-57
political party, 180, 216, 296
political philosophy, 3-17
political power, 187, 192; access to, 196; of elite, 273; struggles, 141-43
politics, 14-15, 46, 233
population, 22-23; as factor in economic development and distribution, 249-51
populism, 49, 243
Positivists, 51, 54
Powell, G. B., 284, 292, 294
prefectorial system, Napoleonic, 221
Press, Charles, 228n
pressure groups, 30
PRI (Mexico), 226, 230
Protestant ethic, 245
public intervention, *see* state intervention
Public Law 480, 251n, 275
Pye, Lucian W., 76, 86, 103n, 106n, 107n, 108n, 109n, 118n, 121n, 124n, 129n, 140n, 145n, 146n, 149n, 157n, 169n, 202, 234n, 235n, 270

Ramachandran, G., 146n
Ranis, G., 251n
Ranney, Austin, 165n
Ranum, O., 222n
rationality, 19-20, 38-40, 55, 138; in development of capacity, 99-100
rebellion, *see* revolution
Redfield, Robert, 171, 268
Reformation, 178
relativism, cultural, 40-41
representation, 59-60, 178, 195-96; demand for corporate, 189-90; as form of political participation, 162
revolution, 136-37; and aristocracy, 193; and legitimacy, 165-66; and political participation, 165-66; role of students, 203n
Ricardo, David, 248
Riggs, Fred W., 75n, 90n, 98n, 180, 265n
Rintala, Marvin, 203n
Rogger, Hans, 170n
Rokkan, Stein, 165n, 294n, 300n, 301
role conflict, 30-33
Rosberg, Carl G., Jr., 88n, 90n, 92n, 94n
Rose, Richard, 108n, 125, 146n, 148
Rosenberg, Hans, 222n, 255n
Rosenstein-Rodan, Paul, 269n
Rostow, Walt W., 246n
Rothan, Stanley, 87n

Rousseau, Jean Jacques, 19
Rudolph, Lloyd I., 110n
Rudolph, Susanne, 110n
rural sector, 226-27, 248-51
Russett, Bruce, 294n
Rustow, D. A., 77n, 80n, 83n, 87, 110n, 121n, 127n, 149, 215n, 284n, 311, 314n

Sahlin, Marshall, 79n
Sartre, Jean Paul, 19
Sawyer, John E., 242n
Schramm, Wilbur, 214n
Schultz, Theodore, 233n, 248, 249, 250, 251, 254, 258, 275, 276n
Schumpeter, Joseph A., 71, 249, 257
Scott, James C., 241, 242
Scott, Robert, 103n
secession, 88, 189, 191
sequence, 5ff; components of, 295-307; of crises, 64, 297-98; relation of institutionalization to, 300-05; issues raised by, 84-93; relationship among stages of, 307-16
sequential models, of development, 284-85; of political participation, 183-85; relationship among stages, 307-08; structure of, 286-88; and underlying developmental problems, 288-95
Service, Elman R., 79n
Seton-Watson, Hugh, 171
Shils, Edward, 29, 89, 90, 95, 119n, 148n
Siffin, W. J., 246n, 255n
Silberstein, J., 129n
Sinai, R. I., 240
Singer, Milton, 171
Singham, A. W., 245
Sjoberg, Gideon, 99n
Smelser, Neil J., 75n, 76, 85, 93n, 99, 100n, 201n
social atomization, 36-37
Social Contract, 54
social development, 27ff; functional specification, and structural differentiation, 27-28
social mobilization, 166-67, 171
social science, and economic development, 27ff; historical change and, 13-15; themes of consciousness and functionalism, 18-20; theory in relation to political development, 27-37; traditional societies, 269ff; views of political development, 14-16
social stratification, 29-30, 242, 279; and identity, 114-15; middle sectors, 33-34; relative deprivation, 168-69; status reversal, 169-70. *See also* elite

socialization, 106-07, 217; alienation arising from, 157-58; disfunctional, leading to legitimacy crises, 144-47; affected by modernization, 166-67; affect on participation, 165-67
Spencer, Herbert, 15, 85
Spengler, Joseph J., 247, 249, 250n, 256, 257, 261n, 271n, 272
state intervention, 173-75, 227, 282
statism, in developing countries, 99; orientation of elites, 89-90
status position, 82n, 167-68; reversal of, 169-70
Stolper, Wolfgang, 247n
Strauss, Leo, 7, 8
suffrage, 59, 96, 176, 178, 184-85, 194
Sukarno, Achmed, 71, 131, 133, 137
Sullivan, Harry Stack, 9
syndrome of modernity, see development syndrome

technological advancement, 54-55, 104, 114; and penetration, 210-15
territory, 112-14, 207-08, 220-23, 231-32
tradition, 153n; and change, 43-46; as an obstacle to distributive change, 267-72; effect on elite, 90; institutions, 230; integration with world culture, 47-48; as opposed to modernity, 20-21, 50-52; role in changing society, 107-08; role in modernization, 86-89; and penetration crises, 219; politicization of culture, 48; preserving or rejecting, 153-54; responses of to modernization, 267ff; societies, 271-72; effect on status, 42. See also leadership
Thompson, J.A.K., 4n
Thorbecke, E., 251n
Tilly, Charles, 183n
Tilman, Robert, 261n
Tinbergen, J., 258n
Tinker, Hugh, 128n, 271n
Tinker, Irene, 146
Titmuss, R. M., 277, 278n
Tobin, James, 253
Tocqueville, Alexis de, 51, 94, 190
Tonnies, F., 41, 42, 218n
Tout, T. F., 222n
Truman, David, 196
Tucker, Robert C., 92n, 148n

Tufte, E., 287n

U Nu, 131, 137
unions, 172, 195
urbanization, 26, 35-36, 271; imbalance with industrialization, 252-53; and political participation, 184-85

values, human, 234-35
van der Mehden, Fred R., 143n
Verba, Sidney, 93n, 103n, 106n, 108n, 129n, 146n, 157n, 163n, 165, 193, 273
Viollet, P., 222n
vom Stein, 222

Ward, R. E., 77n, 80n, 83n, 87, 103n, 121n, 126n, 127n
Waxman, C. I., 239n
Weber, Eugen, 170n
Weber, Max, 14, 34, 42, 50, 71, 80, 233n; authority, 138ff, 228; on bureaucracies, 179-80; system of public bureaucratic organization, 228; on charisma, 149; on history, 19-20; model of administrative neutrality, 35
Weiner, Myron, 69, 70n, 88n, 89, 93, 94, 96n, 103n, 127, 146n, 165n, 167n, 181n, 185n, 234, 238, 240n, 281
Werner, Heinz, 85n
West, education in, 259ff; fear of absorption by, 123; model of equality, 94-95; modernization of, 81; nation-states, 221; preservation of culture from cultural imperialism of, 184-85
Western impact, on developing countries, 12, 111, 150, 272-79
Whitaker, C. Sylvester, Jr., 89n, 93n
Whitehead, A. N., 9
Willner, A. R., 109n, 148n
Wilson, James Q., 202n
Wittfogel, K. A., 220n
Worms, Jean Pierre, 221n
Wriggens, Howard, 130n
Wright, Arthur, 120n

Yanaga, Chitoshi, 151n
Young, Crawford, 143n

Zetterberg, Hans L., 82n
Zimmerman, L. J., 247n
Zolberg, Aristide, 70, 108, 199n

Sponsored by the Committee on Comparative Politics of
the Social Science Research Council

1. COMMUNICATIONS AND POLITICAL DEVELOPMENT
Edited by Lucian W. Pye
395 PAGES. 1963. CLOTH, $8.00. PAPER, $3.45

2. BUREAUCRACY AND POLITICAL DEVELOPMENT
Edited by Joseph LaPalombara
501 PAGES. 1963. CLOTH, $12.50. PAPER, $3.45

3. POLITICAL MODERNIZATION
IN JAPAN AND TURKEY
Edited by Robert E. Ward and Dankwart A. Rustow
508 PAGES. 1964. CLOTH, $10.00. PAPER, $3.45

4. EDUCATION AND POLITICAL DEVELOPMENT
Edited by James S. Coleman
610 PAGES. 1965. CLOTH, $10.00. PAPER, $3.45

5. POLITICAL CULTURE
AND POLITICAL DEVELOPMENT
Edited by Lucian W. Pye and Sidney Verba
616 PAGES. 1965. CLOTH, $11.50. PAPER, $3.45

6. POLITICAL PARTIES
AND POLITICAL DEVELOPMENT
Edited by Joseph LaPalombara and Myron Weiner
496 PAGES. 1966. CLOTH, $10.00. PAPER, $3.45

7. CRISES AND SEQUENCES IN
POLITICAL DEVELOPMENT
By Leonard Binder, James S. Coleman,
Joseph LaPalombara, Lucian W. Pye, Sidney Verba, and Myron Weiner
340 PAGES. 1971. $8.00

Order from your bookstore, or

PRINCETON UNIVERSITY PRESS, PRINCETON, NEW JERSEY 08540